ROUTLEDGE LIBRARY EDITIONS:
ACCOUNTING HISTORY

Volume 40

THE SOCIETY OF ACCOUNTANTS IN EDINBURGH, 1854–1914

THE SOCIETY OF ACCOUNTANTS IN EDINBURGH, 1854–1914

A Study of Recruitment to a New Profession

STEPHEN P. WALKER

Routledge
Taylor & Francis Group

LONDON AND NEW YORK

First published in 1988 by Garland Publishing, Inc.

This edition first published in 2021
by Routledge
2 Park Square, Milton Park, Abingdon, Oxon OX14 4RN

and by Routledge
52 Vanderbilt Avenue, New York, NY 10017

Routledge is an imprint of the Taylor & Francis Group, an informa business

© 1988 Stephen P. Walker

British Library Cataloguing in Publication Data
A catalogue record for this book is available from the British Library

ISBN: 978-0-367-33564-9 (Set)
ISBN: 978-1-00-304636-3 (Set) (ebk)
ISBN: 978-0-367-49448-3 (Volume 40) (hbk)
ISBN: 978-0-367-49450-6 (Volume 40) (pbk)
ISBN: 978-1-00-304623-3 (Volume 40) (ebk)

Publisher's Note
The publisher has gone to great lengths to ensure the quality of this reprint but points out that some imperfections in the original copies may be apparent.

Disclaimer
The publisher has made every effort to trace copyright holders and would welcome correspondence from those they have been unable to trace.

The Society of Accountants in Edinburgh 1854-1914

A Study of Recruitment to a New Profession

STEPHEN P. WALKER

GARLAND PUBLISHING, INC.

NEW YORK & LONDON 1988

For a list of Garland's publications in accounting,
see the final pages of this volume.

Library of Congress Cataloging in Publication Data

■■■■■■■■■■■■■■■■■■■■■■■■■■■■■■■■■

Walker, Stephen P.
The Society of Accountants in Edinburgh, 1854-1914 :
a study of recruitment to a new profession / Stephen P.
Walker.
    p. cm. — (Foundations of accounting)
Revised and expanded version of thesis (Ph.D.)—
Edinburgh University, 1986.
Bibliography: p.
Includes index.
ISBN 0-8240-6121-7 (alk. paper)
1. Society of Accountants in Edinburgh—History. 2.
Accounting—Scotland—History. 3. Accountants—
Scotland—History. I. Title. II. Series.
HF5616.G72S378   1988
657'.06'04134—dc 19   88-16322

Design by Renata Gomes

The volumes in this series are printed on
acid-free, 250-year-life paper.

Printed in the United States of America

This book has been published on behalf of the Scottish

Committee on Accounting History of The Institute of

Chartered Accountants of Scotland

Foreword

Scottish accountants take great pride in the efforts of their predecessors in constituting the earliest professional accountancy bodies. Since the middle of the nineteenth century, the influence of Scottish accountants has been considerable. Today members of The Institute of Chartered Accountants of Scotland are held in the highest regard throughout the world. That this position has been attained is due in no small regard to the early Scottish pioneers of accounting who formed bodies such as the Society of Accountants in Edinburgh.

Dr Walker's study of the earliest recruits to the Society is a most significant piece of social research – not just as a pure historical study but more as a scientific observation of the past in order to provide an understanding of the present and future. In particular in this study, Dr Walker reflects the early 'closed' nature of the Edinburgh accountancy profession followed by its gradual 'opening up' for economic and related reasons.

This is undoubtedly an important piece of work, and is particularly unique in the bringing of social history skills to the relatively unchartered waters of early professional accountancy. It is to be recommended to all serious students of accounting history, and is warmly supported by the Scottish Committee on Accounting History.

Professor T.A. Lee
Convenor
Scottish Committee on Accounting History
The Institute of Chartered Accountants of Scotland

to

Liz

Contents

Tables

Illustrations

Preface

The 1850-1914 period was a crucial one in the growth, development and status of the social group situated at the apex of the British middle class: the professions. Their increasing number, organization and intellectual standing during the era of industrial-urban maturation were factors which were likely to have had a significant impact on the social derivation and composition of their individual memberships.

The occupation chosen for a detailed investigation of the effect of these, and other socio-economic changes, on professional recruitment is accountancy - a vocation, which in recent years, has attracted a great deal more interest concerning its historical development and the practice and nature of its early practitioners. This enthusiasm for understanding the past of this *new* profession has to be a reflection of the contemporary significance and maturation of an occupation, which barely more than a century ago, was spasmodically organized and of questionable professional status in most nations.

Disproportionate attention has naturally fallen on the history of the accounting profession in Scotland. Not only is this because that small country was the scene of the world's first organizations of professional accountants, but also because the members of those societies played an important part in the subsequent development of the infant profession in several other locations.

Fortunately, for the accounting and social historian, the early members of the first Scottish organization of accountants: the Society of Accountants in Edinburgh (formed in 1853-4), have left a comprehensive and fascinating archive of documents. These manuscripts may be utilized to trace the insecure beginnings of a Society, which by the outbreak of the First World War, had assumed an influence and membership that extended well beyond its limited geographical location. Using these professional, and several other historical sources, it is hoped that this book, in its analysis of recruitment to the new profession of Edinburgh chartered accountancy, will provide an insight into the complex origins and behaviour of the emergent professional and of the organization to which he belonged. In addition, investigation of this one vocation may provide pointers to a greater understanding of the wider professional classes during the Victorian and Edwardian era.

Unlike most previous studies of accountants and other professional men - this is a study of *all* recruits, not only of those who succeeded in becoming qualified members.

The emphasis placed on studying all those entering the vocational training system permits an analysis of the whole process of recruitment: of the causes of the expansion in total recruitment, why the occupation was chosen as a career option, and the reasons why some recruits failed to enter the qualifying association.

In the tradition of the *Garland Collection* of providing primary research material not easily available – Appendix D contains copies of ten documents that were highly significant in the development of the accounting profession in Edinburgh, and which are only scarcely available outside Edinburgh or Scotland.

Finally, a word about the misleading title of this book. The Society of Accountants was formed in 1854 though its predecessor, the Institute of Accountants in Edinburgh, which was established in 1853, is included in the study. The first recruits to the profession were registered in the records of the Society as having commenced their vocational training in 1837. The starting date in the title is not, therefore, strictly adhered to in the text.

Historical research is always dependent on the assistance and advice of others. This book is a revised and expanded version of a Ph.D. thesis submitted at Edinburgh University in June 1986. That it appears, in this hopefully improved version, is due entirely to the efforts of Professor Tom Lee to whom I am greatly indebted. Firstly, for providing the opportunity and facilities for undertaking the pleasant task of re-writing the thesis. Secondly, for piloting the revised script through the process of drafting into a publishable form. The financial assistance of the Scottish Committee on Accounting History of The Institute of Chartered Accountants of Scotland is gratefully acknowledged for providing the means to revise the original text.

My thanks are also due to Professor Michael Anderson and Dr Bob Morris, both of Edinburgh University for their supervision of the original research project and to the several others who have suggested revisions of the text any errors remaining in which, are my own.

During the data collection stage of the research, I inevitably received the help of the staffs of several institutions. Those employed in the Scottish Record Office, Edinburgh University Library, the National Library of Scotland, the public libraries of Edinburgh, Glasgow, Aberdeen and Dundee, Cambridge University Library and the British Library, all deserve my thanks.

Mrs Dorothy Hogg and her colleagues in the Library of The Institute of Chartered Accountants of Scotland, Queen Street, Edinburgh, extended a warm welcome and cheerfully supplied me with heavy and dusty books over many months. Mr Nigel Morrison, Clerk of Faculty between 1979 and 1986, and the office staff of the Faculty of Advocates were most accomodating in providing access to Faculty records.

I am obliged to almost all those employed in New Register House, Edinburgh during 1982 to 1985, particularly to the Librarian, Mr Jim Welsh, and those 'RAs' who processed innumerable orders for volumes of census books before the arrival of the microfilm yet still became good friends.

My greatest debt is to my wife Liz whose patience, from the earliest stages of this study to the last, has been limitless and whose encouragement and supportive assistance have been vital to its completion.

S.P. Walker
Edinburgh

September 1987

We are willing according to our rules to admit any person into our Society of good character, who complies with the course of training and the requirements and qualifications of the Society. We do not exclude persons otherwise, who satisfy what we regard as essential to the proper practice of the business.

Thomas Goldie Dickson, CA,
President of the SAE, 1889-1892

(Q.) If anybody wanted to become a chartered accountant or C.A., has he only got to take the steps necessary for entering one of those three bodies ? (A.) Yes, I suppose so. I don't think we are in any sense exclusive, except as regards culture and conduct.

James Howden, CA,
President of the SAE, 1892-1895

We are quite willing to admit as many members into our Society as will come, upon the terms set forth in our rules. (Q.) Do you seek to limit competition in any way amongst persons who, in your judgement, are duly qualified ? (A.) Certainly not. We only require qualification; we don't seek exclusion.

Richard Brown, CA,
Secretary of the SAE, 1892-1916,
President 1916-1918

Court of Session. "Pursuers Proof", Interdict Case, The Chartered Accountants of Scotland Against The Corporation of Accountants Limited, December 7 1892.]

1
Introduction

My father was an eminent button maker -
but I had a soul above buttons -
I panted for a liberal profession.

[George Coleman the Younger, *Sylvester Dagerwood*, 1795]

The object of this study is to provide a greater understanding of the process of recruitment to the professions in nineteenth and early twentieth century Britain. There have been several investigations into the social origins of professional men and of the rate of social mobility in individual vocations.[1] But there has been a distinct lack of intensive historical study of all stages of the recruitment process. Although there is a growing literature on intergenerational rates of mobility (comparing the professional's social status with that of his father), relatively little is known regarding the son's path to professional standing; the obstacles in the system of vocational preparation that might block his achievement of professional status; and the factors which permitted or encouraged his upward mobility.

There is limited empirical evidence of a historical nature concerning the factors which determined levels of recruitment to the professions. Most studies have been content with the traditional explanation for the growth of professional occupations in industrial-urban society - that is, that their services were demanded increasingly due to the growing sophistication and complexity of the economy. This assumes, however, that certain factors which may have engendered a *supply* of recruits to the professions were of much less significance to vocational expansion.

Similarly, although the existence of self-recruitment is regarded as an important determinant of the rate of social mobility, and the number of sons following fathers into a profession has occasionally been studied, the *determinants* of the level of self-recruitment (namely, changes in the age at marriage, in marriage and fertility rates, and in the career preferences of the sons of professionals) have received little quantitative analysis in this context.

The lack of historical studies in this area is all the more surprising considering that the second half of the nineteenth century and the early twentieth century witnessed general economic and social changes which had a potentially significant impact on the origins of professionals, the system of vocational recruitment, and the extent of self-recruitment.

1. **The Expansion of the Professional Class** – the number of professionals increased rapidly relative to general population growth and the labour force employed in manual occupations. In seventeen selected professional or emerging professional occupations in England and Wales, the number employed expanded at a rate of 1.9% *per annum* between 1841 and 1891 compared to 1.2% for the growth of the total population.[2] There were, theoretically, a greater number of professional 'statuses' to be filled. The expansion of the tertiary sector of the economy relative to the secondary sector in urban-industrial societies has consistently been provided as the major explanation for an increase in *collective* upward social mobility.[3]

2. **The Number of Professions Increased** – several occupations attained or began to assert their professional status during the late nineteenth and early twentieth centuries. These *new* professions, such as accountancy, engineering, surveying and dentistry, were alternative vocations to the exclusive *old* professions of physic, law, the church and the armed forces.[4]

3. **The Process of Professionalization** – in order to assert their professional standing, the new professions introduced recruitment regulations, formalized systems of vocational preparation and admission which potentially affected the origins of those who could enter and succeed in them.[5]

4. **Meritocratization** – the introduction of entry based upon competitive examination rather than patronage and the testing of academic abilities in all the professions, especially from the 1850s, implied that the attributes required for recruitment and qualification changed.[6]

5. **The Expansion of the Educational System** – in the private and later in the state sector, elementary and, subsequently, secondary education[7] potentially increased the opportunities available to enter the professions among those in receipt of appropriate schooling.

6. **Changes in the Distribution of Income and Wealth** – this entailed changing perceptions of the vocations deemed suitable for sons, and the financial means to enter them. The increasing relative wealth of large manufacturers,[8] for example, implied that they had an increased ability to secure the upward mobility of their offspring by entering them into desirable professions. The improved socio-economic position of the middle classes in general ensured that: "Relatively few who had come from trade and industry reverted to it for their adult career, except perhaps among the merchant bankers. Such middle-class men were now ready to enter the esteemed professions: the church, the law, the universities, the army or navy, or the civil service."[9]

7. **The Decline of Middle Class Fertility and the Existence of Differential Fertility** – this was potentially of great significance in limiting the rate of self-recruitment to the professions.[10] The reduction in middle class family size from the 1870s hypothetically

resulted in a reduced capacity to produce sons for recruitment to one's own profession in the succeeding generation, and the consequent occupation of vacancies by sons from lower status, high fertility families. As Sorokin was to realize during the interwar years, differential fertility: "Creates a kind of social vacuum within the upper strata. As the performance of the functions carried on by the upper strata continues to be necessary, and as the corresponding people cannot be recruited any longer from a diminishing upper population, it is natural that this 'vacuum' must be filled by the climbers from the lower strata."[11]

In order to investigate fully the process of recruitment to the professions, and the impact of these fundamental changes on the social origins of recruits, a number of matters required analysis for individual professions during the nineteenth and early twentieth centuries. These were: the factors which determined expansion in professional recruitment; the working of the process of vocational decision-making; the nature of, and changes in, the educational, apprenticeship and professional examination systems; the factors which determined the ability of recruits to succeed in the training system; and the marital and fertility experience of existing professionals and the occupations followed by their sons.

DEFINING THE BOUNDARIES : THE CHOICE OF PERIOD, LOCALE AND PROFESSION

Having established the general nature of the topic under scrutiny, it was necessary to make a series of decisions concerning the precise limits of the research.

The period of the study was necessarily determined by the timing of the phenomena outlined above, and was therefore to include the years between 1850 and 1914. The availability of demographic source material was a further consideration in the choice of period. Statutory civil registers and census enumerators' books were likely to prove essential sources. In Scotland, the former began in 1855 and the latter are accessible for 1841 to 1891.

It soon became apparent that Edinburgh was to be the organizational location and geographical base of the vocation(s) studied. This was not simply a choice of convenience given the wealth of repositories for historical research in that city. Rather, it was a consequence of the fact that nineteenth century Edinburgh was a centre in which the professions were of disproportionate numerical and socio-economic significance.

In 1861, 3.9% of the population of Edinburghshire were enumerated under the

Registrar General's 'professional classes' (4.8% in Edinburgh city district) compared to 1.7% for the whole of Scotland. By 1891, the proportion had risen to 5.1% in the county (6.5% in Edinburgh Parliamentary Burgh) as against 2.8% in Scotland. The occupational impact of this large professional class was considerable given the army of clerks and domestic servants that it employed directly and the relatively large number of retailers and craftsmen who depended heavily upon its patronage. Hence, F.H. Groome in 1885 could claim that Edinburgh formed "the greatest retail shopkeeping centre out of London."[12]

With the exception of brewing, distilling, publishing and india-rubber manufacture, Edinburgh was not notable as an industrial city. And, although certain areas of its central business district were dominated by the head offices of the Scottish banks and insurance companies, T. and W. McDowall could assert in 1849 that: "As a place of commerce, it is entitled to little prominence or consideration, as its manufactures are few and on a limited scale."[13] Whereas in Liverpool and Manchester, noted John Heiton in 1861, "Twas cotton that did it", and in Glasgow "Twas pig-iron that did it"; in Edinburgh the most respectable classes, especially the lawyers, considered that "Twas quarrels that did it".[14] The city was also perceived as being dominated by its professionals due to the advances of its medics, the notoriety of its religious leaders, and the reputation of its university professors.

Edinburgh was the organizational headquarters of the traditional professions in Scotland: the Church of Scotland; the Royal College of Surgeons (chartered 1503); the Royal College of Physicians (chartered 1681); the Faculty of Advocates (1532); the Society of Writers to the Signet (organized in 1594); and the Society of Solicitors to the Supreme Courts (incorporated 1797). During the nineteenth century, some new professions became established in the city. For example, the Institute of Accountants in Edinburgh (1853); the Faculty of Actuaries (1856); and the Actuarial Society of Edinburgh (1859).

Professions based in Edinburgh, as opposed to those centred in London for instance, offered the prospect of investigating occupations of manageable proportions, and a geographically-limited field from which recruits were drawn and members could practice. This was an important consideration as the problems of transience and locating recruits and their families throughout Britain in historical sources were potential impediments to a comprehensive investigation.

In order to be able to conduct an intensive survey and obtain a complete picture of recruitment, it was decided to choose one profession for in 'depth study' and minor investigation of at least one other for comparative purposes. The selection of a particular profession for major research was governed by its ability to satisfy the following criteria:

1. The occupation was required to have exhibited a high rate of expansion, at least greater than the rate of population growth.

2. That expansion was traditionally deemed to be the consequence of industrialization and the resultant increased demand for professional services.

3. A comparatively recent organization was necessary so as to enable an assessment of the impact of professionalization upon recruitment.

4. The occcupation was required to have attained the status of a profession or at least be in the process of acquiring it. This was vital to ensure that the distance and extent of any mobility could be measured (with a degree of confidence) as having been from lower or higher status origins.

5. Given the complexity of the issues requiring research and the exhaustive nature of the study, a membership of manageable numerical proportions was important as was a rich archive containing consistent series of relevant information.

The individual professions considered and their rates of growth as revealed in census reports are listed in Table 1.1 below.

Comprehensive study of one of the *ancient* or *traditional* professions was rejected due to their comparatively low rate of expansion as well as their long existence. Some legal societies within the lawyer category suffered a decline of membership in certain periods of the nineteenth century. The armed forces were unsuitable because they could not be regarded as having a separate Edinburgh organization, many of their number in the city were retired, and a high transiency rate was envisaged. The Edinburgh medical profession posed an additional problem of its recruits being drawn from a wide geographical area, and a study of total membership of the medical colleges involved too large a population. The latter problem also applied to the clergy.

The remaining alternatives being *new* professions, although experiencing high rates of growth, were mostly of questionable professional status during the nineteenth century. This was particularly the case with regard to teachers, whose number was also daunting. University lecturers were a potential sub-group for investigation with fewer

TABLE 1.1 Rate of Growth of Professions in Edinburghshire and Scotland 1861-1911

Profession	Total in 1861 Census		Total in 1911 Census		Compound Rate of Growth p.a. (%) 1861-81		Compound Rate of Growth p.a. (%) 1891-1911		Compound Rate of Growth p.a. (%) 1861-1911		% of in Edinburgh
	Edinburgh	Scotland	Edinburgh	Scotland	Edinburgh	Scotland	Edinburgh	Scotland	Edinburgh	Scotland	
Army Officers (full or part pay or retired)	316	841	254	892	-0.89	-0.88	-0.09	0.47	-0.43	0.11	32.57
Naval Officers (full or part pay or retired)	82	304	34	720	-5.11	-0.95	-0.81	6.52	-1.74	1.07	16.39
Established Church Ministers	114	1468	160	1765	0.13	0.23	0.42	0.23	0.68	0.34	8.61
Ministers, Priests of other Churches	266	2340	398	3362	1.05	0.97	0.10	0.10	0.80	0.71	12.19
Advocates, W S 's, Solicitors	787	2219	1267	4219	-0.85	0.48	1.36	1.53	0.95	0.90	31.67
Physicians, Surgeons, G P 's	363	1870	586	5278	-0.21	0.02	0.78	1.09	0.96	1.09	18.50
Dentists	76	192	326	1595	0.96	2.58	3.49	4.69	2.95	4.04	26.92
Architects	122	413	312	1659	3.46	4.67	1.49	1.70	1.89	2.82	21.66
Civil and Mining Engineers	107	454	241	1573	2.91	4.18	-0.26	1.18	1.63	2.51	18.30
Accountants	259	889	506	1988	1.40	1.23	1.74	2.35	1.34	1.53	28.59
Teachers and Lecturers	1812	12452	3731	26780	1.78	1.69	1.14	1.44	1.45	1.54	14.50
Total	4304	23460	7815	47789	0.96	1.33	1.10	1.58	1.70	1.41	17.34
Total excluding teachers	2492	11008	4084	20931	0.28	0.89	1.05	1.51	0.93	1.25	20.87
Total Population	273,997	3,062,294	507,666	4,760,904	1.11	0.99	0.78	0.84	1.74	0.88	-

It should be noted here that the usual problems of occupational definition and changes in classification in census effect some of the above statistics. For example, the excessively high growth rate of Naval Officers in 1891-1911 was caused by the inclusion of Marines in the 1911 figure. Similarly, the rate for Dentists in the same period was partly due to the inclusion of 'dentist's assistants' from 1901.

Membership statistics of professional organizations provide a more reliable guide of occupational growth through these are not always readily available and do not include those practising a vocation outside of their membership. The census therefore provides a general outline of professional expansion and the relative growth of particular occupations.

problems of status though their late organization (the Scottish Association of University Teachers was formed in Edinburgh in 1922) was a disadvantage. Similarly, dentists remained for too long unorganized and also unregistered, while architects did not form a continuous Scottish branch until 1916 when the Royal Institute of Scottish Architects was established in Edinburgh. Questions of status and occupational definition were the major disadvantages of a study of civil or mining engineers.

The Edinburgh actuarial profession formed an attractive high growth alternative and also one in which problems of status determination were less daunting. The Faculty of Actuaries also holds a comprehensive archive. However, the major problem was that of small numbers; in 1914 there were only 225 members of the Faculty.

It was decided to investigate an occupation allied closely to the actuaries, the professional branch of accountancy practitioners: Edinburgh chartered accountants (CAs). The recruits and membership of the Society of Accountants in Edinburgh were to be studied from its origins in 1853 to 1914. This organization with the Institute of Accountants and Actuaries in Glasgow (IAAG) (formed in 1853 and chartered in 1855), together with the Society of Accountants in Aberdeen (SAA) (formed in 1866 and incorporated in 1867), constituted the three branches of the chartered accountancy profession in Scotland which amalgamated in 1951 to form The Institute of Chartered Accountants of Scotland (ICAS). As we shall now discover, the SAE provided an example of a professional organization which satisfied the selection criteria outlined previously.

For comparative purposes, a minor study was undertaken of the Scottish Bar, organized as the Faculty of Advocates, which was of manageable proportions and exhibited a slow rate of growth.

THE GROWTH, DEVELOPMENT AND STATUS OF THE SOCIETY OF ACCOUNTANTS IN EDINBURGH

Professional Expansion

An examination of membership statistics reveals that Edinburgh chartered accountancy was a high growth profession. Figure 1.1 shows the expansion in the membership of the SAE. The trend is illustrated further in Table 1.2.

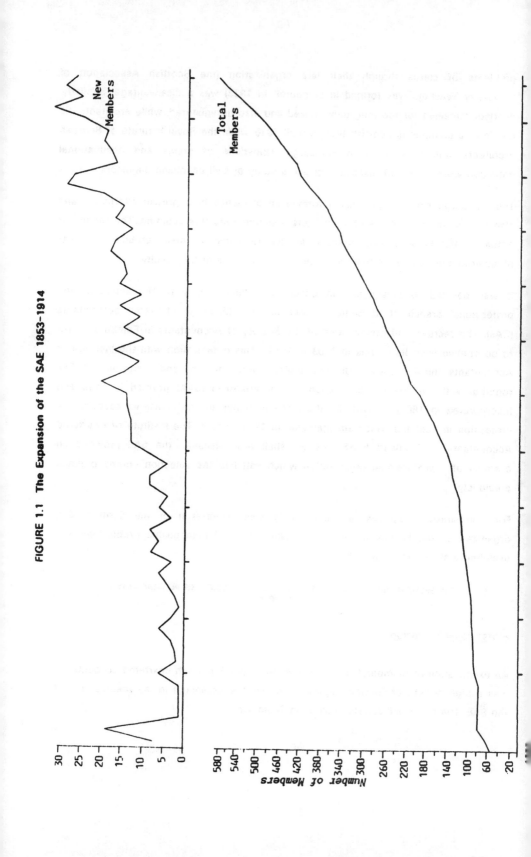

FIGURE 1.1 The Expansion of the SAE 1853-1914

TABLE 1.2
Annual Compound Growth Rate of Membership of the SAE 1855-1914 (percentages)

Quinquennial Rates		Decennial Rates	
1855-59	-0.32		
1860-64	2.31	1855-64	1.07
1865-69	1.84		
1870-74	2.85	1865-74	2.19
1875-79	2.43		
1880-84	6.87	1875-84	4.71
1885-89	5.16		
1890-94	4.01	1885-94	4.59
1895-99	3.46		
1900-04	4.09	1895-04	3.51
1905-09	2.80		
1910-14	3.93	1905-14	3.43
	1855-1914= 3.44		

The variation in growth rates (for instance, the 1870s compared to the 1880s), reveals a profession with changing rates of expansion and, thus, one which can be examined for the causes of these variations. The information contained in Table 1.3 reveals that the rate of growth of the SAE far exceeded that of the local population from which most of its recruits were likely to have originated.

TABLE 1.3
Annual Compound Growth Rate of the SAE Compared to That of the Population of Edinburghshire in Census Years (percentages)

Years	Population of Edinburghshire	Membership of SAE
1861-71	1.83	2.21
1871-81	1.71	3.50
1881-91	1.10	5.63
1891-01	1.19	3.47
1901-11	0.38	3.61
1861-1911	1.24	3.68

Occupational Development and Professional Status

It is not the intention here to provide a thorough description of the organizational development of the SAE nor of Scottish accountancy during the 1850-1914 period. Not only has this been done elsewhere,[15] but it is not necessary given the subject under consideration. A basic outline of the SAE's history and the context within which the organization existed is, however, necessary. It is prudent to reveal occupational developments in terms of the more significant question of ascertaining the status of the vocation and its progress through the process of *professionalization*.

Many occupational sociologists have wrestled with the problem of how to define a profession. Most have relied on the *trait* approach, testing an occupation's claim to professional status by its exhibition and acquisition of certain characteristics.[16] These traits have generally been identified as: the practice of a skill based upon theoretical knowledge; extensive and specialized systems of training; the testing of competence; the existence of an acknowledged organization; public recognition of professional standing; ethical codes of conduct; the provision of an altruistic service rewarded in the form of a fee, and so on. Others have adopted variations of this procedure, measuring an occupation's progress through a series of characteristic developments known as the process of professionalization.

The problem of definition is particularly difficult to assess historically. As Millerson has rightly argued: "Professional status is probably a dynamic quality. Elements composing status may change owing to social and economic changes."[17] This difficulty is especially acute when studying professions during the nineteenth century – a transitional period of occupational and societal change resulting in altered evaluations concerning the attributes of professional status.

In pre-industrial Britain, the professions were characterized by a certain gentlemanly bearing. Professional income was earned neither by manual labour nor by trade. Professions were recruited heavily from the ranks of the landed gentry which formed their major clientele and to whom they aspired and emulated socially. The professions composed the 'ancient three', the traditional or old vocations of the church, the law and physic (some would also include the military). During the twentieth century, by contrast, these societal connections have been of lesser significance in the determination of professional status – that is, compared to the exhibition of academic excellence, meritocratic training and occupational specialization.

The transitional stage between these extremes was one in which some of the old characteristics of a profession became of less importance (such as morality, public service, gentlemanly conduct and origins) relative to those of increasing significance (such as State recognition, open competition in recruitment and the testing of specialized knowledge). The imposition of rigid definitional criteria thus becomes inadequate during the period of this study because of the changing emphasis placed upon the acquisition of certain professional traits in status determination. The professional status of the SAE and other developing occupational aspirants of the nineteenth century has to be examined in the context of this period of changing evaluations.

The Overt Professional Characteristics of the SAE

By purely twentieth century criteria, the SAE might not have been considered to have constituted a profession until the late nineteenth century. Although certain traits were attained much earlier than this, others of increasing significance were gained late in the century.

Despite previous attempts to do so, the first successful venture to organize Edinburgh accountants began on 17 January 1853 when Mr Alexander W. Robertson issued a circular to fourteen practising accountants requesting their attendance at a meeting to discuss: "some definite arrangement for uniting the professional Accountants in Edinburgh".[18]

Eight men responded and resolved to form a society composed of individuals recognized as practising solely as accountants in the city. They prepared a draft constitution which was amended at a second meeting held on 22 January 1853. Forty seven attended the next meeting on the 31 January 1853 when office-bearers were elected and the constitution approved, and it was resolved to admit accountants who were engaged as managers of life assurance companies or who held legal appointments as Honorary members. The new voluntary organization was to be entitled the **Institute of Accountants in Edinburgh**. Legal recognition by the State was obtained on 23 October 1854 when a Royal Warrant was granted to the Institute which was registered and sealed on 11 December 1854.[19] Thereafter the organization changed its name to the **Society of Accountants in Edinburgh**.

As well as organization and incorporation, other professional traits soon became applicable to the SAE. Members resolved to adopt the notation of 'C.A.' after their names on 30 January 1855: in the 1855 issue of *Index Juridicus, The Scottish Law List and Legal Directory*, the following intimation was printed at the foot of the list of members: "NOTE. - *The Members of the Society of Accountants have adopted the distinctive abbreviate letter of "C A," Chartered Accountant*".[20] The exclusive usage of the notation by the members of the three Scottish chartered societies was defended fiercely against the later rival claims of the Scottish Institute of Accountants (SIA) which was formed in 1880, and the Corporation of Accountants formed in Glasgow in 1891. Remuneration for members was primarily in the form of the traditional professional fee, and a certain code of ethics (particularly relating to advertising and the conduct of members) was established early in the Society's existence.[21]

Despite the acquisition of these professional traits, the SAE was deficient by the 1860s and 1870s in others that were of increasing contemporary significance. The charter of incorporation noted that Edinburgh accountants practised on the basis of a specialized knowledge only attainable through the receipt of a liberal education and qualification *via* the Society's training system. Yet, it was not until 1873 that competence was tested adequately on the introduction of a three-tier examination system. Similarly, the claim to an exclusive performance of accounting functions was tainted by the unregulated nature of the occupation - despite Scottish CA's attempts during the 1890s to exclude unqualified practitioners, and by SAE members adopting alternative, though related occupations.

Other status-enhancing projects were late in coming. A student society was formed in 1886, a widow's fund in 1887, and permanent premises were purchased as late as 1891 until which time the library (founded in 1865) did not assume the proportions expected of a *learned profession*. No directory of members was published until 1896 and no journal until 1897.

It would appear then that, by present day criteria, the SAE had not attained the status of a profession until perhaps the 1880s or 1890s. Although this opinion would appear to be confirmed by other writers on the subject of the status of nineteenth century accountants, it is important for in this study to establish that this was not so, and to identify more precisely the occupational standing of the *Edinburgh* CA during the period of the study.

The Occupational and Social Context of Professional Status

In successive published census reports until 1921, accountants were classified as commercial rather than as professional men due to their close occupational proximity to the mercantile and manufacturing community. Similarly, Reader has asserted that: "accountancy scarcely emerged into the professional world until very late in the [nineteenth] century."[22] Not until the increased scale of business resulted in an improvement in commercial morality, he claims, did accountants achieve something approaching complete professional status. This appraisal is perfectly valid in the nineteenth century *national* context, and is an adequate description of the position attained by organized British accountancy during that period. It ignores, however, the development of *local* professions within the national scene, and tends to neglect the fact that this was a transitional period of professional status determination. Only in this context, and by examining the localized occupational and social milieu in which they existed, can an adequate explanation of the timing and nature of the SAE's claim to professional status be examined.

Confusion as to the precise status of Scottish accountants was most obviously displayed in the 1871 census which, in uniquely classifying them into two groups (686 in 'commerce' and 421 in the legal category of the 'professional classes') recognized that some accountants at least deserved to be considered as professionals by that time.

The position of the Scottish accountant was somewhat different to his numerically superior English counterpart during the nineteenth century. Whereas: "In England it appears to have been the Companies Act of 1862 and the Bankruptcy Act of 1869 which caused the emergence of the professional accountant in independent practice",[23] in Edinburgh the *professional* accountant had become established much earlier despite the relatively late exhibition of modern traits. The attainment of professional status was not simply due to the SAE being the first organization of accountants to become incorporated. Rather, it was based on a characteristic of the pre-industrial kind, upon an occupational and social association with a traditional profession of unquestioned standing: Edinburgh lawyers.

During the eighteenth and early nineteenth centuries: "The real leaders of Edinburgh society", claims Smout, were the "professional men: and among the professions there were none, in numbers, wealth or prestige, to equal the lawyers".[24] The legal class confirmed its position through an intimate association with Lothian landowners, and by providing some of the most notable political and intellectual leaders of the period. One English lady on visiting Edinburgh noted that: "Almost every house in the New Town at least, is occupied by some person connected with the law . . . the city is a huge manufactory of litigation."[25]

Edinburgh accountants of the first half of the nineteenth century became classed as an adjunct to this prestigious group of professionals. They, too, resided predominantly in the desirable New Town district of the City. Of 95 accountants listed in the 1840-1 *Edinburgh and Leith Post Office Directory,* 78 (82.1%) had New Town addresses;[26] the majority of the remainder being located in middle class Newington. Almost one half resided with or lived next door to an advocate, Writer to the Signet (WS), Solicitor to the Supreme Court (SSC), writer or solicitor, and only 7.4% did not live or work in a street in which at least one of these legal gentlemen was resident. Table 1.4 shows this close spatial relationship between Edinburgh lawyers and accountants from an alternative perspective and reveals that, fourteen years before their incorporation, Edinburgh accountants were geographically and perhaps socially closer to the highest branches of the legal profession than to the lower status and unorganized writers and solicitors.

TABLE 1.4

Percentage of Edinburgh Lawyers Whose Address is Given as a Street in Which at Least One Accountant was Located in 1840–41

Occupation	N	% of Total in that Occupation
Advocate	118	64.8
WS	312	68.3
SSC	69	71.9
Writer	51	34.9
Solicitor	27	23.5
	577	

Source: *Edinburgh and Leith Post Office Directory 1840-1*

These residential connections with lawyers were compounded by occupational ones. The source of most early Edinburgh accountants' employment was remits from court to consider and prepare accounts relating to insolvent estates and judicial factories. Consequently, the occupational titles of 'writer' and 'accountant' were often interchanged in Edinburgh as much early work of this nature was conducted in solicitors' offices. Some WSs and SSCs and solicitors effectively practised solely as accountants and these were permitted to apply for admission to the SAE if they had been employed in the business chambers of a member of the Society for at least three years under the Regulations adopted in 1855.[27] Many of the original members of the SAE had received their training in law offices, and attendance at the law classes of the University of Edinburgh remained an important component of both a lawyer's and an accountant's training during the early nineteenth century. Accountants were thus regarded as *junior members* of the Edinburgh legal profession.

In 1834, for example, a Bill was presented to Parliament to establish the office of 'Accountant-General' in the Court of Session. It proposed that the individual should: "be chosen from among the Members of the Faculty of Advocates, the Society of Writers to the Signet, or the Incorporation of Solicitors of the Supreme Court, of at least ten years standing."[28] A subsequent report by a committee of the Society of Writers to the Signet rejected these sources of appointees: "because it excludes a most respectable body of *professional* gentlemen, who, although they are not incorporated, are perhaps the most fitted for the duty, viz., the Accountants."[29] [italics added]

Perhaps the greatest testament to the pre-1853 standing of the Edinburgh accountant was the fact that so many fathers in the older, established professions, especially the law, deemed it a suitable vocation for their sons which did not entail a significant loss of family status. One particularly illustrious member of the Faculty of Advocates, Sir Walter Scott, as early as 1820 recommended to his brother that his nephew:

> Cannot follow a better line than that of an accountant. It is highly respectable – and is one in which, with attention and skill, aided by such opportunities as I may be able to procure for him, he must ultimately succeed. I say ultimately – because the harvest is small and the labours numerous in this as in other branches of our legal practice.[30]

Of the 64 original members of the SAE who joined before incorporation, 40 had fathers in occupations that may be considered as having been above the status of the accountant.[31] Twelve were the sons of lawyers, nine the sons of clergymen, and six were the sons of landed proprietors. By contrast, the founders of the Institute of Chartered Accountants in England and Wales (ICAEW) in 1880 were said to have derived predominantly from lesser status – that is, mercantile origins.[32]

Just as it was the case that the status and dignity of the corporate legal organizations of Edinburgh were derived largely from their landed associations and origins of recruits, so the Edinburgh accountant's connections with those in the older professions of established standing threw a lustre of professional and social status over them. John Heiton, in describing the social structure of Edinburgh during the 1850s, noted that, at the top of the hierachy, stood the nobility and landed gentry, then came the lawyers – who were ordered thus:

> The Advocates keep the Writers to the Signet at bay, except when these have a fee in their hands. The Writers to the Signet look askanse at the Solicitors before the Supreme Courts, and also at the *Accountants* who again will have nothing to do with the Solicitors at Law.[33] [italics added]

It would not appear exaggerated to assert that from a contemporary perspective, Edinburgh accountants might be considered as having attained the status of a profession from the date of their receiving a Royal Charter of Incorporation. That event was the final characteristic necessary to have obtained such a standing during the 1850s.

Whereas later accountancy organizations, such as the ICAEW, found it necessary to incorporate in order to assert their occupational presence and professional status, the SAE charter of 1854 was a reflection of an occupational respectability already attained through association with the lawyers. It was not, as in the ICAEW's case, a first institutional measure of many designed to impose a status not founded upon a long-standing recognition by those already established as members of the professional classes and the public. The position of the SAE was summarized adequately by R.A. Witty in 1906:

> It was not until the middle of the century that there was anything like a serious attempt to organize what had already come to be looked upon as an important profession. In 1854 a Royal Charter of Incorporation was granted to the Society of Accountants in Edinburgh, and that was the first date of consequence in the history of accounting as a profession.[34]

Frequent references were made by late nineteenth century commentators, in and outside of accountancy, to the high standing of the Edinburgh profession due to its legal connections. *The Accountant's Journal* in 1893, for example, noted enviously that the greater importance of legal work in the Scottish accountant's business compared to his English counterpart ensured that:

> They are unquestionably accepted by the bench, the bar and the people, as being at all events members of the 'learned profession' [of law], and they are not infrequently found to be practising in partnership with advocates or writers . . . the perfect accord that obtains between law and accountancy in Scotland speaks volumes for the generosity and good sense of both sides, and might well be emulated here.[35]

Their employment by the courts and in law offices resulted in eastern Scottish CAs often being referred to as the 'cousins' or 'junior partners' of the established legal profession. It was in Edinburgh that this connection was at its strongest and, consequently, the SAE was regarded by all as the most eminent branch of the profession.

In Glasgow, by contrast, accountancy, had more commercial origins which reflected the economic structure of the city. It was not uncommon before 1853 to discover an individual practising as a 'Merchant and Accomptant'. This connection with commerce was also evidenced by the close association of the early IAAG with stockbroking; twelve of the first sixteen chairmen of the Glasgow Stock Exchange Association were IAAG members.[36] Glasgow CAs' business bought them into occupational and social contact primarily with merchants, bankers, brokers and shipowners rather than with those occupied in the professions. This association with commerce was reflected in the occupations of the fathers of the early members of the Glasgow Institute.

In the 1871 census, of the 305 accountants enumerated in Edinburghshire, 215 (70.5%) were classified under the legal profession and 90 under 'commerce', whereas in Lanarkshire, 103 (25.9%) were entered in the former category and 295 in the latter. This basic divergence between the two major branches of the Scottish CA profession was reflected also in the fact that Edinburgh accountants were placed in the legal section of their local street and trades directory and appeared in the *Scottish Law List and Legal Directory* from the year of their incorporation. The Glasgow Institute did not appear in the latter until the 1880s.

The professional status of the early SAE was, however, partially tainted by a commercial element due to the employment of almost one-third of its original members in insurance companies. Most were managers, an occupation of higher standing in Edinburgh than the rest of Britain. The post required "a man of gentlemanly bearings"[37], was not infrequently occupied by an eminent lawyer in the larger companies, though more often it was filled by a professional actuary. 15 SAE members were among the 38 original members of the Faculty of Actuaries. Despite the connection with insurance, the popular impression of the Edinburgh CA was of an expert witness before the courts, whereas in Glasgow it was of a businessman in his counting house.

Consequently, James Martin, corporate accountant and life-long critic of the chartered societies claimed that: "the Glasgow Institute was considered on a lower level than the Edinburgh Society".[38] The connection with commerce and trade left some IAAG members open to public suspicion. Their pecuniary motivations were questioned by some due to the alleged unscrupulous and unprofessional tactics (no doubt exaggerated) of gaining business and extracting exhorbitant fees. As a result, Martin concluded in 1896 that: "I do not know whether it is the case that in Glasgow we have a lower type of C.A. than exists elsewhere. If I did say so I should not be the first to record the observation."[39] Although unprofessional activities were undoubtedly common only among a few, their existence could reflect on the standing of all IAAG members. The public were notoriously suspicious of dealers in money, and adverse opinions concerning them were aroused easily during the nineteenth century. In Edinburgh, similar claims of unfair business practices were no doubt lodged from time to time though they were unlikely to have gained such widespread public consciousness in an atmosphere in which the CA was seen as a trustworthy gentleman of the legal classes.

Indeed, the SAE connection with the legal profession was so strong that Martin later claimed that certain CAs could advantageously affect the decisions of the courts in cases where the Society's interests were under threat. In the 'CA case' of 1893 in which the Scottish chartered societies fought successfully in the Court of Session the claims of Glasgow corporate accountants to use the 'CA' notation, Martin suggested that the SAE utilized its legal connections to determine the outcome. "Judges and C.A.'s", he noted "mix in Edinburgh society".[40] A series of "Edinburgh dinners and Edinburgh champagne"[41] won the Court's favour. And, although he could not be certain, he suspected:

> . . . that social environment and family ties had something to do with the decision. The C.A.'s of Scotland are wealthy and influential, but the influence is strong elsewhere– I was not, when the case was raised, aware of the family relationships between the C.A.'s in Edinburgh and the Court.[42]

The difference in status, both professional and social, between the Edinburgh and Glasgow CA societies, despite the timing of their institution and similar organizational progress, reflected the continued significance of social determinants and evaluations of occupational standing during the nineteenth century. The divergence between the commercial and legal orientated branches of Scottish chartered accountancy was evident in their continuous friendly rivalry at best and hostility at worse. The most obvious indication of the divergence of status between the two organizations which apparently exhibited such similar professional traits, was the fact that they remained separate entities for so long. Concerted co-operation between the Scottish CA societies was only encouraged by the existence of a common threat during the 1880s and 1890s when external organizations posed a greater intimidation to the SAE's status than did association with the IAAG. It was not until 1951 that the individual societies formally and completely united as one national organization.

The Scottish situation contrasted with that of accountancy in the rest of Britain. With the partial exception of London, English accountancy organizations had essentially mercantile roots. Late eighteenth and early nineteenth century accountants in England tended to be described in local directories as 'writing masters and accomptants', 'agent and accomptant', 'broker and accomptant', or, 'merchant and accomptant' (depending on city). The location of the earliest organizations reflected their non-legal origins; associations were founded in Liverpool and London in 1870, in Manchester in 1871, and in Sheffield in 1877. Given that: "the profession of accountant did not attain a position of importance in England or in Ireland at so early a period as in Scotland",[43] these disparate societies found it necessary to improve and impose its professional status through the establishment of a national, centralized, incorporated organization - the ICAEW founded on 11 May 1880.

The status of the English CAs was damaged further due to the occupational diversity of the ICAEW's membership compared to the relatively high degree of occupational specialization of CAs in Edinburgh - most of whom were engaged in professional practice. Martin commented ruefully, for instance, that:

> I think if Pharoah's baker and his butler had been living they might have been original members of the English society- so mixed is it- along with his butcher and his barber, his bootmaker and his billsticker, and so on through the alphabet.[44]

Another more persistent blight on the professional standing of the English CA, and to a lesser extent also on that of his Scottish equivalent, was caused by the unregulated nature of accountancy and the unprofessional and commercial orientations of many so called *accountants*. Any unqualified individual could describe himself as an accountant. The position of the professional became tarnished by the activities of the unscrupulous and incompetent. *The Accountant's Journal* noted in August 1892, for example, that:

> Hardly a week goes by without some so-called accountant being brought before the magistrates to answer for some, more or less disgraceful piece of misconduct; and in consequence an honorable profession runs the risk of being considered decidedly 'mixed' as regards the status of its members.[45]

Whereas in Edinburgh the term accountant was a reasonably well-defined occupational title with a definite connection with the legal profession in the second half of the nineteenth century, English accountancy journals were compelled regularly to protest "strongly against the looseness with which the term 'accountant' was applied to any clerk or bookkeeper whose disorderly conduct might bring him into the hands of the police. Almost every crime has thus at one time or another been imputed to our profession."[46] During the 1880-1900 period, and despite their incorporation, members of the relatively infant ICAEW were often indistinguishable in the public imagination from the degraded 'turf accountant', 'football accountant', 'auditor' or 'bookkeeper'. Many undoubtedly concurred with the popular impression that an accountant of any description was a desperate character who had failed in a number of previous vocations and who sought to pay off his debts by fleecing the public - sentiments that were hardly likely to encourage public esteem in the occupation. *The Scottish Accountant* reported in 1893, for example, that

A Welsh Accountant while giving evidence recently before the Select Committee on Building Society Bills stated that in Carnarvonshire it was a common thing for the auditors of building societies to be painters, waiters, brick-builders, coachmen, quarrymen &c., and his experience was that in many cases all the auditors did was "to sign the balance sheet and take their fees.[47]

The source of such public distrust of accountants in England and Wales stemmed largely from the widely-reported and condemned activities of certain accountants in company auditing and insolvencies in the middle years of the nineteenth century. During that period, claimed Jeal in 1937: "accountants were of two classes: men who had established a reputation for integrity and men who were worthy of no confidence".[48] *The Times* in 1868 asserted that it was: "One of the greatest evils of recent times that the occupation had been left without any means provided by which the most reputable members of the body might earn a definite position calculated to exclude the herd of disreputable persons."[49]

Cases bought before the English courts revealed the ineptitude and dishonesty of certain accountants, and frequently included adverse comments from the presiding judge concerning the undistinguished and questionable nature of practitioners. For instance, in 1875, Mr Justice Quain asserted that "The whole affairs in bankruptcy have been handed over to an ignorant set of men called accountants, which was one of the greatest abuses ever introduced into Law."[50] The most famous damnation of English accountants by a lawyer was the much quoted: "An accountant appears to be a man who cannot give an account of himself." Such comments contrasted strongly with the expressed opinions of the established professional classes, especially the lawyers, regarding the integrity and standing of the Edinburgh CA. The confidence of the establishment and the public in English accountants was only gained, claimed Jeal, during the last years of the nineteenth and early twentieth centuries and was recognized in 1900 when the auditing of all limited companies was made compulsory.

Scottish CAs, and particularly the legal orientated membership of the SAE, could stand aloof from such unsavoury connections and criticisms which were especially prevalent in the press. The Edinburgh Society's long standing by the late nineteenth century ensured that, locally at least, most of its clientele and the public might recognize the existence of some distinction between a CA and an accountant. Throughout the second half of the nineteenth century, it can therefore be asserted that the status of the occupation varied in different parts of Britain:

> The import of the word [accountant] in the two countries [England and Scotland] has quite different significations. In the one country we point to an educated, trained and intelligent class of men, bearing the same appellation, which in England is looked upon as a mere keeper of books, and manipulator of elementary calculations.[51]

Evaluating Professional Status

It is apparent from an examination of the nineteenth and early twentieth century accountancy profession that modern methods of determining whether an occupation may be regarded as a *profession* are inadequate for historical purposes. The adoption of certain *traits* varied in their relative importance in different periods. The professional status of Edinburgh CAs derived predominantly from the acquisition of characteristics of significance to occupational standing during the eighteenth century; primarily from connections with a traditional, established profession and its clientele. Incorporation was sufficient to affirm a standing already gained.

By the 1880s, the determinants of professional status had altered, a greater emphasis being placed upon examination and practice based on specialized knowledge. The English accountants, without the foundation of any such prestigious associations upon which to build their occupational stature, had to adopt a series of institutional measures necessary at the time to *assert* their status. A national organization and the immediate introduction of a comprehensive system of examination were vital. The Edinburgh accountants of the 1840s and 1850s had not found it so urgent and indispensable to organize and establish a procedure for the thorough testing of theoretical knowledge. It simply upgraded its examination system in successive steps during the 1860–1910 period to comply with the increasing emphasis that was placed upon meritocratic features as a *professional* characteristic.

It is also evident from the study that, although the trait approach recognizes the significance of occupational standing with the public as important to its professional status, *social* and *professional* status are not always distinguishable – particularly in the historical context. Insufficient emphasis has been placed upon the social standing of the practitioners of an occupation and the opinions expressed by existing professionals, their clientele and the general public concerning its professional status and respectability. Such factors appear to have been particularly significant to occupational standing during the eighteenth and nineteenth centuries. The practitioner must be examined within his own economic and social environment rather than concentrating solely on the development and institutional characteristics of the organization to which he belongs.

It follows that national evaluations of occupational status can be misleading. There could be considerable local and regional variation in professional status within one vocation during the nineteenth century. Certain of the new, marginal status, centrally-organized professions had their origins in local branches, each reflecting and catering for the demands of its own populace and the economic and social structure of its location. Each branch might therefore vary in the nature and sources of its business, its clientele, and in the perceived value of its existence. In nineteenth century accountancy, the status of the profession displayed such regional and local variation. Scottish CAs were considered as having a higher professional standing than English CAs and, within Scotland, SAE members were accorded a greater status than IAAG members – thus rendering inaccurate general assertions concerning the occupational status of *British* accountants during the second half of the nineteenth century.

Having thus outlined the nature of the profession chosen for major investigation, and the nature, timing and sources of its professional status, this chapter proceeds to discuss the methods by which the information relating to the examination of recruitment was collected and analysed.

OPERATIONALIZATION

The most fruitful means of information retrieval was to compile a collective biography of all Edinburgh chartered accountants who gained admission to the SAE to 1914. Additionally, all individuals who became apprenticed though failed to qualify, and who would conceivably have become members by 31 December 1914 had they not been unsuccessful, were included in the data base. The objective was to collect such information concerning the life history of each individual as was pertinent to his recruitment and professional experience. The information was recorded on standardized forms akin to those of a modern social mobility survey to ease later sorting and organization.

To locate the total pool of individuals, a variety of sources were utilized. The indenture registers of the SAE provided the names of all apprentices and the Society's minute books revealed members admitted. The task was also eased by information contained in two works relating to the Scottish profession.[52] A total of 1146 cases were identified as members or failed apprentices. Three SAE recruits were excluded from the investigation due to their later being admitted as members of the IAAG and their careers being centred in Glasgow or the west of Scotland.[53]

It was then considered advantageous, in order to ease the task of searching the primary sources, to collect biographical information concerning each CA as it appeared in the obituarial sections of professional journals. Here, the Scottish CAs' periodical *The Accountant's Magazine* published from 1897 proved to be most useful as was to a lesser extent, the English CAs' equivalent: *The Accountant* (from 1874), mostly for members dying south of the border. Almost all SAE members who were deceased from 1897 received some mention in *The Accountant's Magazine*, the amount of detail varying according to the degree of eminence achieved by the individual in the profession.

The seven volumes of SAE indenture registers relevant to the period of the study were then exhausted. Each indenture was in the form of a contractual agreement between master and apprentice. The following information was collected for each case from this source: duration and dates of the apprenticeship; name of master(s) and cautioner(s) (the guarantor of the apprentice's good conduct, usually his father); the address and occupation (where provided) of the cautioner; date of birth (provided for some later apprentices); progress in compulsory university classes; the indenture fee and its payer; and the names and addresses of the witnesses of the agreement.

Each recruit's progress through the changing professional examination system was then recorded as well as any details concerning later career as contained in the examination and membership books of the SAE and in the minute books of the Council of the Society.

Information relating to family origins and circumstances and basic demographic data not revealed in previous sources was next accumulated. As a prelude to searching census enumerators' books, the addresses of each apprentice's family or guardians was obtained from local street directories for the census years closest to the period of indenture and qualification. The addresses provided in the articles of indenture proved invaluable for locating those from non-urban areas in the census. The apprentice's family was then searched in as many census years as possible between 1841 and 1891 in order to ascertain family size, the occupations of its members, their ages and birthplaces. Certain features of the household were indicative of the recruit's living conditions, such as number of domestic servants and windowed rooms (the latter from 1861).

In cases where it proved impossible to locate a family at all in any census (for example, where the apprentice's family lived outside Scotland) or difficult to compose a complete picture of the recruit's origins and circumstances, as much pertinent information as possible was gained from civil registers of births, marriages and deaths. These sources, as well as local and professional directories, proved most useful in the identification of occupational information.

Further information concerning each CA's career and its location was collected from Scottish legal directories, and from 1896-7, the annual list published by the three Scottish CA societies. Each CA's location, firm, and offices held in the professional organization were recorded as they altered in successive directories. The details provided and the year of final entry proved to be a valuable indicator in identifying those who were eligible to produce sons for future self-recruitment, and in establishing age and place of death.

The educational experience of each apprentice was likely to be of potential significance to his opportunities for professional recruitment. Relevant information was only sparsely provided by the previous sources. The published alumni and rolls of the universities and prominent schools listed an adequate record for some apprentices. Reliance on these sources clearly, however, produced a bias towards those who had attended the higher class educational institutions of the period. In order to overcome this bias, an additional source was consulted. It had become apparent that many qualifying Edinburgh CA's had attended certain law classes at Edinburgh University as part of their vocational training. This was compulsory for all apprentice's from 1866 and had been a convention previously. The matriculation registers of the University were thus examined, these being unique in that, from 1869, they list not only the student's place of birth, age and course, but also the educational institutions attended previous to first matriculation.[54]

In order to examine Edinburgh CAs' potential for securing self-recruitment to their profession particular investigation was undertaken of the marital and fertility experience of 355 members who joined the SAE between 1853 and 1892 (including three ICAEW members who practised in Edinburgh) and their sons. This cohort could feasibly have produced sons for self-recruitment and qualification to the profession by 1914. Details of the methodological approach employed for this analysis and information collection are provided in Chapters 6 and 7.

The information collected for each individual recruit and CA was then organized and prepared for computer analysis. Two major files were constructed, the smaller containing the data on the marriage, fertility and self-recruitment capacity of 355 cases in the form of 111 relevant variables for each. The larger file was composed of all 1146 apprentices and members of the SAE, and related mostly to the input-recruitment aspect of the study. A total of 307 variables for each case were coded. A series of minor files were constructed in order to ease data sorting and coding, and to analyse information collected concerning 651 members of the Faculty of Advocates admitted between 1850 and 1914. The Statistical Package for the Social Sciences was utilized to analyse the data.

A status classification of occupations was an essential requirement in a study that would attempt to measure the distance of social movement. On the basis of the data collected for CA apprentices and from other qualitative sources, nine social status groups (SSGs) were identified. Discussion of this classification appears in Appendix A. The nature of the schools attended by recruits to the SAE and sons of CAs also required ordering into manageable groups. The procedure adopted here and the resultant classification are described in Appendix B.

Having thus outlined the subject of this study, its design, the methods of investigation and analysis and the nature of the particular profession chosen to investigate recruitment, the text now proceeds to examine and discuss the findings of the research. The structure of the book follows the recruitment process from the decision to enter a specific vocation, through qualification and membership of a profession, to the entrance to it of sons in the succeeding generation. The factors that were involved in the decision to enter the recruitment system of the SAE are examined in Chapter 3. Chapter 4 comprises an analysis of the process of vocational preparation and qualification. The determinants of success and failure in the professional training system and post-qualification are investigated in Chapter 5. The potential of Edinburgh CAs to secure self-recruitment to the SAE and the rate of social mobility into the profession are studied in Chapters 6 and 7. The analysis begins, however, with an investigation of the determinants of the expansion of recruitment to the SAE; the demand for professional services and the supply of recruits.

Notes

1 Studies of social mobility to individual professions include the following. R.K. Kelsall, "Self Recruitment in Four Professions", in D. Glass (ed.), *Social Mobility in Britain* (London, 1954). *idem., Higher Civil Servants in Britain from 1870 to the Present Day* (London, 1955). D.H.J. Morgan, "The Social and Educational Background of Anglican Bishops", *British Journal of Sociology* 20 (1969). C.B. Otley, "The Social Origins of British Army Officers", *Sociological Review* 18 (1970). P.E. Razell, "Social Origins of Army Officers in the India and British Home Army", *British Journal of Sociology* 14 (1963).

2 Calculated from data provided by W.J. Reader, *Professional Men: The Rise of the Professional Classes in Nineteenth Century England* (London, 1966). See also R.M. Hartwell, "The Service Revolution: The Growth of Services in Modern Economy 1700-1914", in C.M. Cipolla (ed.), *The Industrial Revolution* (Brighton, 1973). B.R. Mitchell and P. Deane, *Abstract of British Historical Statistics* (Cambridge, 1962), ch. 2. C. Clark, *The Conditions of Economic Progress* (London, 1957). D.C. Marsh, *The Changing Social Structure of England and Wales 1871-1951* (London, 1958). A.L. Bowley, *Wages and Income in the United Kingdom since 1860* (Cambridge, 1937), pp. 127-36.

3 See for instance E. Sibley, "Some Demographic Clues to Stratification", *American Sociological Review* 7 (1942). N. Rogoff, *Recent Trends in Occupational Mobility* (New York, 1953). J.A. Kahl, *The American Class Structure* (New York, 1957). G. Carlsson, *Social Mobility and Class Structure* (Lund, 1958). S.M. Lipset and R. Bendix, *Social Mobility in Industrial Society* (Berkeley, 1959). P.M. Blau and O.D. Duncan, *The American Occupational Structure* (New York, 1967). J.H. Goldthorpe, *Social Mobility and Class Structure in Modern Britain* (Oxford, 1980).

4 See G. Millerson, *The Qualifying Associations: A Study of Professionalization* (London, 1964), pp. 221-58 for the establishment of new professional organizations. For detailed documentation of the development of individual professions, see A. Carr-Saunders and P.A. Wilson, *The Professions* (London, 1933) and also Reader, *Professional Men.*

5 See N. and J. Parry, "Social Closure and Collective Social Mobility", in R. Scase (ed.), *Industrial Society: Class Cleavage and Control* (London, 1977).

6 See Reader, *Professional Men,* chaps. 4-6 and Millerson, *The Qualifying Associations,* Appendix 1, for the introduction of examination systems as the basis of professional qualification.

7 For the general expansion of the educational system see J. Lawson and H. Silver, *A Social History of Education in England* (London, 1973), chaps. 8-10. R.L. Archer, *Secondary Education in the Nineteenth Century* (Cambridge, 1921). For Scotland, see R.D. Anderson, *Education and Opportunity in Victorian Scotland* (Oxford, 1983). J. Scotland, *The History of Scottish Education* (London, 1969).

8 See H. Perkin, *The Origins of Modern English Society, 1780-1880* (London, 1969), pp. 428-36.

9 S.G. Checkland, *The Rise of Industrial Society in England 1815-1885* (London, 1964), pp. 294-5.

10 The existence of differential fertility can be shown by the fact that the 1911 Fertility Census for Scotland revealed that the mean fertility of marriages since 1860

was 5.82 births for the whole population. However, it was 4.17 for the ten professional groups enumerated, compared to 6.29 for general labourers and 7.04 for crofters. British *Parliamentary Papers*, 1914, vol. 99, "Census of Scotland 1911", vol. 3, Table XVII, pp. 284-8. See also British *Parliamentary Papers*, 1948-9, vol. XIX, "Royal Commission on Population". T.H.C. Stevenson, "The Fertility of the Various Social Classes in England and Wales from the Middle of the Nineteenth Century to 1911", *Journal of the Royal Statistical Society* 83 (1920). For the decline in middle class fertility see, J.A. Banks, *Prosperity and Parenthood* (London, 1965). *Ibid., Victorian Values: Secularism and the Size of Families* (London, 1981).

11 P. Sorokin, *Social and Cultural Mobility* (New York, 1964), p. 346. Sorokin first propounded this hypothesis in his earlier work *Social Mobility* (New York, 1927). For the consequences of differential fertility on social mobility, see also J. Westergaard and H. Resler, *Class in a Capitalist Society* (London, 1975), Part 4. J. Matras, "Differential Fertility, Intergenerational Occupational Mobility and Change in the Occupational Distribution", *Population Studies* 15 (1961). S.H. Preston, "Differential Fertility, Unwanted Fertility and Recent Trends in Occupational Achievement", *American Sociological Review* 39 (1974). D.V. Glass and J.R. Hall, "A Study of Inter-Generational Changes in Status", in D.V. Glass (ed.), *Social Mobility in Britain* (London, 1954).

12 F.H. Groome, *Ordnance Gazetteer of Scotland* (London, 1885), p. 517.

13 T. and W. McDowall, *McDowall's New Guide in Edinburgh* (Edinburgh, 1849), p. 11.

14 J. Heiton, *The Castes of Edinburgh*, 3rd ed. (Edinburgh, 1861), pp. 281-2. See also R.Q. Gray, *The Labour Aristocracy in Victorian Edinburgh* (Oxford, 1976), ch. 2 on the social structure of nineteenth century Edinburgh.

15 R. Brown, *A History of Accounting and Accountants* (Edinburgh, 1905). ICAS, *A History of the Chartered Accountants of Scotland to 1954* (Edinburgh, 1954). E. Jones, *Accountancy and the British Economy 1840-1980: The Evolution of Ernst and Whinney* (London, 1981), ch. 3. J.C. Stewart, *Pioneers of a Profession, Chartered Accountants to 1879* (Edinburgh, 1977). For England and Wales see also N.A.H. Stacey, *English Accountancy; A Study in Social and Economic History* (London, 1954).

16 See the following. Carr-Saunders and Wilson, *The Professions*. Millerson, *The Qualifying Associations*. J. Ben-David, "Professions and the Class System of Present Day Societies", *Current Sociology* 12 (1963-4). P. Elliot, *The Sociology of the Professions* (London, 1972). R. Lewis and A. Maude, *Professional People* (London, 1952). T.J. Johnson, *Professions and Power* (London, 1972). J.A. Jackson (ed.), *Professions and Professionalization* (Cambridge, 1970). Series of papers on the professions in *Daedulus* 92 (1963).

17 Millerson, *The Qualifying Associations*, p. 9.

18 Brown, *A History of Accounting and Accountants*, p. 203. For a recent discussion of the motivations behind the organization of Scottish accountants see, J.C. Stewart, "The Emergent Professionals", *The Accountant's Magazine* 79 (1975). K.M. Macdonald, "Professional Formation: the Case of Scottish Accountants", *British Journal of Sociology* 35 (1984). R.J. Briston and M.K.M. Kedslie, "Professional Formation: The case of Scottish Accountants – some corrections and some further thoughts", *British Journal of Sociology* 37 (1986). K.M. Macdonald, "Professional Formation: a reply to Briston and Kedslie", *British Journal of Sociology* 38 (1987).

19 The grant of the Royal Charter, though highly significant to the membership of the Institute of Accountants in Edinburgh, was received with little excitement in the local press. Both the *Edinburgh Evening Courant* and *The Scotsman* were more concerned

with the Crimean War and the Siege of Sebastopol. The charter was granted two days before the Battle of Balaklava and the charge of the Light Brigade.

20 *Index Juridicus, The Scottish Law List and Legal Directory 1855*, p. 612.

21 The early minute books of the SAE reveal that considerable emphasis was placed on maintaining standards of conduct among the membership. One original member, Henry Callender, CA was removed from the Society following some publicised unprofessional activities that induced his fleeing to the USA to avoid prosecution.

22 Reader, *Professional Men*, p. 149.

23 Carr-Saunders and Wilson, *The Professions*, p. 210.

24 T.C. Smout, *A History of the Scottish People, 1560-1830* (London, 1969), p. 373.

25 Heiton, *The Castes of Edinburgh*, pp. 176-7.

26 That is, an address given as within either the St George or St Andrews Registration Districts of Edinburgh.

27 For example, among the original members of the SAE David Cormack, CA was also an SSC; John Hunter, CA was a WS and Auditor of the Court of Session; and, William Myrtle, CA was a writer.

28 "Report of the Committee appointed at the General Meeting of the Society of Writers to Her Majesties Signet, to consider the Details and Report upon a Bill brought into Parliament for the Appointment of an Accountant-General in the Court of Session", preamble. (Special Collections Dept., Edinburgh University Library).

29 *Ibid.*, p. 2.

30 Quoted in Brown, *A History of Accounting and Accountants*, p. 127.

31 That is, had fathers who were employed in the legal, clerical, physic or defence professions or who were described as landed proprietors or other 'independent income'.

32 See L. Hopkins, *The Hundredth Year: The Story of the Institute of Chartered Accountants of England and Wales* (Plymouth, 1980). Jones, *Accountancy and the British Economy 1840-1980*, pp. 35-6, 137.

33 Heiton, *The Castes of Edinburgh*, p. 6.

34 R.A. Witty, *How to become a Qualified Accountant* (London, 1906), pp. 16-17.

35 *The Accountant's Journal* 11 (1893), p. 3.

36 Stewart, *Pioneers of a Profession*, p. 12. The IAAG in 1870 allegedly consisted of 37 stockbrokers, 27 accountants and no actuaries. By 1885 there were only 3 actuaries and "a high proportion of stockbrokers to pure accountants is still kept up." (*The Accountant* 11 [1885] p. 5).

37 Revd. N.L. Walker, *David MacLagan, F.R.C.E.* (London, 1884), pp. 84-5.

38 J. Martin, *The Accountant Profession: A Public Danger* (Glasgow, 1896), p. 37. Similarly, *The Accountant* commented in 1885 that of the three Scottish CA societies,

the SAE "is by far the most important of these bodies, both in number and in the status of its members. They, even at the first, were admitted with care, and the training and qualifications of those who subsequently joined its ranks leave little to be desired." The IAAG, by contrast, "has not done for its members, and consequently for Glasgow, what has been affected by its Edinburgh rival." (*The Accountant* 11 [1885] p. 6).

39 *Ibid.*, p. 18.

40 J. Martin, *The Accountant Squabble: The Government and the C.A. Case, Were the Law Courts Bribed ? A Scathing Exposure* (Glasgow, 1908), p. 19.

41 J. Martin, *The Sanctification of the Lie* (Glasgow, 1897), p. 17.

42 J. Martin, *Did the Devil Win the Toss, or, The Lie Triumphant in the Law Courts: An Exposure* (Glasgow, 1897), p. 31.

43 Brown, *A History of Accounting and Accountants*, p. 232. See also *The Accountant* 17 (1891), p. 846 where it is admitted that compared with the ICAEW, the Scottish incorporated societies "have undoubtedly succeeded in raising the profession in public estimation in that country to a higher pitch than has yet been arrived at here".

44 Martin, *The Accountant Profession: A Public Danger*, p. 5.

45 *The Accountant's Journal* 10 (1892), p. 96.

46 *The Accountant's Journal* 10 (1892), p. 24.

47 *The Scottish Accountant* 1 (1893), p. 123.

48 E.F. Jeal, "Some Reflections on the Evolution of the Professional Practice of Accounting in Great Britain", The *Accountant* 96 (1937), p. 526.

49 Quoted in Jeal, "Some Reflections on the Evolution of the Professional Practice of Accounting in Great Britain", p. 526.

50 Quoted in A.H. Woolf, *A Short History of Accountants and Accounting* (London, 1912), p. 177.

51 J. McClelland, *The Origin and Present Organization of the Profession of Chartered Accountant in Scotland* (Glasgow, 1869), p. 14.

52 These were Brown, *A History of Accounting and Accountants* which contains an appended list of deceased Scottish accountants to 1905, and Stewart, *Pioneers of a Profession* which provides biographical details for 346 Scottish CAs admitted between 1853 and 1879, of whom 180 were SAE members.

53 These were William Hardie, CA, who joined the SAE in 1878 and the IAAG in 1900; John M. MacLeod, CA, who was admitted to the SAE in 1880 and the IAAG in 1894; and, John Laurie, CA who was apprenticed in 1893 to George Lisle, CA in Edinburgh but completed his training with Rattray Bros. & Co. in Glasgow and entered the IAAG in 1899.

54 See Anderson, *Education and Opportunity in Victorian Scotland* for details of the information available in the matriculation records of the Scottish universities.

2
The Determinants of Recruitment to the
Society of Accountants in Edinburgh

Accountants are the products of present economic conditions

[*The Scottish Accountant*, 1892]

Prominent nineteenth and early twentieth century accountants were consistent in their explanations of the origins and expansion of the numbers practising their profession. The increasing complexity of the urban-industrial state and the vast development of manufacturing had:

> . . . called into existence a multitude of new businesses and professions to meet the demands of the most gigantic fabric of trade and commerce which the world has ever seen. Not the least useful or notable of the occupations which have in this way had their origin or development is that of a Public Accountant.[1]

The long-run escalation in the demand for services provided by CAs was viewed, as with the unbounded growth and sophistication of the economy, as an infinitely expanding process. As the wealth of the nation increased and the importance of the accurate compilation and scrutiny of financial accounts became increasingly recognized by government, companies and individuals, it was assumed CAs could envisage an ever-widening field of employment.

A traditional adherence to the free market operation of the laws of demand and supply were deemed by CAs as the short and medium-term regulators of the rate of professional expansion. The growth in CAs' business (demand), in relation to the number of practitioners (supply), determined the level of professional income which, in turn, altered the attraction of entering the profession and therefore the number of recruits.

Successive eminent Edinburgh CAs provided lists of specific economic and legislative events within the increasingly complex infrastructure of the state which had increased the demand for the services of CAs and, consequently, had increased their numbers. The President of the SAE in 1894, for example, noted a serious of developments which had "exercised a very decided influence upon the profession".[2] The railway mania of the 1840s and the establishment by Act of Parliament of railway companies' *limited* status, and the legal requirement for an audit for the benefit of shareholders marked "a supreme moment in the history of the profession".[3] Similarly, the expansion of insurance companies in Edinburgh during the 1840s and 1850s ensured that openings were created for accountants as actuaries and managers. In addition, the establishment in Scotland of seven banks between 1810 and 1838 proved to be "a valuable addition to the business of the profession."[4]

A series of subsequent legislative enactments were assumed as being the major determinants of the growth of the Edinburgh profession and its timing. The Life Assurance Companies Act 1870, the Companies Act 1879, the Bank Act 1891, and the Building Societies Act 1894 established the compulsory, independent audit and inspection of insurance, banking and building society company accounts. The Local Government (Scotland) Act 1889, the Burgh Police (Scotland) Act 1892, and the Local Government (Scotland) Act 1894 represented an augmentation of Edinburgh CAs' workload in instituting the compulsory audit 'by fit persons' of county, burgh and parish council accounts, respectively. The extension of the statutory investigation of local authority books during the first decade of the twentieth century was one of the explanations propounded for the profession's expansion during the same period. *The Accountant's Magazine* noting in January 1912 that a doubling in the number of Scottish CAs since 1897 had occurred, concluding that: "There must have been a great addition during the last fifteen years to the work for which a professional accountant is required."[5] The journal offered a further explanation for the progress in membership in the increasing complexity of recent income tax changes which had demanded a greater accuracy in bookkeeping, and further envisaged that the National Insurance Act 1911 would lead to an increase in actuarial business among its subscribers.

Many of these apparently significant legislative enactments have been grossly exaggerated in their effects upon increasing CAs' business and consequently in their effects on professional recruitment. For example, the audit of banking and insurance company books was conducted almost wholly by CAs before statutory compulsion was introduced. The Local Government Act 1889 had provided only three SAE appointments by 1896.

In order, therefore, to estimate the actual significance for recruitment of escalations in Edinburgh CAs' workload allegedly induced by legislative and economic developments, it is initially necessary to define the major sources of their business and its changes over the 1854-1914 period. The SAE's minute books, together with journals, speeches and experiences of its individual members, the content of its examination papers but particularly, the information presented by the Society in resistance to the SIA petitions for incorporation by royal charter, reveal the pertinent information. The latter source proved particularly useful in its meticulous breakdown and comparison of CAs' total business as against that of the rival SIA membership.

In 1889-90, it was asserted that in Scotland:

> Accountants are largely employed in the winding up of limited and other public companies, as trustees on estates sequestrated under the Bankruptcy Acts, as judicial factors on the estates of deceased persons, as *curators bonis* to persons incapable of managing their own affairs and as factors *loco tutoris* to infants. They are also largely employed in auditing the accounts of public corporations and joint stock and limited companies.[6]

The most lucrative and significant sources of Edinburgh CAs' workload during the 1854-1914 period were judicial factories, bankruptcies and registered companies. It is legislation affecting these that requires particular investigation as to its impact on SAE recruitment.

The appoinment of CAs as **judicial factors** (previously the preserve of writers and solicitors) was a branch of work particularly influenced by legislation introduced *before* the institution of the SAE. The Pupils Protection Act 1849 placed all factories and appointments under the supervision of an Accountant of the Court of Session in Edinburgh. It was under this Act that SAE members received the majority of their factorial appointments. The 1880 and 1889 Judicial Factors Acts do not appear to have affected significantly the workload of Edinburgh CAs; the former permitted factorial appointments outside the Edinburgh-located Court of Session, and increased the business of provincial accountants under sheriff court factories.

The minute books of the SAE reveal that the major concern of early SAE members was with **bankruptcy** business. Again, however, the significant legislation augmenting CAs' business occurred very early and very late in the 1854 to 1914 period. The Bankruptcy Act 1856 permitted the appointment of trustees by creditors to manage and wind-up insolvent estates and remained the prominent legislation important to CAs until the 1913 Act. CAs could be appointed as trustees under the supervision of the Accountant in Bankruptcy. Edinburgh CAs received similar appointments under *cessio bonorum* legislation;[7] and relevant enactments to this branch of business were passed in 1838-9 and 1856. The *cessio* was abolished in 1913.

Of greatest importance during the later years of the period was **registered company** work: the audit and winding-up of joint stock companies. The Limited Companies Act 1855 and the Companies Act 1862 (with its provisions for the formation of companies without parliamentary sanction, and with limited liability as well as a clause relevant to auditing) were not of immediate interest to SAE members. The expansion of new firms and of liquidations under the Act ensured, however, "That it has been of great benefit to the profession by adding largely to the amount of business to be overtaken."[8]

Not until the Companies Act 1900 was the independent audit made compulsory though, well before this time, this branch of business was of considerable importance. "In this field", reported *The Scottish Accountant* in 1893 "the demand for our services is increasing by leaps and bounds."[9] The greater rate of expansion of the membership of the Glasgow CA society relative to the SAE from the 1890s was explained in terms of the rate of company formation and commercial orientation of the "second city of the empire".[10]

Not only did the growth of joint stock company formation also encourage the appointment of CAs as company accountants, managers and secretaries, but their example of employing a professional auditor was emulated by smaller business concerns. By 1894, *The Scottish Accountant* could assert that:

> There has been a remarkable increase in recent years, in the extent to which the commercial world has availed itself of the services of the accountant in the matter of auditing. At first this was largely confined to the books of public bodies or companies where the interests of shareholders and others were involved. More recently, however, private firms, in large numbers, have found it desirable to adopt the wise and salutory precaution of a skilled audit.[11]

Given the timing of the major legislative changes that were likely to have affected the demand for Edinburgh CAs' services and, in the case of the vital Companies Act 1862, its delayed impact upon the profession and its workload, it is clear that a simple examination of the relationship between the dates of relevant legislation and professional growth would not reveal significant conclusions regarding the impact of legislative developments on recruitment. What requires investigation are the long-run impressions that these and other developments made on trends in Edinburgh CAs' business. An analysis comparing the dates of apparently important legislation to the SAE member and the intake of apprentices in the same or following year would be too simplistic and misleading. An alternative approach was consequently adopted.

A quantitative reconstruction of fluctuations in Edinburgh-located CAs' sources of employment was attempted for the 1854–1914 period in order to monitor closely the impact of increased demand for professional services on recruitment.

Statistics of the annual increases in the number of new appointments in Edinburgh and the Lothians in the three major sources of CAs' business were collected where possible, and compared to the annual intake of SAE apprentices. The number of new bankruptcies before the Court of Session and Midlothian Sheriff Court were available for 1857 to 1914 inclusive from the unpublished annual reports of the Accountant in Bankruptcy, and from published *Judicial Statistics of Scotland* in Parliamentary Papers.[12] *Cessio* statistics for Edinburghshire before the Accountant of Court were derived from that official's annual reports;[13] but they are available for the 1883–1913 period only. Court of Session judicial factory statistics were gained for 1883 to 1914 only from *Judicial Statistics of Scotland*.[14] And the annual number of registered companies established or liquidated under company legislation and located in the Lothians was made available *via* the yearly reports of the Board of Trade relating to joint stock companies and the unpublished original books of the Registrar of Companies for Scotland.[15] The total number of new appointments created by some of the minor legislation noted earlier were included where quantifiable.

On the basis of these figures, two series of data were constructed which represent annual changes in the number of new appointments potentially open to Edinburgh CAs. The statistics measure, in effect, changing demand for CA services. *Series A* includes the totals of the data available over the entire 1857 to 1914 period, whereas *Series B* covers all the information available between 1883 and 1913 and is, therefore, a more accurate estimation of changes in total potential new business in that period. The figures are contained in Table 2.1 and reveal the declining importance of bankruptcy and related work relative to company auditing and liquidation.

It should be noted here that there are certain limitations in the usage of these statistics:

1. Each individual appointment is counted as of equal value to all others. No weight is attached to the likely volume of business or income derived from various appointments, though, clearly, the audit of the Commercial Bank of Scotland was of greater significance than that of the Scottish Mushroom Company.

2. Though they represent the major, most lucrative and voluminous sources of Edinburgh CAs' work, a large component of business was composed of small audits, remits from court and actuarial business not legally requiring registration, and therefore remains unquantifiable. This was, however, likely to have constituted everyday, constant, on-going business.[16]

3. It is not possible to account for changes in the interoccupational distribution of appointments. For example, CAs' share of bankruptcy work may have increased relative to that of lawyers and other accountants despite the fact that total sequestrations were declining. The figures in Table 2.1 represent the optimum number of new appointments that Edinburgh CAs competed for and, as will be shown later, they received a high and constant proportion of them.

4. Neither can the figures reveal the distribution of possible appointments among Edinburgh CA firms. It was quite possible that a high proportion of new assignments were received by one or two large firms. Again, however, this would not detract significantly from its hypothetical effects upon recruitment; it would simply result in a concentration of new apprentices in a few firms.

TABLE 2.1
Annual Number of New Appointments Made in Edinburgh and the Lothians in the Major Sources of Edinburgh CA's Business 1857–1914

Year	a	b	c	d	e	f	Series A (a+b+c+f)	Series B (Sum a to f)
1857	64	2	0	–	–	0	66	–
1858	72	3	0	–	–	0	75	–
1859	88	0	0	–	–	0	88	–
1860	84	1	0	–	–	0	85	–
1861	62	4	0	–	–	0	66	–
1862	60	4	0	–	–	0	64	–
1863	67	5	0	–	–	0	72	–
1864	73	5	0	–	–	0	78	–
1865	50	3	1	–	–	0	54	–
1866	69	2	0	–	–	0	71	–
1867	64	1	0	–	–	0	65	–
1868	93	6	1	–	–	0	100	–
1869	100	2	0	–	–	0	102	–
1870	106	2	1	–	–	0	109	–
1871	100	12	0	–	–	0	112	–
1872	77	17	0	–	–	0	94	–
1873	71	16	0	–	–	0	87	–
1874	61	16	0	–	–	0	77	–
1875	99	13	6	–	–	0	118	–
1876	90	16	2	–	–	1	109	–
1877	90	31	3	–	–	0	124	–
1878	107	14	6	–	–	0	127	–
1879	176	11	10	–	–	0	197	–

1880	112	18	8	–	–	0	138	–
1881	94	17	19	–	–	1	131	–
1882	97	20	7	–	–	0	124	–
1883	70	20	3	92	23	0	93	208
1884	85	24	10	81	30	0	119	230
1885	73	17	7	97	22	0	97	216
1886	82	19	10	92	12	0	111	215
1887	78	19	7	82	32	0	104	218
1888	84	18	5	82	33	0	107	222
1889	63	28	13	83	29	3	107	219
1890	74	22	8	66	28	0	104	198
1891	73	19	11	69	21	0	103	193
1892	75	20	9	86	21	0	104	211
1893	75	28	10	94	25	0	113	232
1894	48	31	14	103	19	19	112	234
1895	57	47	17	82	10	0	121	213
1896	47	54	20	87	21	0	121	229
1897	50	63	20	89	13	0	133	235
1898	36	69	19	85	20	0	124	229
1899	47	58	27	81	15	0	132	228
1900	68	62	34	97	16	0	164	277
1901	53	24	22	99	12	0	99	210
1902	51	31	24	75	11	0	106	192
1903	48	53	45	93	10	0	146	249
1904	41	42	17	83	14	0	100	197
1905	40	47	33	94	15	0	120	229
1906	42	36	23	94	11	0	101	206
1907	49	58	31	92	21	0	138	251
1908	63	48	36	108	19	0	147	274
1909	52	76	40	74	15	0	168	257
1910	50	44	37	87	12	0	131	230
1911	36	48	32	97	14	0	116	227
1912	33	74	41	72	11	0	148	231
1913	26	66	33	77	10	0	125	212
1914	43	73	30	74	–	0	146	210
Total	4038	1579	752	2767	565	24	6393	7182

Code:

a = Bankruptcies in Edinburghshire before the Court of Session and Midlothian Sheriff Court.

b = Companies registered with offices in the Lothians under the Company Acts.

c = Companies registered with offices in the Lothians wound-up.

d = Judicial Factories under the 1849 Act before the Court of Session.

e = Cessios before the Accountant of Court in Edinburghshire.

f = Other appointments (under local government, banking legislation &c).

TABLE 2.2
Analysis of Trustees of Sequestrations in Midlothian Depending
(that is, not wound-up) as at 31 October 1881

N of Separate Individuals	Occupation	N of Trusteeships Held
37	Edinburgh CA	144*
9	Glasgow CA	13
2	English CA	27
15	Accountant in Edinburgh	80
1	Accountant in Glasgow	1
3	Solicitor to Supreme Court (SSC)	3
1	Writer to the Signet (WS)	1
3	Solicitor in Edinburgh	4
1	Writer in Edinburgh	1
1	Solicitor in Jedburgh	1
1	Writer in Lauder	4
1	Writer in Stornoway	1
3	Merchant in Edinburgh or Leith	10
1	Wood Merchant	3
2	Wine Merchant in Leith	2
1	Distiller in Bo'ness	3
1	Farmer in Gorebridge	1
1	Manufacturer in Arbroath	1
1	Commission Agent in Edinburgh	1
2	Unspecified	2
87		303

* There were 115 SAE members in Edinburgh in 1881.

Source: Calculated from *Annual Report of the Accountant in Bankruptcy, 1881*

Limitations 3 and 4 above become clearer if the data contained in Table 2.2 above are examined. This reveals the concentration of appointments among a few CAs and the number of positions taken by individuals outside the profession.

Despite the limitations of the data, if the demand for the services provided by CAs was the major cause of the growth in recruitment to the profession, we could reasonably expect that fluctuations in the number of new apprenticeships would follow closely those of the optimum number of new potential appointments in the sources of Edinburgh CAs' business. These fluctuations and the trends in these variables are plotted in Figure 2.1 below.

It is apparent from the graph that the rate of expansion of the Edinburgh CA's potential business was lower than the increase in recruitment to the profession. The annual compound growth rate calculated from the linear trend was 1.0% *per annum* in *Series A* and 0.2% in the more representative *Series B*, compared to 3.1% for the

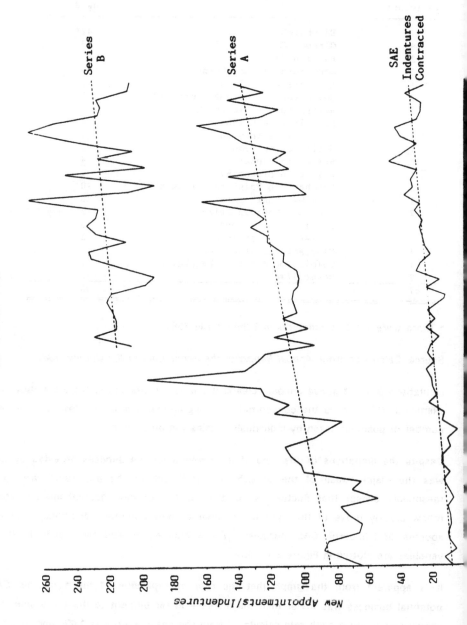

FIGURE 2.1 Growth in SAE Members' Potential Workload Compared With the Intake of Recruits (with linear trend)

annual intake of new SAE apprentices. Only in registered company work was there a higher rate of expansion than in recruitment – the figures being 4.3% *per annum* for the total registered companies established and liquidated, and 4.6% for the former category only. These results would seem to indicate that the supply of new recruits was outrunning the demand for CA services in Edinburgh, and that the amount of business available provided only very loose and generalized limits to the intake of apprentices. This conclusion is confirmed when only the fluctuations in new business and indentures are examined.

Certainly there were periods when recruitment appears to have responded to increased workload; for example, between 1876 and 1883. Yet the extraordinary increase in bankruptcies in Edinburgh in 1879 had a very minor impact upon intake in that or subsequent years. Similarly, the 1898–1914 period was one of great fluctuation in CAs' potential business, reflecting the higher proportion of more cyclical, company appointments; and, although a relationship is discernible in certain years, it is inconsistent.

Indeed, if the hypothetical relationship between the demand for the services of CAs and the supply of recruits to the profession holds, there is an expectation of a high positive correlation between the relevant variables. Table 2.3 shows that the association was positive but relatively weak.

TABLE 2.3

**Annual Increments to Edinburgh CAs' Potential Business
Variables Correlated With the Annual Intake of SAE
Apprentices 1857–1914**

Pearson's Correlation Coefficient Between Recruitment and:	Total Statistics (r)	Detrended Statistics (r)
Series A	0.61	0.09
Series B	0.30	0.12
Total Ltd Co.'s Established and Wound-Up	0.71	0.06
Total Ltd Co.'s Established Only	0.62	-0.21
Mean	0.56	0.01

Increases in Edinburgh CAs' business provide, therefore, only a limited explanation for the short-run timing and causes of the expansion in recruitment to the SAE. There is a significant residual if the raw statistics are correlated and, if the detrended figures are examined (more reliable for time series data), the relationship appears to have been extremely tenuous. It might have been expected that higher positive values for the registered company variables would exist as, of all categories of workload, this was the one which was most representative of CAs' business in that they could claim a near monopoly of company auditing. In 1896, members of the Scottish CA societies audited all 167 Scottish public companies and were responsible for liquidating 87% of all registered companies in Scotland in the three years to 1894 (and 98% of firms by the value of company assets).[17]

The foregoing analysis is not the sole indicator of the apparent inapplicability of the trend in CAs' workload as the major explanation for the SAE's growth. The fact that the profession in Edinburgh soon became overcrowded with practitioners points to the influence of non-market forces in regulating recruitment.

OVERSUPPLY

It was not until the late 1890s and particularly between 1904 and 1908 that British chartered accountants expressed considerable anxiety concerning the excessive numbers entering the profession in relation to the rate of expansion of business. Newly qualified ICAEW members were advised in 1906 not "to live in a fool's paradise and to think that because they passed their final examination successfully, or even with distinction, that they would be sure to get a living. The profession was overstocked."[18]

In Scotland, the problem was more acute given the limited size of the nation compared to its output of CAs. In 1899 *The Scottish Accountant* asked:

> Is it not time that attention were called to the number of young men who are entering on a professional career as accountants ? It seems to us that the market is getting greatly overstocked. The increase has been greatly in excess of the demand.[19]

Six years later, Richard Brown CA noted that the increase in the number of accountants may have outrun available business, concluding that "all who are crowding into the ranks cannot possibly reach eminence or lucrative employment in the profession."[20] The remedy for this situation was simple and universally advocated even though the very mechanism had failed to prevent the emergence of the problem: "The inexorable law of supply and demand",[21] would redress the balance.

Despite the debates on oversupply during the last years of the nineteenth and early twentieth centuries, the problem was not confined to this period; it was an almost constant concern – though one which only received an airing when the medium existed through professional journals for its expression. In *The Accountant's Student*

Journal of September 1884, for example, one correspondent referred to the ICAEW's 70% examination pass rate relative to a decline in sequestrations, and complained that:

> These facts are simply startling; on the one hand we have an immense falling off in our bankruptcy work . . . and on the other we have a continual and growing increase in the number of accountants. That is to say, the field of our labours is being most seriously narrowed whilst the number of labourers is being largely and rapidly augmented.[22]

Given the rate of expansion of business compared to the intake of SAE apprentices, it seems highly unlikely that the Edinburgh profession was not frequently overstocked. This impression is confirmed by a series of pamphlets published in Glasgow by an aggrieved corporate accountant, James Martin, who claimed the existence of a series of corrupt and deceitful practices among CAs there during the late nineteenth century. The underlying cause of unscrupulous activities was the intense competition between CAs for a limited volume of business: "No sooner does an unfortunate individual call a meeting of his creditors than a certain class of accountants are agog, and they swoop down upon the unfortunate like vultures upon a carcase."[23]

The CA societies, claimed Martin, were churning out accountants who: "Enter into the fiercest competition with their professional brethren . . . hawking for business from door to door, and when they fail prey upon the public, try to fleece one another."[24] Undoubtedly, Martin's prejudiced observations were exaggerated but he was not alone in drawing attention to the effects of ferocious competition among practitioners. It also had an impact on the level of professional incomes. *The Scottish Accountant* in July 1896 considered that "the fees paid to Accountants during the last ten or fifteen years have not kept pace with the improved efficiency of the profession. This applies to all departments of accountancy work". The problem had not been brought to the notice of clients "due to the fear that were the question raised it might lead to the discovery that there were not a few young but fully fledged Accountants who would be prepared to do the work at the old rate, and be thankful to get it."[25]

There are other indicators of the existence of an overstocked professional labour market in Scotland and particularly in Edinburgh for CAs. The ferocity with which the CA societies successfully fought the attempts of the SIA to gain a royal charter and the use of the financially vital CA notation in 1884, 1890 and 1896 was one sign of a fear of increased competition. The ultimate effect of a successful SIA petition would have been "to treble or quadruple the number of persons entitled to use that designation."[26] Martin was in no doubt that the CAs' main objections were based upon the potential impact on their already limited business.[27]

No instant success was guaranteed for the newly qualified SAE member during any of the 1854-1914 period; it was never easy for the *unconnected* professional to receive appointments. Consequently, as early as 1869, the President of the IAAG claimed that: "Many men bred to the profession found better, and sometimes more profitable employment in other callings."[28] And, in 1889 it was shown by the SIA that of 204 members of the SAE located in Scotland, only 166 were engaged in practice as accountants or employed as accountant's clerks in Edinburgh. 10 were salaried insurance officials, 7 were stockbrokers, 4 were solicitor's clerks, 3 were solicitors and 1 each was a chamberlain, clerk in a copper company, brewery employee, a printer, and an ex-cab driver.

The experience of individual SAE members also signifies the existence of an overcrowded local labour market. William H. Smith, CA could only obtain an appointment as a bookkeeper in Glasgow at £100 a year once he had entered the Edinburgh Society in 1863. In 1865, he returned to Edinburgh but subsequently rejected his profession (and eventually became Commissioner to the Metropolitian Police) as: "Two years absence made all the difference, I had no business to succeed to, no partnership to expect, and the outlook was far from promising."[29]

Figure 2.2 provides further possible evidence that the Edinburgh CA profession was frequently overstocked. The number of SAE members practising in the organizational centre of the profession exhibits a long-run decline and had reached just below 50% by 1914. It was no coincidence that the periods of greatest increase in membership were also those of escalating emigration. During the 1880-1900 expansion it was England, especially London, which took Edinburgh's excessive professional output. As that location itself became grossly oversupplied, the pioneering areas of the Americas and Asia received much of the excess of new members.

The high rate of emigration among SAE members is also further illustrated in Table 2.4, the data for which were derived from an investigation of the locations of CAs for the majority of the period of their careers using Scottish legal and CA directories as well as obituarial sources. The emigration of Edinburgh CAs from Britain increased significantly among the 1875-1884 and post-1895 entrants to the profession – that is, when there was a large intake of new members to the SAE and a consequent increase in competition for available business.

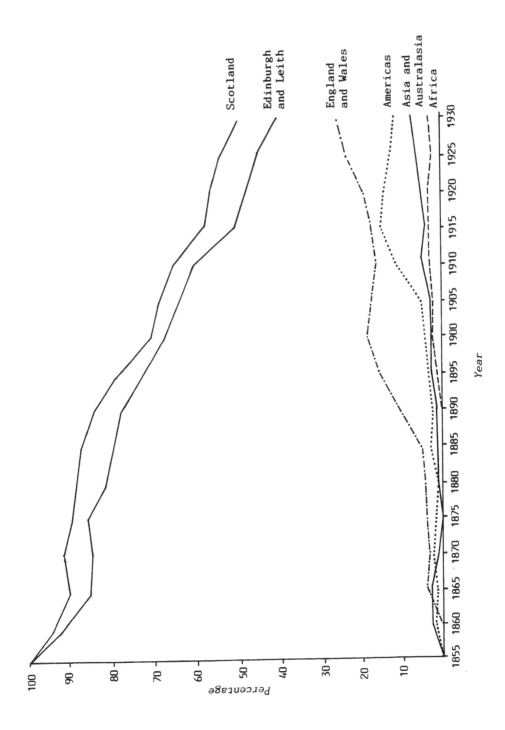

Scotland

Edinburgh
and Leith

England
and Wales

Americas

Asia and
Australasia

Africa

Percentage

100

90

80

70

60

50

40

30

20

10

1855 1860 1865 1870 1875 1880 1885 1890 1895 1900 1905 1910 1915 1920 1925 1930

Year

TABLE 2.4
Major Career Location of SAE Members Admitted 1855-1914
(percentages)

Location	1855 -64	1865 -74	1875 -84	1885 -94	1895 -04	1905 -14
Edinburgh	73.8	63.7	69.2	56.1	47.4	31.7
Rest of Scotland	14.3	4.5	6.6	4.3	5.8	9.3
England, Wales & Ireland	9.5	25.0	13.2	27.4	19.7	22.0
Europe	0.0	0.0	2.2	0.0	1.1	0.8
Africa	0.0	0.0	1.1	3.6	5.2	4.6
Asia	0.0	2.3	1.1	1.4	5.8	8.4
Australasia	0.0	4.5	1.1	0.7	1.1	0.8
North America	2.4	0.0	3.3	6.5	13.3	18.6
South America	0.0	0.0	2.2	0.0	0.6	3.8
Total	100.0	100.0	100.0	100.0	100.0	100.0
British Isles	97.6	93.2	89.0	87.8	72.9	63.0
Overseas	2.4	6.8	11.0	12.2	27.1	37.0
Number of Cases	42	44	91	139	173	237

Before it can be assumed that migration from Edinburgh was evidence of almost continuous oversupply, and of the irrelevance of demand as a major determinant of the expansion in professional recruitment, it has to be established that migrants were a spill-over. It is necessary to prove that transient SAE members were forced out by overcrowding rather than pulled in by the attractions of employment in alternative locations.

SAE MIGRATION AS A CONSEQUENCE OF OVERSUPPLY

Investigations into the motivations of middle class emigrants of the nineteenth century have concluded that transience was a consequence of a combination of *push* and *pull* factors. Musgrove,[30] for example, has drawn attention to the increasing sophistication of the socio-economic systems of overseas territories which resulted in a demand for professional skills. Professional men were, in turn, attracted by high income rewards and the superior social status accorded them in the strict social hierachy of empire nations.

Undoubtedly a myriad of individual circumstances precipitated the exodus of professionals from Britain during the late nineteenth and early twentieth centuries. The indications are, however, that the primary causes of the emigration of large numbers of Victorian professional men lay on the *push* side. Emigration was not contemplated by the majority of the professional classes during the nineteenth century as a desirable objective; the successful remained at home. In 1889 *The Spectator*, reporting on the position of the overstocked professions, asserted that: "It has become a truism to say that of all who start on professional careers, one third *go-under* - that is, get sick, die or *emigrate*".[31] [italics added]

Migration was advocated as the practical solution for those least advantaged in the professional labour market: those without connection, those who had not excelled at school or in occupational training, and those lacking substantial capital. Career guides of the period recommended emigration not for the most able sons but for those who had little hope of succeeding in the more preferable appointments:

> At home the professions are overcrowded and competition for Commissions in the Army or for good civil service appointments is so severe that a large number of our sons, sound in wind and limb, robust, adventurous, and intelligent, find it difficult to secure congenial employment. To all such we would say: 'Why not the Colonies?'[32]

Migration was the alternative propounded for the son unable to pass the simplest of examinations: "In England itself there are very few openings in which headwork is not required; India and the colonies offer a larger field."[33]

The more manual nature of many overseas employments, especially farming, ranching and planting, were averse to the genteel priorities which middle class parents envisaged for their sons. *The National Review* in 1907 noted that emigration was one solution for "unemployed gentlemen" even though their status overseas would be tarnished due to the previous practice of the colonies receiving "many hundreds of British wastrels",[34] who had been shipped out by middle class parents anxious to see the back of them. Similarly, the Public Schools Emigration League was insistent during the 1910s that: "The importance of sending out the right sort of boy cannot be too strongly emphasised; the dumping of Public School failures in the Colonies has in the past worked great injury."[35]

As far as Edinburgh CAs of the nineteenth century were concerned, emigration was a second best, the alternative for the failed apprentice and the disadvantaged, unconnected SAE member. There were of course exceptions, where, for example, a large and successful company established an overseas branch. Such a case was that of John B. Niven, CA, the son of an original member of the SAE, who, in 1900 with Sir George A. Touche, CA, founded the firm of Touche, Niven and Co. in New York. Sir George had been apprenticed to Niven's father and built a substantial practice in London, and was subsequently to open offices in several countries. Niven became

President of the American Institute of Accountants in 1924.

Examples of this type were, however, rare. In general, emigrants appear to have been regarded as the excess capacity of the profession. In 1890, for example, it was asserted by the counsel for the chartered societies in the case against the SIA's claim for incorporation that: "In the Edinburgh Society there is an immense number of young men. If they do not find scope for carrying on their business in Edinburgh or Glasgow, they go to England, or to the Colonies."[36]

As Table 2.5 shows, it was SAE apprentices failing to qualify as CAs who were the first to emigrate in significant numbers – that is, until the British profession became increasingly oversupplied with qualified practitioners and when these too were forced to seek overseas appointments.

TABLE 2.5
Major Career Location of SAE Apprentices According to Whether
They Qualified as CAs or Not (percentages)

| Location | All Indentures Commencing: | | | | | |
| | Pre 1860 | | Pre 1880 | | Pre 1900 | |
	CA	Non CA	CA	Non CA	CA	Non CA
Scotland	94.6	62.1	82.0	43.5	66.6	42.6
Rest British Isles	4.5	3.4	12.1	9.0	17.6	8.1
Europe	0	0	0.8	0.8	0.7	0.4
Africa	0	6.9	0.8	1.6	2.7	3.0
Asia	0	6.9	1.2	5.8	2.7	5.5
Australasia	0	3.4	1.2	5.8	1.0	3.4
North America	0.9	0	1.5	1.6	7.8	3.4
South America	0	0	0.4	1.6	0.9	1.3
Not Known*	0	17.3	0	30.3	0	32.3
Total	100.0	100.0	100.0	100.0	100.0	100.0
% Known Outside British Isles	0.9	17.2	5.9	17.2	15.8	17.0
% Likely Outside Scotland	5.3	37.9	18.0	56.5	33.4	57.4
Number of Cases	112	29	255	122	580	235

*These non-CAs do not appear in Scottish civil registers of marriages or deaths, therefore, a large proportion of them can be assumed as having left Scotland.

Among apprentices who commenced their indentures before 1860, 17.2% of those who did not become CAs are known to have left the British Isles and 37.9% are likely to have emigrated from Scotland; compared to 0.9% and 5.4%, respectively, of those who qualified. Among all apprentices whose indentures began prior to 1900, the proportions of emigrant CAs to non-CAs were similar as the British profession became increasingly overstocked with qualified practitioners.

The emigration of British CAs appears to have been greatest from Scotland, the country where the problem of professional oversupply was most acute. In 1903, there was one CA per 7,000 people in Scotland compared to a ratio of 1:11,000 in England. Similarly, despite the increasing number of SAE members practising south of the border, there was little room in Scotland, and particularly in Edinburgh, for ICAEW members to set up business. During the 1853-1914 period, for example, only 3 members of the English chartered society practised in Edinburgh for any significant length of time, and each of these were established accountants in the city prior to becoming members of the ICAEW.[37] The Society of Accountants and Auditors also expressed a certain disappointment in 1913 concerning the progress of its Scottish branch, and noted that a high proportion of its young members had left for careers in the colonies and the USA.[38] Richard Brown, CA also wrote in 1905 implying that emigrant CAs were a spill-over:

> . . . a considerable proportion of Scottish Chartered Accountants have found it to their advantage to betake themselves to other countries. It may therefore be held that the present needs of the country, so far as professional accountants are concerned, are fully met.[39]

It was not until the second decade of the twentieth century that emigration ceased to be seen in eminent CA circles as an inferior alternative to remaining in Edinburgh. By that time, so many members had been forced abroad that any reduced status attached to the emigrant would have reflected upon that of the whole SAE. In 1924, *The Accountant's Magazine* claimed that appointments overseas were suited only to the most able CAs.[40] Additionally, as Musgrove has pointed out, by 1914 a tradition of elite emigration had become established; the middle class schoolboy or apprentice would have noticed that his reference groups of ex-pupils and professional trainees were increasingly to be found abroad and was likely to have been less averse than previously to following their example.[41] This tendency was exemplified in the existence of the Public Schools Emigration League which was established "to advise and assist Public School boys, who, after leaving school, decide, with the consent of their parents or guardians, to seek a career in one of the Overseas Dominions."[42]

The known experience of one SAE apprentice during this period of changing evaluations of the status of the emigrant professional illustrates the position at that time. While the senior, most able apprentice of the office remained in Edinburgh on qualifying and became a partner in his master's firm: "All the other apprentices were constantly discussing where they would go – always abroad; Canada, Asia, Australia and the United States."[43] Indeed, 36.4% of those admitted to the SAE between 1900 and 1914 were to spend the majority of their careers outside the British Isles.

Until the early twentieth century, however, there were a number of reasons why Edinburgh CAs would have preferred to have practised in Scotland.

The Status of the CA Outside Scotland

It was only in the three major cities of Scotland that the *professional* status of the CA was recognized until the 1880s and 1890s. In any other location, the CA could envisage a lesser recognition of his qualifications and position until such time as accountancy had assumed a similar degree of importance outside the organizational centres of the profession. As one English commentator on accountants noted in 1895: "There can be no doubt that in Scotland accountancy has developed a degree of importance and that Scotch Accountants rank higher than in any other part of the world."[44]

As established in the previous chapter, the origins of the professional status of the English chartered accountant can be traced back only to the incorporation of the ICAEW in 1880, and subsequently the profession there was tarred with the brush of the unorganized, unscrupulous accountant. Overseas, where the profession was not organized consistently, or the value of its practitioners generally recognized until after the late 1890s, the SAE member could expect an even greater degradation of his status compared to that accorded him in Edinburgh.

Upon leaving Britain, the SAE member could expect to effectively drop the CA notation which was the mark of his professional superiority in the city of his training. In most overseas locations, he became an 'auditor' or a plain 'accountant'. In the USA in 1894, for example, one emigrant advised his British colleagues to:

> 'Stay where you are'. There are many old English accountant's clerks here, always ready for a day's work and any number of bookkeepers on the Accountant's list. Permanent positions there are none, and accountancy here is not even classified as a profession.[45]

In India the CA would have to compete for business and be occupationally associated with the low paid and reputedly careless 'Parsee' or indigenous Hindu accountant. In

Australia, he might become associated with unprofessional practitioners: *The Scottish Accountant* reported in July 1894, for example, the trial of an insurance company secretary which had:

> . . . brought to light the fact that the auditor was a school teacher in an elementary school in the district. The writer knows of another auditor who is a plumber to trade, and whose past career has been that of gold digger, farmer, and Member of Parliament in the Colony.[46]

Additionally, a CA emigrant to Chile claimed in 1905 that there the accountant " . . . at first was thought to be a species of travelling bookkeeper."[47] Emigrant CAs also suffered in their exclusion from the affairs of their society, in being unable for a long period to take on SAE registered apprentices,[48] and in not being updated regarding developments in professional practice.

Professional Income Overseas

Higher income rewards offered abroad were the alleged major *pull* factors and attractions of emigration for the professional. Overseas appointments offered high income soon after qualification. In effect, however, it would have become apparent to intending migrant CAs from the reports of colleagues abroad that the standard of life overseas was not significantly higher than it was for those practising at home. This again indicates the greater significance of the hypothesis of enforced emigration due to a saturated professional labour market in Edinburgh.

One major problem was that the pioneer emigrant CA who intended to establish himself in practice had to compete with the local accountant and was unable to claim a monopoly of business on the basis of his superior qualifications in nations where their value was not recognized. Indian accountants were content to work for "a quarter of the salary paid to the white man",[49] and could maintain a major share of available business on the basis of extended familial connections. In the Gold Coast natives would take £40 a year compared to the £240 paid to the CA, while in America qualified accountants were reported to have been accepting $4 a day in order to remain in work.[50]

The cost of living abroad could also severely cut into salaries. *The Accountant's Magazine* reminded its readers that: "Before any young man goes abroad, he should consider the cost. It is not by any means all plain sailing. Much larger salaries will be offered than at home but the expenses will be much higher."[51] In Argentina living costs were reported as having been double those in Britain in 1913, while in the Phillipines the CA's starting salary of £500 in 1925 was in deficit by £175 if the young man were to cover the expenses of necessities as well as keeping up appearances by purchasing a car and joining the polo club.

Qualitative Aspects of Emigration

Despite the greater opportunities available overseas for a gentlemanly existence in the form of a plentiful supply of cheap domestics as well as hunting and riding,[52] few Scottish CAs found that these advantages outweighed those of remaining at home. Almost all confessed to *The Accountant's Magazine* that they had felt isolated. One emigrant in South Africa reported that:

> . . . However much he may be entertained, however delightful he may find his friends, there always remains the bitter feeling that he is cut off from 'Home', ties and civilization, and that he is spending the best years of his life in a country which he detests more every day.[53]

In Canada the formation of new friendships and associations was reputed to have been slow including making the necessary business contacts. Additionally, the emigrant CA had to contend with a catalogue of inconveniences depending on his precise location: language difficulties, cultural differences, the multiplicilty of problems caused by an unsophisticated economic infrastructure, and, the possibility of political instability. Not the least of these problems was the possible threat to health.

The voyage could be hazardous enough. In October 1902, for example, Norman Balgarnie, CA died on board the *s.s. Dominion* bound for South Africa. On arrival, an inhospitable climate could prove threatening. In India, reported a Scottish CA "the heat is something dreadful" with potentially "uncertain and deadly effects";[54] in China during the summer "there is a danger of cholera and other diseases";[55] in the Gold Coast, those who remained for long "do not make 'old bones'"; while in Japan, CAs were unlikely to have relished the prospect of experiencing an earthquake.[56] The average age at death of emigrant SAE members who practised in Africa and Asia was indeed lower than that of those who remained in Scotland as shown in Table 2.6. It is doubtful that apprentices were not aware of the risks of emigration but apparently felt that they had to leave in order to secure suitable appointments not available to them at home.

TABLE 2.6
Mean Age at Death of SAE Members 1854-1914 by Location for the Major Part of Their Career (where known)

Location	Mean Age at Death	Number of Cases
Edinburgh	65.89	410
Rest of Scotland	65.37	51
England, Wales & Ireland	65.98	146
Europe	65.77	7
Africa	59.06	26
Asia	62.72	34
Australasia	65.64	8
North America	64.83	76
South America	65.15	12
Mean/Total	65.38	770

Having asserted and shown that the numbers entering the SAE exceeded those required in the local professional labour market, it is important to investigate the reasons why market mechanisms were apparently unable to prevent the supply of recruits exceeding the demand for the services provided by CAs. To that end an initial examination is made of an interference with the operation of a free labour market which ensured that recruitment levels persisted irrespective of the need for more members; the process of professionalization.

PROFESSIONALIZATION AND THE RECRUITMENT POLICY OF THE SAE

On initial investigation the recruitment policy of the SAE would appear to have been inherently restrictive. The desire to ensure a status on a par with the legal profession of Edinburgh warranted the emulation of the high indenture and membership fees exacted by the legal societies, while the quest for *learned* standing entailed the introduction of ever-more sophisticated examination and training regimes.

Beyond these not inconsiderable impositions, and for those who could satisfy such demands, recruitment was limited only by the willingness of youths to present themselves as apprentices and of masters wishing to train and employ them. The SAE policy (which was not expressed officially) was outwardly consistent throughout the 1854-1914 period. It has rightly been described as having been *conservative* in its pecuniary obstacles though *elastic* in its unlimited intake of recruits.[57] The objective was simply to exclude "incompetent persons from their ranks",[58] who might degrade professional status. Beyond that the doors of the Society were considered to have been open. *The Accountant's Magazine* summed up the SAE position in 1907:

> In our opinion any artificial restrictions upon the numbers of those who may be trained for a profession are undesirable, and savour of trade-unionism. The ordinary rule of supply and demand should be left to regulate the matter, and the profession should be in all respects free and open to those who are willing to acquire the qualifications.[59]

Consequently, whereas in the ICAEW members were only permitted to train two apprentices at any one time, in Scotland there were no such restrictions. Even during the early twentieth century debate within the profession on oversupply, the SAE made no outward attempt to limit the intake of new recruits. The underlying reasons for this simplistic and non-interventionist attitude to the CA labour market were self-interested attempts to assert professional position, and an infinitely escalating vision of the demand for the services of SAE members.

The World View

Despite its highly localized organizational structure, the SAE adopted a national and world-wide perspective when considering the employment opportunities of its increasing membership. There was no need to limit entrance to the profession because, even if Edinburgh quickly became saturated with accountants, they were increasingly required outside the boundaries of the City. In the long-run, the Empire and industrialising nations overseas would, it was assumed, follow the British experience and realize the value of *professional* accountants, the CA's superior qualification, and demand their services as a result. Recruitment was based on the assumption of an upwardly-spiralling demand for CAs outside Scotland. For example, *The Accountant's Journal* in 1890 claimed that: "The Australian colonies and the US . . . afford good openings, and in years to come, the, at present unbuilt cities and trading centres of our African territories will stand in need of the CA."[60] Similarly, the SAE could assert that it "Welcomes candidates not merely with a view of carrying on business in Edinburgh, but in any part of the world where there is scope for a highly trained accountant."[61]

It was possible for the SAE and other accountancy organizations to adopt this attitude because, unlike the national limitations of a lawyer's training, the universal usage of figures ensured that a CA's training was relevant almost anywhere.[62] The Edinburgh society was also partly motivated by its own colonization pretentions. It was the world's first organization of professional accountants and was keen to assert its presence and influence in the areas where the occupation was in its embryonic stages. In 1906, for instance, Scottish CAs' reacted strongly to the claim of the ICAEW's President that his Institute formed the model upon which 38 overseas accountancy bodies had been established. *The Accountant's Magazine* was quick to point out that the SAE was the mother of all subsequent societies including the English.[63]

Inter-Occupational Encroachment

The long-term demand for the services of CAs was also contemplated as being ever-escalating as individuals and institutions became increasingly aware of the necessity of presenting accountancy business to *professional accountants* rather than to lawyers, auditors and bookkeepers who had received much work before the organization of the SAE. *The Accountant's Students Journal* claimed in 1884 that: "There will be an increase in bookkeeping work as people realize clerks are not to be entrusted with such important work that could only be entrusted to honest qualified accountants."[64]

A considerable amount of potential CAs' business was undertaken by others in Scotland during the whole of the nineteenth century. In 1896, the three Scottish CA societies presented the following analysis of their legal business for the previous year.

TABLE 2.7
Distribution of Scottish CAs' Legal Business in 1895

Nature of Appointment	% Held by SAE Members	% Held by All Scottish CAs
Judicial Factories in the Court of Session	19.3	28.1
Judicial Factories in Sheriff Courts	5.3	16.3
Judicial Factories (Guardianship Cases)	2.4	9.8
Judicial Factories (Common Law Cases)	36.1	52.9
Judicial Factories (Bankruptcy Cases)	39.3	60.7
Sequestrations Awarded	19.8	53.0
Cessios Wound-Up	10.5	24.2

Source: calculated from the 1896 Petition of the Scottish CAs against the SIA.

It is apparent that 35% of these legal appointments were held by CAs. As their superior qualifications to undertake this business was increasingly recognized by the courts, CAs could expect a greater proportion of this work would be remitted to them.

It was also envisaged that CAs would discover new areas of employment requiring their specialized skills, ousting those who had previously performed the function. In manufacturing and commerce, for example, the appointment of CAs as managers, secretaries and company accountants could be entertained as the production process became increasingly complex, resulting in the employment of professional staff. The field was viewed as being a "large and expanding one"; young CAs, claimed the President of the SAE in 1894, "are ready on the slightest provocation to undertake any piece of general business which may offer itself to them".[65]

It was also difficult to predict specific developments that might widen the future field of employment.

Unpredictability

Comparatively recent attempts to foresee the future demand for accountants and other professionals have proved largely unsuccessful.[66] In medicine or teaching, for example, future personnel requirements can be partly envisaged on the basis of projections derived from demographic statistics. In accountancy, given the widening boundary and diversity of business and, the legislative sources of work, future recruitment planning during the nineteenth century would have proved particularly hazardous. The imposition of restrictions on recruitment might have ensured labour shortages if unforeseen legislation resulted in a sudden or even gradual increase in the demand for CAs.

There were, however, other reasons for the SAE to permit an unlimited supply of apprentices to became indentured which were less the cause of employment conditions and more to do with the attainment of occupational pre-eminence and the assertion of professional status.

Monopolistic Engrossment – The Exclusion of Professional Competitors

As an unregulated occupation, it was and is possible for any individual to set up in business as an accountant – whether qualified or not. The resultant ever-present pool of unorganized and unqualified auditors during the 1854-1914 period which attracted a certain amount of lower class business provided a safety valve to possible CA oversupply. The chartered societies could increase membership at the cost of greater competition as its effects were most likely to have been detrimental to unqualified accountants than to themselves. As the superior nature of the CA's qualification became increasingly recognized, it was assumed that the non-CA would suffer. While this pool persisted and a monopoly of business remained unsecured, the CA societies could provide any number of practitioners in order to dislodge competing unqualified *accountants* who remained a 'stain' on their attempts to assert the status of the whole profession.

In Edinburgh during 1854-1914, there existed a substantial presence of non-chartered, competing accountants as illustrated below.

TABLE 2.8
Average Decennial Number of Non-CAs Practising
in Edinburgh and Leith 1855-1914

Year	Average Number
1855-64	60.0
1865-74	82.4
1875-84	92.9
1885-94	87.1
1895-04	78.9
1905-14	64.3

Source: *Edinburgh and Leith Post Office Directory* 1855-1914.

The number of *unorganized* accountants in Edinburgh declined from a peak of 95 in 1880 to 31 in 1914, as many joined the SIA and, later, the London Association of Accountants Limited; societies which adopted a similar attitude as the CAs in attempting to increase recruitment to exclude the unqualified. But these organizations were dislodged increasingly by the SAE. In 1884 there were 28 SIA members in Edinburgh, and by 1914 there were 16. The CAs' attempts to monopolize business ensured that Scottish incorporated accountants: "Had not the same kind of field for expansion as the society had in England and Wales."[67]

The expectation of an eventual business monopoly as public confidence in the abilities of CAs increased was actively encouraged by the SAE through its jealous preservation of the exclusive use of the CA notation despite the claims of the SIA and Corporation of Accountants. The desire to maintain their position in the face of an alleged weakness has also to be examined as a possible cause of unlimited recruitment to the SAE. This weakness was exploited by the SIA in its petition of 1889-90 when it referred to the Scottish CA societies being:

> Strictly local in character, and can only be regarded as professional organizations for the three cities . . . Nor are they, even in this limited area, completely representative of the profession, for in each of the cities named, there are many persons practising as Accountants, who, having been trained there or elsewhere, in the offices of non CAs, did not, and could not enter the profession through the Chartered Societies.[68]

The three societies, in claiming to represent the accountancy *profession in Scotland*, had to assert that they were at least numerically dominant in their own centres and more than purely *local* in character and membership. This was only feasible by increasing membership to outnumber and dislodge local non-CA competitors and by establishing a large supply of CAs distributed widely throughout Scotland and beyond its borders. By comparison, not only were SIA members "resident in all parts of Scotland", they were, between 1880 and 1890, also increasing rapidly in number (110 members in 1884 and 160 in 1889), giving added force to their claim of representing the *national* profession and therefore entitled to consultation with government on matters of occupational interest. There were, indeed, more accountants outside the CA societies in Scotland than within them throughout the second half of the nineteenth century. As late as 1910-11, there were 1227 Scottish CAs, of whom 822 practised in Scotland, while the 1911 census enumerated a total of 1908 accountants north of the border.

According to James Martin, corporate accountant in Glasgow, the result of the threat of alternative organizations to the Scottish CA societies was the expansion of their membership irrespective of the demand for professional services, in order to assert their numerical strength. The scenario, he claimed, was as follows:

> Up till 1880, a quarter of a century after the date of the first charter, the admissions to the societies were few in number; but the Scottish Institute of Accountants was formed in that year, and the chartered societies discovered a new danger. Since that time they have increased their numbers rapidly, but not so fast as the number of accountants outside their bodies have increased.[69]

Additionally, the establishment of the joint examination system in 1893 was an attempt, argued Martin, to unite three divided and local CA societies in Scotland as a response to the common threat posed by the SIA. The high success rate in CA examinations compared to those of the legal societies was Martin's proof that the occupation was being deluged with an unrequired supply of CAs.

Although an increase in recruitment certainly did occur following the formation of the General Examining Board (GEB), the reasons for this, as shall be discovered later in the chapter, were not solely due to Scottish CA fears of competition. The desire to develop a professional monopoly and maintain it was a longer term cause of unlimited recruitment. In order for the SAE to assert and maintain its professional status and position, it required a constant supply of new members for a further reason.

The Financial Advantages of Unlimited Recruitment

The system of apprenticeship provided an excellent investment for the practising CA. Not only did it confer the status of *master,* but the limited obligations it imposed were outweighed by its financial advantages. The master received a fee and was (usually) under no compulsion to pay a salary though it was customary to return the fee over the period of the indenture in increasing annual emoluments. By the fourth or fifth year, the master benefitted from the services of a skilled man who was better qualified than a clerk and did not require a high salary or any guarantee of employment once the contract of service was discharged. It seems likely under these circumstances that a CA would have been averse to rejecting a recruit presented for apprenticeship whatever the state of his business.

From the perspective of the SAE, an increasing membership was a highly desirable financial objective. A newly-established professional organization was heavily dependent on admission and membership fees to meet the expenses of status enhancing acquisitions such as the purchase of permanent premises, a library, the employment of secretarial staff, the establishment of a teaching facility, publications, and investments to ensure long-term security. As late as the year ending 31 December 1914, the SAE was still dependent for 30% of its income from the entrance fees of new members, the fees imposed for the registration of indentures and the library subscriptions of apprentices. The remaining 70% of income derived primarily from stocks, mainly in Scottish railway companies.

Even in some of the oldest established professions, income derived from members and recruits could form the major determinant of the state of the organization's finances and its ability to expend on various projects. The minute books and Treasurer's accounts of the Faculty of Advocates, which can trace its origins back to 1532, illustrate the dependence upon the supply of recruits for income. The Treasurer of the Faculty noted in 1847, for example, that: "The Faculty would have nothing to depend on in the future but the annual fees of Intrants, whose average number had greatly fallen off of late years. The most rigid economy would therefore be indispensable."[70]

In 1847, 96.6% of Faculty income was derived from entrance fees. Subsequently, committees investigating Faculty funds were established regularly and, on occasion, extra income was raised by appeals to members in years of few *intrants.* Eventually, annual recruitment was so low that sufficient funds to maintain the Advocates' Library could not be secured, resulting in its reorganization as the National Library of Scotland

---

financed by the State in 1925. A series of other desirable projects had to be postponed until the number of intrants increased: library extension, electric lighting, the purchase of new books and salary increases for Faculty staff.

Except in occupations where the State imposed limits on intake, such as in the civil service and the armed forces, other nineteenth century professional organizations, according to their own peculiar circumstances, were generally under similar pressures as the SAE to ensure that recruitment continued at a level determined by the supply of individuals presenting themselves for entry rather than by the level of demand for professional services. Architects and engineers, for example, were, during the nineteenth century, undergoing the process of professionalization and were occupied in a vocation which, like medicine, could be practised world-wide. Given then, that recruitment to the professions was not generally limited by the demand for services or by organizational impositions beyond those necessary to maintain professional status, how can levels of recruitment be explained ? What factors generated the supply of recruits inducing nineteenth century professional expansion ?

THE SOCIAL FORCES OF OCCUPATIONAL EXPANSION

The answers to these questions and the reasons why the professions experienced such growth despite their numbers outrunning the demand for their services and thus producing frequent overcrowding, lie in the very nature of nineteenth and early twentieth century society and the relationships between the strata within it. Changing evaluations of the status attached to certain occupations, and the aspirations of parents from lower ranking vocations with the means to ensure that their sons could enter those of a higher prestige than their own, were the central factors which generated the supply of recruits to the professions including the SAE.

Status, Social Aspiration and the Supply of Recruits

A major social status division of the Victorian and Edwardian period, and one of especial significance to this study, was that existing in the middle class between the *professions* and *trade*, the latter comprising the mercantile and shopkeeping strata. The distinction rested partly upon the fact that the professions had been long associated with, and patronized by, landed families and were the desired occupations for their younger sons. The altruistic nature of the professions, and the source of their income being derived from fees as opposed to the profits of trade, likened them to the gentry. As Crew recognized as late as 1925:

> The difference between trade and a profession is clear. The essence of the former is that its only criterion is the financial return which it offers to the individuals concerned. The essence of the latter is that though men enter it for the sake of livelihood, the measure of their success is the service which they perform, not the gains which they amass.[71]

Tradesmen were tainted with their pursuit of money, the absence of honourable professional rules and lack of public usefulness and worth. According to Checkland, the shopkeeping, small manufacturing and lower white collar strata of nineteenth century society also suffered from "a triple opprobium. Dealing in small quantities, being in intimate contact with, and even touching the goods themselves, and directly receiving money payments from hand to hand constituted the trinity of shameful acts."[72] In the later nineteenth century, as increasing value became attached to the receipt of a liberal education and meritocratic qualification as a determinant of occupational standing, tradesmen also became distinguished from professional men by their comparative lack of academic training. The popular vision was of the self-made tradesman, an uneducated profitmaker as against the highly trained, specialist, professional. Hence, in 1870, it was asserted that "It used to be thought that the professions only required brains, and that for trade anyone would do."[73]

Further status divisions were evident throughout the remaining levels of the social structure between classes, occupations and neighbours. The shopkeeper was distinguished from the artisan by the non-manual nature of his labour, the latter being recognized for his manual skill, income and respectability by the labourer. The crucial point with regard to recruitment is that individuals were conscious of their social placement and of the reference groups which occupied a higher or lower status position than their own. The socially ambitious among these groups were determined to improve their position in the status hierachy. A contributor to *Blackwood's Magazine* in 1867 pointed out that: "However humiliating the fact may be, the truth, I suppose is undeniable: we do all of us, with very few and remarkable exceptions, make either the maintenance or the improvement of our social standing a very important object of life".[74]

One means of achieving social status improvement was to adopt certain chracteristics of lifestyle or the acquisition of relevant material consumables that were associated with those occupying a higher rank in the social scale. A further, more enduring and desirable mark of social advancement with the potential for generational status enhancement, was to attempt the entrance of a son into a higher occupation than one's own. The aspirations of increasing numbers of middle class, and later, upper working class, parents for the upward mobility of their sons combined with the financial means to carry through their desires, largely explain the expanding supply of recruits to the professions during the 1854–1914 period.

The occupational consequences of these intergenerational ambitions can be illustrated by examining the position of the late nineteenth century clerk.[75] The quest for genteel status, and the social aversion to *trade* among many middle and upper working class parents, ensured many sons were entered into training for an occupation irrespective of the demand for their services. The resultant overcrowding was tolerated due to its financial benefits for employers in the form of low salaries. The situation was portrayed admirably by F. Devanant in 1870 who quoted correspondence form *The Daily News* concerning the lamentable plight of the city clerk and the explanations for his position. Anxious parents and unemployed or underpaid clerks complained of an overstocked labour market due to the results of "the false pride of genteel people",[76] and:

> . . . A growing dislike to manual labour amongst the lower section of the middle class which is painfully apparent to those who see much of commercial life. Parents are eager to get their sons into houses of business where they may maintain the appearance if not the standing, of gentlemen. The City is crowded with well educated lads, who are doing mens work for boys wages.[77]

Furthermore, the problem was worsening:

> It is quite useless to argue with parents and urge the propriety of sending boys to learn a trade; the idea of a lad returning from his work in the evening with dirty hands and clad in fustian or corduroy, is quite shocking to the respectability of Peckham and Camberwell, and so the evil is perpetuated, and the prospect of the clerk becomes more gloomy from year to year.[78]

One individual recalled that his entrance into trade due to the lack of opportunities in clerking resulted in: "My clerk friends gave me up. 'Wearing an apron!' they remarked, and brushed their seedy black when passing."[79] This was despite the fact that his income rose from £60 to £800 *per annum* in six years compared to their constant £180-200. The demand for clerking appointments among an increasing pool of eager candidates was said to be "like a scramble of minnows for a piece of bread."[80]

The similar social distinction between professions and trade explains largely the excessive growth of the former. As Devanant continued:

> . . . In spite of much levelling that has gone on, an ideal difference still exists between the class of traders and the class of professionals . . . it is certain the opinion prevails, that a member of the trader class gains by transfer to the professional . . . Many and varied talents are lost to society by this insane worship of mere gentility; boys whether well or ill adapted for a commercial career are forced into houses of business.[81]

Others noted that such social distinctions were worsening. *The Spectator* claimed in 1889 that: "Caste feeling, which always feeds the professions, grows stronger than ever in certain sections of the community."[82] And such sentiments were not confined to London. In 1900, for example, it was asserted that:

> Prosperous retail shop-keepers in our provincial towns send their sons to college, with the exalted notion that they must never demean themselves by soiling their hands, by wearing an apron, or by standing behind a counter as their fathers have done; but must seek for 'appointments' in the civil service or in one of the increasing number of what are euphoniously called 'professions', by which they will be able to earn large salaries with little work, to wear a frock coat and a silk hat, and be addressed as 'Esquire'.[83]

The consequence of this 'absurd prejudice' was a glutted labour market over a long period as there were "hundreds of applicants for almost every clerical or professional situation."[84]

One particular trait of professional occupations was increasingly attractive to parents who were considering vocations for their sons; their claim to *learned* status which was reflected in the spread of entrance by examination in the professions and the consequent expansion of middle class education to accomodate the change. As increasing numbers attended appropriate schools, a further supply of potential recruits was generated. Parents, having incurred the expense of acquiring the required education for their children, were likely to have been eager to ensure that sons entered a *learned* vocation irrespective of the necessity for more practitioners in the professions.

The Expansion of Middle Class Education and the Supply of Recruits

Just as the emulation of certain lifestyles, consumption patterns and the occupational advancement of sons were status-enhancing attributes, so the education of offspring at certain institutions was a significant imitation. The attendance of sons at prescribed schools enhanced parental status in that it associated them with a higher social milieu and allowed sons to gain the necessary paper and social qualifications for entry to an occupation of greater standing. Consequently, during the second half of the nineteenth century especially, increasing numbers of middle class sons entered schools which prepared their scholars for entrance to the professions.

Musgrove has explained the situation in England.[85] During the early nineteenth century, increasingly wealthy middle class parents, anxious that their sons should secure social advancement through association with the offspring of landed families, sent them to public schools. This resulted, after the 1820s, in a great expansion of such institutions and in the number of sons attending them. The nature of school society and curricula was designed to prepare individuals for a high expenditure and genteel future and produced generations of scholars with attendant expectations. As the numbers at public schools expanded, so did the numbers of scholars expecting to enter suitable areas of employment in order to satisfy the necessary financial and social conditions of the career for which they had been prepared.

This pressure was compounded by a further development. The reforming movement from the 1850s to base professional entrance upon examination and merit developed from the marginal professions (which were keen to establish their *academic* standing) to the traditional, and meant that the public schools needed to provide their scholars with the necessary certificates. This they were first to do. Consequently, not only did increasing numbers of sons attend schools which imbued them with expectations of entering a profession, but they were also educationally prepared for future *learned* professional status, and envisaged entrance to occupations of a nature commensurate with that standing. Fathers were likely to have been increasingly averse to sending suitably educated, academically-qualified sons into non-professional, non-learned occupations. The result of these tendencies were, so Musgrove claims "a formidable increase in the output of educated young men after the mid-nineteenth century."[86]

Contemporaries noted the same consequences of educational expansion in increasing the number of "The educated who desire to live by their brains, and, if possible, by the professions recognized as conferring a diploma of presumable culture . . . or desire for 'a life in which ability tells'".[87] Furthermore, as meritocratization extended into non-professional occupations, and education was increasingly recognized as a means of improving social status, and as increasing numbers of scholars from wider social origins gained expectations of upward mobility, the process had filtered down beyond the middle classes by the late nineteenth century. In 1889, *The Spectator* noted the increased numbers expecting to enter higher, mainly professional, occupations due to: "That thirst for education which it is in our day the ambition of legislators to gratify, and from that desire for refined life which is its necessary result."[88]

The consequence was that the number of educated men desirous of entering learned vocations "bears no proportion to the increasing numbers of those who contend for it".[89] Parents complained increasingly during and after the 1880s of not being able to place educated sons: "The journals mention almost every week the hundreds of applicants for the smallest vacancy which an educated man can fill."[90]

A futuristic piece by Walter Besant which was published in 1893 provides an excellent example of contemporary attitudes toward the impact of educational expansion on social ambition and the supply of recruits to the professions. Besant argued that the expansion of educational provision for the working class would create a social revolution during the twentieth century resulting in the *Conquest of the Professions by the People*. During most of the nineteenth century, the professions were closed to all but a few scholarship-winning working class sons. The extension of post-elementary and technical education from the mid 1880s created a considerable increase in the number of ambitious manual workers' sons.

Attenders at such institutions: "Thought that to be a man of books was better than to be a man with a saw or a plane. Ambition seized them - seized them by tens of thousands; they would rise. Learning was their stepping stone."[91] Educated sons would strive to enter the middle classes. No one having learnt integral calculus, claimed Besant, would desire to adopt his father's occupation of cabinetmaker. As working class education expanded so the number of social aspirants would increase to create an 'upward pressure' to enter the professions regardless of the need for their services: "Then followed a rush into the Professions as had never before been witnessed. Already too full, they became at once absolutely congested and choked. Every other man was either a doctor or a solicitor."[92]

In the very long term, the ultimate result envisaged was a devaluation of professional income and status ensuring a return of working class sons to the more remunerative trade and craft employments. Although a far sighted perspective, the significance of Besant's work lies in its constant assumption that the demand for professional services would not limit the flood of recruits except in the very long-term. Besant was not alone in focusing attention on the education system as a cause of overcrowding in the professions. Public schools, in particular, received considerable criticism concerning their inability to satisfy the expectations that they had imbued in scholars and their unsuitability for preparing sons for a more lucrative career in commerce rather than in the professions.

The Cornhill Magazine in 1903 summed up the concern expressed by dissillusioned parents expecting that a public school education was the avenue to a secure professional employment for their sons:

> "My youngster's a good steady fellow, did capitally at school, took a high class in Mods, and his tutor says he'll do the same in Greats; but what's the practical value of a so called liberal education in the real struggle of life ? He has to earn his own keep, and to make his own way. The open professions are hopelessly crowded . . . Are the Public Schools a failure, or is the 'Varsity played out'? for neither of them seems to have fitted him for the future." How often one hears this bitter wail from a distracted parent ![93]

The Supply of Recruits and Occupational Expansion

Late nineteenth and early twentieth century journals and career guides were universal in their assumption that the interrelated forces of status acquisition and educational expansion resulted in an oversupply of sons qualified for, and entering, the professions. The ever-increasing numbers of professional men relative to the amount of business available ensured increased competition and adversely affected income levels. The problem was considered to be one of deepening severity and was not being remedied by the laws of supply and demand in the professional labour market. As early as 1868 *Chamber's Magazine* reported that:

> What is to be done with a gentleman's sons, is a question of growing difficulty. The old genteel professions are getting overdone . . . Educate him to be a lawyer – he may never get a brief, or miserably hang on for years, picking up now and then a few guineas. Make him a doctor – what a struggle to get into practice. Rear him for the Church – worse and worse.[94]

Twenty one years later impressions were that the situation was unchanged if not worse:

> . . . Everyone knows that in every profession the young are more and more disappointed, that the competition grows ever keener, and that the numbers who admit that they make absolutely nothing is becoming bewildering. The Bar declares itself starving; the solicitors lament the proportion who remain clerks half their lives; the State service is besieged with applicants for examination; and medicine is positively choked with men who strive, contend and intrigue for appointments and 'practices' of £50 and £100 per year.[95]

Partnerships were reported as becoming more expensive and the increased cost of living in the face of demands to lead a *civilized* lifestyle were such that there was great financial and psychological pressure on many professional men. *The Spectator* in 1895 estimated that the chances of a professional earning £800 *per annum* were 50% less in that year than they had been thirty years previously.[96] In 1907 it was claimed that many educated sons of excellent families were "straining every nerve to get work", and that:

> There probably never has been a time . . . when so many men of good education and good social standing, the majority between the ages of 20 and 40 were in want of work as now; and certainly there was never a time when there seemed to be so few vacancies suitable for men of this class.[97]

The advice given to these unfortunate individuals was consistent throughout the period: ignore social prejudice and enter trade. This was the sector of greatest opportunity for financial reward. Yet, despite the guidance, few appeared to have followed it and the journals which advocated it were themselves sceptical of the impact of their own message.[98] The antipathy toward a career in trade only very gradually diminished due to the economic necessity of entering it as an alternative vocation. As late as 1907 *The National Review* was still asserting that:

> . . . . Very soon many well educated men who primarily were intended to be barristers, doctors, solicitors, clergymen, Army officers, and so on, will begin seriously to consider the advisability of entering trade. For the disdain with which our fathers and grandfathers used to look upon men engaged in trade is rapidly dying out.[99]

The continual relevance of such social prejudices is indicative of the insignificance of salary equilibrium in regulating occupational expansion during the nineteenth and early twentieth centuries. Career choice was consistently based largely upon parental preferences concerning perceived status acquisition for themselves and for their sons. The ability to make a living was of secondary and not of immediate importance to parents considering the occupational destinations of their sons. For example, an article entitled "Social Ambitions" which appeared in *Blackwood's Magazine* in 1867, considered that the activities of all were governed by three motivations: working for money; working to secure leisure; and:

> . . . . Aiming at position, rank, influence in some shape; and with a view to this, we are willing to spend freely the money which some hoard, and to sacrifice personal indulgences which make all the happiness of others. No one can doubt that this last class of motives is the highest of the three.[100]

Hence, the supply of sons entering the professions which did not set limits to annual intake, remained unabated despite the obvious financial advantages of entering alternative vocations. *Blackwood's Magazine* in 1894, referring to the legal profession, noted that: "It seems incomprehensible that people should keep crowding into a profession which, if we are to judge from the average earnings of its members, is certainly the least remunerative in the world."[101] Twenty four years previously, Devanant had suggested a reason for this situation. He challenged aspiring lawyers who were essentially motivated by the *influence* attached to the profession to consider "whether his forte, his genius, his taste, or whatever else he may call it that leads him on, be real or spurious."[102] In 1903 *The Cornhill Magazine* noticed that although barristers expressed displeasure at their level of earnings, they were satisfied with their occupational and cultural status.[103] Similarly, one clergyman expressed a fear in 1899 that the Church might be elected as a vocation by those seeking influence and social importance rather than by those motivated by their Christianity.[104]

Besides the continued maintenance of occupational status differences and prejudices, other social factors should be recognized in explaining why the supply of recruits to various overstocked professions remained unabated despite the financial disadvantages. Firstly, recruitment preferences toward the overcrowded professions were probably perpetuated by interfamilial competition. Having uncles, cousins or brothers in professional occupations ensured that entering any alternative form of vocation was a derogation of family and individual status: "The lad who has brothers and cousins in the Church, the Army, the Civil Service, at the Bar, or in Medicine, will not, as a rule, become a police court reporter."[105]

Secondly, parents perhaps placed too much faith in education and in the professional qualification system. Many middle class parents appear to have assumed that once their sons had attended a desirable public school and gained a professional diploma, the field of employment opportunity was relatively open and some progress and a decent living were assured. These perceptions were reinforced by the many examples of those who had reached the pinnacle of their vocations. Career handbooks often claimed that despite overcrowding there was always room for the most able in the professions, and those who failed to excel were generally assumed to have suffered from personal defects which might be remedied by some strict parental discipline or individual improvement: "Hundreds have only themselves to blame for failing to succeed, yet it is a truism that many seem not to be aware of."[106]

THE SUPPLY OF RECRUITS TO THE SOCIETY OF ACCOUNTANTS
IN EDINBURGH 1854-1914

The Social Background

It is clear from the above analysis that the expansion in recruitment to the professions has to be examined in the context of the underlying social forces and relationships which generated a supply of potential recruits. The growth of the SAE has therefore to be analysed in these terms.

Edinburgh, in the 1850-1914 period, the source of the majority of SAE recruits (see Table 3.15), was noted for a social structure and a popular mentality that was especially likely to have ensured a high level of parental motivation and ambition in favour of the entrance of sons to the local professions. The acute division between many distinct status strata and social snobbery were renowned characteristics of the population of the Scottish capital. An obsession with social status and its enhancement led to the citizens being characterized by 'pride and poverty' or 'piecemeal and pianos': expenditure on conspicuous material acquisitions and social progress was given priority over a balanced diet. An Edinburgh lamplighter described the social pretence of his city thus in 1911: "Its the one being better than the other, and having a grander 'ouse than the other and general 'puttin' on. My wife says its aal red 'errings and pianofortes in Edinburgh."[107]

Heiton observed a mid-nineteenth century population that was highly conscious of social placement coupled with a fierce desire to improve its position in the hierachy. He claimed that "the pressure upwards has become a war of pride and envy between caste and caste, and the entrenchments become the firmer and firmer as you ascend".[108] Writing half a century later, Keith considered that the social scale could be divided in Edinburgh not on the basis of occupation or social class, but into four classes of varying levels of motivation and aspiration. At the head were "people who count in the social scale"[109] – the old nobility and professional groups who had effectively reached the top. Secondly, "people who think they count" – successful professionals and wealthy tradesmen, "creepers" seeking entrance to the first class. Thirdly, "people who hope to count" – the ambitious, snobbish and arrogant. Fourthly, "people who don't care a brass farthing whether they count or not, so long as they are happy" – despised by those above them though unpretentious, honest and hardworking.

The distinction between the professions and trade was also particularly acute in a city that was socially and culturally dominated by the former, and in which a high regard was held for academic excellence. Income derived from commerce was considered inferior to that from professional fees. According to Heiton: "of all the places in the kingdom Edinburgh is that in which the 'New Man' has the least chance of being received into the old ranks."[110] This prejudice persisted at the turn of the century. Keith noted that, although outsiders recognized the importance of brewing in Edinburgh: "As for the inhabitants of that city, they make no boast of brewing or anything else which smacks of trade or traffic."[111] Similarly, shopkeepers, with their marginal middle class status were reputed to have been striving constantly at the social emulation of the professional classes in terms of residence and consumption patterns. Their children were apparently highly motivated toward social advance out of the *trade* class.

There appears to have existed then, in Edinburgh, a highly status-conscious population, with attendant designs to move up the social scale *intra* generationally through material improvement, and *inter* generationally by ensuring that sons moved into more respectable, mainly professional occupations.

This quest for social advancement was reflected in Edinburgh's position as a major and expanding centre of middle class education during the nineteenth century. The local public schools and the university produced large numbers of sons motivated to professional recruitment, particularly from the 1870s expansion in private secondary education. Additionally, many aspiring sons from outwith the city were reputed to have migrated to Edinburgh to take advantage of the educational facilities available and to enter the Edinburgh-based professions. Not surprisingly, these factors generated a substantial supply of entrants to the local professions with the result that they became overstocked. In 1908 the aspiring professional was said to have had:

> . . . So many cultured rivals to contend with that we often find him content to hold his cravings for fame and distinction as satisfied with the position of teacher, law clerk, newspaper reporter, Civil Service clerk, or druggist's assistant.[112]

Edinburgh was said to have had an "abnormally large" number of unemployed professional people.[113] It was almost considered more respectable to remain as an idle impoverished professional maintaining a certain independence than it was to dirty one's hands with *trade*.

Though these socially-induced pressures to professional recruitment were especially virulent in Edinburgh, they were not exclusive to the Scottish capital. Despite a less rigid social structure in Glasgow and Dundee, for example, increasingly wealthy merchants and manufacturers often desired an improvement in their family's social standing by the entrance of certain of their sons to the professions.

These social forces should be recognized prior to an examination of the growth of one of Edinburgh's newer professions which accomodated a proportion of the supply of eager recruits: that is, chartered accountancy.

The Expansion of the SAE

The major periods of expansion in SAE recruitment, as revealed in Figure 2.3, were the 1850s and 1860s, the mid 1870s to the early 1880s, and the mid 1890s to the late 1900s (see also Figures 7.1 and 7.2 for annual recruitment trends). Preceding each of these periods of growth, a vital event occurred which effectively induced a subsequent increase in the number of indentures contracted by improving the attractiveness of the profession as a vocation to parents and sons.

The formation of the Institute of Accountants in 1853, and its subsequent incorporation, confirmed the professional status of accountants in Edinburgh, and the occupation consequently was perceived by parents as a suitable vocation for sons. An organized profession with entrance based on the acquisition of a liberal education induced more parents to consider the occupation for sons than its unorganized, lower status predecessor.

From the late 1860s to the early 1870s, the rate of expansion in recruitment declined. The likely cause of this was that, compared to alternative professions, the SAE's unsophisticated system of examination and qualification was increasingly less attractive to parents who desired that their sons enter occupations which would take advantage of their expensive education (this is further discussed in Chapter 4). This SAE deficiency was remedied, and the trend in recruitment arrested, from 1873 when a comprehensive three-tier system of professional examination was introduced. Thenceforth, any son qualifying for admission to the SAE could claim membership of a *learned profession*. The SAE thus became a more alluring career alternative to parents anxious that their sons should enter such an occupation for which they had been academically prepared. The extent to which the SAE attempted to present itself as a learned organization to middle class parents can be measured by the emphasis placed on the encouragement of academic excellence among apprentices through the introduction of money prizes and bursaries to the most successful performers in examinations. These awards constituted 40% of the total expenditure of the Society between 1873 and 1879.

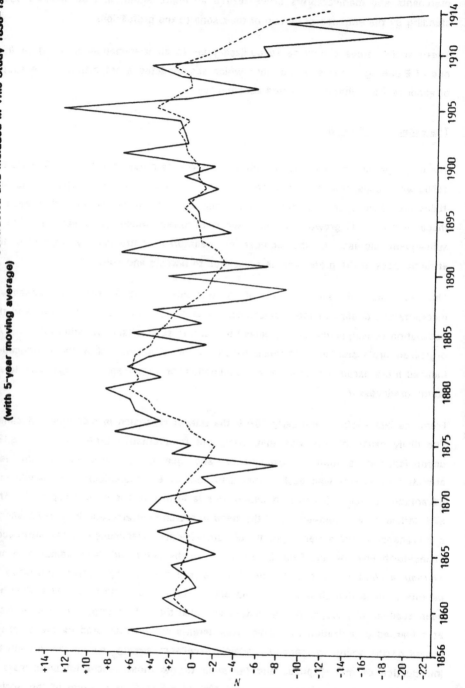

FIGURE 2.3 Deviation From Linear Trend of the Number of SAE Indentures Contracted and Included in This Study 1856-1914 (with 5-year moving average)

Similarly, the expansion in recruitment of the mid 1890s and 1900s also appears to have been triggered by a significant event in the history of the SAE; the establishment of the General Examining Board in 1892. In introducing a centralized and uniform system of examination and entrance to the three Scottish CA societies in 1893, this enhanced the perceived academic and professional value of a CA qualification to parents considering the occupation as a possible career option for their sons.

Additionally, the 1893 changes increased the attractiveness of the CA profession in a further respect. It was an expression of national unity among three separate societies, and formed the first institutional move in the development of a *Scottish* CA organization. As Woolf was to point out in 1912:

> In 1893 the three existing Societies of Accountants in Scotland entered into an agreement "providing for uniform Rules for Qualification for and Admission to Membership of their respective corporate bodies, and for the Establishment of a General Board for the Examination of Apprentices, &c." This joining of forces has proved of immense benefit in many ways, and since the "amalgamation" the three constituent Societies have become known as the "**Chartered Accountants of Scotland**."[114]

The English and Irish chartered societies had been strengthened and their qualification become more widely recognized due to their singular, centralized structure. Prior to 1893, the separate Scottish societies had been accused, as we have seen, of localization by the *national* SIA. Any son entering the SAE during the 1880s, when the Society was threatened by a series of petitions and litigations, would have been trained for a profession with an uncertain future. From 1893, however, the SAE apprentice could envisage becoming a member of a more united profession. As James Martin claimed in 1897:

> Before the action of the Scottish Institute of Accountants and Corporation of Accountants the three CA societies were separate entities. Perhaps I ought to say non- entities . . . But when the Corporation of Accountants was formed, the three societies found it convenient to combine against the common danger.[115]

The 1893 reforms were recognized as having been of great significance within the CA profession both in Scotland and in England. *The Accountant's Magazine* in 1901 considered that they had marked:

. . . The commencement of a new era in the history of the profession in Scotland. From that time the societies, in all public questions have acted as one body, and, so united, have become of tenfold greater public importance. The title 'Chartered Accountant' has become of one value throughout Scotland and that value is now universally known as of the highest.[116]

South of the border the organ of the English Institute, *The Accountant*, had commented in 1893 in an uncharacteristically harmonious vein:

For all practical purposes (*i.e.,* so far as the outside public is concerned) there will, in the future be but one class of Chartered Accountants in Scotland – a class with definite qualifications, and of untainted reputation. It is beyond question that the real gainers in the long run will be the community whose affairs will be supervised by a body of upright, vigilant, and intelligent gentlemen – the Scottish Chartered Accountants.[117]

The official centenary history of the ICAS recognized the potential impact that these events had had upon recruitment to the profession. While acknowledging that there had been an increase in the business of CAs during the post-1893 period, it also admitted that "it is probable that the parents of young men now realized that the profession offered a discipline and a system of training and examination that were progressive and constructive."[118]

CONCLUSIONS

The foregoing analysis illustrates that traditional explanations of nineteenth and early twentieth century professional expansion in terms of the growth in the demand for occupational services resulting from the increasing sophistication of the urban-industrial economy are much too simplistic. Changes in workload only partly influenced recruitment, and the regulating mechanism implied by the hypothesis and adhered to by contemporaries was prevented from perfect operation. The laws of demand and supply were effective in determining the rate of professional growth in only the very long-term, their impact was delayed or rendered insignificant, and they imposed only very indefinite upper limits to occupational expansion in the short and medium-term.

A number of features of the professions themselves and of society prevented the demand for professional services acting as the prime determinant of the intake of recruits. The forces of professionalization acted to permit the entrance of all qualifying applicants in order to assert organizational strength and security irrespective of their need in the labour market. Underlying social and educational pressures generated an increasing supply of candidates motivated to, and qualified for, recruitment. These social forces were so virulent that the level of professional income did not always act as a regulator of the intake of recruits; income considerations were secondary to those whose main objective was to attain *professional* status.

The SAE experienced its greatest periods of expansion in recruitment following institutional changes which enhanced its professional and learned standing, and therefore satisfied the demands of increasing numbers of parents who determined their sons' vocational direction on the basis of status acquisition and chose for them occupations which offered these social attributes. How was it though that parents became aware of this relatively new profession of chartered accountancy as a career option for their sons ? This is a vital question which requires investigation in order to understand fully the process of occupational expansion and the factors which determined the social origins of recruits to the profession.

Notes

1 *A Guide to the Accountancy Profession* (London: Gee & Co., 1895), p.1.

2 J. Howden, CA, "The Profession in Scotland", *The Accountant* 20 (1894), p. 646.

3 *Ibid.*, p. 646.

4 *Ibid.*, p. 649.

5 *The Accountant's Magazine* 16 (1912), p. 1.

6 Privy Council, "SIA Petition", Appendix to the Petition of the Scottish Institute of Accountants for Grant of a Royal Charter, (1889), p. 2. (ICAS Collection, National Library of Scotland).

7 A *cessio bonorum* differed from a sequestration in that the bankrupt conveyed to his creditors not only his assets at the date of sequestration, but also his subsequent income. It provided relief from severe laws of imprisonment for debt – the pursuer could claim in court that his debt was due to innocent misfortune and had to present a statement of his affairs to prove it. Originally *cessios* were brought exclusively before the Court of Session from which source most SAE appointments were derived. See W. Bell, *A Dictionary and Digest of the Law of Scotland* (Edinburgh, 1861), pp. 148–50.

8 Howden, "The Profession in Scotland", p. 650.

9 *The Scottish Accountant* 1 (1893), p. 96.

10 See *The Accountant's Magazine* 2 (1898), p 492.

11 *The Scottish Accountant* 1 (1894), p. 158.

12 The Annual Reports of the Accountant in Bankruptcy are contained in West Register House, Edinburgh (CS 322 series). The statistics are for the year ending 31 October. Court bankruptcy statistics do not include liquidations of registered companies which are recorded by the Registrar of Companies for Scotland. "Judicial Statistics for Scotland" appear from 1868 to 1914 in *Parliamentary Papers.*

13 *Cessio* statistics from the Accountant of Court are also available in West Register House (CS 322 series); they represent new *cessios* brought before the Court of Session.

14 Privy Council, "SIA Petition", In the Matter of the Petition of the Scottish Institute of Accountants for Incorporation by Royal Charter, (1896) (Scottish Dept., Edinburgh Central Public Library). This document claimed that the Edinburgh CAs received the bulk of factory work under the 1849 Act, that is, Court of Session factories. From 1881 the sheriff courts could also award factorial appointments though only a small proportion of this (mainly provincial) work went to SAE members. Similarly, appointments under the 1889 Act were not numerically significant to Edinburgh CAs compared to those under the 1849 Act. See Table 2.7.

15 Statistics of the number of joint stock companies registered with offices in the Lothians were derived from the annual reports of the Board of Trade in *Parliamentary Papers* until the firm's address ceased to be provided (from 1900). Thereafter figures were taken directly from the books of the Registrar of Companies for Scotland which

are held in West Register House (BT.1 series). The number of liquidations could be derived only from the latter source.

16 Minor appointments formed the major component of workload in the small offices. In 1896, Mr W.C. Smith speaking on behalf of the SIA in its claim for incorporation stated that: "The greater mass of the accountancy business by which the profession lives and makes its money, is the private audit of commercial books." W.C. Smith, Privy Council, "Speeches by Counsel", In the Matter of the Petition of the Scottish Institute of Accountants for Incorporation by Royal Charter, (1896), pp. 92-3. (Scottish Dept., Edinburgh Central Public Library).

17 Privy Council, "SIA Petition" (1896), pp. 65-6.

18 *The Accountant's Journal* 23 (1906), p. 383.

19 *The Scottish Accountant* 3 (1899), p. 57. Similarly, a meeting of the Edinburgh CA Students' Society were informed in an address by an IAAG member in 1892 that: "when one sees so many young men applying for admission into Accounting Societies, one cannot help wondering where they are all to find lucrative employment . . . When one surveys the host of competitors this, at least, is clear – all cannot hope to succeed." J. Muir, CA, "A Chat about Accounting", *The Accountant* 18 (1892), pp. 108-9.

20 Brown, *A History of Accounting and Accountants,* p. 332.

21 *The Scottish Accountant* 3 (1899), p. 57.

22 *The Accountant's Student Journal* 1 (1884), p. 347.

23 Martin, *The Accountant Profession: A Public Danger,* p. 15.

24 *Ibid.,* p. 21. See also *The Scottish Accountant* 1 (1893), p. 70.

25 *The Scottish Accountant* 1 (1893), p.104.

26 Mr Finlay, QC, MP, Privy Council, "Speeches by Counsel", In the Matter of the Petition of the Scottish Institute of Accountants for Incorporation by Royal Charter, (1890), p. 25. (Scottish Dept., Edinburgh Central Public Library).

27 See Martin, *The Accountant Profession: A Public Danger, Idem., The Accountant 'C.A.' Case: Was there a Misapplication of the Law* (Glasgow, 1896); *Idem., Did the Devil Win the Toss, Idem., The Sanctification of the Lie; Idem., The Accountant Squabble.*

28 McLelland, *The Origin and Present Organization of the Profession,* p. 11.

29 W.H. Smith, *From Constable to Commissioner* (London, 1910), p. 28.

30 F. Musgrove, *The Migratory Elite* (London, 1963), ch. 2.

31 "The Outlook of the Professional Classes", *The Spectator* 63 (1889), p. 363.

32 W.C. Gully, *Careers of Our Sons: A Practical Handbook for Parents* (Carlisle, 1904), p. 201.

33 M.L. Pechell, *Professions for Boys and How to Enter Them* (London, 1898), p. 142.

34 B. Tozer, "The Unemployed Gentleman", *The National Review* 49 (1907), p. 598.

35 H.F.W. Deane and W.A. Evans (eds.) *The Public Schools Year Book, 1913* (London, 1913), p. 587.

36 Finlay, "Speeches by Counsel" (1890), p. 8.

37 These were Thomas Steven Lindsay, ACA, a former writer, accountant and partner in a CA firm in Edinburgh who established his own firm in London and Edinburgh. Robert Murdoch Rose, ACA, who was born in Fife and was in practice as an accountant in Edinburgh before entering the ICAEW. John MacFarlane Cook, ACA was born in Edinburgh and had a firm in Edinburgh before entering the English society. Each of these gentlemen were also members of the Scottish Institute of Accountants. Lindsay was its Chairman for a period and Cook was Convenor of its Edinburgh Council.

38 *The Incorporated Accountant's Journal* 24 (May, 1913).

39 Brown, *A History of Accounting and Accountants*, p. 335.

40 *The Accountant's Magazine* 28 (1924), p. 509.

41 Musgrove, *The Migratory Elite*, p. 28.

42 Deane and Evans, *The Public Schools Year Book, 1913*, p. 586.

43 Personal letter, 20 November 1984 from a CA apprenticed 1907-12 who wishes to remain anonymous.

44 B. Worthington, *Professional Accountants* (London, 1895), p. 41.

45 *The Accountant* 20 (1894), pp. 693-4.

46 *The Scottish Accountant* 1 (1894), p. 214.

47 *The Accountant's Magazine* 8 (1904), p. 245.

48 *The Accountant's Magazine* 7 (1903), p. 187.

49 *The Accountant's Magazine* 9 (1905), p. 30.

50 *The Accountant* 20 (1894), pp. 693-4.

51 *The Accountant's Magazine* 28 (1924), p. 510.

52 For instance, see: G. Orwell, *The Road to Wigan Pier* (London, 1937), ch. 8.

53 *The Accountant's Magazine* 9 (1905), p. 29.

54 *The Accountant's Magazine* 7 (1903), p.32.

55 *The Accountant's Magazine* 28 (1924), p. 285.

56 *The Accountant's Magazine* 29 (1925), pp. 290-2.

57 A.A. Garrett, *History of the Society of Incorporated Accountants 1885-1957* (Oxford, 1961), p. 3.

58 Finlay, "Speeches by Counsel" (1890), p. 34.

59 *The Accountant's Magazine* 11 (1907), p. 137.

60 *The Accountant's Journal* 8 (1890), pp. 125-6.

61 Finlay, "Speeches by Counsel" (1890), p. 35.

62 See "Is a C.A. fit to Practice in any part of the World", *The Accountant's Magazine* 11 (1907), pp. 85-7.

63 *The Accountant's Magazine* 11 (1907), pp. 1-4.

64 *The Accountant's Student Journal* 1 (1884), p. 347.

65 Howden, "The Profession in Scotland", p. 646.

66 For example, see D. Solomons with T.M. Berridge, *Prospectus for a Profession: The Report of the Long Range Enquiry into Education and Training for the Accountancy Profession* (London, 1974), pp. 130-1.

67 Garrett, *History of the Society of Incorporated Accountants*, p. 64.

68 Privy Council, "SIA Petition" (1890), p. 1.

69 Martin, *The Accountant Profession: A Public Danger*, p. 19.

70 Treasurer's Statement, Annual General Meeting of Faculty, 20 January 1847, "Minute Book of the Faculty of Advocates 1843-61", p. 119.

71 A. Crew, *The Profession of an Accountant* (London, 1925), p. 12.

72 Checkland, *The Rise of Industrial Society in Britain 1815-1885*, p. 301.

73 F. Devanant, *What Shall My Son Be ?: Hints to Parents* (London, 1870), p. 6.

74 "Social Ambitions", *Blackwood's Magazine* 101 (1867), p. 541.

75 See G. Anderson, *Victorian Clerks* (Manchester, 1976) and D. Lockwood, *The Blackcoated Worker: A Study in Class Consciousness* (London, 1958).

76 F. Devanant, *Starting in Life: Hints to Parents on the Choice of a Profession or Trade for their Sons* (London, 1881), p. 160.

77 *Ibid.*

78 *Ibid.*

79 Devanant, *What Shall My Son Be ?*, p. 196.

80 Devanant, *Starting in Life*, p. 160.

81 Devanant, *What Shall My Son Be ?*, pp. 7, 162.

82 "Outlook of the Professional Classes", p. 363.

83 Mercator, *Reasons of Failure and Roads to Success* (Walsall, 1900), p. 1. See also

"Maxims by a Man of the World", *Chamber's Journal,* 4th series, 45, p. 468.

84 Mercator, *Reasons of Failure,* p. 1.

85 F. Musgrove, "Middle Class Education and Employment in the Nineteenth Century". *Economic History Review,* 2nd series, 12 (1959-60). For ensuing debate see H. Perkin, "Middle Class Education and Employment in the Nineteenth Century: A Critical Note", *Economic History Review,* 2nd series, 14 (1961-2). F. Musgrove, "Middle Class Education and Employment in the Nineteenth Century: A Rejoinder", *Economic History Review,* 2nd series, 14 (1961-2).

86 Musgrove, "Middle Class Education and Employment", p. 102.

87 "Outlook of the Professional Classes", p. 363.

88 *Ibid.*

89 *Ibid.*

90 *Ibid.*

91 W. Besant, "The Upward Pressure", *Scribner's Magazine* 13 (1893), p. 592.

92 *Ibid.,* p. 595.

93 "Prospects in the Professions", *Cornhill Magazine,* n.s., 15 (1903), p. 118.

94 "What to do With My Sons", *Chamber's Journal,* 4th series, 5 (1868), p. 342.

95 "Outlook of the Professional Classes", p. 363.

96 "The Professions versus Trade", *The Spectator* 75 (1895), p. 720.

97 Tozer, "The Unemployed Gentleman", p. 600.

98 "The Professions versus Trade", p. 720.

99 Tozer, "The Unemployed Gentleman", p. 599.

100 "Social Ambitions", p. 541.

101 H.E.M. Stutfield, "Celibacy and the Struggle to Get On", *Blackwood's Magazine* 156 (1894), p. 783.

102 Devanant, *What Shall My Son Be ?,* p. 25.

103 "Prospects in the Professions", *Cornhill Magazine,* n.s., 13 (1902), pp. 471-83.

104 D. MacLeane, "The Church as a Profession", *The National Review* 33 (1899), pp. 945-55.

105 A Veteran Journalist, "Journalism as a Career", *The National Review* 32 (1898-9), p. 212.

106 Tozer, "The Unemployed Gentleman", p. 598.

107 J. Bone, *Edinburgh Revisited* (London, 1911), p. 250.

108 Heiton, *The Castes of Edinburgh,* p. 7.

109 A. Keith, *Edinburgh of Today* (Edinburgh, 1908), pp. 204–11.

110 Heiton, *The Castes of Edinburgh,* p. 280.

111 Keith, *Edinburgh of Today,* p. 9.

112 *Ibid.,* p. 30.

113 *Ibid.,* p. 37.

114 Woolf, *A Short History of Accountants and Accounting,* p. 166.

115 Martin, *The Sanctification of the Lie,* p. 37. One year after the first unsuccessful application of the SIA for a Royal Charter, *The Accountant* also commented as follows on the hitherto disunity among the three Scottish chartered societies: "As far as we can learn, no community of action or indeed of sentiment, has ever been displayed by these local societies, though the petition of the Institute has at least been provocative and indeed productive of concerted action on their part upon this occasion. The Glasgow Society was formed out of jealousy of its older Edinburgh rival; they never before acted in harmony or made common cause". *The Accountant* 11 (1885), No. 537, p. 4.

116 *The Accountant's Magazine* 5 (1901), p. 140.

117 *The Accountant* 19 (1893), p. 4.

118 ICAS, *History of Chartered Accountants of Scotland,* p. 45.

3
Career Selection : Why Chartered Accountancy ?

Tinker,	Army,	Army,
Tailor,	Navy,	Navy,
Soldier,	Peerage,	Medicine,
Sailor,	Trade,	Church,
Richman,	Doctor,	Architect,
Poorman,	Divinity,	Lawyer,
Beggarman,	Law.	Left in the Lurch.
Thief.		

[*The Oxford Dictionary of Nursery Rhymes*]

Newly instituted professional organizations of the nineteenth century were confronted with the problem of advertising themselves as an alternative career option to the supply of sons aspiring to enter the professions. This was due to the often localized and relatively small scale of their operations during their early existence.

The new occupational organization, however, depended on a constant influx of members. Not only was this a financial necessity, it was also vital to maintaining the provision of services, and to the assertion of occupational presence and status. Professional status also depended increasingly on exhibiting certain organizational traits which contradicted effectively the objective of increasing membership. Recruitment was restricted by the existence of entrance fees and an examination system to ensure the proficiency of practitioners. It was desirable, therefore, to interest large numbers of potential recruits in the profession in the expectation that some might satisfy the financial and educational conditions of entry. A relatively new vocation was confronted with a problem of communication between itself and those it needed to recruit for its expansion.

From the perspective of the potential recruit, there existed also a communications barrier. Awareness of opportunities in newly organized occupations during the nineteenth century was limited and still is today:

> The job information to which a young person has access is strictly limited. The division of labour has produced a multiplicity of occupations, and in industrial societies work is performed in special organizations normally out of the gaze of the general public. Under these circumstances it is difficult for a young person to acquire any sort of comprehensive job knowledge . . . Consequently school-leavers know little about the occupations that are open to them.[1]

Occupational choice in an open society is founded ideally upon access to information concerning opportunities in all available vocations. The individual has perfect knowledge of options and forms a preference on the basis of the relationship between his own qualifications and abilities, and those necessary to fulfill the demands of the occupation. Given freedom of choice, the candidate presents himself for admission to the vocations on offer.

Before the availability of mass literature concerning vocational openings, and in the absence of a sophisticated career and appointments service for school leavers (the latter has its British origins in the Education [Choice of Employment] Act 1910), occupational preferences could not be determined on the basis of perfect knowledge and free choice.[2] Not only was job placement during most of the nineteenth century seldom the result of open competition based on merit, it was also hindered by a lack of information on a national scale concerning the occupations available.

The range of career options was likely to have been considerably limited by parental perceptions of the occupational structure and these, in turn, were determined and probably manufactured by their own occupational experience; and, by inadequate information of opportunities from other agencies in the career-determining process (that is, teachers, relatives, neighbours and peer groups).

There were, however, some professions which were well-established vocational options for sons even if parents had no immediate connections with or within them. Law, medicine, divinity and the armed forces were long-standing professional vocations with a national distribution of practitioners. They were also occupations with which most middle class parents would have some, often infrequent contact on a professional or social level. By contrast, some of the new professions, such as chartered accountancy, were not so well self-advertised. Not only did these alternative career options often originally have a localized existence, they also had a clientele whose occupational and social composition was limited. Professions experiencing this situation could not be seen as possible vocational choices for school leavers over the whole nation. This was particularly the case when considering the inadequacy of information concerning the nature of the occupation and how to enter it.

Under these conditions of ignorance concerning career alternatives, occupational choice during the nineteenth century was more than anything else a function of *connection.* Youths were placed in vocations determined by the range of parental occupational and social associations and by their ability to exploit them.[3] For example, one SAE original member's route to chartered accountancy was as follows:

> What to do with seven sons must have been something of a
> problem even for a man with so many friends as Dr MacLagan. For
> David, however, who had elected to go into business, there was
> by-and-by found an opening in the Scottish Union Insurance Office, to
> which Dr MacLagan stood in relation of medical adviser.[4]

The importance of influence in securing openings was as significant in the new as
well as the old professions despite the meritocratic tendencies of the second half of
the century. As late as 1908, to enter the legal profession a youth required not only
considerable funds but also a father with a "certain amount of influence in some
particular class of society."[5] Similarly, it was considered a great advantage if a
potential engineer had a father who held shares in a firm where his son might be
apprenticed. Parents contemplating the entrance of a son to auctioneering were
recommended to address themselves to certain questions:

> A parent will want to know, How am I to get a boy into an
> auctioneer's office ? This is certainly where the shoe pinches. There are
> but three ways of doing so. First, Have you any personal influence with
> any auctioneer, land surveyor, valuer, house and estate agent? Have
> you any relative engaged in the business? Or, does any of your relatives
> know a friend so occupied ?[6]

It was the multiplication of such connections and points of influence between
chartered accountants and parents that largely explains the social origins of the
supply of SAE apprentices, and played a significant part in determining the timing of
the expansion in recruitment. There were a number of reference points which
increased the *visibility* of accountants and accounting to the public. It was through
this route that information concerning the profession as a career alternative became
more widespread. What were these points of reference and increasing connections
that resulted in greater numbers of sons opting for chartered accountancy ?

Recent investigations into the processes of occupational decision-making have
identified a range of definite influences upon the choices of school leavers.[7] An
historical study is unable to discover precisely the relevant motivating factors for each
case in the same manner as a modern investigation - except where individual
biographical evidence is available directly pertaining to the subject.

It is also difficult to impose value judgements as to which factors may have been the
most significant in the career decision-making process of individual SAE apprentices

who commenced their indentures between 1837 and 1911. Clearly, some influences were of greater importance that others. Having a father in the profession was likely to have been a more powerful inducement to recruitment than information concerning the vocation obtained from a career guide. In other cases, more than one potentially significant factor can be identified, and it would prove a highly problematical exercise to attempt to distinguish which was the most important. For example, Thomas Scott's indenture of 1876 could have been induced by his mother taking a lodger who was an accountant or by his employment as a CA's clerk some months previous to the commencement of his apprenticeship. What is feasible is to identify a number of variables which may have been of relevance to individual decisions concerning occupational choice towards chartered accountancy.

The methodology employed involved utilising computer-sorting techniques. A list of the names of the 1067 SAE apprentices who commenced their indentures between 1837 and 1911 was prepared to reveal possible familial relationships. Along side each case, biographical information considered potentially relevant to the career decision-making process was collected. This included: the occupations of identified relatives; previous employment of apprentices; schools attended; and place of residence in relation to the location of professional accountants and other apprentices at the time of indenture. On the basis of the analysis of this data and other information from sources such as career guides, it was possible to identify the potential relevance of a number of influencing factors upon vocational choice among SAE apprentices. This also permitted a study of the increasing prevalence of points of connection between Edinburgh CAs and parents and the consequences of this for professional expansion. The aspects of occupational decision-making to be examined in turn are: familial determinants of occupational choice; educational influences; the significance of pre-apprenticeship work experience; occupational information, and residential and spatial factors.

FAMILIAL DETERMINANTS OF OCCUPATIONAL CHOICE

Post-war studies of the individuals that influence career decision-making and aspirations have revealed that the most important determinants in western societies are familial.[8] Potentially, the most significant single influence toward a decision to enter the CA profession was to have:

a) A Relation Employed in Professional Accountancy

Individuals who have a relation in a vocation are in an advantageous position with regard to entering it themselves. Not only do they gain intimation of vacancies before others, they also learn something of the nature of the employment and its rewards. Information concerning the new profession of chartered accountancy with its limited clientele and localized urban existence would have been most available during the 1854-1914 period to youths with a practising relative. Most importantly, a father in the profession could form a great inducement to occupational inheritance. The consistently high proportion of SAE apprentices who had a relation in accountancy is an important indicator of the supply-led nature of the intake of recruits and the profession's growth. In a newly organized occupation, it might be expected that the extent of nepotism would decline as it expanded and became increasingly regarded as a career alternative by those unconnected with it. Table 3.1 shows that widespread consideration of the CA profession as a career option was unlikely to have occurred by 1911. The constant proportion of apprentices who had a relation in the profession, despite its rate of expansion, illustrates that as family connections multiplied among SAE members so did recruitment from this source.

TABLE 3.1
SAE Apprentices 1855-1911 with an Identified Relation in Chartered Accountancy, Accountancy or as a CA Apprentice

Year of Indenture Commencement	Relation to Apprentice								As % Total Recruits
	F	FB	B	GF	U	C	BL	Total	
1855-64	8	0	4	0	4	0	2	18	20.9
1865-74	2	2	4	2	5	3	0	18	17.0
1875-84	15	3	7	1	5	4	4	39	20.0
1885-94	20	2	8	0	10	7	0	47	22.5
1895-04	15	1	15	1	10	5	1	48	16.2
1905-11	9	2	8	0	7	2	0	28	18.9
Total/Mean	69	10	46	4	41	21	7	198	19.0

Code: F = Father; U = Uncle; FB = Father and Brother; C = Cousins and Cousins Removed; B = Brother; BL = Brother-in-law; GF = Grandfather.

There are examples of family succession and self-recruitment which suggest clearly that some sons were destined to become CAs from birth in order to carry on their father's firm. For example, three generations of Robertson/Robertson-Durhams, Pearsons, and Martins entered the profession during the 1853-1914 period. Also of interest are the number of apprentices who followed brothers into the profession. This was higher among CAs than in the major and established branches of the Edinburgh legal profession.[9]

b) A Relation in an Occupation in Which Accountancy Was Practised as a Secondary Occupation

Before the usurpation of most accounting business by professional accountants, a variety of legal practitioners in Edinburgh acted as accountants. Some, indeed, devoted their careers to it prior to the 1850s. As was shown in the preceding chapters, Writers to the Signet, writers, Solicitors to the Supreme Courts, solicitors and, to some extent, advocates, not only had considerable occupational and social contact with CAs through their mutual concern with certain branches of legal practice but also were one of the few sections of Edinburgh society to recognize the importance of the accountancy profession and its practitioners. Consequently, the CA profession formed a visible career alternative for the sons of lawyers before it became a recognized option for the sons of fathers in occupations with fewer connections with accountancy. Table 3.2 reveals that a high proportion of early SAE recruits were the sons of lawyers.

TABLE 3.2
SAE Apprentices 1837-1911 With a Father in the Legal Profession

Year of Indenture Commencement	Occupation of Father						As % Total Recruits
	Advocate	WS	SSC	Writer	Solicitor	Total	
1837-54	2	3	0	0	0	5	19.2
1855-64	0	16	3	4	1	24	27.9
1865-74	6	15	5	4	1	31	29.2
1875-84	1	10	4	1	2	18	9.2
1885-94	1	5	1	2	1	10	4.8
1895-04	9	7	7	2	6	31	10.4
1905-11	4	4	3	1	3	15	10.1
Mean/Total	23	60	23	14	14	134	12.6

The interdependent relationship between law and accountancy in Edinburgh was so strong by the mid-nineteenth century that a convention in vocational choice became established among parents which was imitative of a recruitment custom among landed proprietors in Scotland. Just as "it was a good old Scottish custom for younger sons of the lairds to go early into commerce, trade, and the various professions - the Bar being generally reserved for the eldest son",[10] so with the sons of Edinburgh lawyers. It was deemed a 'good variety' for the eldest son to follow his father into law and for any subsequent male offspring to be found a position in chartered accountancy. 52.2% of sons with a father in an occupation where accountancy may have been practised as a secondary occupation also had an elder brother either training for, or in, the legal profession. The practice was especially common among Writers to the Signet. James Balfour, WS, for example, had three sons. In 1835 John became a member of the Society of Writers to the Signet, and began business with his father in Picardy Place. James also became a WS on 6 June 1839. Robert was trained to be a Chartered Accountant. Robert had been " . . . influenced largely by his fathers advice."[11]

Fathers in non-professional occupations also tended to emulate the recruitment fashion of sending an elder son into law. Consequently, the profession of chartered accountancy became apparent to, for example, merchants, through the legal occupation of the older son, and was subsequently considered as a possible vocational option for younger sons.

c) Relation in an Occupation Practised by CAs as a Secondary Occupation

As established in Chapter 1, a number of early Edinburgh CAs, in addition to practising accountancy, also acted as actuaries, insurance managers, insurance and bank agents, and later, as stockbrokers. 2.6% of all SAE apprentices had a father in one of these occupations. There was a long-run tendency for this feature of Edinburgh CAs work to suffer relative decline though the professional relationship between CAs and actuaries remained close. There was, during the 1854-1911 period, a constant intake of apprentices from these sources, reflecting the increasing importance of the actuarial profession in Edinburgh and its connections with the SAE. One route of particular significance to a CA indenture for sons from non actuarial-insurance origins was to have an elder brother as an insurance clerk or apprentice. This again revealed accountancy to the sons of parents with little previous knowledge of it as a career option. Almost one-fifth of SAE recruits with a relation in an occupation classified in this section had an older brother employed as an insurance clerk or apprentice.

d) Relation in an Occupation Likely to Employ a CA

The precise nature of the clientele of Edinburgh CAs over the 1854-1914 period is difficult to define though, from the evidence presented in the previous chapter, there were clearly general changes that bought SAE members into contact with individuals from an increasingly broad range of occupational groups. This pattern is reflected in the origins of SAE apprentices. For example, outside legal-orientated business, early CAs were often employed by landed proprietors or estate managers and agents to scrutinize estate accounts. Later in the nineteenth century, the expansion of auditing work brought CAs into contact with manufacturers and the officials of public limited companies. Table 3.3 illustrates that the changing clientele of Edinburgh CAs in these branches of business was reflected in the recruitment of apprentices from these sources.

TABLE 3.3
SAE Apprentices 1837-1911 With an Identified Relation as:

Year of Indenture Commencement	A Landed Proprietor, Landed Proprietor's Factor or Manager	A Large Manufacturer, Employed in a Ltd. Co., or a Banker
1837-54	15.4 (4)	0 (0)
1855-64	5.8 (5)	1.2 (1)
1865-74	4.7 (5)	3.8 (4)
1875-84	6.7 (13)	6.7 (13)
1885-94	6.2 (13)	8.1 (17)
1895-04	2.4 (7)	8.4 (25)
1905-11	1.4 (2)	4.7 (7)
Total/Mean	4.6 (49)	6.3 (67)

As well as providing an alternative profession for the younger sons of Scottish landowners, an SAE indenture also constituted a good introduction to estate management for future landowning sons. Other recruits from landed origins, such as James Maxtone-Graham (indentured in 1881 and son of the 13th Laird of Cultoquhey) may have entered chartered accountancy for rather different reasons:

> James was the third and youngest son. His father considered that there was no chance of any opening anywhere for younger sons, and having taken up this attitude held out no prospect to James of anything but life at home, a dull affair, in spite of chances of sport for a young man full of energy and ambition . . . Acting on his own initiative James left home at nineteen for an accountant's office in Edinburgh, and qualifying as a CA started out on a life that . . . . offered opportunities to win a place for himself in the world of affairs.[12]

If manufacturing on any scale of operations is considered, the increasing connections with, and recruitment to, the Edinburgh CA profession from this source can be further illustrated by the fact that only 2.3% of SAE apprentices whose indentures commenced between 1837 and 1879 had a father in the manufacturer (SSG 3) status group compared to 10.3% of those recruited between 1880 and 1911. The escalation of auditing work and the increasing importance of company accounting could precipitate a chain of recruitment into Edinburgh chartered accountancy. For example, in 1894, the son of Henry J. Younger (John A.C. Younger), a major Edinburgh brewer, entered into an SAE indenture followed, in 1902, by the son of the company secretary and in 1905 by the son of a manager in the same firm.

As the employment connections between large businesses and CAs increased and, as the importance of account keeping became ever more evident, a training in a CA's office was seen by some of Edinburgh's principal manufacturers as providing an adequate introduction to company management and accounting for sons who would eventually inherit the family firm. In the preceeding instance, John A.C. Younger did not become a CA but entered the service of William Younger and Co. The case of John J. Cowan provides a further example. He was the son of Alexander Cowan, paper manufacturer, and " . . . spent most of the summer of 1864 in the office of Kenneth MacKenzie, CA . . . getting some experience of office work."[13] and later became chairman of Alexander Cowan and Sons Ltd. The connection with the profession was thus established. In 1895 Cowan was cautioner of his nephew's indenture (Alexander Cowan) and in 1897 his own son (Francis Cowan, CA) was apprenticed to Richard Brown and Co. (a firm with an association with John J. Cowan's old CA employer, see Figure 3.2). Francis Cowan, CA never practised the profession but spent twenty-five years as Secretary to the family company in Edinburgh.

e) Relation in an Occupation Where Account Keeping Was a Major Work Task Though the Individual Was Not an Accountant

This group of occupations includes relations who were bookkeepers, cashiers, customs officers and clerks in the commercial sector (the majority are classified as lower white collar, SSG 7 occupations). These were expanding occupations during the second half of the nineteenth century in which the employee was acquainted with account keeping and may have had some contact with a CA through, for example, preparing books for audit. These individuals may well have observed chartered accountancy as a known occupation of high status and therefore as an advantageous career option for those with professional aspirations for sons. The number of recruits who had a relation employed in such occupations is shown in Table 3.4 below. The significance of occupational connections between the CA profession and those for whom account keeping was a minor work task should also not be discounted as a possible cause of increased awareness of the vocation and consequent recruitment to it. Shopkeepers, commercial travellers and craft employers may not have experienced direct interpersonal and functional relationships with CAs but the keeping and scrutiny of accounts was an increasingly important component in the performance of their occupations. When combined with other forms of association with a CA, such as the presence of a neighbour in the profession, this group of lower middle class parents, who were highly geared to the generational social advancement of their sons, may well have considered chartered accountancy as an ideal, comparatively cheap-to-enter, professional occupation.

Table 3.4 illustrates how all of the occupational contacts between the apprentice's family and CAs, outlined in the foregoing analysis, changed over the 1837-1911 period. The final column reveals the constant potential importance of occupational connections in explaining the origins of SAE recruits.

TABLE 3.4
**Familial Occupational Connections of SAE Apprentices
1837-1911 With Chartered Accountancy**

Year of Indenture	% With Identified Relation in Occupational Group					
Commencement	a	b	c	d	e	Total
1837-54	3.8	34.6	3.8	15.4	7.6	65.2
1855-64	20.9	32.5	5.7	7.0	5.7	71.8
1865-74	16.9	35.6	3.7	8.5	7.5	72.2
1875-84	20.0	21.1	8.2	13.3	12.3	74.9
1885-94	22.4	19.2	9.0	14.3	8.6	73.5
1895-04	16.1	17.5	6.7	10.8	9.0	60.1
1905-11	18.9	14.8	7.4	6.1	10.8	58.0

Note especially column (b) which reflects the long-run relative decline of apprentices who had relatives in the legal profession as the occupational associations between lawyers and CAs weakened. The expansion in column (e) illustrates that increasing numbers of lower middle class parents who worked with accounts were recognizing the profession as an occupational alternative for their sons.

EDUCATIONAL INFLUENCES IN VOCATIONAL DECISION-MAKING

The individual's school experience, attendance at particular educational institutions, and the influence of teachers may all be hypothesized as likely to have acted as the second major set of agencies in the career determination process. Schools and teachers may not only be seen as instrumental in establishing value orientations and aspirations but during the nineteenth century assumed a further significance.

Considering the lack of national and, to some extent local, information concerning occupational opportunities, the school seems likely after the family to have been the most notable source of information concerning the range of career options. As far as middle class parents were concerned, teachers were often considered as the best-qualified individuals to assess their sons' abilities and suitability for entrance to certain professions. "What is my son to do ? is a question very frequently addressed by a parent to a schoolmaster."[14]

In order to identify a possible relationship between educational factors and career choice toward chartered accountancy, and to address the question of the significance of scholastic institutions in the occupational decision-making process, it is necessary to establish the existence of certain *connections* between Edinburgh schools, their staffs and the SAE. There appears to have been a number of possible points of contact.

Connections Between Individual CAs and Certain Schools

The appointment of leading Edinburgh CAs as school governors, treasurers, secretaries and/or auditors might be expected to have increased individual schools cognizance of accountancy as a career option for scholars and therefore increased recruitment from that institution.

This is best examined by individual examples. Thomas B. Whitson, CA was Secretary to Loretto School during the first quarter of this century; he also compiled the *Loretto Register.* His appointment at the school, however, did not imply any favouritism towards the recruitment of Loretto scholars to the SAE. Similarly, between 1891 and 1911 George A. Jamieson, CA and John T. Smith, CA were auditors and governors of Fettes College, yet there was no increase in the recruitment of apprentices from that school during their term in those positions. This is shown in Table 3.5 over.

The SAE had a particularly strong connection with two Edinburgh schools from 1873 when external examiners were first appointed to prepare and mark the new professional examinations. In December 1873, Mr A.M. Bell of Fettes College was employed to conduct the preliminary examination: "With such assistance from his colleagues as he may consider necessary having in view the subjects of the Examination."[15] Between 1875 and March 1883, two masters from the Edinburgh Academy were appointed, and from 1883 to 1892 a former mathematics master of Fettes College replaced them as Examiner.

TABLE 3.5
SAE Apprentices 1837-1911 Whose Last School
Was Fettes College or Loretto

Year of Indenture Commencement	Fettes College (opened 1870)	Loretto
1837-54	-	1
1855-59	-	2
1860-64	-	0
1865-69	-	3
1870-74	0	1
1875-79	1	3
1880-84	4	4
1885-89	4	1
1890-94	3	0
1895-99	5	2
1900-04	3	0
1905-11	2	2

These connections do not appear, however, to have resulted in chartered accountancy becoming a more advertised career option in these schools. During the seven years in which masters from the Academy held the position of Examiner, 20 scholars left the school to enter an SAE training. In the seven previous years, 14 apprentices had derived from the Academy, and during the seven subsequent years 18 had done so. Any effect on recruitment deriving from these connections was therefore marginal.[16] Similar conclusions apply with regard to Fettes College. No SAE apprentices derived from that institution in 1873-75, 5 did so between 1883 and 1892 and 7 did so in the same period subsequently.

Advice from Teachers Concerning Career Choice Based upon Scholastic Abilities

Proficiency in mathematics was the most obvious indicator in the nineteenth century mainstream school curriculum that a scholar might be suited to a career in accountancy. Potential CAs were advised in 1885:

. . . . that the duties devolving on a CA are of a nature not suitable to all intellects. Although exceedingly varied, they all require a knowledge of accounts, an aptitude for figures which is only enjoyed by a proportion and they are most likely to succeed in the profession who at school or college select mathematics for their principal study in preference to classics.[17]

Certainly, there existed cases where career choice in favour of chartered accountancy was likely to have been based on the acquisition of numerate skills. George Lisle, CA, the son of a master butcher and prize winner in mathematics at the Edinburgh Institution in 1881 was an example. There was, however, no established tradition among Edinburgh schools that good, able mathematicians should be directed towards an SAE indenture. An examination of the occupations followed by maths prize winners of the Edinburgh Academy between 1855 and 1899 confirms this point.

TABLE 3.6
**Occupations of Prize Winners in Mathematics
at the Edinburgh Academy 1855–1899**

Occupation of Son		Occupation of Father							
	a	b	c	d	e	f	g	h	NK
a Law	4	2	1			1		1	3
b Church		1							
c Medicine		2	1						1
d Defence	2		1	2					1
e Govt. Service	1								
f Teaching	1	1		1					1
g Actuarial					1		1		
h Banking	1								1
Engineering		1	2		1	1			
CA	1								
Merchant									1
Farmer			1						1

It is clear from the table above that not only were 41 Academy prize winners in maths more likely to enter the *old*, high status professions, engineering or commerce, but it also appears that decisions concerning occupational destination were based not on particular abilities in relevant disciplines but rather by the career preferences of parents.

The relative lack of emphasis placed upon matching a son's skills in certain subjects with his vocation is further evidenced by an investigation of the education received by SAE apprentices. Despite the importance of mathematics in the vocational training system and to professional practice, most apprentices had received a schooling dominated by arts and literature subjects. Of the 40 apprentices who left school with Higher Leaving Certificates between the 1890s and 1911, the subjects listed were: English (28), Mathematics/Arithmetic (19), French (11), Latin (11), German (8), Greek (5) and, Science/Dynamics (3).

Schools With a Bias Toward Educating Pupils for Recruitment to Specific Occupations

Certain schools have developed curricula designed for the entry of its scholars to specific vocations. During the nineteenth century, for example, the Edinburgh Academy with its emphasis on classical subjects was believed to be the route to the Scottish legal profession. Similarly, there existed two Edinburgh Merchant Company schools which, during the last third of the nineteenth century, offered the most suitable pre-accountancy education and had long standing links with the profession.

The most important of these schools was George Watson's College. Not only was this school instituted through an endowment of one of Edinburgh's first (some claim *the* first) accountants in 1741, it also provided from its inception a commerce-orientated curriculum which included bookkeeping. Despite the fact that CAs were often critical of the nature of bookkeeping teaching in schools during the later nineteenth century as a preparation for entering the profession, most accepted that: " it would be of immense benefit to a lad who enters an accountant's office if the principals of double entry bookkeeping were lucidly and fully explained to him before he goes into business."[18] Bookkeeping was potentially the most relevant school subject to chartered accountancy, and it was a necessary skill that constituted a significant proportion of papers in the SAE examination system.

If evidence is to be sustained of SAE apprentices having attended schools in preparation for entry to chartered accountancy, then it would be expected that a significant number would have had attended George Watson's subsequent to 1870 (when the institution was expanded on opening as a day school). Table 3.7 below illustrates that this did in fact occur.

Despite the obvious increase in Watsonian recruits to the SAE it appears doubtful that this was a reflection of occupational determination *via* education. What was more important were changes in middle class parental evaluations based on socio-economic considerations as to the most desirable school for their sons to attend.

The expansion in the number of Watsonian apprentices was indicative of the increasing popularity of the school itself. Individual educational institutions in nineteenth century Edinburgh were subject to intense competition.[19] Established schools could suffer a decline of numbers as a new school was built to satisfy a local accomodation or curricular deficiency offering low fees, or simply because it became less fashionable. The Royal High School, for example, suffered with the opening of the Edinburgh Academy in 1824.[20]

TABLE 3.7
Schools Attended by More Than 50 SAE Apprentices 1837–1911 at Some
Stage in Their Educational Careers (percentages)

Year of Indenture Commencement	School/College				
	George Watson's	Edinburgh Academy	Royal High School	Edinburgh Institution	Daniel Stewart's
1837–59	2.2	43.5	8.7	2.2	–
1860–69	0	41.0	5.0	6.0	–
1870–79	10.4	22.2	11.1	4.9	4.2
1880–89	16.9	15.9	7.7	9.7	3.6
1890–99	25.3	11.5	5.1	5.1	7.9
1900–11	29.1	12.3	5.2	5.8	9.4
Number of Cases	203	191	69	64	62

The timing of the increase in Watsonian recruits to the SAE correlates closely with the general trend in numbers on the school roll.

TABLE 3.8
Total Pupils on the School Roll of George Watson's College
Compared to the Number of SAE Apprentices From That
Institution Whose Indentures Commenced 1870–1911

Total on School Roll in:		Total SAE Apprentices Who Attended George Watson's in:	
1870	800	1870–74	2
		1875–79	13
1880	1236	1880–84	12
		1885–89	21
1890	1604	1890–94	32
		1895–99	32
1900	1722	1900–04	49
		1905–11	41
1910	1209		

Not only did the opening of George Watson's as a day school fill a local educational gap in the southern area of Edinburgh, its low fees (around £8 a year compared to £16 at the Academy and £13 at the Royal High School) together with its middle class status ensured its increasing attractiveness at the expense of other secondary educational institutions. As a result, it was alleged that not only did schools in the southern districts of the City suffer a withdrawal of pupils but additionally "A number of boys have also been removed from the High School and certain well known institutions on the north side of the town [Edinburgh Academy and Fettes College] have suffered a diminution of their numbers."[21]

The same applies to the increase in apprentices from Daniel Stewart's. Stewart's offered a curriculum closely resembling that of Watson's. But the expansion in the number of SAE recruits from the school again reflects trends in its popularity rather than its ability to prepare sons for entrance to the accountancy profession. In sending sons to these two Merchant Company schools parents entertained certain generalized perceptions as to the career destinations of sons in the broad direction of *commerce*. There is little evidence to suggest that all but a few parents anticipated the entry of their sons to a specific profession.

Support for this assertion that middle class parents during the nineteenth century seldom entered sons in schools on the basis of pre-determined career preparation is provided by evidence of the schools attended by the sons of CAs who also became CAs. These sons were likely to have had their occupational inheritance established from birth, and it might be expected that they would have attended schools that would ensure that they would fulfill their destinies and become proficient successors to the family practice. The educational preferences of CAs for future CA sons seem, however, to have been indicative of choices made on the basis of considerations of school status, own school attended, location and efficiency rather than on occupational preparation.

Among 50 SAE apprentices who were the sons of CAs, and whose educational backgrounds are known, the most popular schools attended were those run on the English public school model (Edinburgh Academy, Fettes and Loretto), or English public and grammar schools themselves (Winchester, Cheltenham, Repton), most of which would have provided a classical-orientated education. Only 6 CA sons who became CA apprentices had attended Watson's or Stewart's as their last school before indenture commencement (5 at Watson's and 1 at Stewart's). The remainder had attended the following institutions: Edinburgh Academy (17), Fettes College (4), Loretto (3), Edinburgh Collegiate School (3), Royal High School (2), Edinburgh Institution (2), Winchester (2), Cheltenham (1), Repton (1), Craigmount (1), Tettenhall College (1), St. Ninian's (1), Merchiston Castle (1), Stirling High School (1), Moreland's (1), Trinity College, Glenalmond (1), Sedbergh (1), and Wellingborough Grammar School (1).

Schools, Occupational Choice and Parental Aspirations During the Nineteenth Century: The Timing of Career Decision-Making

The evidence suggests that middle class educational institutions were, in most cases, irrelevant agencies in the process of specific occupational determination. Teachers may well have been important in elevating the vocational aspirations of lower middle and upper working class sons whose parents were likely to have had only a limited knowledge of opportunities for recruitment in the professional labour market. Even in such instances, however, the preferences of school peers were likely to have proved equally, if not more significant reference groups.[22]

The majority of middle class, status conscious parents, seldom made educational preferences for their sons on the basis of preparation for entry to specific systems of vocational training, and contemporaries recognized this. The choice of school was heavily dependent upon cost, opportunities provided for access to gentlemanly circles, the potential for the formation of advantageous connections, and the acquisition of appropriate social graces. *The Cornhill Magazine* in 1864 noted that on the question of a son's education:

> The rich bankers and merchants settle the matter from the beginning. Before the babes are out of long-clothes they are destined for a public school and university education; and it makes no difference in this respect whether they are likely to be lawyers or legislators, or simple country gentlemen, or merchant princes.[23]

The priorities placed upon status acquisition and fostering connections tended toward sons receiving tuition in subjects potentially irrelevant to their ultimate career destinations. The *Schools Inquiry Commission* reported in 1867-8 that it had discovered much ignorance and indifference among parents on the subject of education, noting that "Too often the parents seem hardly to care for education at all. Too often they give an inordinate value to mere show."[24]

This was reflected in parents desiring that their sons receive instruction in the classics even though they might be destined for a career in commerce or trade. Latin in particular was recognized as having had: "a distinct social value, being supposed to mark a man as having received a liberal education, and therefore in so far belonging (and even in his youth belonged), to the more cultivated classes."[25] Given the overcrowded nature of the traditional professions during the late nineteenth century a number of classical scholars consequently found it difficult to obtain positions in vocations for which their schooling had prepared them and were unsuited to entering alternative occupations in business. *The National Review* in 1907 commented thus:

> Listen to the conversation of twenty men who have had a good classical education, and you will hear a dozen or more openly expressing regret that their fathers should have squandered . . . so many hundreds of pounds upon having them taught subjects that have proved to be of no practical use to them whatever.[26]

Career handbooks of the late nineteenth and early twentieth centuries considered that "Parents usually take too little interest in directing the studies of their boys, and only perceive the effect of their negligence when it is too late to be remedied."[27] Additionally, a view was expressed frequently that it was inadvisable for parents to start considering specific occupations for sons until the final year of their education at the earliest:

> Neither parents nor teachers should attempt to turn out men and women of business in their teens. A child goes to school not to learn how to get his living, but to learn how to learn in later life. Education at school should aim at the training of the faculties, rather than at instruction in certain branches of knowledge.[28]

With regard to the timing of the decision to enter an SAE indenture, the limited evidence suggests that it was made after the completion of education and often well after. The known experience of two SAE apprentices confirms this.

Following two years at Edinburgh University, William H. Smith in 1857 was vexed by the question of having to decide on his future vocation:

> What to devote myself to after that I could not decide, but it was decided for me, and before I knew where I was I found myself an apprentice in the office of Brown and Pearson, the eminent accountants in George Street.[29]

In 1909, Alexander Harrison was confronted with the same dilemma. Following a school career in which future vocations were not discussed, he visited Germany and while there determined to consider entering forestry. This vocation, however, required an Oxbridge education which was not possible or desirable. On returning to Scotland therefore he entered the office of Robert C. Millar, CA to learn some business. Millar was an admired friend of his father, both being members of the Edinburgh Savings Bank Committee.[30]

To this point it may be concluded that not only were career choices made predominantly after the completion of education, they were also more likely to have been influenced by familial connections than by educational experiences. There was, however, a further possible source of information concerning vocational openings; published guides to occupations.

PUBLISHED OCCUPATIONAL INFORMATION

The widespread diffusion of comprehensive, updated and accurate information concerning occupational opportunities and career options has always been recognized as being deficient. Even with today's employment advice infrastructure, there are difficulties in providing adolescents with a thorough insight into the increasingly complex nature and range of professional occupations.[31]

During the 1850–1914 period, knowledge of employment prospects and job requirements was limited to that gained through the restricted occupational and social associations of the family, the localized information of educational institutions and media, and the more national approach of parent's handbooks and career guides. The latter were the only reasonably reliable and updated source of information concerning opportunities in a wide range of professions. Given the inadequacy of sources of information concerning the range of occupational options available and how to enter them, it is not surprising that parents relied heavily on the more comprehensive knowledge provided by associates already employed in the professions, and determined vocational choice for sons on the basis of it.

With regard to chartered accountancy, career guides to the professions would only have had a very limited and delayed impact on determining the supply of recruits. The tendency was for published surveys to be written by individuals with limited comprehension of the full range of opportunities available, particularly in the case of the emerging, often highly localized *new* professions. Many authors of handbooks were, for example, teachers. Consequently, the first specific discussion of *chartered* accountancy in a national career guide appears to have been published as late as 1898.[32]

The dearth of information concerning the profession prompted the ICAEW to publish its *Guide to the Accountancy Profession* in 1895.[33] The first mention of the Scottish profession appeared as late as 1906 in *How to Become a Qualified Accountant* and its advice was unlikely to have induced a supply of eager recruits, for not only did it consider that the final examinations were difficult but also "The entrance fees are considerably higher than in England and are prohibitive to all save those who are possessed of considerable means."[34]

Nevertheless, some Scottish middle class parents, on the basis of some subsequent reports of opportunities in chartered accountancy, may well have considered an SAE indenture for their sons despite the expense. Few professions were given such an alluring description in the British career guides of the 1890s to 1910s:

> The profession of a Chartered Accountant as a future career for a smart, well educated youth is one well worthy of serious consideration by parents and guardians. . . The prospects on completion of the term of apprenticeship are most favourable.[35]

Career handbooks during this period were united in their enthusiasm for this relatively new, open and lucrative profession. Not only did it offer a contrast to the greatly overcrowded medical and legal professions but, as there was less competition than for commissions and civil service appointments, the comparatively more favourable rate of examination success ensured that parental outlays for training would be wise investments in their sons' futures.[36]

Additionally, the financial sacrifice required for a CA's training was much less than that necessary for vocational preparation to other professions. In 1908, the estimated average cost of training and entrance to a range of occupations (exclusive of the cost of subsistence) was given as follows.[37]

TABLE 3.9
Cost of Training and Entrance to Selected Professions in 1908

Profession	Average Cost (£s)	Cost at 1983 Prices	Years of Training Required
Navy and Marines	1000	31,000	4
Barrister	860	26,660	3
Army	750	23,250	2 or 2+
Solicitor	500	15,500	5
Engineer	470	14,570	5
Doctor	300	9,300	5
Dentist	280	8,680	4
Church	250	7,750	3
Chartered Accountant (ICAEW)	160	4,960	5
Chartered Accountant (SAE)	230	7,130	5
Veterinary Surgeon	112	3,472	4

It is not inconceivable that some parents gained their information concerning the accountancy profession from these published sources alone and sent their sons into it as a result from the turn of the century. This is impossible to estimate since the readership and influence of career guides is difficult to assess, and there were no individual examples of SAE recruits who specified that they or their parents had referred to published sources in deciding upon the profession. What they may have done, however, was to reinforce opinions already made on the basis of occupational and social contacts with accountancy or accountants concerning the profession as a possible vocation for sons. Alternatively, they may have encouraged fathers to examine whether their occupational or social acquaintances included any CAs or those connected with the profession as a prelude to investigating the possibility of entering a son into an apprenticeship.

PRE-APPRENTICESHIP WORK EXPERIENCE : JOB REHEARSAL

The ideal source of information concerning an occupation is actual experience in its work situation. This may be hypothesized as forming a potentially powerful inducement toward entering an occupation on a permanent basis. Job rehearsal permits a testing of abilities against the requirements necessary for the practice of the vocation.

Pre-apprenticeship employment in accountancy or related fields formed a stable and important channel of recruitment to the SAE. The appointment of a youth as a clerk or junior clerk to a CA, WS, solicitor or actuary could lead to these individuals subsequently taking out an SAE indenture in a profession of which otherwise they might well have been ignorant. The connection between chartered accountancy and potential recruits could thus be established through direct employment contacts and experience.

There are a number of examples of individuals who probably *discovered* the profession through having been previously employed in related occupations, since they had no other obvious direct familial or occupational connection with the SAE membership. This was particularly the case with some apprentices from outside Edinburgh who originally entered a lawyer's office or bank in their own locality, and who subsequently found a more suitable appointment in the capital - which, in turn, resulted in contact with CAs and those occupations associated with them. An instance is provided by the career of Francis More, CA. He was the son of a jute mill manager and commenced employment in a writer's office in Dundee, subsequently entered an Edinburgh law firm in 1862 followed by nearly seven years as clerk to Lindsay, Jamieson and Haldane, CAs to whom he became apprenticed in December 1870. Other apprentices served long periods of clerkship in the offices of CAs and were recommended to serve indentures as the next logical step in their careers. Peter S. Warden, CA, for example, the son of a commercial clerk, "was for a time assistant to the late George Auldjo Jamieson, who, on the occasion of the vacancy in the office of City Chamberlain of Edinburgh, gave the opinion that Mr W. had qualities which marked him out for a much more important vocation."[38] Therefore, following over five years in the office of Lindsay, Jamieson and Haldane, Warden was apprenticed in 1886 and entered the SAE in 1890.

Certain recruits had fathers in occupations allied closely to accountancy but entered professional training following previous employment in a related vocation. Thomas Whitson, CA, for example, was the son of a writer in Blairgowrie, spent ten years in the service of a firm of Edinburgh Writers to the Signet before entering into a CA indenture with Lindsay, Jamieson and Haldane in 1867 when aged almost 33 years.

TABLE 3.10
SAE Apprentices 1855-1904 Employed in Related Occupations to
Chartered Accountancy Previous to Indenture Commencement

In the Office of a:	Year of Indenture Commencement				
	1855-64	1865-74	1875-84	1885-94	1895-04
CA	10	16	34	36	48
Accountant	0	3	1	0	0
Writer to the Signet	4	1	0	0	4
Writer	1	2	0	0	0
Solicitor Supreme Court	4	0	0	0	0
Solicitor	2	0	0	1	1
Insurance Official	0	0	2	1	1
Banker	0	0	2	0	0
Stockbroker	0	0	0	0	2
Total	21	22	39	38	56
% of all Apprentices	24.4	20.8	20.0	18.2	18.9

15% of the sons of CAs and accountants who became SAE apprentices (and who had access to information concerning the profession as a career option) undertook some pre-apprenticeship employment compared to 19.7% of all apprentices whose indentures commenced between 1855 and 1904. The constant proportion of recruits who entered the SAE training system *via* related occupations is indicative of the dearth of available information concerning the vocation, and reinforces the earlier point that apprentices were derived from occupational sources which had some association with CAs or their business.

It would appear from this evidence that the CA profession had not become established by the turn of the century as a nationally recognized career option for sons. The experience of one SAE apprentice from Ireland in 1907 would seem to confirm this:

> I visited relatives in Edinburgh and while there a senior member of
> the family died. This completely changed the family's way of life. My
> original intention was to go to Canada but before I did so they said that
> I should have a CA degree. I accepted the proposal even though it was
> the first time that I had heard of such a profession.[39]

RESIDENTIAL AND SPATIAL CONNECTIONS

During the nineteenth century the most cohesive social attachments among the
Edinburgh middle classes beyond institutional acquaintances were neighbourhood ties.
These social relationships were encouraged by the high degree of geographical
segregation between the classes in the city and by occupational concentration in
certain districts. The mid and western areas of the *New Town* were, as established in
Chapter 1, dominated by lawyers during the first half of the century. Similarly, by 1908
it was noticed that on the southern side of Edinburgh:

> The Newington residents are, for the most part, representatives of
> the aristocracy of the retail trade in Edinburgh . . . They are supposed
> to be rather clannish and much given to discussing the affairs of their
> fellow citizens, not only those of their district, but also those inhabiting
> other localities.[40]

These relatively close neighbourhood relationships (embodied in the assertion that
"there are more dinner parties in Edinburgh than there are in any town, except London,
in the Kingdom"[40]) appear to have been particularly significant in explaining why some
sons entered chartered accountancy. Given the limited range of CAs' occupational
contacts and the restricted dispersal of information concerning the profession, the
presence of a resident CA in the neighbourhood might have been the only revelation
to some parents concerning the occupation as a possible career option for their sons.

The precise working of this potentially important residential connection between CAs
and parents is difficult to assess and accurately quantify. We may however assume,
as a working model, that it was, for example, direct if a son was found a position in
the CA next door's office; and, indirect in the case of a CA neighbour who, living
some doors away in the same street, was observed as a distant acquaintance whose
presence and conspicuous affluence formed a powerful inducement to consideration
of his profession as a suitable one for a son.

What is a plausible deduction from an examination of the relationship between the
addresses of SAE apprentices at indenture commencement and the residence of CAs

is that, for parents with a tenuous or non-existant occupational connection with CAs, living close to a practitioner could induce recruitment. This is shown in Table 3.11.

Among Edinburgh-based SAE apprentices who had no relative in the profession and who lived in a street where a CA or an accountant was resident, 72.1% lived within nine doors of CA and 50.3% lived within four doors or opposite. Considering that the null hypothesis here would be a random distribution of CAs and apprentices among Edinburgh streets in middle class residential districts, the relationship between CAs' and apprentices' residence was clearly more than coincidental.

TABLE 3.11
Edinburgh-Based SAE Apprentices 1837-1911 With No Identified Relation in Chartered Accountancy or Accountancy, Resident in the Same Street as a CA or an Accountant at Indenture Commencement

Year of Indenture Commencement	Number of Doors From the Nearest CA or Accountant					
	1	2-4	Opposite	5-9	10 and 10+	Total
1837-54	1	1	0	1	0	3
1855-64	2	6	0	2	9	19
1865-74	1	6	2	3	5	17
1875-84	3	12	5	8	10	38
1885-94	2	5	3	5	8	23
1895-04	11	11	5	13	12	52
1905-11	5	7	1	7	5	25
Total	25	48	16	39	49	177

Not only could it prove significant in career determination to live near a CA, there were also seven examples of apprentices who lived next door to a CA's widow or to a CA's brother who had entered a different occupation.

A close CA neighbour could potentially have induced the recruitment of a succession of apprentices from one street. Belgrave Crescent is not an isolated example. From here, Alexander T. Hunter became an SAE apprentice. The original connection with the profession derived from the fact that his grandfather had been employed by the East India Company, his father was a Major in the Madras Medical Service and an elder brother was a civil engineer in India. Hunter was apprenticed to C. and D. Pearson, CAs who

> . . .were agents for the Chartered Mercantile Bank of India, London and China, and my father's original idea was that I should serve in that bank's branch for a year or two, be transferred to the London office and

> eventually go to India in their service as several of my predecessors
> had done. After some months of argument with my parents, and telling
> them that nothing would persuade me to go to India . . . I was then
> apprenticed to Mr Pearson to become a C.A.[41]

Hunter's family also resided two doors from a CA. In 1878, Atheling A.E. Glennie, also the son of a father employed in the overseas service (a consular official in Santos, Brazil) who lived three doors from Hunter, entered into an indenture. Within the next eleven years four other SAE apprentices came from this one street. Three were next door neighbours to each other.

To parents living in Edinburgh's central business district, the CA profession was a particularly visible vocation that their sons might enter. St Andrew's Square and Castle Street had the greatest concentration of CA offices in Edinburgh during the 1880s and 1890s. From among the few private residents of these areas came three apprentices between 1880 and 1899.

An important point follows from the latter example. Many of the original members of the SAE and accountants before them practised their vocation and resided in the same premises within the business centre of the city. For instance, from 1848 as Alexander T. Hunter, CA, recalled, his master:

> Mr Pearson had his dwelling house and office in the same building
> (128 George Street) as a good many professional men of that time had.
> The dining room was used as such for breakfast and late dinner, but
> during business hours, it became the cash room.[42]

During the 1860s and 70s, however, this practice broke down. Home and workplace became separate for increasing numbers of CAs reflecting their increasing wealth and adherence to middle class assumptions concerning residence. In the *Edinburgh and Leith Post Office Directory 1854–5*, 58.1% of CAs lived and worked at the same address but, by 1874–5, this was reduced to 35.7% and to 16.9% by 1894–5. With regard to the supply of SAE recruits, this feature was of likely significance. Increasing numbers of CAs were moving from the business centre of Edinburgh with its few private residents to the residential areas of the city and its suburbs, and in doing so multiplied their visibility to parents considerably. CAs were their own best advertisements to potential recruits who might otherwise have known little about the profession, its practitioners and the opportunities that it offered had there not been a neighbour in the vocation.

This enhanced visibility factor in explaining some of the expansion in SAE recruitment is compounded by a further residential trend. By the end of the nineteenth century, CAs were evenly distributed over the major middle class residential areas of Edinburgh. During the 1850s, the majority of SAE members had lived in the *New Town,* on the north side of the city, an area with a heavy concentration of lawyers, that is, the group who would have been already aware of accountancy as a potential vocation for their sons through occupational connections. The residential shift of CAs to the south side of Edinburgh not only distributed them over a greater area but also ensured their visibility to social groups that might otherwise have had only a limited knowledge of the profession. This, as will be shown Chapter 7, is reflected in the occupational origins of apprentices during the post 1870 period.

Table 3.12 shows the increasing residential dispersal of CAs in Edinburgh compared to the districts of the city from which SAE apprentices were derived, and Table 3.13 illustrates how the changing residential distribution of CAs and their north to south migration was reflected in the areas of the city from which Edinburgh based apprentices were drawn over the entire 1837 to 1911 period. The merchants, shopkeepers and clerks of the Newington, Bruntsfield, Merchiston and Morningside districts of Edinburgh, whose occupational connections might lead them to consider chartered accountancy as a possible vocation for their sons, increasingly had a visible CA reference in their midst to confirm their preference.

TABLE 3.12
Areas of Residence of Edinburgh CAs and SAE Apprentices in Selected Years Where Known (percentages)

Registration District in 1891	CAs	Indentures Commencing	CAs	Indentures Commencing	CAs	Indentures Commencing
	1854-5	1850-9	1874-5	1870-9	1894-5	1890-9
St George	25.5	31.0	28.6	23.9	24.2	21.2
St Andrew	65.5	38.1	52.4	32.5	31.6	17.9
Canongate	0	0	0	2.6	0	0
St Giles	0	7.1	0	8.5	3.7	3.3
Newington	3.5	14.3	16.6	24.8	31.6	47.3
North Leith	5.5	0	2.4	4.3	1.0	1.6
South Leith	0	0	0	0	1.0	2.2
Outside City Boundary	0	9.5	0	3.4	6.9	6.5
Number of Cases	55	42	84	117	190	184

TABLE 3.13
**Edinburgh–Based SAE Apprentices Who Commenced Their Indentures
Between 1837 and 1911 Whose Parents Resided in the
Three Districts of the City (percentages)**

Year of Indenture Commencement	New Town (St George & St Andrew)	Old Town (Canongate & St Giles)	South (Newington)
1837-74	77.7	6.4	15.9
1875-94	54.3	7.8	37.9
1895-1911	37.7	3.3	59.0

More difficult to assess is the potential significance of having had neighbours in related occupations to accountancy leading to career choice in the latter direction. 33 Edinburgh-based SAE apprentices, for example, lived next door to a lawyer at the commencement of their indentures. It might not have proved unlikely that, for instance, WS neighbours would direct inquiring parents toward chartered accountancy rather than to their own more crowded and expensive-to-enter profession. There are other examples of apprentices having had close neighbours in other occupations connected with CAs or accountancy; actuaries, insurance managers and bankers were seemingly the most significant.

One particularly influential connection and factor in career decision-making appears to have been the example provided by an SAE apprentice in the vicinity. This was perhaps a more powerful inducement to entering a son into the profession than the presence of a CA in the local community, in that parents and sons had in their midst a practical and current example of an entrant to the system of vocational training, its cost, impact on the apprentice's family, employment opportunities and chances of success.

There are many examples which illustrate the importance of this residential contact; of a number of apprentices deriving from one street within a short period. In 1903, James Smith, the son of a plumber of 10 Leslie Place became an SAE apprentice followed by the next door neighbour's son, William M. MacDonald, the son of a tailor, two years later. The indenture of William Burnet in 1885, the son of a commercial traveller probably precipitated, within three years, the apprenticeship of his next door neighbour in Millerfield Place, the son of a retired farmer. This was followed by the recruitment of the next door neighbour of the latter later in the same year.

On another occasion, the direction of a son's vocation may have become entangled with economic competition between fathers in the same trade. In 1897, the sons of two bakers and confectioners from Haymarket Terrace became SAE apprentices. Daniel D.F. MacKenzie of 60 Haymarket Terrace (who had an elder brother training as a solicitor) and Leslie B. Dalgleish of 84 Haymarket Terrace were born and indentured within days of each other and passed the final examination at the same sitting.

Table 3.14 provides some evidence of the potential importance of the existence of an apprentice in close proximity to parents in determining occupational direction toward chartered accountancy. It is apparent that, especially from the 1870s, increasing numbers of apprentices were derived from streets where other apprentices were resident. It is also worthy of note that the periods of greatest expansion in new SAE indentures were also those of greatest residential concentration among Edinburgh based apprentices.

TABLE 3.14
Edinburgh-Based SAE Apprentices 1837-1911 Resident in a Street
at Indenture Commencement Where at Least One
Other Indenture Was Current

Year of Indenture Commencement	Number of Apprentices	As % of all Edinburgh-Based Apprentices
1837-54	1	7.1
1855-64	14	22.6
1865-74	18	23.1
1875-84	52	37.4
1885-94	38	30.4
1895-04	71	35.5
1905-11	37	41.6

The residence of a CA or CA apprentice in a street may have induced a self-accumulating effect on recruitment leading to the existence of localized *clusters of recruitment*. For example, 50 apprentices came from the Grange district of Newington (and from 13 of the 16 streets contained within this area) between 1880 and 1909. 11 apprentices derived from only one street in the district: Lauder Road (which contained 51 houses). The first was the son of a brewer, the remainder had no obvious connections with chartered accountancy except that a residential chain of recruitment to the profession had become established so that an SAE indenture was the most visible career choice on display to parents.

Among all SAE apprentices commencing their indentures between 1837 and 1911 and who resided in the City of Edinburgh, only 22.1% derived from a street where no other apprentice was residing or had resided. 705 apprentices living within the Parliamentary boundary of the capital resided in 323 different streets (a mean of 2.18

per street). 19.3% resided in a street in which one other apprentice had resided or was residing; 17.0% from streets where 2 others had resided, and; 23.3% where 3 to 5 apprentices had previously or were currently residing; 15.7% where 6 to 10 others resided. 18 SAE recruits or 2.6%, derived from one Edinburgh street (Great King Street) between 1862 and 1901 (an average of one apprentice every 2.2 years) – 3 of whom were next door neighbours.

Similarly, in the districts just outwith the boundary of Edinburgh residential connections were evident. 40 apprentices resided in Leith at indenture commencement, 21 of these derived from a street where one or more SAE apprentices had also lived during their period of training. 20 recruits came from Portobello of whom 10 derived from streets where other apprentices had lived or were residing. 6 of the 9 apprentices who listed Murrayfield addresses lived in locations where others had resided or were residing.

It may be inferred, that for some youths, the fact of living in close proximity to a CA or CA apprentice formed the major inducement to entering the Edinburgh-based profession. For others, it confirmed opinions already developed or formed an additional inducement to recruitment on top of occupational or familial connections. What is evident is that the increasing diffusion of SAE members and apprentices over the major middle class residential areas of Edinburgh was an act of unconscious self-advertisement that precipitated consideration of a new profession as a career option among increasing numbers of parents and their sons.

Non Edinburgh-Based SAE Apprentices

As Table 3.15 and Figure 3.1 show, increasing numbers of SAE apprentices were derived from outside Edinburgh. If residential connections were significant to the process of vocational decision-making, how can it be explained that so many recruits chose the profession when they lived some distance from its organizational centre ? Few, if any of the parents who resided in remote rural areas of Scotland would have had a practising CA in their midst. Apprentices from Aberdeen, Perth and London (38 in total) derived from urban centres where CAs were resident and the concentration of, for example, Dundee apprentices in the West Ferry district indicates that similar revelation effects were evident as in Edinburgh.

An analysis of recruits from Midlothian suburban villages and small towns such as Dalkeith, Lasswade and Corstorphine reveal that similar processes were at work.

For example, 4 apprentices came from the Pathhead Ford area of Dalkeith between 1892 and 1907.

TABLE 3.15
Location of SAE Apprentices' Parents or Guardians at Indenture Commencement Irrespective of the Location of the Indenture (percentages)

Census District	1837 -54	1855 -64	1865 -74	1875 -84	1885 -94	1895 -04	1905 -11	Total
Scotland								
Northern								0
North Western	3.8		0.9		0.5	3.7	2.0	17
North Eastern		2.3		2.0	1.4	2.0	1.4	17
East Midland	7.7	4.6	5.7	5.1	7.2	4.1	7.4	60
West Midland		1.2	0.9	0.5	1.4	1.3	1.3	12
South Western		3.5	0.9	0.5	1.4	1.7		13
Edinburghshire	76.9	80.2	83.0	83.1	75.6	75.8	71.6	828
South Eastern (exc Edinburghshire)	3.9	4.6	1.9	2.0	4.8	3.0	3.4	35
Southern		1.2	2.9	2.0	1.4	2.7	3.4	21
England & Wales								
London				2.0	0.5	1.7	2.0	10
South Eastern					0.5	0.3	0.7	3
South Midland					0.5			1
Eastern								0
South Western			0.9					1
West Midland				0.5	1.0		0.7	4
North Midland							0.7	1
North Western						1.0		3
Yorkshire	3.8							1
Northern		1.2		0.5				2
Wales						0.3		1
Overseas								
Ireland							1.3	2
Europe					0.5	1.0	0.7	4
South Africa							1.3	2
China							0.7	1
Not Known	3.9	1.2	2.9	1.3	2.8	2.4	1.4	28
N of Apprentice	26	86	106	195	209	297	148	1067

Given the size and distribution of the Scottish population and the number of SAE indentures contracted between 1837 and 1911, and also the fact that Edinburgh was the centre of the profession, it was not expected (on the basis of a random selection of recruits from outside Edinburghshire), to discover the kind of residential concentration revealed by the following examples in Table 3.16.

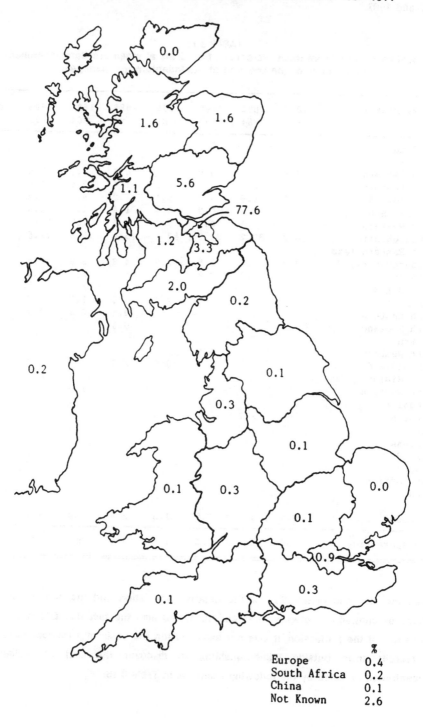

FIGURE 3.1
Location of SAE Apprentices' Parents or Guardians 1837–1911

	%
Europe	0.4
South Africa	0.2
China	0.1
Not Known	2.6

TABLE 3.16
**Geographical Clusters of SAE Recruits From Selected Scottish
Locations Outside the Lothians**

Year of Indenture Commencement	N of Apprentices from	Location	Population in 1891	Miles from Edinburgh
1859-85	3	Dolphinton	248	28
1875-76	2	Tulliallan	1982	28
1895-04	3	St Boswell's	962	41
1865-97	4	Campbeltown	5455	130
1897-05	2	Foveran	1945	147

Fathers aspiring for the entrance of their sons to professional occupations were at a distinct disadvantage if they lived in remote rural areas during the nineteenth century. Information concerning career opportunities and the range of options available in urban centres (the scene of professional training and organization) was distinctly limited. This problem arose not only through distance, but also because the rural occupational composition was unlikely to have provided a range of visible professional references for parents.

The majority of the 135 SAE apprentices whose indentures commenced between 1837 and 1911 and who were derived from relatively small Scottish settlements (with a population of less than 15,000 in 1891), were the sons of: churchmen (16.3%), farmers (16.3%), landed proprietors or others of independent income (11.1%), lawyers (8.9%), manufacturers (6.7%), and merchants (6.7%). These were the most socially and economically significant individuals within their particular localities and were most likely to have desired a professional future for certain sons. Indeed, 83.0% of apprentices from small settlements had fathers in SSGs 1-5 compared to 65.3% of all SAE recruits.

This would seem to suggest that, outside the main urban centres, recognition of the CA profession as a career alternative for sons from lower middle class and working class backgrounds was limited. Many of the high status parents of rural Scotland seem likely to have had a relation or connection with professional men in the capital who might provide an opening for a son or intimation of career prospects in the range of urban centred occupations. In fact, of the apprentices who were derived from rural Scotland and whose parent's place of birth is known, 18.1% had at least one parent who was born in Edinburghshire. Given the social cohesion and interrelationship between local notables within their own districts, the discovery of a new professional vocation for one of their sons (perhaps through an occupational or familial connection in Edinburgh) was likely to have constituted an inducement or an example to others. More detailed investigation of the five pockets of recruitment provided in Table 3.16 suggests that processes of this nature operated during the period studied.

1. **Tulliallan** (Fife) – the first apprentice from this location who was apprenticed in 1875 was the son of the principal landowner of the parish who had a WS uncle in Edinburgh. In 1876 the son of the parish minister followed into an SAE indenture.

2. **St Boswells** (Roxburghshire) – the son of a merchant was followed into the profession by the son of the parish minister, and he by the son of a local farmer and butcher. The years of indenture commencement were 1895, 1904 and 1904.

3. **Campbeltown** (Argyll) – a writer's son departed for Edinburgh in 1865 followed by the son of a distiller in 1889. The first apprentice's nephew (also the son of a distiller) was then indentured in 1890 followed by the brother of the second apprentice in 1897.

4. **Foveran** (Aberdeenshire) – the first SAE recruit, apprenticed in 1897 was the son of the parish schoolmaster who had discovered accountancy through pre-apprenticeship employment in an Aberdeen solicitor's office. The second, indentured in 1905, was the son of a local merchant and JP who had a merchant brother in Edinburgh.

5. **Dolphinton** (Lanarkshire) – this provides an excellent example of how one initial connection could result in a supply of recruits from one small parish as well as illustrating the full interplay of familial, occupational, spatial and *recruitment fashion* aspects of career determination during the nineteenth century.

FIGURE 3.2
Recruitment Connections to the Edinburgh CA Profession:
Dolphinton, Lanarkshire

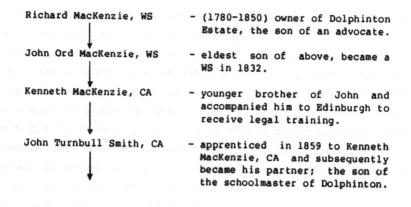

Richard MacKenzie, WS — (1780-1850) owner of Dolphinton Estate, the son of an advocate.

John Ord MacKenzie, WS — eldest son of above, became a WS in 1832.

Kenneth MacKenzie, CA — younger brother of John and accompanied him to Edinburgh to receive legal training.

John Turnbull Smith, CA — apprenticed in 1859 to Kenneth MacKenzie, CA and subsequently became his partner; the son of the schoolmaster of Dolphinton.

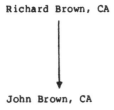

Richard Brown, CA — apprenticed to MacKenzie and Smith, CAs in 1872; the son of a local farmer who lived next door to the parents of Turnbull Smith and was taught in the parish school.

John Brown, CA — apprenticed to a CA in 1885 who had been trained by MacKenzie the nephew of a local farmer and probable cousin of Richard Brown.

CONCLUSIONS

Investigation of the determinants of career choice among SAE apprentices between 1837 and 1911 reveals a number of significant characteristics of the occupational and social structure of the period.

Firstly, the expansion of the SAE and perhaps some other *new* professions during the nineteenth century was largely a process of self-propogation. Given the inadequacy of the agencies of occupational information, career choice was a function of the physical revelation of professional practitioners leading to their acting as references upon which decisions were made. The discovery of an alternative vocation for sons was made chiefly through occupational, familial, social and residential connections. These connections between parents, sons and CAs escalated as the work of the practitioner became important to a wider distribution of occupational groups, and as their increasing number and geographical diffusion extended over a greater area.

Secondly, the supply of recruits to a profession was also a function of the establishment of *recruitment fashions* among middle class parents. These were instituted as a result of parental assertions of their own social status and through the desire to enhance it through the entrance of sons to certain occupations. Such conventions concerning the vocational placement of sons were emulative of practices adopted by those at the head of the social hierachy. Similarly, some lower middle and upper working class parents also manipulated the career choices of their sons for status enhancing reasons by aspiring for their entrance to professional occupations. This also tended to increase the supply of recruits, irrespective of the demand for professional services.

Thirdly, educational institutions played a minor part in the career determining process. Educational and career choices reflected parental decisions based on status acquisition and generalized notions concerning the occupational destination of their sons.

Fourthly, the inadequate nature of career and vocational information and the consequent reliance on parental connections in occupational determination implied that the upward mobility of the sons of manual workers was restricted. Working class parents of the nineteenth and early twentieth centuries might aspire for their sons to become doctors, lawyers or clergymen; these were visible vocations to all though entry was expensive. Knowledge of opportunities in cheaper-to-enter new professions, such as accountancy, surveying and architecture by contrast, seem likely to have been limited by a lack of occupational and social contact with practitioners, which was in turn encouraged by the division between manual and white collar work and by the urban segregation of social classes. Consequently, the major avenue of recruitment to the professions for the working class son was into the known, visible vocation of school teaching. The alternative route into a higher status profession such as chartered accountancy was through the revelation effect of clerking in it first.

It may be concluded that the processes of career selection were important to an explanation of the expansion of the SAE and were instrumental in determining the precise social origins of CA recruits.

For those parents and sons who were conscious of the profession as a career alternative and aspired to enter it, a further process of testing and selection had to be contemplated. Before entering the vocational training system of the SAE and the achievement of full professional status, a son had to successfully proceed through the process of apprenticeship and examination. It is to this aspect of recruitment to the Edinburgh CA profession that the next chapter is directed.

Notes

1 K. Roberts, "The Entry Into Employment", *Sociological Review* 16 (1968), p. 155.

2 For discussion of the inadequacy and efficiency of the present day career information service see Roberts, "The Entry Into Employment". J. Haystead, "Social Structure, Awareness Contexts and Processes of Choice", *Sociological Review* 19 (1971).

3 On the importance of *connections* in the career decision-making process during the nineteenth century see "On Relatives and Connections", *Temple Bar* 1 (1861), pp. 381–86. C. Dickens, *Bleak House* (London, 1862), ch. 13.

4 Walker, *David Maclagan, F.R.C.E.*, p. 28.

5 D. Cross, *Choosing A Career* (London, 1908), p. 231.

6 R.W. Atkinson, *Popular Guide to the Professions* (London, 1895), p. 22.

7 See W.L. Slocum, *Occupational Careers* (Chicago, 1966), ch. 11. Open University, *Occupational Structure and Placement* (1976), DE 351, "People and Work" (Unit 5).

8 On the importance of familial and other factors in occupational choice see Slocum, *Occupational Careers*, ch. 11. W.M. Williams (ed.), *Occupational Choice* (London, 1974).

9 Sir F.J. Grant, *The Faculty of Advocates 1532-1943* (Edinburgh, 1944); *Idem., History of the Society of Writers to His Majesties Signet* (Edinburgh, 1936). The information contained in these two works show that fewer advocates and WSs had brothers already in the profession compared to SAE members.

10 *The Accountant's Magazine* 1 (1897), p. 496. The prevalance of eldest sons in the Edinburgh-based legal profession can be shown by the fact that 42.8% of new members of the Faculty of Advocates admitted between 1850 and 1914 were eldest sons (excluding those who were only sons) compared to 25.6% of SAE apprentices indentured between 1837 and 1911.

11 B. Balfour-Melville, *The Balfours of Pilrig* (Edinburgh, 1907), p. 217.

12 M.E. Maxtone-Graham, *The Maxtones of Cultoquhey* (Edinburgh, 1935), pp. 196-7.

13 J.J. Cowan, *From 1846-1932* (Edinburgh: By the Author, 1933), p. 23.

14 Kelly College, Tavistock, *On the Choice of a Profession* (Oxford, 1891), p. 1.

15 Minute Book of the SAE, vol. 1, p. 203.

16 During the seven years in which a master from the Academy held the appointment, of the 20 Academy apprentices: 11 had a relation in the profession, 2 had WS relations, 1 was the brother of a stockbroker, 1 was the son of an audit clerk, 1 the son of a bank manager, and, the other was the son of a manufacturer. All, therefore, had some occupational-familial connection with the CA profession thus indicating that attendance at the Academy was of secondary importance in the decision to become an SAE apprentice.

17 F.W. Pixley, *The Profession of a Chartered Accountant* (London, 1885), p. 3.

18 *A Guide to the Accounting Profession,* p. 31.

19 See Anderson, *Education and Opportunity in Victorian Scotland,* pp. 180-1.

20 See *The Edinburgh Academy Register 1824-1914 and War Supplement* (Edinburgh, 1921), pp. xi-xiv. M. Magnusson, *The Clacken and the Slate: The Story of Edinburgh Academy* (London, 1974).

21 H.L. Waugh (ed.), *George Watson's College 1724-1970* (Edinburgh, 1970), p. 55. This work was also the source for the total numbers on the Watson's school roll contained in Table 3.8, p. 206.

22 An example is provided by the case of Charles E.W. MacPherson, CA, the son of a Church of Scotland minister and who attended the Royal High School and was apprenticed in August 1876. His next door neighbour, Thomas F. Gibb, CA, followed him into the profession in October of the same year and was the son of a cabinetmaker. Gibb had also attended the Royal High School.

23 "Middle Class Education in England", *The Cornhill Magazine* 10 (1864), p. 411. See also "Maxims by a Man of the World", *Chamber's Journal,* 4th series 45, pp. 465-9.

24 British *Parliamentary Papers,* 1867-8, vol. XXVIII (*Reports,* vol. 1), "Report of the Commissioners appointed by Her Majesty to inquire into the education given in schools in England, not comprised within Her Majesty's two recent commissions on popular education and on public schools", p. 15.

25 British *Parliamentary Papers,* 1867-8, vol. XXVIII (*Reports,* vol. 9.), Burgh Schools in Scotland, "Report of the Commissioners appointed by Her Majesty to inquire into the education given in the schools in England, not comprised within Her Majesty's two recent commissions on popular education and on public schools", p. 640.

26 Tozer, "The Unemployed Gentleman", p. 600.

27 *The Student's Annual and Guide to Employment* (Dublin, 1897-8), p. 1.

28 *What Shall I Be ?* (London, 1900), p. 11.

29 Smith, *From Constable to Commissioner,* pp. 20-1. See also L.R. Dicksee, *The Student's Guide to Accountancy* (London, 1907), p. 15.

30 Interview with Alexander Harrison, CA (admitted to the SAE in 1914), Edinburgh, 13 December 1984.

31 For example, see S.R. Timperley and A.M. Gregory, "Some Factors Affecting the Career Choice and Career Perceptions of Sixth Form School Leavers", *Sociological Review* 19 (1971).

32 H. Jones, *Guide to the Professions and Business* (London, 1898).

33 *A Guide to the Accountancy Profession.*

34 Witty, *How to Become a Qualified Accountant,* p. 30.

35 Jones, *Guide to the Professions and Business,* p. 89.

36 Compare the rate of failure in examinations for higher civil service cadetships with those of chartered accountant preliminary examinations: (percentages)

Year	Civil Service	SAE	ICAEW
1896	57	36	30
1897	59	32	32
1898	52	33	31
1899	61	42	26
1900	64	36	22
1901	62	37	35
Mean	59.2	36.0	29.3

Civil Service statistics calculated from "Prospects in the Professions", *Cornhill Magazine* 15 (1903), p. 120.

37 Statistics in Table 3.9 calculated from information provided in Cross, *Choosing a Career*

38 *The Accountant's Magazine* 20 (1916), p. 411.

39 Personal letter, 20 November 1984 from a CA apprenticed 1907-12 who wishes to remain anonymous.

40 Keith, *Edinburgh of Today,* p. 144.

41 A.T. Hunter, CA, "Rambling Reminiscences of an Old Edinburgh Citizen", *The Weekly Scotsman* (October-December 1936), p. 25.

42 *Ibid.*

4

Occupational Preparation : Apprenticeship and Examination

> Above all we would direct the attention of its members to the
> education of young men for the profession of Accountant. The
> Faculty of Advocates, the Society of Writers to the Signet,
> and other Law societies require a certain course of education
> and why should not the Accountants? It is a most important
> profession, and a proper education in that department of
> business, should under proper regulations, fit a member for
> employment in various capacities, where sound business-
> knowledge, especially in connexion with accounts or finance
> generally, is required. If this is not attended to,
> Accountants will become what they are in England
> "bookkeepers".

[*Index Juridicus, The Scottish Law List and Legal Directory, 1853*]

It is the intention in this chapter to provide an outline of the changing system of
professional training through which SAE recruits had to proceed before becoming CAs
(more detail is provided in Appendix D). This is designed as a prelude to an analysis of
the factors tending to secure success in the process of occupational preparation, and
the extent to which the imposition of increasing numbers of obstacles to qualification
acted as barriers to recruits from various social origins. The nature and complexity of
the system of professional training were of potential significance in determining the
possibility and extent of upward social mobility to the profession. The analysis is
preceded by a discussion of the major form of SAE instruction during the 1853-1914
period: apprenticeship.

APPRENTICESHIP

A nineteenth century CA training laid considerable emphasis on gaining professional
knowledge through practical learning and experience. As with the system of its close
associate, the solicitor's profession, an SAE vocational preparation was in the form of
an apprenticeship, a formal contract binding a potential member to a qualified
practitioner for a predetermined period of service.

This method of training had not only been traditional before 1853, it also offered
advantages to the new organization and its members. For a master it ensured a
means of relatively cheap labour while the apprentice benefitted from long term,
consistent training in one office. From the perspective of the professional organization,

the indenture provided a means of occupational socialization and of inculcating new members with the conduct of the vocation as well as encouraging an *esprit de corps* among its number.

Despite the increasing movement towards a more theoretical training in the SAE, by the standards of the modern accountancy profession, the emphasis during the 1853-1914 period was heavily on the practical side. Indeed, it was not until the institution of a preliminary examination in 1873 that there was any test of a potential apprentice's knowledge or suitability to the vocation except from a generalized requirement of having received a *liberal education*. The assessment of an apprentice's qualifications and abilities rested with the master. The experience of aspiring Edinburgh CAs was dominated by that of indenture, of their training in the offices of existing members and from learning on the job.

The mechanics of the SAE indenture were simple and regulated soon after incorporation in the *Constitution and Laws* of the Society, ratified by a general meeting of 7 February 1855. The articles of apprenticeship were to be of a standardized format and consisted of a contractual agreement between master and apprentice. No youth desirous of entering the Edinburgh profession could do so "except under regular deed of Indenture"[1] which was recorded in a book by the Secretary of the Society at the cost of one guinea. A date of commencement was determined and a date of expected expiry: no apprentice was eligible to sit the examination for admission to the SAE until his master had formally discharged him, and that event had been recorded before witnesses in the SAE register of indentures. A fine of £50 was imposed upon any party failing to abide by the terms and obligations of the agreement.

In addition, the indenture had to be served with an SAE member; the apprentice was required to serve for a minimum period, and had to have attained a certain age, appointed a cautioner and paid an indenture fee to his master. Each of these aspects of apprenticeship will be examined in turn.

The Choice of Master

With the exception of a few instances where a long-standing and promising CA's clerk had advanced his career through the logical step of becoming apprenticed to his employer, discovering an office in which a son might be indentured appears to have been a matter of arrangement between parents or guardians and potential masters.

The choice of particular office was based ideally upon a number of practical criteria. As an initial consideration, it was advised that: "careful inquiry should be made as to the precise extent of the practice of the Accountant with whom it is contemplated entering into articles."[2] This was deemed necessary on the grounds that the possibility existed of there being insufficient business in the office to occupy the existing staff let alone a new apprentice thus providing an inadequate training. Parents were recommended similarly to consider the relative advantages and disadvantages of recruitment to large as against small offices.

A large firm offered the prospect of gaining experience in a variety of work and a career-enhancing reputation and clientele after qualification. Against this were the disadvantages of possibly being allocated and restricted to training in one department of a large business. Thus, a lack of personal attention from masters and the division of labour would mean that training was effectively under the supervision of a managing clerk rather than the master. By contrast, a small office might permit a close and more personal relationship between the parties as well as a more rapid advancement from menial work tasks. Yet, a small firm was unlikely to have provided a familiarity with all the branches of a CA's business and offered limited opportunities for advancement in the office once qualified.

Most accountancy journals of the late nineteenth century recommended a training in a medium to large firm. In England, it was considered that "the balance of the argument is on the side of the fairly large firm - one employing 10 or 15 clerks is a very good size."[3] In Edinburgh it appears that apprenticeships were disproportionately conducted in larger offices. The 1067 SAE apprenticeships included in the study (those commencing between 1837 and 1911) were contracted between 214 separate masters, a mean of 4.98 apprentices per master. It is shown in Table 4.1 below that 55 CAs acted as masters to 10 or more apprentices and 24 to 20 or more apprentices; while only 51 recruits were trained in the office of a CA who was not a master to any other apprentice.

Seven firms dominated the training of SAE apprentices whose indentures commenced between 1837 and 1911, each training 30 or more recruits. These were Lindsay, Jamieson and Haldane; A. and J. Robertson; Howden and Molleson; F.H. and F.W. Carter (later Carter and Greig); Richard Brown and Company; Moncreiff and Horsburgh; and Barstow and Millar.

Each of these firms appear to have produced to some extent a different kind of training and professional education reflecting its specialization in certain types of business. This was an additional consideration for parents in deciding upon a suitable master. Lindsay, Jamieson and Haldane, for example, was an old firm with traditional business in remits from court, management of landed estates and insurance; Howden and Molleson appear to have had a bias toward banking and insurance work; while F.H. and F.W. Carter conducted more company auditing. A parent had to consider, therefore, whether to place a son in an office whose business was of a declining or expanding nature as well as the reputation of the firm. There were advantages in entering a son into a *modern* office in which the partners were recently qualified, and practised updated methods. Graham, Smart and Annan was reputedly such an Edinburgh firm. Whether or not the apprentice could expect to receive a salary (and its amount) were also likely to have been important factors in the choice of office and master, as was, in later years, a firm's record at ensuring the success of its apprentices in the professional examinations.

TABLE 4.1
SAE Members Who Were Listed as Having Been a Sole or Joint
Master of an SAE Indenture That Commenced 1837-1911

Number of Indentures in which CA Appeared as a Master	Number of CAs
1	51
2-4	47
5-9	61
10-19	31
20-29	11
30-39	9
40-49	4
Total	214

A parent also had to consider post-qualification. The nature of a father's employment could be important: if occupied in the law, his connections might secure for his son some legal business; and a manufacturer might be disposed to find his son a position as a company auditor. The nature of the CAs business was potentially important in this context. As one career guide noted in 1908:

> Influence is of some importance to a young accountant when he has passed through his novitiate. If possible, an office should be chosen which does a good deal of the kind of business which may be expected to come in the pupil's way later.[4]

Despite these potentially important considerations, it would seem that perhaps the major influences in the determination of the choice of office for training were those alluded to in the previous chapter: the range of connections and associations between parents and CAs. Not only could occupational, familial and social connections play a part in career choice, they might also have determined the precise location of professional training. *The Scottish Accountant* was quite adamant in 1893 that in order to secure for a son a CA indenture: "The first qualification . . . for all applicants was not ability to pass successfully the prescribed examinations, but influence to obtain a situation with a CA."[5] Though it undoubtedly occurred, it would appear to have been exceptional that a parent approached a master with the offer of an indenture fee on the basis of no connection, recommendation or introduction, however distant the association might have been.

In a number of cases where no apparent reason existed why an SAE recruit should have received his training in a specific office, detailed study and cross-referencing revealed frequently a connection between master and apprentice. One such case was that of Henry W. Jamieson who was indentured in 1901 for no obvious reason to Archibald Langwill, CA. Further investigation revealed that both parties resided in Portobello, and that Langwill was an elder in the local parish church to which Jamieson's father was Minister.

Pre-Apprenticeship Training and the Duration of the Indenture

Once a suitable firm had been discovered, it was recommended practice in most occupations with apprenticeship training systems for the potential recruit to spend a trial period in his principal's office before the entrance examination was taken or the articles signed.

For the SAE apprentice and his parents this was a prudent procedure. Before investing in an indenture fee, it was wise to test a son's suitability to the profession and his master's ability to train him. Hence the apprentice might "attend at the office for a few hours daily and obtain some little insight into business matters."[6]

The prevalence of this practice among potential SAE apprentices is difficult to estimate as, if the trial was a success and an indenture resulted, the period was often included as part of the full term of the apprenticeship. Even if a trial period was not contemplated, pre-apprenticeship employment in a CA's office presented a further advantage. It resulted in a reduced duration of the indenture which may have lessened the financial burden of professional training for the sons of low status parents.

The Constitution of the SAE adopted in February 1855 established that the usual period of service would be five years and this remained so throughout the 1855-1914 period. The 26 indentures registered in the books of the SAE that commenced between 1837 and 1854 were expected to run for an average of 4.27 years illustrating that previous to organization the usual indenture ran for four years. Thereafter the mean expected duration at the commencement of training was 4.76 years, and this deviated little over decennial cohorts 1855-1911. The majority of indentures (82.8%) had terms of five years, 9.7% were projected to run from four to five years and 7.5% from three to four years. The two latter groups constituted those qualifying for reduced periods of service and training.

Apprentices who had been previously employed in the office of an SAE member (or from 1893 by any CA) or a law agent (WSs, SSCs, enrolled solicitors or writers) were entitled to a reduced term calculated on the basis that, for every year or part year of previous employment in the offices of these practitioners, the term of service could be reduced from five years by half that duration. For example, if an apprentice had been employed as a WS's clerk for two years he was entitled to one year less than the usual term. No apprentice could, however, have his term reduced to less than three years and, from the 1880s, only previous employment after the age of seventeen was taken into account. From the late 1890s, university graduates were entitled to a four year indenture, a provision which applied to 15 cases contained in the study to 1911.

The rules concerning the nature of pre-apprenticeship employment permitting a reduced period of indenture do not appear to have been applied strictly in all cases. Previous engagement in insurance, for example, was a grey area. Though an insurance office might employ a CA as a manager or auditor so that a future SAE apprentice might have been considered as having been "in the business chambers of a Member",[7] it seems unlikely that the 5 apprentices in Table 4.2 who claimed a reduced term through employment in such firms were under the direct supervision of a CA or were engaged in business highly relevant to accountancy.

The 189 apprentices whose previous term-reducing occupations are known spent on average 2.61 years in related employments. It is also apparent that 83% of the time by which indentures were reduced was due to previous employment in the offices of CAs, and that 14.1% was due to previous engagement in lawyers' offices. As will be shown in Chapter 5, pre-apprenticeship employment had potential ramifications for the recruit's success in the system of professional preparation.

TABLE 4.2
Occupations of 189 SAE Apprentices 1837-1911 Provided as Reasons for Reduced Terms of Indenture (where known)

Previous Occupation	N of Periods of Employment Cited by 189 Apprentices	Total Period Spent in Employment (Years)	Mean (Years)
In CA's Office	130	256.66	1.97
CA's Clerk	35	89.66	2.56
Clerk to Accountant of Court	2	12.08	6.04
CA Apprentice	2	3.58	1.79
CA's Cashier	2	9.00	4.50
Actuary Apprentice	1	4.00	4.00
In WS's Office	8	27.16	3.39
WS's Clerk	5	16.83	3.36
In SSC's Office	5	10.83	2.16
SSC's Clerk	1	1.00	1.00
SSC Apprentice	1	5.00	5.00
In Writer's Office	1	1.00	1.00
In Solicitor's Office	2	3.25	1.62
Solicitor's Clerk	1	1.33	1.33
Solicitor's Apprentice	1	5.00	5.00
Lawyer's Clerk	2	8.50	4.25
Clerk in Teind Office	1	4.00	4.00
In Insurance Office	1	3.83	3.83
Insurance Clerk	2	15.00	7.50
Insurance Apprentice	2	8.00	4.00
Banker's Clerk	1	8.00	8.00
Total	206	493.71	2.39

Age

No person who is under sixteen years of age shall be taken by any Member of the Corporation as an Apprentice.[8]

So stipulated article 30 of the 1855 Constitution of the SAE. The minimum age was raised to seventeen years under the Rules and Regulations adopted in 1889 and remained so under the GEB agreement of 1893. Previous to the introduction of the 1889 regulation, the odd underaged apprentice appears to have become indentured. In March 1864, Peter Ronaldson, born on 14 August 1848 was indentured as was Frederick Falkner in August 1868 though he was born on 21 November 1853.

In cases where it has been possible to identify the apprentice's date of birth, it appears from Table 4.3 that before the introduction of the age limit in 1855, recruits were on average one year younger at the date of the commencement of their training than subsequently.

TABLE 4.3
Age of SAE Apprentices 1837-1911 at Recruitment
(where date of birth is known)

Year of Indenture Commencement	Mean Age at Commencement	N of Apprentices
1837-54	16.80	25
1855-59	17.81	38
1860-64	18.06	43
1865-69	18.48	53
1870-74	18.23	50
1875-79	18.19	90
1880-84	18.13	103
1885-89	18.29	91
1890-94	18.47	116
1895-99	18.55	136
1900-04	18.97	161
1905-11	19.02	148
1837-1911	18.45	1054

The mean age of SAE recruits increased until the early 1870s and declined until the late 1880s, which may have been a response to the introduction of the comprehensive examination system from 1873 which essentially codified the qualification system and established a standard of education necessary for success in it. The rise in the average age from the late 1880s can be explained by the raising of the minimum age in 1889, and by the desirability of remaining in eduation for a longer period in order to maximize chances of succeeding in the increasingly difficult examinations of the overstocked professions including Scottish chartered accountancy.

As the statistics contained in Table 4.3 would suggest, the majority of SAE recruits (84.6%) were aged between 15 and 19 years at the commencement of their indentures. A further 12.9% were aged between 20 and 24 years, 1.8% were aged between 25 and 29 years, and 0.7% were aged 30 years or over.

The oldest apprentice contained in the study was Henry Lees who was 46 at the commencement of his three year period of service with Kenneth MacKenzie, CA in 1864. Lees, however, was no ordinary recruit to the profession. The SAE Sederunt Books reveal that he was employed previously in the office of a WS between 1838 and 1844, and had acted subsequently as Secretary and General Manager of the Edinburgh, Perth and Dundee Railway Company which was taken over by the North British

Railway Company in 1862. In 1864, Lees was actually a practising accountant in Edinburgh but had entered into a CA apprenticeship following the loss of a public office which presumably led to a drastic decline in his business. Fortunately, Lees had married the daughter of Adam Black, publisher and MP for the City of Edinburgh under whose influence (Black was the cautioner of the indenture) he entered MacKenzie'e office. The Sederunt Book records that MacKenzie contracted Lees in order to oblige him subsequent to the loss of the public office which had been "through no fault of his own". Needless to say, the 'indenture' was not discharged and Lees did not become a member of the SAE. His fortunes were presumably restored as he soon returned to practice on his own account in York Place, Edinburgh.

6 other apprentices were aged over 30 years at the start of their professional training and of these, 3 provide excellent examples of how sons from relatively humble origins were recruited to the SAE, and succeeded in becoming CAs following the *revelation effect* of previous employment in menial white collar work and consequent income accumulation to afford professional indenture fees. John B. Lewis, the second oldest apprentice identified in the study, was the son of a messenger to the National Bank of Scotland in Edinburgh. Lewis entered into an indenture with A. and J. Robertson in 1910 aged 37 years following several years employment as a general clerk and five years previous service with his future masters.

Similarly, George H. Rimer was the orphaned son of a low ranking customs officer, and had begun his career as a mercantile clerk followed by four years as clerk to Ebenezer Erskine Scott, CA to whom he was apprenticed in 1885 aged 32 years. Robert Ritchie was the son of a commercial traveller. He was indentured in 1907 to Frederick Marshall, CA at the age of 32 who he had served as clerk for four years. Ritchie's vocational direction was also likely to have been influenced by the fact that his eldest brother was a clerk in the accountant's department of an Edinburgh insurance company.

The Location of the Indenture

In order to be eligible to sit SAE examinations and admission to the Society, an apprentice had to receive his training in the office of a qualified member. Consequently, potential recruits were extremely limited in the range of locations in which they might complete an indenture, and this provided a not inconsiderable obstacle to the apprenticeship of non-Edinburgh based sons. All but 26 of the 1067 apprentices contained in the study were trained in the Edinburgh offices of SAE members. It was not until 1894 that the first SAE indenture to be conducted outside

Edinburgh was registered (that of Edward A. MacKay to George C. Harrower, CA in London) and the practice remained exceptional until the turn of the century (19 of the 26 non-Edinburgh-based apprenticeships commenced between 1903 and 1908) despite the increasing geographical diffusion of the SAE membership.

10 SAE apprentices received their training in Inverness (all in the office of Robert F. Cameron, CA), 5 in Perth (4 in the office of Ernest Jack, CA), 1 was located in Glasgow and 8 in London (under a variety of masters), and 1 each in Cape Town and Johannesburg.

For the youth desirous of entering the CA profession but living at some distance from Edinburgh, the proximity of a local SAE member able to take an apprentice was a great advantage for those not wishing to leave home or incur the expense of lodging in the capital. The necessity of migrating to the three major Scottish cities to receive a CA training was a source of criticism of the chartered societies by the rival accounting organizations. The Edinburgh, Glasgow and Aberdeen societies, claimed the SIA in 1889-90: "Are to a large extent special and exclusive . . . it is unjust to require the youth desirous of following the profession of an accountant to leave their homes in the provinces."[9] Similarly, in 1896, the Scottish CA societies were accused of fostering a monopoly of professional training:

> . . . Outside of these towns with the exception of one or two offices in Scotland there is no facility for a lad entering this profession at all unless he is in a social position, such as will enable him to be sent from his home during the five years of his youth and attend an office in these three towns.[10]

The SAE defended its position in typical altruistic terms:

> It is for the benefit of the profession and the public that the Accountants of Scotland should receive their education and training in the University towns, where the great bulk of the legal and general business of the country is conducted, and where the education and training are more varied and efficient than in small provincial towns.[11]

Unless there was in, or near the town of indenture a university providing SAE approved law classes (as there was only in London, Glasgow and Dundee) as an alternative to those deemed compulsory at Edinburgh University, the provincial apprentice could not avoid residence in Edinburgh. Both South African-based recruits were compelled to spend at least one year in Edinburgh to attend lectures and gain experience in an Edinburgh office. The Inverness apprentices spent from one to two years in the capital for the same reasons, some having their indentures formally transferred to an Edinburgh master for the last two years of their term of service.

The Cautioner

Each indenture had to be signed by a cautioner or guarantor of the apprentice's good conduct and to ensure that he would bind by the terms of the agreement. In 18 indentures, no cautioner was assigned due to the apprentice being of adult age and usually having served long periods of pre-apprenticeship employment in the office of the future master.

In this study, the cautioner was of potential significance for two reasons. Firstly, he provides proof of the existence of living parents which may be hypothesized as of possible importance to the successful completion of an SAE indenture. Secondly, the possibility exists that the cautioner was the individual who was of greatest influence in the decision to enter the profession: the person with CA connections who was best placed to guarantee the apprentice's behaviour and measure his progress.

Table 4.4 reveals that, in most cases, the cautioner was the apprentice's father. Of those apprentices whose cautioner was their mother, 91.7% appear to have lost their fathers by the date of recruitment. Yet, of the 186 who did not have a father or step father as cautioner, 40.9% had living fathers at the outset of their indentures, possibly indicating that some other individual (such as an uncle or brother) was of more significance in directing the career destination of the apprentice.

The increasing number of apprentices with fathers acting as cautioner over the period and the decline in the number of uncles reflects not only the improved life expectancy of parents but also the changing social origins of apprentices. Increasing numbers of apprentices were derived from families where career choice in favour of chartered accountancy had been based not upon primary, interfamily, personal connections with a CA (through having a WS uncle, for instance), but rather through *revelation effects* and more remote occupational and residential associations so that the father remained the obvious cautioner.

TABLE 4.4
The Relationship Between the Apprentice and Cautioner in SAE Indentures 1837-1911

Relationship to Apprentice	% of Total Indentures Commencing Between:							% of Total
	1837 -59	1860 -69	1870 -79	1880 -89	1890 -99	1900 -11	1837 -11	
Father	65.2	59.0	62.5	64.1	73.1	69.6	717	67.1
Step Father	0	2.0	0.7	0	0.8	0	5	0.4
Mother	12.1	14.0	16.0	11.8	12.7	14.6	145	13.6
Brother	3.0	5.0	4.8	5.7	4.7	5.9	55	5.2
Sister	0	0	0	0	0	0.3	1	0.1
Grandfather	0	2.0	0	1.0	0	0	4	0.4
Grandmother	0	0	0	0.5	0	0	1	0.1
Uncle	10.6	9.0	7.6	10.3	5.1	4.9	75	7.0
Aunt	1.5	0	0.7	1.0	0.4	0	5	0.4
Cousin	0	0	0	0	0	0.3	1	0.1
Father-in-Law	0	1.0	0	0	0	0	1	0.1
Brother-in-Law	0	0	0.7	0	0	0	1	0.1
Father's Cousin	0	0	0.7	0	0	0	1	0.1
Master	0	1.0	0	0	0	0.3	2	0.2
A CA	4.6	3.0	0	0.5	0	0	7	0.7
Executor of Father's Estate	3.0	0	0.7	0	0.4	0.6	6	0.6
Family Solicitor	0	0	0.7	0.5	0	0	2	0.2
Headmaster	0	0	0	0.5	0.4	0	2	0.2
A Neighbour	0	0	0	0	0	0.6	2	0.2
Landlady	0	0	0	0.5	0.4	0	2	0.2
No Cautioner	0	3.0	3.5	0.5	0.8	2.3	18	1.7
Not Known	0	1.0	1.4	3.1	1.2	0.6	14	1.3
Total Indentures	66	100	144	195	253	309	1067	100

Apprenticeship Fees

The payment of an indenture fee to the master was a potentially significant financial obstacle to the recruitment of sons, depending on their social origins. The imposition of an apprenticeship fee was established practice before the organization of the Scottish accounting profession. In 1784, the firm of Gibson and Smellie placed this advertisement in *The Glasgow Mercury.* "Wanted an Apprentice: None need apply unless they intend to give an Apprentice-fee.[12]

9 indentures commencing before 1855 that mention the indenture fee and its amount were registered in the SAE books; they reveal a wide variety of experience according to the master. The fee imposed ranged from £40 to 150 guineas with an average of £120. The firm of Moncrieff and Baillie, who were masters of 2 of these early

apprentices, charged 150 guineas while Watson and Dickson, who also trained 2, charged £150. There are indications that masters adjusted the fee according to their acquaintance with the apprentice or his family. David Robertson Soutar, CA, charged John Ogilvy £105 in 1848, Charles H. Hughes £10 in 1863, while Patrick Turnbull in 1852 paid nothing. Soutar added the following to the articles of indenture of the latter apprentice: "For the regard he bears to David Turnbull, WS, the uncle of the said Patrick Turnbull, [the master] dispenses with the usual apprentice fee."

During the pre-1955 period of unregulated fees, it was likely in Edinburgh accountancy, as in other professions, that the quality of training depended on the amount of the fee paid. A low cost indenture was available from some accountants though the possibility existed that the discharged apprentice could expect little in the way of business connections or professional standing. Such a case was that of Archibald Lumsdaine, CA, the son of a Gilmerton surgeon who was apprenticed to Henry Callender, CA in 1853 for the premium of £40. Lumsdaine had a particularly unsuccessful career which culminated in his widow applying to the SAE for assistance. Callender was removed from the roll of members in 1873 following his desertion to America to escape jurisdiction following some illicit business practices.

Article 33 of the 1855 Constitution of the SAE regulated and standardized apprenticeship fees, the amount remained static during the 1855-1914 period: "The Apprentice - Fee shall be One Hundred Guineas, and shall be paid when the indenture is entered into."[13] Despite this standardization, there were some deviations from it in practice. On a number of post-1855 indentures, the fee is not mentioned, possibly indicating that none was imposed. While, in 1905, one apprentice was charged £63 for a three year term and another, based in London, was charged £200.[14]

One hundred guineas, though comparatively low by the standards of other professions (see Table 3.9) undoubtedly prevented the recruitment of many sons to the SAE from families of limited means. The imposition of a single rate also removed the possibility of receiving a low cost training in some of the inferior offices. By comparison, the ICAEW did not regulate the amount of the fee though the figure was seldom below £100 and could be as high as £500 in a firm with a notable reputation. The SAA charged 25 guineas and, for an IAAG apprenticeship, no fee was usually imposed. Significantly, this divergence in fees between the three Scottish CA societies did not result in a flood of recruits to the Glasgow and Aberdeen societies at the expence of the SAE. The higher status of an Edinburgh CA's training and qualification was probably considered as more important to a son's long-term prospects than short-term financial disadvantages in the form of a greater burden of fees.

SAE articles of indenture record the individual who paid and advanced the apprenticeship fee on the signing of the contract of service. It is difficult to evaluate the significance of this variable, as there is no indication that the payee was responsible for earning or raising the money and whether or not, for example, the cash was simply forwarded by the apprentice but was derived from his father's bank account.

Table 4.5 reveals the fee payees listed on indentures, over one half of apprentices are recorded as having paid their own training costs.

TABLE 4.5
**The Relationship to the Apprentice of Fee Payers Listed
on SAE Indentures Commencing 1837-1911**

Relationship to the Apprentice	Number of Indentures	As a % of all Apprentices
The Apprentice	577	54.1
Father	295	27.7
Apprentice and Father	9	0.8
Step Father	1	0.1
Mother	41	3.8
Apprentice and Mother	1	0.1
Brother	10	0.9
Uncle	11	1.0
Apprentice and Uncle	1	0.1
Aunt	3	0.3
Executor of Father's Estate	6	0.6
Apprentice's Last School	1	0.1
School Governors and Apprentice	1	0.1
No Mention of Fee	96	9.0
No Fee to Pay	2	0.2
Not Known	12	1.1
Total	1067	100.0

Remuneration

The apprenticeship fee might appear to have been less restrictive to the recruitment of sons from low status families if it were returned in whole or in part to the apprentice as salary during the term of service. The question of remuneration was of considerable importance to apprentices from non-wealthy origins given that the cost of their training and support constituted a net drain on family resources. Unlike the present-day system whereby student accountants receive a self supporting salary, the SAE did not regulate the payment of apprentices by their masters.

Before the standardization of the form of the indenture in 1855, 10 contracts of service contained provisions for the remuneration of the apprentice, thus indicating that this was the conventional practice before, and perhaps also after, the organization of the Edinburgh profession. The most comprehensive arrangements were made for James Watson who was apprenticed between 1847 and 1852 in the office of Donald Lindsay, CA. Watson had been dux of George Heriot's Hospital in 1845, a school that provided the payment of apprenticeship fees for certain of its pupils. The indenture established that Lindsay would pay the Governors of the Hospital or whoever: "Shall furnish the said James Watson with Bed, Board, washing and clothing, viz., the sum of £20 sterling for each of the first and second years of the said apprenticeship, the sum of £25 sterling the third year, and the sum of £30 sterling the fourth and last year."[15] In addition, the school was to pay £10 a year toward Watson's keep and award him £5 on the discharge of his indenture "to purchase clothes", provided that he "abstain from bad company and vicious practices, and behave himself discreetly at all times to his said master."[16] A similar arrangement was made for Archibald Lumsdaine as an apprentice; his £40 fee was paid by George Watson's Hospital which was to be repaid as salary to Lumsdaine at the rate of £10 *per annum* with additional payments of £5 in the first year, rising by a further £5 in each successive year of service.

The remaining 8 early indentures in which remuneration was specified illustrate, that as with fees, the amount of salary varied according to the firm. The usual procedure was for the apprentice fee to be repaid in full in increasing annual instalments over the period of the term. There were, however, exceptions. Patrick Turnbull who paid no fee to his master as we have seen, received £90 in salary while John Ogilvy, who had paid £105 to the same master received £120. Patrick Morrison, CA charged James Smeal £100 but paid back only £45 between 1853 and 1856; David Cormack, CA, SSC, by contrast charged Dugald C. Kerr £99 and 19 shillings but returned £115 in salary between 1849 and 1854. In almost all these cases, remuneration was on the condition that the apprentice maintained good conduct and was faithful to his master.

Only 7 indentures that commenced after 1854 included provisions for an apprentice's salary. In the earliest, John F. Moffatt paid the usual fee but received a total of £190 from Alexander T. Niven , CA between 1856 and 1861; comprising "a salary for his services" which was paid quarterly. 4 other of the relevant indentures were contracted during the late 1860s and 1870s. In two cases the £105 fee was returned in increasing annual emoluments. In the other 2 instances, John F. Moffatt, CA was himself the master and paid one apprentice £20 per year and another a total of £265. The former apprentice was the son of a wealthy brewer, and the latter the son of a small builder, indicating that some masters may have taken the apprentice's circumstances into account when considering remuneration.

The remaining 2 relevant indentures commenced in 1897 and 1905. These, however, are unrepresentative of conditions in the Edinburgh profession as one was located in Glasgow (no fee, £70 salary) and the other in London (£200 fee, £100 salary) and reflected local conventions concerning the remuneration of apprentices. In London, for example: "A very usual arrangement with high-class firms is to fix the premium at from 250 to 300 guineas, and the salary paid during the course of the last three years at about £100 or £150."[17]

Despite the lack of information on this subject for Edinburgh CA indentures, it seems likely that apprentices did receive a salary though the provisions and the amount varied among firms. It is known, for example,[18] that Barstow and Millar paid their early twentieth century apprentices in instalments of £20, £24, £28, £32 and £36 over the five years, constituting the repayment of their fees *with interest*. Martin and Currie and Co. had similar arrangements. In these circumstances, the imposition of an apprenticeship fee does not appear to have been such a potential obstacle to recruitment. However, the raising of the lump sum at indenture commencement remained a barrier to the sons of low income families aspiring to enter the local CA profession.

The Experience of Apprenticeship

The experience of the SAE recruit, whether in or outside the office, altered over time and depended considerably upon individual circumstances. The position of the apprentice within the firm varied according to its size and the division of labour within it. Increasingly, however, given their expanding number and concentration in a small number of larger CA offices, apprentices formed a distinct group within the employment structure of the firm.

The medium-sized late nineteenth century Edinburgh firm of CAs consisted of two or more partners, a head or managing clerk (who was frequently a recently qualified CA who had trained with the firm), a cashier, perhaps four or five clerks, a junior *trotter* or messenger, and a number of apprentices of whom one was usually considered to be the senior. Despite their employment in work tasks that were often similar to those of the clerk, a series of common interests distinguished the apprentices from the other office staff. These were: their relationship with the partners and employment status; a mutual concern with examinations and qualification; membership of the SAE student society; and their comparatively transient position with the firm.

Over the period of the indenture, the standing of the apprentice improved reflecting his increasing knowledge and involvement with the more sophisticated business. During the initial period of training, however, the apprentice performed the most menial and routine tasks to familiarize himself with the office system – such as filing, letter copying and indexing:

> During the first twelve or eighteen months of his service, an articled clerk will, in the usual course, be engaged in the most simple and elementary work of the office, such as copying accounts, writing up books, making additions, calculations of interest, and other similar matters.[19]

Such monotonous and rudimentary work could, claimed Dicksee in 1907, breed disappointment, the apprentice wondered "how it is that his work differs so little from that of a mercantile clerk."[20]

Once the basic skills of bookkeeping had been mastered, the apprentice might advance to assist with audits, and in the final years of training was given sole charge of less complex audits or remits and received introductions to the wider areas of business. The major change over the period of the indenture was that of increasing responsibility: "He may also be deputed to take charge of an undertaking or on behalf of his principal acting as receiver, liquidator or trustee, often on his own away from the main office."[21]

The practical work of the office was supplemented by the increasing burden of examination preparation. As the standard of professional education required for examination success rose, so apprentices were compelled to spend more time at university law lectures, evening classes and meetings of the student society. Apprentices of the 1850s to early 1870s could recall a more relaxed era of training. William H. Smith, CA, who was indentured between 1857 and 1862 to Brown and Pearson recalled that:

> I was as happy as the day was long. But here circumstances conspired against me. The racket court was a little too contagious, and in it I spent as much time as I did at the desk. I also joined the St Andrew Boat Club.[22]

Similarly, B. Worthington wrote in 1895 that some years ago English apprentices learnt nothing from the first day of their indenture to the last except a taste for sport and wine appreciation. These days were long gone, now "application to work reign in their stead".[23]

Despite their apparent cohesiveness during working hours (which by the late nineteenth century were generally nine to six on weekdays and nine till one on Saturdays), the office apprentices dispersed at the close of business. One SAE apprentice of the early 1900s recalled that: "Time in the office was busy and friendly, after hours we went our separate ways."[24]

Social intercourse between staff and between staff and apprentices appears to have lessened as the scale of the SAE and the CA office expanded. Alexander T. Hunter, CA, writing in 1936 recalled that in 1876, when the profession was a comparatively small affair, "its necessities for hospitality were amply satisfied by a series of dinner parties in the President's house. Compare this with the superior splash now made in the Freemason's Hall. The President honoured me, still an unfledged apprentice with an invitation to one of his dinner parties."[25] The President of the Society (Charles Pearson, CA) was, incidently, one of Hunter's masters.

The social experience of the apprentice varied widely according to his means and distance from the parental home. The relatively prosperous recruit could take advantage of the opportunities for sport, club membership and entertainment available in Edinburgh. By contrast, his poorer colleague, living at some distance from home and without family or old school friends, could envisage a basic and isolated existence. One such apprentice of the 1900s with parents in Ireland recalled that during his indenture:

> I moved to one room in a tenement block. The landlady was elderly and very poor. She gave me breakfast and dinner (tapioca, 5d.); lunch was two buns and a glass of milk (3d.). My only asset was a gold watch which was inherited. I pawned it once. I studied every evening for the examinations as I had no money to do anything else.[26]

However impoverished, it is clear from the addresses provided by recruits at the commencement of the indentures and at examination, that most at least benefitted from the hypothetical advantages of residing in the parental home during their apprenticeship. 857 of the 1067 (80.3%) apprentices contained in the study and who began their indentures between 1837 and 1911 appear to have done so. 9 resided with one or both of their parents in the Edinburgh home of a relative; 28 lived with brothers and sisters (most of these had deceased parents); 4 resided in their own marital homes; and, 1 lived with his CA master who was also his brother-in-law. 3 resided with grandparents, 34 with an uncle, an aunt or both, and 1 with a cousin. Of the 38 who resided with a relative, at least 11 were orphaned and 6 were fatherless. The remainder appear to have taken advantage of lodging with a relation in Edinburgh, their parents living well outside the city. Most also derived from lower middle and working class origins and were perhaps unable to afford the high costs of separate accomodation.

Those apprentices who were beyond commuting distance from Edinburgh and without relatives in the city took lodgings: at least 65 did so (their parents living an average of 119.8 miles from Edinburgh). Nineteenth century Edinburgh contained a disproportionate number of lodging and boarding houses reflecting its status as a major centre of educational and occupational preparation. In 1881, the ratio of lodging house keepers to total population was 1:259 in Edinburgh compared to 1:518 in Glasgow. A few SAE apprentices lodged in houses that specifically accomodated university students and medical or legal trainees. Most, however, were the only lodgers resident in the household.

18 SAE apprentices took *rooms* or apartments. These were mostly the sons of landed proprietors and professional men living on average 92.3 miles from the capital. A further 7 apprentices appear to have experienced an even more comfortable period of indenture residing with a brother or brothers in a separate household in Edinburgh with parents living on average 79.2 miles away. Most of these individuals derived from SSGs 1-3 and had been provided with independent accomodation for the period of their vocational training. It was a common practice during the nineteenth century for the younger sons of landed proprietors and wealthy farmers to move to Edinburgh and learn a profession while elder brothers benefitted from the inheritance of the family property. Donald Lindsay, CA, an original member of the SAE, was a case in point; the son of a Forfarshire landed proprietor, he and his brother accompanied by a servant moved to Edinburgh and received a training in a WS office. His brother qualified as a WS and he became an accountant. A later example is provided by William S. Buttar, CA (admitted in 1891), the third son of a Forfarshire farmer of 510 acres. His elder brother entered farming while he and his younger brother were trained in Edinburgh, he as a CA and his brother as a merchant's clerk. During their training, they were accomodated in a separate household with one domestic servant.

Of the remaining apprentices, 2 resided in university halls, 1 in the hostel of his last school, and 3 lodged with their ex-schoolmasters. Information concerning the remaining 34 recruits is lacking though it is likely that the majority resided in lodgings during the period of their indentures. As will be discovered in the subsequent chapter, the apprentice's place of residence during professional training was significant in terms of his success in the system of occupational preparation.

EXAMINATION

Despite the heavy reliance upon practical training, it became increasingly obvious to the SAE and other professional organizations during the second half of the nineteenth century that the vocational preparation of a *professional* required the testing of theoretical knowledge. The resultant trend toward more academic testing of the apprentice's abilities culminated in a questioning of whether the emphasis in the qualification system placed upon examinations had become too great. In 1909, for example, one CA asserted that:

> Examinations of all kinds have become a feature of the age, and it is worth while to inquire whether they have not been exalted to too important a place. After all, the object of examinations should be to test to what extent a candidate has profited by the teaching and training which he has received.[27]

It was the increasing importance attached to the testing of the acquisition of theoretical knowledge that distinguished the experience of the SAE recruit of the 1900s from that of his 1860s counterpart, and placed in his path a greater number of obstacles to the achievement of full professional status.

The SAE Examination System of 1855-73

The Constitution which was ratified by the newly-formed Institute of Accountants in 1853 made no provision for the entrance of members on the basis of examination. As Martin rightly pointed out in 1896, the original members of the Institute were not required to pass any formal test of their abilities as accountants.[28] This defect aroused some adverse criticism of the infant society from the established legal profession which was keen to ensure that an organization of its 'junior partners' with which it would be unavoidably associated, was composed of *learned* gentlemen. The *Index Juridicus* of 1853, in commenting on the Institute's Constitution, advised that:

> There should be a test - at least of ability and respectability - to entitle a person to join. Cases are far from rare where men, after having failed in their ordinary pursuits, suddenly bethought themselves of having the word "Accountant" engraved on their brass plates, and, under this designation, have either carried on a very miscellaneous sort of business, or like Mr Micawber, waited patiently "for something to turn up". This should be provided against.[29]

The resultant examination procedure instituted in 1855 by the, now incorporated, SAE was, by present day standards in the professions, very rudimentary. Article 39 of the 1855 Constitution provided for a single examination to be taken as the final stage of training upon which entrance to the SAE depended.

> Candidates for admission shall undergo examination by the Examinators at such time and place as they may appoint. The Examinators shall examine Candidates for admission in such form and to such extent as they may consider necessary upon subjects usually occurring in the practice of the profession, such as algebra, including the use of logarithms – annuities – life assurances – liferents – reversions – book-keeping – framing of states under sequestrations, trusts, factories, executries – the Law of Scotland, especially that relating to Bankruptcy, private trusts and arbitration, rights and preferences of creditors in rankings.[30]

As this would suggest, the subjects of the examination were of a highly practical nature, testing an apprentice's acquisition of specific skills during his indenture and his ability to utilize them efficiently as a future member. The examination procedure reflected this objective in that it was conducted orally before a Committee of Examiners (the President of the SAE, with the Council and three elected CAs) and consisted of an interrogation of the apprentice of no predetermined duration. The candidate, having satisfied the Committee was 'found duly qualified' and permitted to apply for admission. Significantly, no one appears from the SAE minute books, as ever having failed or requested to re-appear subsequent to a first examination. The procedure and the lack of emphasis placed upon examinations for qualification to the profession during this period was well explained by one senior CA writing in 1909:

> The examinations were of secondary importance and were to a great extent oral, which enabled the Examiner to bring his personal observation of the candidate into play. His judgement, therefore, rested on wider grounds than a mere report of the value per cent of a candidate's answers to certain questions put to him. Weight was attached, and rightly, to the character of the instruction he would be likely to receive in the office in which he was trained and to the intelligence shown in oral examination; and if in certain branches of his profession the candidate revealed deficiency, he was informed of his defects and told how best to remedy them.[31]

This rudimentary method of evaluating a future professional's abilities was not unique at the time. Indeed, the SAE attitude toward examinations reflected that existing among the Edinburgh profession that it most aspired to and desired to emulate: the lawyers.

An intrant to the Faculty of Advocates in 1861 was required to hold a degree in arts or pass an oral examination in general scholarship as evidence of his receipt of a liberal education. This was followed by attendance at four university courses in law, a private, oral examination in law, and submission of a thesis which was publically defended before the Faculty membership. A Writer to the Signet was similarly obliged to attend four law courses, serve a five-year indenture and then sit a private oral examination in Scots Law before three examinators and a public examination in Conveyancing before the whole membership. Solicitors to the Supreme Courts were obliged to attend two sessions of university courses in arts, at least one law course at Edinburgh University, and serve a five-year apprenticeship. In all the legal and related professions, a similar system of qualification and suitability assessment was evident during the mid nineteenth century. The receipt of a *liberal education* had to be proven and was sufficient proof of a candidate's academic abilities; examinations were a test of the acquisition of the basic skills and knowledge required to practice the vocation. The payment of entrance fees was evidence of the suitability of the recruit's social status and commitment to the organization and its membership.

It was as Reader has asserted,[32] the lower status, aspiring professions that initiated the move toward comprehensive and written examinations in order to affirm their standing on the basis that their members provided informed and expert knowledge. Within the horizons of the SAE, it was such a profession that may have encouraged Edinburgh CAs to adopt a more rigorous examination system. The Faculty of Actuaries, incorporated in 1856 and whose membership consisted primarily of insurance company managers (many of whom were also CAs), had its aspirations to professional status tainted by the commercial associations of its members. Consequently, from 1856, it introduced a comprehensive examination system and placed a greater emphasis on the acquisition of theoretical knowledge as a condition of qualification.

Potential "Actuarial Students" (the title *student* as opposed to *apprentice* is significant, the former has an academic connotation, the latter implies a practical training) had, before indenture, to pass a matriculation examination consisting of elementary subjects. The student was required to attend lectures and prescribed classes, and admission to the Faculty depended on succeeding in two *written* final examinations on professional subjects. Following the first sitting of the matriculation examination in which all seven candidates passed, the Council of the Faculty reported with some pride in the following terms which illustrates how novel this system of qualification was by contemporary standards:

> The examination was conducted in writing, and occupied an entire
> day, a series of questions on each subject having been placed before

the candidates, who were required to give in written answers before
leaving the room and without receiving assistance of any kind.[33]

Perhaps in the light of the actuaries' example, the SAE in late 1863 proposed a
relatively minor reform. As with the entrance examination of the Writers to the Signet,
the final examination was divided into two diets, to be taken by the apprentice in
October and January. Despite the provision that examinations were now to "be
conducted *viva voce* or in writing, or both, at the discretion of the Examinators", the
emphasis appears to have remained on the oral procedure. As previously, no one
appears to have failed. William H. Cook, CA, seems to have qualified under this
procedure and his recollections to an apprentice of the 1920s illustrates how the
examination for admission to the SAE had been radically different in his day.

> I was admitted to the Society without sitting any examinations.
> One day when my indenture was at an end I dressed myself in a frock
> coat and silk hat and presented myself before the members of the
> Council. They all shook me by the hand and said they were sure I would
> be a credit to the profession, and that is how I became a Chartered
> Accountant.[34]

Given the comparatively small membership of the SAE during this period and the
close association between members practising within a limited geographical area
(there were never more than 100 SAE members located in Edinburgh between 1854
and 1873), it is not surprising that this elementary process of ability assessment was
considered as sufficient. Examiners were undoubtedly known to the apprentice's
master and, in many instances the master was an examiner. An apprentice's practical
abilities were well known before he entered the examination room and his success as
an apprentice had been monitored. Indenture was the process by which practical skills
were acquired and tested. If the apprentice completed his term he was as good as
qualified. Examination was a test of basic understanding and, perhaps more
importantly, an assessment of professional respectability. From 1873, however, the test
of ability upon which admission depended moved increasingly away from indenture
and toward more sophisticated examination as the SAE sought to affirm its
professional status and to broaden its appeal to parents as a vocation for their sons.

The 1873-93 Examination System

Although the single final examination was considered to have been adequate and to
have worked satisfactorily, it was quite clear by the early 1870s that it was insufficient
by the the standards of other *new* professions laying claim to a membership of highly

qualified men. Not only was the SAE lagging behind current trends in vocational preparation that would improve its own status, it was also at variance with the aspirations of increasing numbers of parents seeking careers for sons who had been educationally prepared for, and expected to enter, professions which could claim a sophisticated examination system and a recognized qualification of high academic standing.

It was in response to such pressures that at the annual meeting of the SAE in 1872, the President and Council were remitted to consider alterations to professional examinations which might improve efficiency in the education of apprentices and, apply the 'soundest test' of their abilities in order that the Society might 'keep pace' with educational developments in other professions. The consequent report and its recommendations were endorsed at the annual meeting of 1873 and a new three-tier system was implemented during the same year. The report considered that the major defect of the existing system was that: "No preliminary Examination is at present required before an Apprentice enters his indenture; nor is any test applied during the currency of the indenture to ascertain either the fitness of the Apprentice or his application to his professional studies."[35] The following examinations were established as a result of this identified deficiency: the preliminary, intermediate and final examinations.

The **preliminary examination** was essentially a matriculation examination and a test of the aspiring apprentice's general education. Through most of the 1873-93 period, it consisted of two written papers: a two hour test of Dictation, Grammar and Arithmetic followed by a three hour examination in three subjects of the candidate's choice, selected from History, Geography, Latin and French or German. As noted in Chapter 3, external or *professional* examiners were appointed from among the staff of eminent Edinburgh schools to mark the papers and prepare the syllabus. The first sitting of the examination was held on 2 June 1873. After 1889, BA or MA degree holders of a British university as well as those with school-leaving certificates in at least three subjects including Mathematics were exempt from the preliminary examination. Equivalent qualifications to the latter were continually added to the list permitting exemption as shown in Table 4.6 over.

The **intermediate examination** was to be taken by all apprentices after the commencement of their third year of indenture. The examination was written and conducted over two days. The specific subjects of the papers changed over the 1873 to 1893 period. Originally, candidates sat papers in Algebra, Arithmetic, Euclid, Geography, History and Essay; in January 1883, History and Geography were excluded and Logarithms added though this was itself removed in January 1884. Until October 1889, the examination was not a test of professional education, rather, it was an advanced preliminary examination dominated by school rather than vocational subjects. From 1889, however, it became directly relevant to professional practice consisting thereafter of two components: Mathematics which included papers in Arithmetic and Algebra, and; Professional Knowledge which was comprised of papers in Financial Accounting, Letter Writing and Bookkeeping.

TABLE 4.6
Reasons Why SAE Apprentices 1890-1911 and Included in the Study Were Exempt from Sitting the Preliminary Examination

Exemption Due to	1890 -94	1895 -99	1900 -04	1905 -11	Tota
Held Scottish School Leaving Certificate	33	38	38	37	146
Held Oxbridge Local Examination Certificate	1	2	2	2	7
Passed Matriculation Exam of a University	0	2	3	4	9
Held a University Degree	0	4	4	9	17
Passed ICAEW Preliminary Examination	0	0	1	1	2
Passed Law Agents' Examination	1	0	0	0	1
Passed Royal Military Academy Entrance Exam	2	1	0	0	3
Passed Army Preliminary Examination	1	0	0	0	1
Held College of Preceptors' Certificate	0	0	0	1	1
Passed London County Council Preliminary Exam	0	0	0	1	1
Total	38	47	48	55	188
As % of all Apprentices	32.5	34.6	29.8	37.2	33.

In order to encourage academic excellence and enthusiasm for the written examinations, a number of financial inducements were offered to successful candidates from the introduction of the new system in 1873. The intermediate examinations had an 'imperative' and a 'voluntary' component (the former is that described above). The apprentice with the highest marks in both sections was awarded a £20 bursary over two years, while the most successful individual in the 'imperative' was given £10. Due to a lack of interest for the optional 'voluntary' examination, it was abolished in 1882. Thereafter the highest achiever in the 'imperative' received the £20 bursary and the apprentice in second place was awarded £10.

Having passed the intermediate examination, completed his indenture and (from 1866) attended the compulsory law classes at Edinburgh University, the apprentice could apply to sit the **final examination**. This was a two day affair consisting of a written component and a traditional oral component. The subjects of the examination were:

1. **The Law of Scotland**: which "shall consist of written papers as well as a *viva voce* Examination" before an external examiner (who was usually an eminent advocate).

2. **Actuarial Science**: all written papers to be conducted "by a gentleman of actuarial attainments" (usually an insurance company manager and member of the Faculty of Actuaries).

3. **The General Business of an Accountant or Professional Knowledge**: to be conducted by "Members of the Society Exclusively".[36] Half of the examination was oral before a board of at least three examiners.

Emphasis was placed increasingly upon the written papers especially in borderline cases. A fellowship of £30 was awarded to the best performer in the final examination which was often, in practice, split between two or three candidates gaining equal marks.

The General Examining Board 1893 Onwards

The establishment of the GEB in 1892 and the joint agreement of the three Scottish CA societies in February 1893 which unified regulations of apprenticeship, examination and admission has to be analysed in the context of wider developments in the accounting profession.

The agreement was reached during a period of great pressure on the chartered societies in Scotland from competing organizations claiming equal, and a right to, incorporated status. The chartered societies consistently justified their professional superiority over other accountants and their advantageous position in securing business on the grounds that the public chose to employ them due to their having received a higher standard of training and qualification. It had become obvious from the petitions of the SIA for a charter in 1884 and 1889-90 that the standard of examination between the competing organizations was an important issue. The three CA societies each had individual systems of examination (though they did not vary significantly in effect) which appeared contrary to their joint claim of superiority through having obtained a uniformly exceptional professional education. It was important, therefore, for the CAs to provide a regular system of training and examination and to assert standards applicable to all three societies. This would prevent any future exploitation by the SIA of the divergent *local* examination systems of the individual organizations. As *The Scottish Accountant* claimed of the CAs in

1893, the establishment of the GEB in 1892 appeared as "a desire to strengthen their position for the purposes of opposing the new comers."[37] Martin, writing in 1896, was more vociferous: "The pretended examinations of the accountants are a sham, designed to mislead the public into the belief that the chartered societies are carefully selecting and preparing a class of highly qualified men for the profession."[38]

The pressure on the chartered societies became even more immediate in October 1892 when the SIA revised its competing system of examination claiming that: "A glance at it will suffice to show that the standard of excellence which the Council are resolved to maintain for admission to membership, is of a high order, and is, to say the least of it not inferior to that of any other Society or Institute in the Kingdom."[39] The CAs' reply came in the form of a revised syllabus and the institution of an organization constituted specifically to monitor examinations and maintain standards of professional training.

The GEB consisted of five members elected by the SAE, five by the IAAG and two from the SAA as well as the Presidents of each who were *ex officio* members. The Board had the power to regulate and conduct all examinations, to set papers, and to determine whether a candidate had passed or failed. Examinations were held in Edinburgh, Glasgow and Aberdeen on the same days.

The structure of the pre-1893 SAE examination system remained essentially intact and formed the model for the GEB syllabus. The preliminary examination altered little in form from 1893. A Shorthand paper was introduced as an additional option in 1893. Thereafter the range of choice became ever more restricted. In 1897, Algebra was introduced as a compulsory subject as was a foreign language from 1907 so that, by then, the candidate for recruitment took six subjects, four of which were compulsory. The exemption qualification was adjusted; in 1897 a leaving certificate had to include English as well as Mathematics.

In June 1910, the preliminary examination was abolished in response to the increasing numbers entering apprenticeships on the basis of holding leaving certificates. In 1912, it was claimed that the preliminary had become obsolete and unnecessary "chiefly on the ground that tests of general education were more suitably conducted by educational authorities, who now make ample provision for doing so."[40] Those not in possession of leaving certificates could, thereafter, take the Mathematics, English and Language papers of the preliminary examination in Arts of the Scottish universities.

Of all the GEB examinations, the intermediate received least criticism over the 1893-1914 period and remained similar in structure to its pre-1893 SAE equivalent.

Five papers were taken over two days: Arithmetic and Algebra were both two hour papers, and three hours was permitted for questions on Bookkeeping, Framing Accounts, and Correspondence.

Under the GEB, the number of papers in the final examination was increased to eight, and it became a totally written test of four days duration. In the late 1890s, the papers were on:

1. **Law of Scotland**: Bankruptcy, Judicial Factories, the Company Acts (2.5 hours); Partnership, References and Arbitrations etc. (2.5 hours).

2. **Actuarial Science** (2 hours).

3. **Political Economy** (2 hours).

4. **General Business of an Accountant**: Theory and Practice of Bookkeeping (3 hours); Audit of Accounts and Books (3 hours); Management of Estates and Factories (3 hours); Public Companies (3 hours).

Alarmed by a rising failure rate among apprentices caused by the considerable mental strain placed upon the candidates, the diversity of subjects and the fact that many had to combine office work with examination preparation, the GEB divided the final examination into two divisions in 1903. It was made possible for the apprentice to sit the whole examination at once as before or take either the first or second division at one sitting and the outstanding division at a following diet. Both divisions had to be passed within 26 months of each other or the candidate was required to resit both divisions. If the candidate took the whole examination he could be passed in one division and failed in the other which he would have to retake subsequently. The first division was composed of four papers in the more academic and theoretical subjects while the second consisted of four papers in practical or professional subjects.

The re-arrangement of the final examination was not considered to have been an immediate success. Two-thirds of candidates continued to sit the whole examination soon after the introduction of the two divisions. It failed to arrest the declining pass rate, and incurred criticism from other accountancy organizations to whom it appeared as a reduction in Scottish CA entrance standards – a claim which the GEB denied.

Having thus described the nature and development of the SAE examination system its changing impact upon recruits will be discussed, particularly in the context of the increasing burden and pressures of examinations.

The Examined

The major developments over the 1855-1914 period in examinations from the perspective of the SAE apprentice was the increasing emphasis placed upon them in order to qualify, their increasing number and apparent severity. By the 1920s, the focus had moved so far from the practical side of vocational preparation that *The Accountant's Magazine* had to assure its readers that:

> . . . The 'be all and end all' of apprenticeship is not the passing of examinations. The daily practical training in the office, is, in our opinion, of far more use, and the apprentice who avails himself of this practical training is almost certain to do well.[41]

There was a considerable divergence in the experience of the apprentice of the 1860s compared to his successor of the 1900s. The former was obliged to appear for a single oral examination in his final year, and did not have to contemplate the possibility of failure; the latter was presented with the prospect of having to sit a series of increasingly difficult papers at three stages of his professional preparation. This contrast is illustrated in Table 4.7.

TABLE 4.7
Percentage of Scottish CA Apprentices Failing at Separate Sittings of Examinations 1855-1914 With the Total Number of Candidates Taking the Examination

SAE

(only apprentices included in the study and where the
date of sitting the examination is known)

Year Examination Taken	Preliminary Examination	N	Intermediate Examination	N	Final Examination	N
1855-59	-	-	-	-	0	13
1860-64	-	-	-	-	0	28
1865-69	-	-	-	-	0	31
1870-74	13.6 [1]	22	0	6	0	56
1875-79	23.0	113	14.9	47	17.2	29
1880-84	22.6	146	17.7	124	7.6	66
1885-89	21.9	114	28.4	109	7.1	84
1890-94	5.1	78	25.4	130	22.8	92
1895-99	17.2 [2]	87	35.1	194	12.0	92
1900-04	-	-	29.1	189	22.6	146
1905-09	-	-	24.9	209	42.3	286
1910-14	-	-	51.4	72	52.5	343

GEB
(all Scottish CA Apprentices)

1894-99	34.3	694	30.6	708	25.9	359
1900-04	39.3	675	31.6	573	34.6 [3]	564
1905-09	45.3	898	27.2	779	45.5	989
1910-14	53.9 [4]	152	43.8	915	53.5	1289

[1] = 1873-4 only. [2] = for 1895-8 only, thereafter SAE records only provide the date of passing the preliminary examination. [3] = from 1903 failure rate of all those sitting whole or part of the final examination. [4] = 1910 only.

Among recruits who entered the profession on the basis of examination between 1855 and 1875, CAs sat an average of 1.6 diets in the final examination. Those who entered the Society between 1876 and 1896 sat a mean of 2.2 diets of intermediate and final examinations before passing them, compared to 2.9 for those admitted between 1897 and 1914. It should be established at this juncture that Scottish apprentices were not alone in having to contemplate sitting increasing numbers of ever more difficult examinations before they could acheive membership of the CA profession. Failure rates in the ICAEW examinations also displayed a long-run increase.

TABLE 4.8
Percentage of ICAEW Apprentices Failing at Separate Sittings of Examinations
1882-1914 With the Total Number of Candidates Taking
the Examination

Year Examination Taken	Preliminary Examination	N	Intermediate Examination	N	Final Examination	N
1882-84	38.4	190	19.4	155	35.7	224
1885-89	38.0	484	21.9	393	34.7	631
1890-94	44.2	873	24.1	758	30.0	597
1895-99	31.1	1523	26.5	1136	34.2	968
1900-04	34.2	1752	32.4	1811	37.2	1526
1905-09	32.6	1935	33.2	1871	37.8	1766
1910-14	39.3	2444	37.9	2098	39.5	1923

Source: Calculated from statistics in Dicksee, *The Student's Guide to Accountancy,* 2nd ed. and *The Accountant* 1907-15.

Despite the introduction of a more sophisticated examination structure by the SAE in 1873, its working was at first dominated by the mentality of the old basic system, it was almost a cosmetic exercise conceived and enacted for the benefit of parents and public. The examinations were not particularly exacting, and those who marked them were notably lenient and inconsistent, appearing to sieve out all but the very worst candidates that the practical training of indenture had failed to remove.

In this earlier period, examinations existed to be passed and every opportunity was provided to ensure that result. In the final examination of December 1878, for example, John Brewis and Robert MacNair were passed on the condition that they return to complete a paper which had not been finished due to a lack of time. If a candidate failed in one paper of the examination, he usually had to resit only that single paper. If, however, his overall performance was considered to have been more than adequate, he might be excused the obligation. In the final examination of December 1882, James A. McLaren, for example, gained an overall mark of 56% and was passed despite a "very disappointing" actuarial paper. It appears that the previous procedure remained of passing candidates though advising them to study their weaker subjects, and of masters' opinions concerning apprentices being taken into account by examiners.

No specific pass mark was fixed though it seems to have been around 45% to 50% between 1873 and 1893. Borderline cases were often given the benefit of the doubt especially in years when the general performance of candidates was good. In the intermediate examination of December 1886, Ernest N. Paton was passed with 41% of the marks and came sixteenth out of the 19 candidates. Two years previously James MacPherson gained the same mark but was failed and had to retake the whole examination being twelfth placed out of 21 candidates. And, in December 1887, James M. Stewart also failed with 41% and was requested to resit only the specific subjects in which he had performed badly.

The whole relaxed attitude toward early SAE examinations is well summed up by the following comments, one from an examiner and the other from an examinee. James A. Molleson, CA, in his report to the Council of the SAE concerning the Professional Knowledge paper of the 1883 final examination asserted that:

> The answers and relative states, of course, varied in degree –
> some of them excellent, others feeble, but as the whole of them
> exhibited some knowledge of the profession and the evidence of study, I
> have to recommend that the thirteen candidates should be passed.[42]

Alexander T. Hunter, CA, recalled that in 1881 he had to sit up "night after night until two and three a.m., swotting up Scots Law, Conveyancing etc., in preparation for my final examination." He arrived at the house of Lord Pearson, advocate and Senator of the College of Justice, for his oral in Scots Law wearing full evening dress en route for a dance at 9 p.m.:

He then proceeded to question me. I remember I made one bad 'bloomer' at which he smiled and said quietly "Do you really think so ?" I replied "No, I mean exactly the opposite". I got to my dance not too late; passed my final, and became a full-fledged CA.[43]

From the generation of apprentices who commenced their indentures from the 1880s onwards, the examinations appear to have become more exacting. This was undoubtedly a response by the SAE to present to the SIA and the courts a picture of CAs as highly qualified professionals who had succeeded in passing through a severe system of occupational preparation and, from the turn of the century, may also have been the result of acute overstocking in the profession. The rising rate of examination failure was not attributed to a decline in the standard of recruit entering into indentures, though there was criticism of the ability of schools to prepare apprentices for entrance to the profession. This latter point has potential implications for the successful recruitment of sons from families only able to afford a basic secondary education as will be revealed in the next chapter.

The most convincing explanation propounded for the worsening examination failure rate appears to have been a lack of adequate preparation by apprentices for the more demanding SAE and GEB examination systems.

The GEB and *The Accountant's Magazine* were united in their claim that examination preparation was deficient among apprentices. The preliminary examination, for example, produced higher pass rates at its December sitting than at its June diet as school leavers had five months available to study for the former. The examination was not particularly difficult, involving the study of only one prescribed textbook per subject. Yet, the GEB complained year after year of poor spelling and an inability to correct elementary grammatical errors in the English paper; "a tendency to make absurd blunders" in the History paper; "extraordinary distortions of information" in Geography; and "poor translation" in the languages.[44]

It was recommended that apprentices should prepare for the intermediate examination utilizing prescribed textbooks and advice from masters at least six months before presenting themselves. For the final, a year of private study was prescribed in the late nineteenth and early twentieth centuries of at least three hours a day and more as the examination approached. Despite such guidance, the examiners complained in 1897 of: "A disposition to come forward too hurriedly- before sufficient experience has been acquired, and without adequate preparation."[45] There were similar complaints concerning the lack of examination technique displayed by candidates. In the preliminary examination of June 1899, the GEB noted that "in many cases the candidates seemed to be unable to grasp intelligently even the terms of the question put."[46] *The Accountant's Magazine* found it necessary to print articles such as "Hints to Examinees",[47] and "How to Pass Examinations".[48]

The high failure rate in CA examinations, and the reasons propounded for the phenomenon, are suggestive of the existence of generations of recruits from the 1870s simply not geared to the process of comprehensive examination and the testing of their abilities through this medium despite the fact that their parents increasingly desired that they should enter professions in which their sons would be academically certified. It has to be borne in mind that apprentices of this period were being indentured to masters whose own qualification had been dominated by *practical* training. Apprentices indentured to such such principals were not always employed in an office geared to examination preparation.

It must also have proved difficult for those generations of apprentices who were passing through a transitional period in the importance of factors that determined vocational success. Qualification had depended until the early 1880s on the ability to raise an indenture fee and a good practical training which were paid and provided for the apprentice. Examinations were a completely different kind of test, one that depended more on academic ability, individual effort and private study.

The response of SAE apprentices to the increasing importance of examination, and the escalating failure rate, illustrate admirably this nineteenth century dependence on paid services as the determinant of qualification. It was no longer sufficient to pay only a CA master, the apprentice sought the services of the tutor or *crammer* who it was expected would ensure success in the examinations. The recollection of one SAE apprentice of the 1900s illustrates this point:

> The exams were not difficult if you were prepared to study without interruption . . . Apprentices who could afford it used tutors- some for every subject. I think the busy tutors could not have done other work. I knew one apprentice who used tutors for every subject and failed to pass the final exam, he thought that *tutors would put him through*.[49]

The SAE discouraged *coaching* due to the existence of variable teaching standards among tutors. By 1918, however, they effectively formed an important feature of a CAs training. In 1917, one contributor to *The Accountant's Magazine* declared that: "The examiners do not find what the apprentice has been taught by the master, but what has been crammed into him by the coach who has sized up the examiner."[50]

For ICAEW examinations, a tutor was recommended to apprentices by the published guides to the profession. The expense (about £20) was considered to be a wise investment, especially considering that prize-winning students of the Institute were reputed to have availed themselves of the services of a proficient coach.

University Law Classes

The apparent lack of adequate preparation by apprentices before examination provides one likely explanation for the SAE decision in 1866 to initiate compulsory attendance in prescribed law classes at Edinburgh University. This move must also be regarded, again, as part of the general attempt of the SAE during this period to upgrade its system of theoretical training in order to parallel its system of qualification with that current in the Edinburgh law societies. Article 37 of the Constitution in 1889 stated that in order to apply for admission SAE apprentices now had to "have produced Certificates to the Secretary that they have attended the Classes of Scots Law and Conveyancing in the University of Edinburgh for one complete session."[51] The GEB regulations of 1893 resolved that courses could be taken at any Scottish university whose lectures had been approved and in Edinburgh Mercantile Law replaced Conveyancing from 1908-9. Additionally, apprentices were recommended to take other university classes such as Political Economy and Commercial Law, though these were not deemed compulsory.

The SAE had close links with Edinburgh University much earlier than the 1860s and the source of the association was accountants' connection with, and emulation of, the established legal profession. As mentioned earlier advocates, WSs, SSCs and even ordinary writers and solicitors were required to attend university lectures in Law as part of their vocational preparation. It would appear that, even before organization and incorporation, Edinburgh accountants adopted the same practice (see SAE original members in Table 4.9).

Although the 1855 Constitution made no provision for the compulsory attendance of SAE apprentices at university classes, it was a convention that they ought to if possible. The indenture of Henry Budge, CA, which commenced in January 1855 was unique in containing the following:

> As it may be thought advisable for the said Henry Budge to attend the Law Classes at the University it is agreed that he shall be allowed to do so, and the requisite time shall be afforded to enable him to attend during the different sessions, one of the three law classes.[52]

Despite this provision, Budge does not appear in the matriculation registers of Edinburgh University.

Table 4.9 shows that increasing numbers of apprentices did attend Edinburgh University during the period of their indentures previous to compulsion. It is significant that the long-term increase in university enrollment was boosted from the mid 1870s by the introduction of the 1873 examination system of the SAE.

TABLE 4.9
SAE Apprentices 1837-1889 Who Attended Edinburgh University During Their Indentures

Attended Course In	Original Members	Year of Indenture Commencement							
		1837 -54	1855 -59	1860 -64	1865 -69	1870 -74	1875 -79	1880 -84	188 -8
Law	42	12	15	19	30	29	63	71	6
Arts	0	0	1	2	5	1	5	2	
Literature	1	1	4	0	0	0	0	0	
Medicine	0	0	0	0	1	0	0	0	
Mathematics	0	0	0	0	0	0	0	1	
Law + Literature	6	0	6	6	2	2	3	3	
Law + Medicine + Arts or Agriculture	0	1	0	2	1	0	0	0	
N Who Did Not Attend	30	12	14	17	15	20	21	26	1
% Who Did Attend	53.2	53.8	65.0	63.0	72.2	61.5	77.2	74.8	85
Mean Duration if Attended (sessions)	1.9	1.6	1.5	1.6	1.2	1.1	1.1	1.1	1

Source: calculated from Edinburgh University Matriculation Registers

It is also notable that SAE apprentices were spending less time at the University though studying more relevant subjects (Law) to the practice of accountancy and to succeeding in the final examination. It was not uncommon, especially among the pre-1870s cohorts, for apprentices to study a wide range of subjects during the period of their indentures. Charles H. Hughes, for example, attended courses in Arts, Medicine and Law between 1864 and 1868; Patrick Turnbull studied Agriculture, Medicine and Law between 1852 and 1857 as well as preparing to become a CA. Whether such recruits were simply extending their education or keeping their vocational options open in the event of their being unsuited to this rather unusual alternative profession is difficult to determine.

What is clear, however, is that attendance at the compulsory classes from their institution shows gradual improvement as success in the final examination became more difficult to achieve. This was especially the case regarding the Scots Law course with its direct relevance to two of the papers of the final examination. The following statistics illustrate the point.

TABLE 4.10
Percentage of SAE Apprentices Who Attended Compulsory Lectures at Edinburgh University (for cases where information is available)

Year of Indenture Commencement	% of Apprentices Who Attended N % of Possible Lectures					
	SCOTS LAW (52-60 Lectures)					
	20-39	40-59	60-79	80-89	100	N
1885-89	0	9.1	36.4	54.5	0	11
1890-94	2.2	7.9	37.1	48.3	4.5	89
1895-99	0.8	3.4	29.1	59.0	7.7	117
1900-04	0	2.4	24.2	69.5	3.9	128
1905-11	0.8	0.8	19.5	75.6	3.3	123
	CONVEYANCING/MERCANTILE LAW (24-28 Lectures)					
1885-89	0	9.1	18.2	45.4	27.3	11
1890-94	0	9.0	41.6	38.2	11.2	89
1895-99	0	2.6	35.0	54.7	7.7	117
1900-04	0.8	1.5	39.1	45.3	13.3	128
1905-11	0	0.8	22.1	57.4	19.7	122

The increasing numbers of apprentices who attended more than 80% of the lectures in Scots Law is particularly notable among the 1900 to 1911 groups who were confronted by ever-more daunting examination failure rates.

The trend toward improved attendance is also borne out by the increasing numbers of apprentices who sat the periodical class examinations that were attached to the university courses. In Scots Law, 94.3% of apprentices whose indentures commenced between 1905 and 1911 sat 80-100% of the examinations, compared to 43.3% of the 1890-4 intake. The corresponding figures for Conveyancing or Mercantile Law were 88.5% and 45.5%, respectively.

In addition to compulsory university courses, the SAE instituted from 1896 its own evening classes for apprentices which, according to Brown in 1905, "have been found most helpful in enabling apprentices to acquire that theoretical knowledge and book-learning which they can hardly be expected to obtain in their office work."[53] Previously, there had existed a series of lectures for apprentices provided in conjunction with the Institute of Bankers. The post-1896 classes were held at the SAE's Queen Street premises and covered subjects of direct import to the examinations such as: Auditing, Bankruptcy, Mathematics and Actuarial Science. 63 apprentices enrolled on the first course of lectures which were delivered by experts from the relevant professions.

CONCLUSIONS

It is apparent that over the 1854-1914 period an increasingly complex infrastructure was established by the SAE for the testing of the academic and practical abilities of recruits. This trend was precipitated largely by the rival claims of external accounting organizations to have provided for the training of a membership of equal competence, and was also a response to contemporary changes in the traits deemed necessary to have acquired in order for an occupation to deserve *professional* status. It is also unlikely to have escaped the attention of the policy-making office bearers of the Society that recruitment to the profession increased when more sophisticated systems of vocational preparation were introduced.

The individual most affected by these fundamental changes was the trainee professional. As the occupation proceded through the process of professionalization and parents demanded that their educated sons enter *learned* professions, apprentices were confronted with increasing numbers of obstacles to their qualification. This development had potentially far reaching consequences for the recruitment of sons from various social origins and their ability to achieve professional status.

Notes

1 *Index Juridicus: The Scottish Law List 1857* (Edinburgh, 1857), p.706.

2 Dicksee, *The Student's Guide to Accountancy,* p. 10.

3 Cross, *Choosing a Career,* p. 4.

4 *Ibid.*

5 *The Scottish Accountant* 1 (1893), p. 87. See also Reader, *Professional Men,* ch. 8.

6 Dicksee, *The Student's Guide to Accountancy,* p. 16.

7 *Index Juridicus* (1857), p. 706.

8 *Ibid.,* p. 705.

9 Privy Council, "SIA Petition" (1890), p. 3.

10 Finlay, "Speeches by Counsel" (1896), p. 17.

11 Privy Council, "SAE Petition", Appendix to the Petition of the Scottish Institute of Accountants for Grant of a Royal Charter, (1889), p. 73. (ICAS Collection, National Library of Scotland).

12 ICAS, *History of the Chartered Accountants of Scotland,* p. 12.

13 *Index Juridicus* (1857), p. 706.

14 These were the indentures of Norman M. Hart who was apprenticed (1905–10) to Andrew D. Fairbairn, CA in London, and; John M. MacDonald, apprenticed (1905–8) to Beilby and Gregor in Edinburgh. Neither became CAs.

15 SAE Register of Apprentices, vol. 1.

16 *Ibid.*

17 Dicksee, *The Student's Guide to Accountancy,* p. 11.

18 Information from interview with Alexander Harrison, CA, (admitted to the SAE in 1914), Edinburgh 13 December 1984; personal letter, 20 November 1984 from a CA apprenticed 1907–12 who wishes to remain anonymous.

19 *A Guide to the Accounting Profession,* p. 28.

20 Dicksee, *The Student's Guide to Accountancy,* p. 33.

21 *Ibid.,* p. 64.

22 Smith, *From Constable to Commissioner,* pp. 20–21.

23 Worthington, *Professional Accountants,* p. 3.

24 Personal letter, 20 November 1984 from a CA apprenticed 1907–12 who wishes to remain anonymous.

156

25 Hunter, "Rambling Remininscences", p. 25.

26 Personal letter, 20 November 1984 from a CA apprenticed 1907–12 who wishes to remain anonymous.

27 *The Accountant's Magazine* 13 (1909), p. 543.

28 Martin, *The Accountant Profession: A Public Danger,* p. 4.

29 *Index Juridicus, 1853,* p. xi.

30 *Index Juridicus* (1857), p. 706.

31 *The Accountant's Magazine* 13 (1909), p. 543.

32 Reader, *Professional Men,* ch. 3.

33 Report by the Council of the Faculty of Actuaries to the Meeting of the Faculty, 30 January 1857. From *Index Juridicus* (1857), p. 694. The mere fact that this report was printed in a law directory indicates that the Council of the Faculty were keen to publicize the nature of their new system of qualification to the legal profession and the public.

34 *The Accountant's Magazine* 78 (1974), p. 324.

35 SAE Annual General Meeting Minute Book, vol. 2, p. 11.

36 Constitution and Laws of the SAE 1889, reprinted in Privy Council, "SAE Petition" (1889–90), p. 109.

37 *The Scottish Accountant* 1 (1893), p. 79.

38 Martin, *The Accountant Profession: A Public Danger,* p. 21.

39 *The Scottish Accountant* 1 (1893), p. 50.

40 *The Accountant's Magazine* 16 (1912), p. 225.

41 *The Accountant's Magazine* 28 (1924), p. 311.

42 J.C. Stewart, "Qualification for Membership a Hundred Years Ago", *The Accountant's Magazine* 78 (1974), p. 265.

43 Hunter, "Rambling Reminiscences", p. 26.

44 Reports of GEB and examiners in *The Accountant's Magazine,* vols. 1–4.

45 *The Accountant's Magazine* 1 (1897), p. 125.

46 *The Accountant's Magazine* 3 (1899), p. 523.

47 *The Accountant's Magazine* 1 (1897), p. 653.

48 The *Accountant's Magazine* 14 (1910), p. 256.

49 Personal letter, 20 November 1984 from a CA apprenticed 1907-12 who wishes to remain anonymous.

50 *The Accountant's Magazine* 21 (1917), p. 268.

51 Privy Council, "SAE Petition" (1889–90), p. 109.

52 SAE Register of Indentures, vol. 1.

53 Brown, *A History of Accounting and Accountants,* p. 217.

5

Vocational Success and Failure : Professional Training, Qualification and Careers

> What is the most valuable asset for success as an accountant ?
> Five leading accountants replied, in effect,
> "common sense and business connections".

[D. Cross, *Choosing A Career,* 1908]

Having outlined the nature and process of vocational preparation to the SAE, this chapter investigates the extent to which the system acted as a barrier to the recruitment of sons from various social origins. The identification of the ascriptive and achievement factors that determined success or failure in the professional training system is a vitally important aspect of recruitment to the profession of Edinburgh chartered accountancy.

The emphasis in this chapter is placed upon identifying the likely reasons why apprentices commencing SAE indentures failed to become qualified CAs, and the conditions that permitted the remainder to succeed. The degree of success achieved by individuals in the training system and in susequent careers in relation to their social origins will also be subject to examination in order to further illuminate the conditions that ensured vocational advancement.

PROFESSIONAL TRAINING

For a small number of early recruits, the SAE indenture records provide the precise reason why an apprentice failed to qualify or at least indicate a possible explanation. In the majority of such cases, the alternative occupation adopted by the apprentice is provided as the cause ("joined Army", "Actuary to Caledonian" [insurance company], for example) or his location was listed ("in India" for instance). With the exception of those who ceased their apprenticeship through death or illness, these simple descriptions reveal little regarding the underlying reasons why an apprentice, for example, found it prudent to reject his professional training in favour of alternative employment or continually failed in the qualifying examinations.

Recent studies of trends in social mobility and the obstacles to upward movement have identified and attempted to measure the relative importance of a range of inequalities of opportunity on individual achievement.[1] Father's occupation, age, sex, ethnicity, family size, and overcrowding have all been hypothesized as ascriptive factors influencing individual ability to secure achievement at various stages of the attainment process (school, further education, occupational entrance, training and career). These factors have been considered as potentially significant to individual ability to secure upward social mobility, its distance and aspirations for status improvement.

It is the intention here to assess the relative importance of the demographic, occupational, residential, geographical, educational and vocational factors that were of possible significance in ensuring the success or failure of SAE apprentices in the system of vocational training. The analysis begins, however, with a chronological investigation of the number of recruits failing to qualify as CAs and become members of the SAE.

The Failure Rate 1837-1914

356 of the 1067 SAE apprentices contained in the study failed to qualify, that is 33.4%. If 9 indentures commencing between 1837 and 1849 are excluded (being recorded in the SAE books in 1854-5 to ensure that they were eligible for membership as having been past or current apprentices to original members so that all had essentially completed their training on registration), the failure rate was 33.6%. Figure 5.1 reveals that the failure rate over the 1850-1911 period exhibited considerable fluctuation. In general, the number of apprentices not becoming SAE members declined as a proportion of the total intake of recruits. Three relatively distinct periods in apprenticeship failure rates are discernible: those commencing indentures between 1850 and 1871, those recruited between 1872 and 1897 and those who entered SAE training between 1898 and 1911.

The 1850-71 period was characterized by high and fluctuating rates of failure. 53.3% of apprentices who embarked on an indenture failed to become CAs. Given the relatively simple system of examination and entrance during this period, the high rate was perhaps a surprising discovery. It can, however, be adequately explained.

Many, perhaps the majority of those not apparently succeeding in their apprenticeships during the 1850-71 period cannot justifiably be classed as having been *failures*. Their not becoming SAE members was predominantly a voluntary decision. During the 1853-60s period, when the SAE was in its infancy, it was not necessarily an occupational or social advantage to adopt the CA initials which were only attainable through membership of the Society. The public did not at first recognize the distinction between an SAE member and an ordinary accountant.

Consequently, it proved difficult during the early years of the Society, to encourage some members to pay annual subscriptions.[2] The letters **CA** "when originally used, merely expressed the simple fact that the person using them was a Member of a Body or Society of Accountants Incorporated by Royal Charter."[3]

Little pecuniary advantage appears to have accrued originally to the **CA** compared to the accountant. In these circumstances, it was difficult for a recruit who had completed his indenture to justify payment of a membership fee which would be better expended on helping to establish himself in practice. The pre-organization qualification of simply completing a practical training was sufficient to embark on a career as an accountant during this early period. Taking an examination and incurring the cost of membership were largely unnecessary inconveniences. This point is confirmed by the data presented in Table 5.1 which show that a high proportion of apprentices during the 1850-71 period who completed their training, did not join the SAE but became accountants. 22.8% of all apprentices whose indentures were discharged (that is, formally completed their indentures) but who did not become SAE members were known to have become accountants, compared to 7.7% of those apprentices whose indentures were not discharged between 1850 and 1911.

TABLE 5.1

SAE Apprentices Who Commenced Their Indentures 1850-1911 Who Were Discharged (completed their term of service) but Who Did Not Enter the Society

Year of Indenture Commencement	Number Discharged	As % of all Failing Apprentices	Number Known to have Become Accountants or Auditors
1850-54	2	11.8	0
1855-59	13	32.5	4
1860-64	14	30.4	4
1865-69	5	9.3	1
1870-74	4	7.7	2
1875-79	6	6.5	0
1880-84	10	9.7	2
1885-89	9	9.8	2
1890-94	8	6.8	3
1895-99	20	14.7	4
1900-04	29	18.0	7
1905-11	29	19.6	5
Total/Mean	149	14.0	34

It would appear that it was not until the late 1860s and early 1870s that SAE apprentices who completed their indentures (year of commencement plus 4 to 5

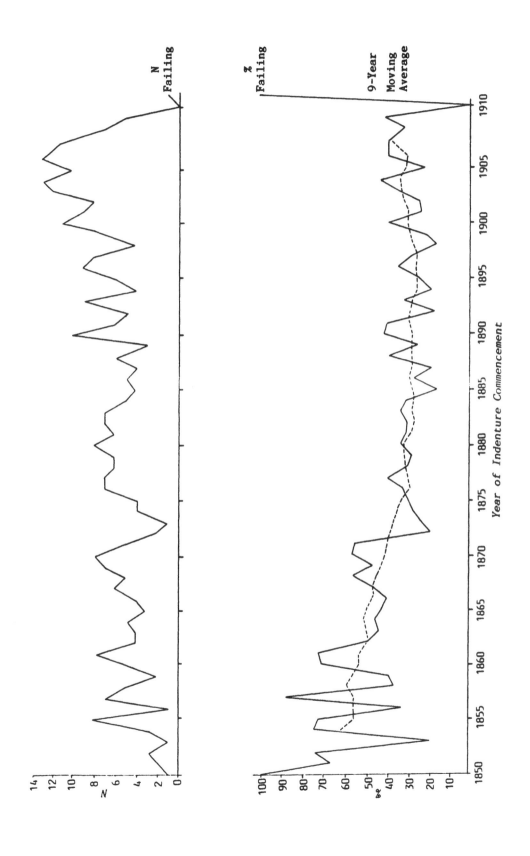

years) found it more desirable to apply for admission to the Society. The value of the CA notation seems to have become increasingly recognized by that time and, in the context of increasing professional competition, the accountant could expect to fare worse than the expanding numbers of qualified CAs.

From the intake of recruits of 1872, there was evidently a dramatic and sudden decline in the proportion of apprentices failing to qualify as SAE members. Thenceforth, until the late 1890s the failure rate was consistently low at 29.1%. The crucial event that precipitated this improvement in qualification was the introduction of the comprehensive examination system in 1873. Apprentices commencing their indentures from 1872 were subject to the conditions of the new regulations. Rather than acting to worsen the rate of qualification, the imposition of an additional structure in the process of vocational testing and selection at first worked to improve it.

Having passed through a complex system of examination, the successful apprentice could, from 1873, justifiably lay claim to superiority over the unqualified and inadequately prepared accountant. Membership of the SAE and the adoption of the CA letters were of considerably more value to the apprentice from the early-mid 1870s than they had been previously. Given the increasing competition for business during this period (see Figures 2.1 and 2.2), the individual claiming pre-eminence through holding a qualification that was a mark of academic as well as professional distinction was likely to benefit more than the individual relying solely on testimonials.

The initials CA were perceived increasingly as being of greater significance than a simple badge indicating an accountant's membership of an incorporated organization. By 1889, the SAE could assert that the notation "is a generally known and appreciated guarantee to the public of professional efficiency and good standing and conduct."[4] Consequently, it claimed that the designation CA came to have a definite meaning in the minds of the Scottish public as belonging to those fit to be entrusted with the most important business. "The letters CA after a few years at once marked out a man as belonging to the highest branch of the profession and for that reason lead to his getting work."[5]

Potential clients were disposed increasingly to take their business to the qualified practitioner in a period when professional qualifications gained on the basis of academic training were assuming greater importance. The counsel for the Scottish CA societies in 1890, for instance, noted that: "The public naturally conclude that an unchartered is in some way professionally inferior to a chartered accountant."[6]

The importance of the acquisition of the CA designation had become so great by the

1880s and 1890s that, as mentioned in Chapter 1, rival organizations fought fiercely against their exclusive usage by the three Scottish chartered societies who were gaining more business as a result. According to Martin, CAs took maximum advantage of their delineation of professional status over the **accountant**. The initials were used by SAE members not only for business purposes "but you see them used in all sorts of ways in their private life and conduct. They put them upon their intimations of births, their marriages and deaths, nay, even on their tombstones."[7]

From 1873, the qualification and membership of the SAE was a more essential requisite to a successful career in accountancy; it was no longer sufficient for the recruit to have simply completed an apprenticeship and deem himself an *accountant*. There now existed two grades of accountant and one was significantly superior in status to the other. It would appear reasonably safe to assume, therefore, that non-qualifiers during the 1872-97 and the following period were *involuntary* failures.

The institution of the GEB examinations in 1893 and a more exacting examination procedure, briefly acted to further reduce the SAE failure rate in that it also increased the value of a CA qualification as a mark of professional knowledge and distinction, ensuring that apprentices were even less inclined to contemplate not becoming members of the Society. From the late 1890s, however, as professional competition reached its peak, there existed a growing dichotomy between apprentices' aspirations for qualification and the examination standards required for success. The failure rate during this 1898-1911 period rose steadily reflecting the increasing severity of examinations. The mean failure rate of apprentices commencing their indentures in this period was 30.3%.

With these trends in the qualification rate in mind, the chapter will proceed to investigate some of the more specific determinants of individual success or failure in the professional training system.

<u>Demographic Factors in Vocational Success and Failure: Mortality and Morbidity</u>

From a search of statutory registers for deaths in Scotland, and in a few cases, from the records of the SAE, it was discovered that 19 of the apprentices contained in the study died during their indentures or previous to qualification. Table 5.2 provides details pertaining to each case.

Mortality as a cause of indenture cessation declined over the 1850-1911 period. 2.0% of apprentices who commenced their indentures between 1850 and 1889 died compared to 1.6% for the 1890-1911 group (1.3% for 1900-11 indentures only). The social origins of recruits who died during training (see final column of Table 5.2) were generally reflective of trends in the social origins of all apprentices. The nature of the causes of death also indicate that mortality was largely independent of the income of the apprentice's family. The major killers of apprentices until the 1880s were diseases that were associated with inadequate urban sanitation. From then until 1898, the main causes of death were respiratory and related to office conditions. Subsequent deaths were caused mainly by congenital disorders.

TABLE 5.2
SAE Apprentices Whose Indentures Commenced 1837-1911 Who
Failed to Qualify as Members Due to Mortality

Year of Indenture Commencement	Period of Indenture Expired at Death (Years)	Age at Death	Cause of Death	SSG of Father
1855	2.35	19	Typhus Fever	2
1858	1.99	20	Tuberculosis	2
1865	4.81	21	Enteritis	2
1866	4.18	23	Pleurisy	4
1869	3.91	22	Phthisis	5
1869	1.04	21	Typhoid Fever	2
1870	3.47	20	Typhoid Fever	4
1870	3.08	..	...	4
1882	4.83	23	Tuberculosis	3
1884	2.23	20	Phthisis	4
1890	4.29	21	Peritonitis	2
1893	4.25	21	Empyema	2
1896	3.47	21	Pulmonary Tuberculosis	2
1897	4.99	22	Phthisis	6
1898	4.67	21	Brain Disease	4
1900	0.87	19	Nephritis	6
1901	2.12	20	Syncope	1
1903	3.32	21	Pulmonary Tuberculosis	2
1907	1.96	22	Mitral & Aortic Disease	2
Mean	3.25	20.94		

The most prevalent causes of mortality over the whole period were related to conditions in the apprentice's work place. Pulmonary Tuberculosis or Phthisis was a notorious killer among white collar workers in the nineteenth century.[8] The CA apprentice was employed in an environment akin to that of the law clerk who the Registrar-General for Scotland in 1895 and 1905 considered to be particularly subject to those diseases spread by the inhalation or ingestion of the tubercle bacilli in dust laden atmospheres.[9] In 1890-2, Phthisis accounted for 16.8% of all male deaths between the ages of 15 and 65 in Scotland, compared to 34.2% for law clerks and

24.6% for bank and insurance clerks.[10]

Edinburgh CAs' offices were not likely to have been any safer places in which to work than those of legal practitioners. Alexander T. Hunter, CA recalled for instance, how long hours were spent in confined spaces working on dusty books during the period of his indenture (1876-81): "We clerks and apprentices (five in number) worked in the room behind the cash room, so that, when some of the apprentices were not engaged on an outside audit, we were pretty cramped."[11] During the early part of the 1853-1914 period the problem of limited space was aggravated by the tendency of CAs to reside and work in the same premises.

7 apprentices appear to have failed to complete their indentures due to illness though, if the information was available, there would undoubtedly have been a greater number. The specific illness preventing qualification is not provided in SAE apprenticeship records though in 2 cases a search of the death indexes for Scotland revealed that the apprentice died soon after the termination of the indenture due to Phthisis Pulmonalis (1884 and 1905 were the years of death). 2 others, whose training was ended through illness, are also known to have died young but appear to have done so in England.

Those 26 SAE recruits whose professional training was essentially curtailed by the *visitation of Providence* are mostly excluded from the remaining analysis of this chapter as their failure to qualify does not appear to have been related to their social status origins or other potentially significant determinants of vocational success. The failure rate excluding this group over the whole period was 31.7% of apprentices who commenced their indentures between 1837 and 1911.

The existence of living parents may be hypothesized as a further possible demographic factor that potentially influenced the apprentice's ability to succeed in the system of professional training in that their loss had implications for the provision of family stability and finance. The death of a parent during the term of an indenture was a catastrophic event with many attendant consequences for the recruit and his vocational preparation.[12] Information contained in SAE indenture books and civil registers as well as the census permitted the computation of the Table 5.3 over.

It would appear from the evidence provided in the table that the existence or otherwise of living parents at the outset of recruitment had little impact on the apprentice's ability to qualify as a CA. A father was the parent whose loss was potentially the most disruptive to training in that he was frequently the payer of indenture and entrance fees. Yet, the failure rate among apprentices who had a living father or step father at the commencement of their indentures was, at 30.8%, only marginally below the general mean of 31.7%. The failure rate among those without fathers was 31.9%.

TABLE 5.3
Parents of SAE Apprentices 1837–1911 Living at the Commencement of Indentures (excluding apprentices who failed to qualify due to death or ill health)

Parents of the Apprentice Living at Indenture Commencement	% Failed to Qualify	% Qualified	N of Cases
Both Alive	31.3	68.7	387
Father Alive, Mother Dead	31.9	68.1	47
Father Alive, Mother Not Known	30.0	70.0	293
Father Alive with Stepmother	0.0	100.0	6
Stepfather Alive with Mother	60.0	40.0	5
Father Dead, Mother Alive	32.7	67.3	208
Father Dead, Mother Not Known	0.0	100.0	2
Both Dead	29.0	71.0	38
Not Known	43.6	56.4	55
			1041

These figures, together with the large number of apprentices who embarked on a CAs training without a living father indicates that, given prevailing mortality conditions, considerable foresight was exercised by middle class fathers in the adequate provision for their wives and children following death.[13] It was highly unlikely that a costly SAE indenture would have been entered into unless it was expected to have a successful conclusion given the existence or non-existence of certain parents or guardians at its commencement.

Losing a parent *during* the term of the indenture was potentially a more disruptive event in an apprentice's vocational preparation. Table 5.4 shows that for the categories where enumeration has been possible, 8.3% of all apprentices who commenced their training between 1837 and 1911 lost at least one parent during the term of their indentures, though the proportion declined as the general mortality rate improved over the period. It appears from the table that the loss of a parent was only catastrophic to an apprentice's career if the death left him orphaned. 30.3% (column b) of apprentices who lost their father though their mother survived during the term of service (excluding those who died or ceased training through illness themselves) failed to qualify as CAs, compared to 53.3% (columns a+c+d) of those who were left with no parents.

TABLE 5.4
Identified Mortality Among the Parents of SAE Apprentices
1837-1911 During the Term of Their Son's Indentures

Year of Indenture Commencement	a	b	c	d	As % of all Indentures
1837-54	0	3	0	0	11.5
1855-64	0	7	3	1	12.8
1865-74	1	16	1	2	18.9
1875-84	0	14	0	4	9.2
1885-94	0	15	1	0	7.7
1895-04	0	10	1	1	4.0
1905-11	0	11	0	0	7.4
Total	1	76	6	8	
Failed to Qualify	0	23	4	4	

Code:

a = both alive at commencement, both died during term.

b = both alive at commencement, father died during term.

c = only father living at commencement and he died during term.

d = only mother living at commencement and she died during term.

Demographic Factors in Vocational Success and Failure: Fertility and the Distribution of Familial Resources

Family size has long been regarded as an important factor in the ability of offspring to achieve upward social mobilty. The original hypothesis which has since undergone some refinement was expounded by Dumont in 1890: "Just as a column of liquid has to be thin in order to rise under the forces of capillarity, so a family must be small in order to rise in the social scale."[14]

Families with few children are in a good position to concentrate resources and provide opportunities for the achievement and upward mobility of their offspring. Large families have to divide limited resources among more children thus reducing parental ability to provide advantages in the attainment process. Blau and Duncan, for example, have shown that in the US men from small families tend to achieve greater occupational status than those from large families, principally because their parents were able to devote more resources to providing their sons with a good schooling.[15]

It would therefore seem desirable to examine the possibility that SAE recruits from small families were more successful in the professional training system than those from large families.

Table 5.5 suggests that, except in very large families, the rate of non-qualification did not increase with the number of children. The failure rate among apprentices from families of between one and four children was 30.8% compared to 30.5% for those from families of between five and nine children, and 34.4% from those containing ten or more offspring.

TABLE 5.5
Total Known Fertility of the Parents of SAE Apprentices 1837-1911
(excluding those who failed to qualify due to death or ill health)

Total Children in Apprentice's Family	N of Apprentices From Such a Family	% of Apprentices Failed to Qualify	Total Sons in Apprentice's Family	N of Apprentices From Such a Family	% of Apprentic Failed t Qualify
1	41	34.1	1	147	32.0
2	105	39.0	2	227	31.3
3	145	30.3	3	224	29.5
4	147	24.5	4	175	36.6
5	144	26.4	5	103	26.2
6	119	34.5	6	48	20.8
7	100	24.0	7	19	21.1
8	79	32.9	8	5	60.0
9	36	47.2			
10	17	30.8			
11	9	33.3			
12	6	66.7			
Not Known	93	40.9		93	40.9
Total	1041			1041	

Clearly, the capillarity hypothesis did not apply among SAE apprentices during their training (though it may have done so in earlier stages of the attainment process; in the educational system, for example). Indeed, the statistics for sons provided in Table 5.5 (which were most significant in terms of the cost of vocational preparation) would appear to indicate that the greater the number of siblings, the lower was the rate of failure.

Table 5.6 attempts to assess whether family size had any impact upon qualification among SAE apprentices from various social status origins. We might expect to discover evidence of the relevance of family size to achievement among recruits from lower status groups due to the greater effect on family resource distribution of additional children in situations where income was more limited.

TABLE 5.6
Percentage Failure Rate Among SAE Apprentices 1837–1911 From Various
Social Status Origins According to Family Size (excluding apprentices
who failed to qualify due to death or ill health)

| Total Known: | % Failing to Qualify From SSG | | | | | | | | | |
	1	2	3	4	5	6	7	8	9	N
Children										
1–4	32.1	27.2	39.4	22.0	54.2	20.5	26.0	35.0	35.4	425
5 or 5+	38.7	34.8	25.5	33.8	32.0	23.1	15.6	31.0	75.0	509
										934
Sons										
1–2	42.1	32.2	29.0	26.1	60.0	25.0	25.8	30.6	50.0	366
3 or 3+	25.8	31.0	32.7	30.6	35.3	20.0	17.9	36.4	44.4	568
N of Families	50	344	80	118	49	91	118	69	15	934

Again, at either end of the status hierarchy, no such relationship between family size and non-qualification is discernible. If the failure rate of apprentices from each social status group is examined according to the number of children and number of sons in the family, the fluctuations seem to be random. Only among apprentices from SSG 4 (commerce) was the failure rate lower in families which contained a small number of children and a small number of sons.

The apparent insignificance of family size to success in vocational preparation would appear to indicate that the parents of SAE apprentices deliberately restricted their fertility to a level which enabled them to provide resources for the recruitment of their sons to desirable occupations. Alternatively, their ability to enter sons in a professional vocation may have been a fortuitous consequence of unplanned factors preventing the birth of large numbers of children.

Table 5.7 is an attempt to illustrate that the fertility of parents in the lower social status groups (SSGs 5–9) who bore a son entering an SAE indenture was below that of the mean for that social status group as a whole as revealed by the 1911 Fertility Census for Scotland.

TABLE 5.7

**Mean Fertility of the Parents of SAE Apprentices 1837–1911 (where known)
by That for Comparable Occupational Titles Enumerated in the 1911
Fertility Census[16]**

SSG of Father	a 1911 Fertility Census	b Apprentices' Parents	a-b	Mean Sons of Apprentices' Parents	N of SAE Parents
1	4.71	5.19	-0.48	3.05	51
2	4.34	5.33	-0.99	3.29	355
3	5.83	5.40	0.43	3.27	81
4	4.92	5.21	-0.29	3.23	119
5	6.12	4.94	1.18	3.10	50
6	5.41	4.76	0.65	3.15	93
7	4.75	4.20	0.55	2.62	120
8	5.74	4.15	1.59	2.80	70
9	6.66	3.73	2.93	2.46	15

Evidently, the fertility experience of SAE apprentices' parents in the lower middle class and working class status groups was at variance with the Scottish national differential fertility profile of the 1860–1911 period. It is clear that, among apprentices' parents earning higher incomes, family size was less of a hindrance to commencing a CA indenture than for those on lower incomes. For working class parents (SSGs 8-9), in particular, the entrance of sons into SAE indentures was only possible through an intentional or accidental drastic reduction in marital fertility.

The question of whether or not the below-average fertility of lower status parents was planned in order to secure the upward mobility of fewer sons to the professions is difficult to answer. Some recent commentators have suggested that fertility restriction among lower white collar workers, for example, was deliberate. Goldthorpe *et al.* noted in *The Affluent Worker in the Class Structure* (1969) that:

> The explanation of this phenomenon that has found widest acceptance is that lower white-collar couples tend to be highly status-conscious and thus restrict the size of their families stringently in order to conserve their resources for forms of consumption consistent with their status aspirations, and also to give the children they do have the best possible chances for achieving further mobility.[17]

Those parents of marginal middle class status in nineteenth century Edinburgh; the shopkeepers, clerks and artisans observed in this study were, as illustrated in Chapter 2, also highly motivated to the generational improvement of social status.[18] It would seem doubtful that socially ambitious parents in these status groups were not aware of the advantages that might accrue from the distribution of resources among fewer sons given the contemporary importance of finance in securing an appropriate education and entrance to the local professions.

The example of the opportunities available to sons from small families was provided by the higher middle class groups to whom those of marginal status most aspired and emulated. It is not inconceivable that increasing numbers of lower middle class and upper working class parents adopted practices of fertility restriction to allow for the possibility of the upward movement of sons, before the rest of their status group adhered to family limitation following the example provided by those of greater social status. *Blackwood's Magazine* in 1867 recognized that the socially ambitious among the lower classes " are copying us daily in more points than either they or we are willing to allow."[19]

Gray has shown that the labour aristocrat of Victorian Edinburgh occupied a social position that "pre-disposed him to envisage a relatively long run project of improvement in his personal situation."[20] This was achieved through delayed marriage, thrift and temperance, and although few contemplated *intra* generational mobility out of the working class, an *inter* generational improvement was desired. Given the large number of SAE apprentices who derived from these marginal social status groups (as will be shown in Chapter 7), it would not seem exaggerated to suggest that some highly motivated parents were extending these restrictive practices into their fertility experience to secure the mobility of their offspring.

It may have been the case, as Banks has suggested, that some lower status parents anxious to secure the social improvement of sons through reduced fertility achieved for them greater upward mobility than originally envisaged. An Edinburgh shopkeeper, for example, might have limited family size in order to provide opportunities for his sons to enter commerce. The increasing availability of a cheap secondary education in Merchant Company schools coupled with an awareness of, and connections with, CAs permitted the unexpected though desirable entrance of a son to one of the local new professions.

The likelihood that fertility was reduced deliberately among many lower status parents of SAE apprentices on the basis of the emulation of practices adopted by higher social groups is confirmed if those recruits that derived from semi and unskilled manual families (SSG 9) are examined.

6 of the 17 apprentices from this category were the sons of domestic servants and these formed the parentage of all but one apprentice from SSG 9 origins indentured between 1873 and 1890. Domestic servants were not only in direct residential and

occupational contact with the middle classes, they were also notoriously emulative of their employers (where possible) and highly aspirant toward social advance. 2 other SSG 9 apprentices were, similarly, the sons of a music hall caretaker, an occupation associated with higher society. From 1890, 4 SSG 9 sons were derived from a comparatively well-paid and socially aspirant section of the lower working class; railway workers on the margins of labour aristocratic standing.

As well as family size, sibling position in the sequence of births has been found to be a significant determinant of the attainment of offspring. Studies have shown that the eldest and youngest children have tended to be more successful in the educational and occupational processes than middle children.[21] Eldest sons, in particular, for whom parents are usually most ambitious, have been considered as being highly motivated to achievement at school and provided with a disproportionate share of family resources to encourage their social advancement.

During the nineteenth century, it was likely to have been the ordinal position of sons that was of greatest potential importance to attainment in that a comparatively small proportion of resources was necessary for the occupational preparation of daughters: elder sons were the principal bearers of family status in the succeeding generation. Table 5.8 reveals the ordinal position of SAE apprentices according to their social origins.

TABLE 5.8
The Position of SAE Apprentices 1837-1911 in the Sequence of Known Male Births of Their Parents (where known)

Ordinal Position of Son	SSG of Father (%)									N
	1	2	3	4	5	6	7	8	9	
Eldest and Only	11.8	13.0	16.0	13.6	16.0	9.7	21.7	26.1	26.7	14
Eldest of 2-3	13.7	13.3	13.6	18.6	16.0	17.2	25.8	14.5	20.0	15
Eldest of 4-4+	9.8	6.2	6.2	5.9	4.0	3.2	2.5	5.8	0.0	5
Middle of 3-4	13.7	20.7	18.5	17.0	34.0	17.2	10.0	14.5	26.7	17
Middle of 5-5+	9.8	12.5	16.1	14.4	6.0	14.0	5.8	10.1	6.6	11
Youngest of 2-3	31.4	21.8	18.5	23.7	12.0	29.0	28.4	20.3	20.0	22
Youngest of 4-4+	9.8	12.5	11.1	6.8	12.0	9.7	5.8	8.7	0.0	9
Total	100.0	100.0	100.0	100.0	100.0	100.0	100.0	100.0	100.0	95
Total Eldest	35.3	32.6	35.8	38.1	36.0	30.1	50.0	46.4	46.7	35
Total Middle	23.5	33.1	34.6	31.4	40.0	31.2	15.8	24.6	33.3	28
Total Youngest	41.2	34.3	29.6	30.5	24.0	38.7	34.2	29.0	20.0	31
Total	100.0	100.0	100.0	100.0	100.0	100.0	100.0	100.0	100.0	95
Number of Cases	51	353	81	118	50	93	120	69	15	

It is difficult to remove the effects of differential fertility from the above statistics. For example, the lower fertility of SSG 6-9 parents increased the possibility that the SAE recruit from these origins would be an eldest or a youngest son. Allowing for this, it would still seem apparent that a higher proportion of apprentices from the marginal, socially aspirant SSGs 7-9 were eldest sons. This suggests that these lower middle and working class parents were eager that their eldest sons should enter the CA profession to improve the generational status of the family. When the rate of non-qualification was examined according to ordinal position in the sequence of known male births, four distinct social groups of apprentices emerged. These are revealed in Table 5.9.

TABLE 5.9
The Failure Rate Among SAE Apprentices 1837-1911 From Various
Social Status Origins According to Position in the Sequence
of Known Male Births (excluding those apprentices who
failed to qualify due to death or ill health)

Ordinal Position	% Failing by SSG of Father				
of Son	1+5	2+3	4+6+7+8	9	All
Eldest	55.6	31.9	23.6	57.1	31.1
Middle	43.8	32.9	30.7	40.0	31.1
Youngest	25.8	30.5	26.0	66.7	30.7
N Sons Failing	42	134	104	8	288

The table shows that apprentices from landed and agricultural families (SSGs 1 and 5) were more likely to qualify as CAs the lower down they were in the sequence of male births. The most convincing explanation for this was that the younger sons of parents in these groups were less affected by primogeniture and occupational inheritance that could disrupt or render unnecessary the alternative career of an elder son. Additionally, a proportion of eldest sons from these social origins can be assumed as having entered an SAE indenture in order to gain experience in estate or farm management as a prelude to inheritance with no real intention of entering the CA profession (as was suggested in Chapter 3). By contrast, the eldest sons (and to a lesser extent the youngest) of parents in the commerce, distribution and processing, white collar, and, skilled manual groups (SSGs 4, 6-8) who entered into an SAE apprenticeship exhibited a lower rate of non-qualification compared to middle sons. Parents of recruits from these social groups were located well below professional (SSG 2) standing in the status hierarchy, and were likely to have been the most eager that it was their eldest son who should have been intergenerationally upwardly mobile to improve the social standing of the family.

Among apprentices who had parents in or on the borders of professional status (SSGs 2-3), there was probably less social pressure to ensure the success of an eldest son entering the CA profession for the generational enhancement of family status, as they were either close to, or had already attained, SSG 2 standing. Ordinal position was, in these circumstances, of less importance. The pressure to succeed within these families was likely to have been greatest on elder sons who entered the older, higher status, traditional professions. Among the few SAE apprentices from semi or unskilled manual families (SSG 9), any preference for the upward social mobility of the eldest son was probably outweighed by material disadvantages to qualification, though the small numbers involved make any firm conclusions hazardous for this group.

The Occupation and Social Status of the Apprentice's Father

Given the importance of possessing adequate funds in order to embark on an SAE apprenticeship in the form of indenture, examination, class and entrance fees, the occupation of the apprentice's father and its associated level of remuneration might be hypothesized as having been a significant determinant of success in the SAE system of vocational preparation. The information contained in Table 5.10 suggests that this was the case.

TABLE 5.10
Social Status Group of the Fathers of SAE Apprentices 1837-1911 (where known and excluding apprentices who failed to qualify due to death or ill health)

	SSG of Father	N of Apprentices Qualifying	N of Apprentices Not Qualifying	% Failed to Qualify
1	Independent Means	31	24	43.6
2	Professions	246	117	32.2
3	Manufacturers	59	25	29.8
4	Commerce	88	36	29.0
5	Farmers	31	21	40.4
6	Distribution & Processing	76	21	21.6
7	White Collar	102	30	22.7
8	Skilled Manual	52	25	32.5
9	Semi & Unskilled Manual	9	8	47.1
	Total/Mean	694	307	30.7

There was evidently quite a considerable variation in the rate of success according to the apprentice's social origins from which some important conclusions can be deducted. Contrary to expectations, there was not an inverse relationship between father's social status and the failure rate. The high proportions of SAE recruits not qualifying from high income, independent means (SSG 1) origins appears to have been the result of a low emphasis placed on the need to qualify to the lower than parental status occupation of chartered accountancy. The pressure on sons from this group to enter the SAE was reduced by the knowledge that future income was likely to be derived primarily from inheritance rather than through professional practice. The same applies to apprentices from farming origins (SSG 5); the necessity of qualification being lessened when it was clear that the elder sons could revert to the family holding.

Excluding SSG 5, the rate of failure declined with social status in SSGs 1-6 as the pressure to qualify increased. The son of a high earning professional was likely to have been more confident than that of a lower salaried clerk that, if his CA indenture was not successfully completed, his father had the means available to enter him into an alternative high status occupation. It may be inferred that the pressure on sons from origins on the margins of middle class status was particularly virulent. Not only had their parents undergone some financial sacrifice in order to pay for training costs, they expected reward for their efforts and ambitions through the upward mobility of their offspring which was attainable by their entering the professions. The increased pressure on lower middle and working class SAE apprentices to succeed and perform well in vocational preparation was reflected in their record in winning examination prizes and distinctions from 1873. 12.2% of recruits from SSGs 6-9 won a prize for examination performance or passed their final with distinction, compared to 10.1% of apprentices from SSG 1-5 origins.

Parents and apprentices from working class origins (SSGs 8-9) had most to lose if an SAE indenture was not completed successfully in terms of expenditure and investment in their son's future. The higher failure rate among these apprentices suggests that certain material obstacles to qualification were too great to be overcome, especially for those who derived from semi and unskilled manual families (SSG 9). One of these disadvantages was probably the deleterious consequences of overcrowding as indicated in Table 5.11. If the rate of non-qualification is examined during the 1850-1911 period by the social status group of the apprentice's father, certain indicators emerge that lead to a possible identification of other barriers to a successful indenture. It seems desirable to combine certain social status groups which exhibited a similar experience in Table 5.10. Table 5.12 shows that the failure rate of apprentices from various social origins fluctuated over the period.

TABLE 5.11

Ratio of Number of Windowed Rooms in SAE Apprentice's Parent's or Guardian's Household to Number of Children (from Censuses of 1861-91)

	SSG of Father	Windowed Rooms / N of Children	Number of Children
1	Independent Means	3.79	73
2	Professions	2.92	511
3	Manufacturers	3.41	97
4	Commerce	2.73	170
5	Farmers	2.46	59
6	Ditribution & Processing	1.90	135
7	White Collar	2.07	149
8	Skilled Manual	2.00	88
9	Semi & Unskilled Manual	1.28	23

TABLE 5.12

Percentage of SAE Apprentices Who Failed to Qualify by Social Status of Father (excluding apprentices who failed to qualify due to death or ill health)

SSG of Father	Year of Indenture Commencement					
	1850-59	1860-69	1870-79	1880-89	1890-99	1900-11
1	100.0	80.0	36.4	31.3	44.4	57.1
2	44.8	46.4	36.9	29.1	20.5	27.8
3+4	60.0	50.0	25.0	29.5	28.1	27.7
5	85.7	33.3	16.7	28.6	45.5	42.9
6+7	33.3	25.0	18.5	15.0	14.3	29.6
8+9	50.0	57.1	54.5	26.3	24.0	36.7

The lack of success among apprentices in the 1850-59 and 1860-69 cohorts indicated in Table 5.12 can be explained largely by the low pecuniary advantage to be gained from SAE membership as explained earlier in the chapter. The most significant statistics are those for 1890 to 1911. With the exception of recruits from independent means (SSG 1) origins, for whom qualification was less of a financial necessity, the impact of the development of a more severe standard in examinations from the late 1890s was markedly different between those of high and low status origins. The failure rate among recruits from lower middle and working class families (SSGs 6-9) in 1900 to 1911 rose by 73.0% on its 1890 to 1899 figure, compared to 4.6% for those who had derived from upper middle class origins (SSGs 2-5).

It would seem that the success of SAE apprentices from lower status origins was sensitive to the standard of professional examinations. The rate of non-qualification was generally much lower during the 1880s and 1890s when examinations were less severe and required only a basic scholastic and vocational education to pass. As the standard required for examination success rose, the superior education received by those from higher middle class origins and their ability to afford personal tuition and coaching ensured that they were much better prepared to cope with the more exacting papers of the final examination in particular and, therefore, to successfully complete an SAE indenture.

Rather than to widen the opportunities for the recruitment of sons from lower status origins, the movement to place entrance to the profession increasingly on the basis of meritocratic success tested by examination, acted in the opposite direction. As one correspondent to *The Scottish Accountant*, commenting on CAs opinions of their examination system, noted in 1893:

> I was left with the impression that the only conception these writers had of the benefit of the Institute's examinations was, not that the culture of knowledge which it was necessary to undergo and acquire in order to pass them might better qualify them for performing with credit their duties as accountants, but as a means of preventing persons with perhaps less favourable opportunities becoming members of the Institute, and thereby restricting the privileges of such membership to a favoured number.[22]

This proposition is confirmed if the educational origins of SAE recruits commencing their indentures between 1837 and 1911 are examined.

Education

The failure rate among apprentices according to the last type of school attended previous to indenture recruitment (which was that most likely to have been of greatest importance to preparation for occupational entrance) is provided in Table 5.13. It is clear from the final column of the table that a secondary education was of great importance to the SAE recruit's ability to qualify as a CA. Among those who received a secondary schooling only those who attended the eminent public schools of England, who were derived predominantly from the highest income families and for whom a successful indenture was not so vital, exhibited an excessive rate of failure. Similarly, a foreign education or private education appears to have provided an inadequate preparation for a successful SAE indenture.

TABLE 5.13

The Failure Rate of SAE Apprentices 1837–1911 by Last Known Type of School Attended (excluding apprentices who failed to qualify due to death or ill health)[23]

Type of School	Number Attended	% Attended	% Failed to Qualify
Scottish			
Parish or Board School	35	3.8	37.1
Private or State Aided Elementary School	30	3.3	30.0
High Class Public School (Secondary)	90	9.8	21.1
High Class Private School (Secondary)	658	71.4	26.9
Technical School or College	4	0.4	25.0
English and Welsh			
The Great Public Schools	34	3.7	35.3
Grammar, Cathedral or County Schools	25	2.7	24.0
Other Private Secondary Schools	13	1.4	30.8
Professional and Scientific Institutions	4	0.4	25.0
Other			
Foreign Schools	12	1.3	33.3
Private Tuition or Classes/Educated at Home	17	1.8	47.1
Total	922	100.0	

Table 5.14 illustrates that, with the exception of those who received only an elementary schooling, apprentices from lower status origins did not generally derive from schools that produced the higher rates of failure in SAE indentures.

4.7% of apprentices from lower middle and working class origins (SSGs 6–9) completed their scholastic careers at a Scottish parish or board school, compared to 3.4% of apprentices from upper middle class origins (SSGs 1–5). Of those whose last school was a Scottish higher class *public* school which offered the best preparation for a successful indenture, 8.7% derived from SSGs 1–5 compared to 12.2% from SSGs 6–9. Of those who attended the most numerically significant kind of school, the Scottish high class *private* type, 72.1% of SAE recruits were from SSGs 1–5 backgrounds compared to 70.3% from SSGs 6–9. Evidently, lower status parents of SAE apprentices were distributing their available resources to enable their sons to enter schools that were considered generally to have been the preserve of the middle classes.

TABLE 5.14
Last Known School Attended by All SAE Apprentices 1837-1911 by
Social Status Group of Father (where known)

School Type in Descending Order By Success in SAE Indentures	% of Apprentices with Father in SSG									N
	1	2	3	4	5	6	7	8	9	
High Class Public	10.4	10.2	7.3	7.0	2.3	12.6	9.2	14.9	14.3	89
Grammar/Cathedral/County	4.2	2.4	1.2	3.5	7.0	1.1	2.5	3.0	0.0	24
Technical	0.0	0.3	0.0	0.0	0.0	0.0	2.5	0.0	0.0	4
Professional and Scientific	0.0	0.0	1.2	0.9	0.0	0.0	0.0	0.0	7.1	3
High Class Private	62.5	69.7	73.2	83.3	69.8	78.9	69.2	61.2	64.3	655
Private/Aided Elementary	4.2	2.1	1.2	0.9	2.3	2.1	8.3	10.4	7.1	32
Other Secondary	0.0	2.1	1.2	1.7	0.0	0.0	0.8	0.0	0.0	11
Foreign	2.1	1.5	2.4	0.9	0.0	0.0	0.8	1.5	0.0	11
The Great Public	14.5	5.7	3.7	0.9	2.3	0.0	0.8	0.0	0.0	32
Parish or Board	0.0	3.6	3.7	0.0	14.0	2.1	4.2	9.0	7.2	35
Private Tutor/Classes/Home	2.1	2.4	4.9	0.9	2.3	3.2	1.7	0.0	0.0	20
Total	100	100	100	100	100	100	100	100	100	916

What Table 5.14 fails to show is the impact that an education in the various types of institution had on the failure rate of those from certain social origins. Among apprentices whose indentures were not terminated by death or ill health, the failure rate of those from lower middle and working class origins (SSGs 6-9) who attended a high class *public* school at some time during their school career was 18.6% compared to the general failure rate of 26.0% for those from these origins. Similarly, if an apprentice of low status parents attended at some period a high class *private* school, the failure rate fell to 19.8%. For those apprentices with SSG 6-9 origins who attended a Scottish parish or board school, the rate of non-qualification rose to 30.2%. The effect of an adequate secondary education on vocational success was particularly marked among apprentices from distribution and processing and white collar families (SSGs 6-7). The material disadvantages suffered by apprentices from unskilled and semi skilled manual origins (SSG 9) were apparently too great to be favourably outweighed by a suitable education.

A secondary education was clearly of great benefit to SAE apprentices from the lower half of the status hierarchy who were less likely to have had access to sufficient funds to pay for items to improve a son's performance *during* training such as coaching and private tuition should his schooling have proved deficient. This is confirmed by the following analysis. The major schools attended by 20 or more recruits during their school careers with information pertinent to each is provided in Tables 5.15 and 5.16.

Table 5.16 indicates that, if apprentices from low social status origins could gain entrance to one of these major schools (all of which were essentially secondary schools or had secondary departments), their opportunities for success, in the majority of cases, were improved. For those who derived from upper middle class families (SSGs 1-5) and who attended the more expensive or exclusive institutions, the impact of the nature of the school attended on qualification was of less significance to their success in vocational training. Note that the rate of non-qualification was affected much less by their education for apprentices who had fathers in SSGs 1-5 compared to those who derived from SSGs 6-9. The information contained in Table 5.16 also reveals a further significant point. It is apparent that, if sons from the lower middle or working classes could gain access to the high fee, upper middle class institutions (where over 70% of attenders had SSG 1-5 fathers), their ability to qualify as a CA were improved dramatically. Of the 44 apprentices from SSG 6-9 families who entered Fettes College, Edinburgh Collegiate School, Edinburgh Academy, Edinburgh Institution, Loretto or Merchiston Castle School which had an average annual fee of £27.8, only 18.2% failed to qualify, compared to 28.0% of recruits from the same social groups who did not attend these six institutions.

TABLE 5.15
**Schools Attended at Some Time by Twenty or More SAE Apprentices
(where known and excluding apprentices who failed to qualify
due to death or ill health)**

School in Descending Order by SAE Failure Rate	Number Attended	% Failed to Qualify	Annual Fee[24] (non-Boarding in c.1880 (£s)
James Gillespie's School	24	16.7	2
George Watson's College	203	19.2	·7
Daniel Stewart's College	62	24.2	7
Royal High School	69	24.6	13
Fettes College	25	28.0	41
Edinburgh Collegiate School	46	28.3	18
Edinburgh Academy	191	33.0	16
George Heriot's School	42	33.3	4
Edinburgh Institution	64	35.9	21
Loretto	20	40.0	66
Merchiston Castle School	34	44.1	5
Total/Mean	780	27.9	13.7

TABLE 5.16
The Failure Rate of SAE Apprentices Who Attended Major Schools by Social Status Origins

School Name	% Attended by SSG of Father			Failure Rate by SSG of Father if Attended (%)	
	1-5	6-9	NK	1-5	6-9
James Gillespie's	8.3	87.5	4.2	50.0	9.5
George Watson's	56.7	39.9	3.4	17.4	18.5
Daniel Stewart's	32.3	64.5	3.2	45.0	12.5
Royal High School	59.4	39.1	1.5	24.4	25.9
Fettes College	88.0	12.0	0.0	31.8	0.0
Edinburgh Collegiate	78.3	19.6	2.1	33.3	11.1
Edinburgh Academy	92.7	6.8	0.5	31.6	15.4
George Heriot's	14.3	83.3	2.4	16.7	36.1
Edinburgh Institution	71.9	23.4	4.7	34.8	26.7
Loretto	95.0	5.0	0.0	36.8	100.0
Merchiston Castle	88.3	8.8	2.9	50.0	0.0
Mean				30.0	20.1
% Failed by all with Father in SSG				32.9	26.0

It is clear from these findings, and from the information presented in Table 5.15 and the first section of Table 5.16, that the success of the lower middle and working class SAE recruit depended quite considerably on the availability of a relatively low cost secondary education, a subject to which the final chapter will return.

Attendance at a university previous to indenture commencement appears to have been of relatively minor significance in determining an apprentice's ability to qualify as a CA during the second half of the nineteenth and early twentieth centuries. The rate of non-qualification among 149 SAE apprentices (excluding those who died or whose indentures were terminated through illness) who attended university before apprenticeship was 30.9% compared to 32.0% of the 892 who did not. This is perhaps not surprising considering that those who did attend university did so for an average of only 1.8 years in order to finish their school education.

Of all those apprentices who attended university before indenture, only 20.0% gained a degree (15 at Edinburgh University, 2 at Glasgow, 8 at Oxford, 4 at Cambridge and 1 at Samonigh). But among those for whom university was a more serious attempt to improve personal academic standards and qualifications, only 23.3% failed to qualify as CAs. All but one graduate apprentice had a father in SSGs 1-4. The high cost of supporting a son over three to four years of study without his contributing to family income was too great for those of lower status parents to sustain.

Similarly, short-term attendance over one or two sessions was beyond the means of the parents of apprentices in low income occupations. Only 6.2% of all apprentices with lower middle and working class origins (SSGs 6-9) attended university for a period before indenture without gaining a degree, compared to 13.9% of those from upper middle class origins (SSGs 1-5). Incidentally, 88.7% of all SAE apprentices who attended university before indenture commencement went to Edinburgh University.

A sustained period of university study which was advantageous to the completion of an SAE indenture was therefore relatively closed to those of lesser means. This suggests that the availability of a low cost secondary education was of even greater significance to those sons desiring to enter the Edinburgh CA profession from the lower status hierarchy.

Pre-Apprenticeship Employment

The significance of an adequate school education in order to succeed in professional examinations and qualify as an SAE member has been established. Considering the importance of the practical component of a CA's training during the 1850-1914 period some pre-apprenticeship employment in related employments might be considered to have been of advantage. Indeed, the fact that the failure rate among apprentices not engaged in previous occupations which reduced the term of their indentures was 33.9%, compared to 24.5% for those who did, suggests that this was the case.

These statistics hide considerable variation between the success rate for those employed previously in particular occupations. The worst rate of non-qualification among those recruits who were previously occupied in term-reducing employments was among the 37 apprentices who had been a CA's clerk or cashier; 37.8% of this group failed to become CAs (42.4% for clerks only). 28 recruits who were previously employed in a lawyer's office had a rate of failure of 28.6% compared to 16.7% for the 6 apprentices who had been occupied in banking and insurance offices. The lowest rate of failure among apprentices where significant numbers were involved was 26.2% for the 130 who were described as having been "in the office" of a CA as a prelude to indenture in order to gain preliminary experience.

These apparent differences in the qualification rate appear to have been largely symptomatic of the recruit's social status origins. Apprentices of lower status fathers tended to follow a different path into chartered accountancy than those from higher status families.

TABLE 5.17
Major Term Reducing Pre-Apprenticeship Occupations of SAE
Apprentices 1837-1911 by Social Status Group of Father

SSG of Father	Insurance or Banking	'In CA's Office'	Lawyer's Office	CA's Clerk or Cashier	Total as % of all from SSG
1	2	5	0	0	12.5
2	3	33	11	9	14.9
3	0	12	0	2	16.5
4	0	10	3	1	10.9
5	0	7	3	2	22.6
6	1	13	4	3	21.0
7	0	25	1	12	28.4
8	0	13	3	5	27.3
9	0	2	2	2	35.3
Not Known	0	10	1	1	28.6
Total/Mean	6	130	28	37	18.8

Table 5.17 illustrates that although those recruits from lower middle and working class origins (SSGs 6-9) tended to have been previously employed in greater numbers than those from upper middle class origins (SSGs 1-5), they were engaged primarily in occupations that were not likely to have improved their apprenticeship performance. 25.6% of apprentices from SSGs 6-9 had previously acted as CAs' clerks or cashiers compared to 13.6% of those from SSGs 1-5. In other occupational groups noted above where the failure rate was low (insurance, banking, law and "in the office" of a CA), 86.4% of SSG 1-5 apprentices with previous occupations were employed compared to 73.5% for SSGs 6-9. The differences were particularly marked for the legal and insurance-banking categories reflecting the connections of higher status fathers with these occupations compared to those of lower standing.

What is indeed significant here is that the success of the apprentice from inferior status origins was related to the channel by which he discovered the profession of chartered accountancy as a career option. As noted in Chapter 3, many recruits with lower middle and, particularly, working class parents devoid of direct interpersonal connections with the professional classes only found accountancy as a possible vocation following clerkship in it. The opportunity to embark on an indenture was essentially an extension of a career already established in clerking. The apprenticeship was consequently contracted later in life with the knowledge that in the event of failure one could revert back to the original vocation. By contrast, those sons who entered a CA's office to gain some brief experience previous to indenture did so on the understanding that this was a *prelude* to preparation for a career in the *profession.*

Spatial Factors in Vocational Success

As was suggested in Chapters 3 and 4, as the network of interpersonal connections between those associated with chartered accountancy and those seeking career options for sons increased, the geographical base of SAE recruitment broadened. Table 5.18 shows that although the proportion of apprentices training in their home towns remained relatively stable, increasing numbers travelled greater distances to serve an indenture over the 1837–1911 period.

It would not seem implausible to suggest that those apprentices having to reside long distances from their parental homes suffered material and emotional disadvantages compared to those indentured in their home towns that may have adversely affected their ability to successfully complete an SAE training.

TABLE 5.18
Percentage of SAE Apprentices 1837-1911 Who Trained in Locations at Certain Distances From the Residence of Parents or Guardians[25]

Year of Indenture Commencement	Distance (miles)								N
	0	1–9	10–49	50–99	100–199	200–499	500+	Not Known	
1837–59	66.7	9.1	9.1	7.6	1.5	3.0	0.0	3.0	66
1860–69	73.0	9.0	5.0	7.0	3.0	0.0	0.0	3.0	100
1870–79	75.0	10.4	6.2	3.5	2.1	1.4	0.0	1.4	144
1880–89	65.1	12.3	6.2	6.7	4.1	1.0	0.5	4.1	195
1890–99	67.8	7.9	9.9	3.2	3.9	3.2	0.9	3.2	252
1900–11	67.1	12.3	8.4	3.5	3.2	2.9	1.0	1.6	310
N of Cases 1837–1911	731	112	83	49	35	23	6	28	1067
	68.5	10.5	7.8	4.6	3.3	2.1	0.6	2.6	100.0

Certainly, the SIA considered this to have been so:

> . . . It is unjust that young men desirous of following the profession of an Accountant and of belonging to a Chartered Society should be compelled (as is now often the case) to leave their homes for training in these privileged towns . . . Parents feel strongly that the advantages of belonging to a Chartered Society ought to be open to their sons without the necessity of incurring the extra expense and of being exposed to the risks of leaving home at an early age.[26]

Table 5.19 lends support to this assertion.

Those apprentices who trained in close proximity to their parental homes (below 10 miles) did tend to exhibit an above average rate of qualification which was reduced among those apprenticed 10 to 49 miles distant. The figures for apprentices between 50 to 199 miles from their homes at first sight appear to be baffling. What is plausible here, however, is that many of those in the 10 to 49 mile cohort were daily rail commuters who found it more desirable for financial or other reasons not to reside in Edinburgh though the long periods of travel may have affected adversely their ability to qualify.

TABLE 5.19
SAE Apprentices 1837–1911 who Failed to Qualify According to Distance Place of Indenture and Parental Home (excluding apprentices who failed to qualify due to death or ill health)

Distance (miles)	N of Apprentices	% Failed to Qualify
0	717	31.0
1-9	108	31.5
10-49	80	35.0
50-99	47	27.7
100-199	33	21.2
200-499	22	45.5
500+	6	66.7
Not Known	28	42.9
Total/Mean	1041	31.7

Apprentices who had parents resident between 50 and 199 miles away from the location of their CA training were beyond commuting distance and therefore found separate accomodation. Given the financial outlay necessary for an indenture in a city at such a distance, there was undoubtedly greater pressure on this group of SAE apprentices to qualify. For those apprentices at a considerable distance from home, with parents residing in England or overseas, the ability to have only infrequent contact with immediate kin provides the most likely explanation for the high failure rate among those over 200 miles from their parents.

These variations in qualification according to their distance from home were not a reflection of those noted earlier regarding the social status origins of recruits. This is revealed by the information contained in Table 5.20.

TABLE 5.20
Social Status Origins of SAE Apprentices 1837-1911 by Distance From Parent's Residence to Place of Indenture (percentages)

SSG of Father in Descending Order by Highest Failure Rate	Distance (miles) in Descending Order by Highest Failure Rate							
	500+	200-499	10-19	1-9	0	50-99	100-199	N
9 Semi & Unskilled Manual	0.0	0.0	12.5	18.8	62.5	6.2	0.0	16
1 Independent Means	1.9	5.7	20.7	13.2	45.3	11.3	1.9	53
5 Farmers	0.0	1.9	21.2	7.7	42.3	19.2	7.7	52
8 Skilled Manual	0.0	3.9	5.3	9.2	73.7	6.6	1.3	76
2 Professions	0.3	2.4	7.3	6.5	77.0	2.4	4.1	369
3 Manufacturers	0.0	0.0	5.9	16.7	65.5	7.1	4.8	84
4 Commerce	0.8	0.0	7.3	9.8	73.2	4.9	4.0	123
7 White Collar	0.8	1.5	0.8	10.7	81.7	3.0	1.5	131
6 Distribution & Processing	0.0	0.0	13.2	23.2	62.6	1.0	0.0	99

The table shows that the failure rate of apprentices according to distance from home was not a simple function of the location of parents from various social status groups. For example, apprentices from the high failure semi and unskilled manual group did not derive disproportionately from distances associated with high rates of non-qualification.

What appears to have been more significant in explaining failure according to distance from home was its effect on the apprentice's place of residence during his indenture. Recruits who were at such a distance from their parents location that they were compelled to take independent accomodation exhibited a comparatively low propensity to fail to achieve SAE membership. The failure rate among unmarried apprentices who resided in lodgings or in households with brothers and sisters was 23.2% (excluding those who died or whose indentures were terminated through illness) compared to 32.0% of those living in the homes of parents or relatives.

Independence from parents and elder relatives probably improved the apprentice's performance through the increased pressure to justify the considerable expence of professional training in a distant location. The limited opportunities for diversionary activities from study for the apprentice in a strange city, and being unable to perform family duties such as visits to relatives, were also perhaps beneficial to qualification.

Masters and the Office of Apprenticeship

It is clear from the advice offered to prospective recruits to the CA profession which was outlined in the previous chapter, that there was variation in the quality of training provided by certain masters and types of office during the late nineteenth and early twentieth centuries. The possibility exists, therefore, that the standard of vocational preparation and education received by the apprentice could have influenced his ability to qualify.

The broadening syllabus and increasing severity of SAE examinations, placed an even greater emphasis on the correct choice of office for training and engendered some contemporary comment concerning the duties of masters in ensuring the success of their apprentices. During the 1890s, as ICAEW examination failure rates rose, *The Accountant's Journal* noted that: "Articled clerks are complaining that their principals perform their duties towards them in a very inadequate manner."[27] The evasion of obligations by certain masters was not confined to England. In 1908 'An Old Accountant' of Glasgow wrote that the CAs were preparing inadequately their apprentices for GEB examinations.

> How many of the youths who will present themselves for the Intermediate and Final have had the benefit of practical experience or demonstration of the subjects in which they are to be examined ? The smallest number I believe.[28]

Another Glasgow CA, reflecting the lack of uniformity in training standards between different offices, replied:

> Personally I take a serious view of my obligations, and consider myself responsible for the business career of the youth until he completes his apprenticeship and becomes a member of the Institute. The work given corresponds with the time of service, and when the examinations come he is prepared to meet all demands from the practical side, – failures have been the exception.[29]

In 1925, *The Accountant's Magazine* recognized such variability in training and requested employers in whose offices large numbers of apprentices had failed to regard this as "a slight on his office and . . . ascertain the cause."[30]

It will be recalled that the larger firms were recommended as likely to have ensured the most suitable CA training. Given that the number of apprenticeships contracted to individual masters was a good indicator of firm size, the following Table 5.21

illustrates that an indenture in a large business was advantageous to qualification.

TABLE 5.21

**Firm Size and the Failure Rate as Indicated by the Number of Indentures
1837-1911 in Which SAE Members Acted as Masters or
Joint Masters (excluding apprentices who failed
to qualify due to death or ill health)**

N of SAE Indentures in which CA was Master/Joint Master	N of Masters	N of Apprentices Trained under these Masters	% of Apprentices who Failed to Qualify
1-4	98	188	32.4
5-9	61	421	33.5
10-14	17	197	38.1
15-19	14	232	26.3
20-29	11	247	27.1
30-49	13	450	23.1
Total	214	1735	

The larger office not only had a greater throughput of apprentices and a wide variety of business, but also the number of staff employed and consequent specialization ensured frequently that one partner or senior clerk had sole responsibility for the training of apprentices. This was not always possible in the small-medium firm though the very small office could offer more personal contact and tuition by the master. The largest offices also, as was suggested in the previous chapter, produced more apprentices who achieved notoriety through winning a prize or gaining distinction for examination performance after 1873. 34.6% of apprentices under a master of 30 or more indentures won such an award though these constituted 25.9% of all apprentices.

The statistics in the preceding table, however, disguise variation in the rate of non-qualification attributable to differing standards in certain offices and by certain masters in them. 11 principals, for example, indentured 5 or more apprentices of whom over half failed to qualify as CAs. Henry G. Watson, CA, was master to 8 apprentices whose indentures commenced between 1837-1911 of whom only one entered the SAE. Conversely, 5 masters took 5 or more apprentices all of who qualified. James Romanes, CA, was master or joint master to 9 youths; all became members of the Society. Even the 7 very largest firms and the 13 major masters who owned or were partners in them, displayed different rates of success in the training of their apprentices.

TABLE 5.22
**The Rate of Non-Qualification Among All SAE Apprentices 1837-1911
Trained in the Offices of CAs who Acted as Master or Joint
Master to 30 or More Apprentices**

Master Ordered by Lowest Failure Rate	Firm	N Indentures Under	% Failed
R.C. Millar	Barstow & Millar	36	8.3
J.A. Molleson	Howden & Molleson	38	13.2
J.A. Robertson	A & J Robertson	49	16.3
J.M. Howden	Howden & Molleson	30	16.7
R. Brown	R. Brown & Company	35	20.0
J. Howden	Howden & Molleson	48	20.8
P.C. Robertson	A & J Robertson	35	22.9
A.W. Mosman	A & J Robertson	30	23.3
J.S. Gowans	A & J Robertson	37	24.3
F.J. Moncrieff	Moncrieff & Horsburgh	32	28.1
F.W. Carter	Carter, Greig & Company	49	28.6
G.A. Jamieson	Lindsay, Jamieson & Haldane	43	30.2
J. Haldane	Lindsay, Jamieson & Haldane	43	30.4

Clearly, the range in qualification rates is indicative of the existence of variable standards in preparation by individual masters in certain firms. Alexander Harrison, CA, for instance, who was trained under Robert C. Millar, CA, who appears at the head of the list in Table 5.22, recalled that in that office the prospect of examination failure was not contemplated by early twentieth century apprentices: "We passed as a matter of course, there was not any question of it . . . I expect we got a good training."[31]

The relatively low failure rate among recruits who received their training in the largest offices was not a simple reflection of their social origins. Only 16.2% of sons from the distribution and processing and lower white collar status groups (SSGs 6-7), who exhibited the lowest rate of failure, were trained under the 13 major masters.

What is apparent from an examination of the social origins of apprentices who trained in the largest firms was the fact that 80.3% of them were from the upper middle classes (SSGs 1-5) though these constituted 68.0% of all SAE apprentices whose father's occupation is known. Only one apprentice from semi or unskilled manual origins (SSG 9) received a training in one of the 7 largest CA offices, and only 3.4% of apprentices who were indentured to the above masters were from working class (SSG 8-9) origins, though these constituted 9.2% of all apprentices whose father's occupation is known.

The significant revelation here is that fathers in higher status groups were not only aware of what were the best offices in which a son might receive a CA training, they were also better placed to ensure the entrance of a son into these offices. Once again, we revert to the likely significance of the network of connections and associations between apprentices' fathers and CAs. Parents in SSGs 1-5 were likely to have been in closer proximity to the occupational and social world of CAs than were parents of lower middle class and working class status. Consequently, upper middle class parents were aware of which were the firms of repute and those that were most likely to ensure that their son achieved success in his training and career. The eminent firms were averse to employing apprentices of whom they had little knowledge. They too had a reputation to maintain that could not be tarnished by an incompetent apprentice or CA who had trained in their offices. Among parents in the lowest status groups, with distant and non-personal connections with the profession, one CA or firm of CAs was probably considered as indistinct from others.

QUALIFICATION AND CAREER

Qualification

Having completed an apprenticeship and succeeded in the prescribed examinations, the prospective CA, depending on his financial state or that of his parents, was confronted by an obstacle to his achievement of full professional status: the fee of admission to the SAE.

That this was effectively a barrier to those recruits of lesser means was undoubted and the resulting exclusivity was an accusation continually lodged at the CAs of Edinburgh by their rivals. "The Edinburgh Society requires an apprenticeship with a fee of one hundred guineas, and an entrance fee of like amount, and thereby their ranks are closed to any but the sons of the wealthier classes."[32] The fees exacted by the SAE, claimed Sir Horace Davey, counsel for the SIA in 1890:

> . . . act as they obviously must as a deterrent to persons however able, however richly endowed by nature with all the qualities which fit a person to become an Accountant, but are not richly endowed with that other species of wealth which is so useful in this world which would enable them to attain the privilege of membership of these Societies.[33]

During the 1890s, attacks on the archaic barriers maintained by the three local chartered societies became particularly vociferous; the CAs were out of tune with the universalist tendencies of the age. The remarks of a correspondent of *The Scottish Accountant* from Banff in 1894 were typical:

> Obstacles of an insurmountable kind bar the entrance to these Societies of young men of limited means, however keen of intellect, and this is altogether at variance with the spirit of the times, and ought not so to be: 'The rank is but a guinea stamp, The man's t gowd for a' that.' The whole tendency of modern legislation is in the direction of liberalizing our institutions, breaking down monopolies and privileges, and making the highest position in every walk of life accessible to the humblest subject, who by individual merit shows himself qualified to efficiently discharge his duties.[34]

The CA societies of Scotland defended the imposition of monetary qualifications for admission on the grounds that by comparison with other professions, their entrance fees were low (in 1873 admission to the Faculty of Advocates cost £ 336; and admission to the Society of Writers to the Signet cost approximately £210) and that entry to "any of the learned professions cannot be obtained free of expense".[35]

Not only did the cost of admission to the Edinburgh Society act as a deterrent to those considering an SAE training, it also prevented the admission of some recruits who undertook a CA apprenticeship and succeeded in the professional examinations. The high rate of non-qualification among working class apprentices can undoubtedly be partly explained by the financial requirement of having to pay a substantial sum to gain the privilege of using the CA notation. This can be demonstrated on the basis of the following evidence.

Until the establishment of the SAE Endowment and Annuity Fund in 1887, the admission fee for candidates who had proceeded successfully through the usual route of indenture and examination was £52 and 10 shillings. For apprentices who commenced their indentures from 1888 the fee was increased to £ 105, one half of which was allocated to the Endowment Fund. This effective doubling of the sum required for admission to the Society resulted in a halving of the qualification rate among apprentices from lower middle and working class origins (SSGs 6-9) in the first five years of the new regulations. This is illustrated in Table 5.23. By contrast, qualification among recruits to the SAE from upper middle class origins was not affected by the increase in admission fees.

TABLE 5.23
**The Impact of Increasing SAE Admission Fees on the Qualification of
Apprentices From Various Social Origins**

SSG of Father	% Failing 10 Years Previous Fee Increase (Indentures Commencing 1878-87)	% Failing 5 Years Subsequent to Fee Increase (Indentures Commencing 1888-92)
1-5	29.6 (42)	30.2 (19)
6-9	15.3 (9)	31.1 (9)

The differential impact of admission fees on the qualification of sons from various social status origins is further shown in Table 5.24. The statistics in the second column illustrate that apprentices from the lowest social status groups were more likely to complete their indentures but not seek admission to the SAE. Data in the third column reveal that, if they did become members of the SAE, it took time to raise the necessary funds.

TABLE 5.24
**The Impact of Admission Fees on the Membership of Apprentices 1837-1911
From Various Social Origins (excluding apprentices who failed to
qualify due to death or ill health)**

SSG of Father	% whose Indentures Were Discharged but Did Not Become SAE Members	N	Date of Passing Final Examination Minus Date of Admission (years)	N
1	14.5	8	0.15	31
2	11.3	41	0.20	248
3	13.1	11	0.27	59
4	13.7	17	0.22	89
5	15.4	8	0.25	31
6	13.4	13	0.46	76
7	14.4	19	0.46	103
8	19.5	15	0.73	53
9	17.6	3	0.53	9

Some individual apprentices who could not afford the admission fees of the SAE were fortunate in having a benevolent master. One CA who was apprenticed during the 1900s recalled that: "I had no money to pay the Institute entrance fee. The firm paid it for me. I repaid them when I was a war casualty in Cambridge Hospital on full pay but with no expenses!"[36]

As will now be seen, the significance of money and the legacy of the recruit's social origins also remained important subsequent to admission to the SAE during the 1854–1914 period.

The Determinants of a Successful Career

The qualitative contemporary evidence suggests that the most significant attributes necessary to achieve a successful career in chartered accountancy during the 1854–1914 period were financial resources and connections. Ability, though important in building and maintaining a professional reputation, was not by itself sufficient to the accrual of appointments or clientele – particularly if the CA aspired to enter into practice.

The newly qualified CA was advised to remain as a clerk for a few years with an established practitioner commanding a salary of at least £100 *per annum* (during the 1890s), in order to gain a wider knowledge of the various branches of business as a prelude to setting up on his own account or buying into a partnership.[37] That a career in professional practice was the most desirable vocational direction to be followed was undisputed during most of the 1854–1914 period: "An ambitious young man would not consider the possibility of ending his days as a chief clerk, but would, before beginning his career, decide very clearly that by some means he must have a partnership or business of his own."[38] The cost of following this preferred course could be high. *The Pall Mall Gazette* in 1890 claimed that it was inadvisable to become a chartered accountant unless one had £2000 to £3000 or "influential friends in business circles" to assist in the setting up of a practice.[39] According to James Martin, establishing a clientele was based upon the following:

> It is all a matter of personal connection. The public employ accountants they have confidence in and of whom they have personal and individual knowledge. In all my experience of eighteen years as an accountant, only once did a man come to my office because he saw the name, accountant, on the door; and I make bold to say all other accountants, in this respect, have a similar experience.[40]

The career of David MacLagan, CA (1824–1883), was a case in point. He became manager of The Alliance British and Foreign Fire Assurance Company in Edinburgh through an arrangement with John Hamilton, advocate, who was an acquaintance of his father at St George's Church, Charlotte Square, Edinburgh. Having received that appointment, MacLagan ensured the increasing prosperity of the company as:

> He had also the advantage of an extensive connection and acquaintance by means of which access could be had to the most influential residents of any particular locality. His connection in Edinburgh itself was of vast importance in giving a standing to the office and in securing for it a position which, as a branch of an English company, it could never otherwise have attained.[41]

Later, he became manager of the Edinburgh Life Assurance Company on the recommendation of his father-in-law who had previously held the position.[41]

The whole network of familial, occupational and residential associations of the CA and his parents were vital to his success. Those SAE members who practised in Scotland and had connections in the legal profession had a distinct advantage:

> Solicitors are the gentlemen through whom the employment of the accountant usually comes. Whether an Accountant is employed as Sequestrator on a Bankrupt's Estate, or as Liquidator of a Joint Stock Company, which is being wound up, or as Judicial Factor, or as a private receiver in a private trust estate, it is through the Solicitors generally, that the employment comes.[42]

Similarly, those proposing to practice elsewhere in Britain were recommended to take note of the fact that:

> It frequently happens that instructions are received from family connections and private friends, in their capacity as Executors and Trustees, Directors of Public Companies, or owners of property; but as a rule by far the greater number of the matters transacted in a C.A.'s chambers are introduced by Solicitors. It is therefore evident that success depends upon obtaining the confidence and support of members of this profession.[43]

It is apparent from these and similar comments that CAs from lower status origins was at a considerable disadvantage in entering into the most desirable career directions. Not only were they largely without the necessary means, except through that gained by their own labour as CAs' clerks, but also their social and occupational origins precluded their entrance to the nexus of relevant associations so vital to the establishment of a thriving practice. Their disproportionate training in the smaller, less renowned firms did not aid the formation of highly lucrative business connections or provide an opportunity for rising within one of the larger businesses where partnerships were more often than not reserved for sons entering the profession or, in a few cases, for a brother (as in Barstow and Millar) or a nephew (as in Chiene and Tait). An analysis of the partners of the largest firms during the 1854–1914 period (as measured by their having taken over 40 apprentices) also reveals that non-relatives who became partners were always ex-apprentices of the firm and took longer to attain that status than did the sons of existing partners.

The firm of **A. and J. Robertson**, for example, was formed when Alexander W. Robertson assumed his son, James A., as his partner in 1870. James had entered the SAE in 1869. A second son, Patrick C. qualified as a CA in 1886 and was made a partner in 1887. Two of James A. Robertson's sons were also apprenticed to the firm: Alexander W. entered the SAE in 1900 and became a partner in the same year and James A. qualified in 1913 and was partnered c.1921. Two other apprentices and subsequent partners of the firm, John S. Gowans and Allan W. Mosman took four and ten years to achieve that status during the 1880s and 1890s.

Lindsay, Jamieson and Haldane was formed in 1858. George A. Jamieson had two CA sons who remained with the firm, James Haldane's son Herbert W. entered the SAE in 1895 and was made a partner in 1898. Three other partners, Donald Lindsay, Findlay B. Anderson (admitted 1872, partnered 1873) and Charles J.G. Paterson (admitted 1882 and partnered in 1889) remained unmarried though Francis More (admitted 1875 and partnered 1879) had a son who was admitted to the SAE in 1901 and assumed as a partner in 1905. All the above named were founders or apprentices of the firm.

The firm of **Carter, Greig and Co.** had its origins in 1869 when Frederick H. Carter (who had practised on his own account for ten years) assumed his son, Frederick W. as his partner. Frederick W. entered the SAE in 1868. James Greig became a partner in 1893, ten years after his admission to the society as did Matthew C. McEwan who had qualified in 1888. Both were ex-apprentices of the firm.

Howden and Molleson was constituted in 1863. James Howden's son, John M., became a CA in 1881 and a partner in the same year. James A. Molleson never married.

These obstacles, as well as the prohibition of advertising professional services as an alternative source of attracting business, ensured that, although Edinburgh CAs from lower status origins could enter into practice, it was only possible to succeed after long periods of salaried employment (mainly as CAs' clerks). Additionally, any such practice would tend to have been on a relatively small scale (many appear to have used their parental home as their business premises) and years might elapse before an extensive clientele was gained.

Newly qualified *unconnected* CAs with limited funds had to rely heavily on associations formed during the relatively short period of their apprenticeship, or at least that later part of it in which direct contact with clientele was more likely.

Masters were particularly important in the establishment of a career footing for those trained in their offices. For example, one apprentice who was indentured to Martin & Currie and Co., with parents in Ireland and no business connections, depended solely on one master's associations and frequent visits to North America as the source of employment for the whole of his career. On entering the SAE in the 1910s:

> Mr Currie had a business connection with a small trust company and knew its president personally. The company selected mortgages for the investment trusts which Mr Currie organized and were reviewed by the trustees in Edinburgh. Mr Currie told the president that I intended to go to Canada and he immediately offered me a position with his company.[44]

It was extremely difficult for the CA of low status origins to achieve eminence in the profession through entering the organizational elite of the SAE. Office-holders tended to be the most notable practitioners of their day from the largest, established and successful firms where family succession determined largely career progression. Hence, from among the partners of the four companies mentioned above came the following family continuation of senior office-bearers: Alexander W. Robertson was Secretary of the Society (1853-63), its Treasurer (1863-79) and his son James A. was President (1907-09). James Howden was Secretary (1863-92) and President (1892-95), and his son John M. was also President (1922-25). James Haldane was President (1895-98) as was his son Herbert W. (1934-37). Also from among the above firms, George A. Jamieson and Frederick W. Carter were Presidents of the SAE (in 1882-88 and 1904-07, respectively). In addition to the named firms, David Pearson (President 1898-1901) was the son of Charles Pearson (President 1876-79) and James McKerrell Brown (President 1918-22) was the grandson of the first President of the Society, James Brown (1853-64).

It is apparent from Table 5.25 that the professional organization of the SAE also was dominated by those CAs who had derived from higher status origins. Members from independent means and professional families (SSGs 1-2), in particular, were no doubt favoured for the social lustre that their office holding threw over the Society. If individual offices are examined, the distribution was equally as disproportionate. 56.4% of the 114 SAE Council or Joint Committee members from among the 1853-1914 membership were originated from SSGs 1-2, 22.2% from SSGs 3-5, 16.4% from SSGs 6-7 and only 5.0% from SSGs 8-9. All Secretaries and Treasurers among the 1853-1914 membership were from SSG 1-6 origins.

Also of significance was the fact that merit (as measured by prize winning during indenture in examinations) was not a passport to entering the organizational elite. Only 4 SAE Presidents had been awarded a prize during their apprenticeships. 23.4% of the 1853-1914 membership held an office and, among those who had passed their examinations with distinction, the rate was only marginally higher at 26.1%.

TABLE 5.25
SAE Members 1853-1914 Who Became an Office-Bearer of the SAE, GEB, ICAS
or Joint Committee of the Chartered Accountants of Scotland
According to Their Social Status Origins

	SSG of Father	% Holding Any Office	N	N Who Became President of the SAE or ICAS
1	Independent Means	40.5	17	2
2	Professions	32.1	92	20
3	Manufacturers	25.0	15	2
4	Commerce	20.6	20	2
5	Farmers	17.6	6	1
6	Distribution and Processing	16.0	13	1
7	White Collar	11.9	13	0
8	Skilled Manual	16.7	9	1
9	Semi and Unskilled Manual	0.0	0	0

A further indicator of the comparative lack of vocational success achieved by SAE members who were derived from inferior social origins was the fact that of the 4085 indentures registered in the books of the SAE between 1837 and 1939, CAs from upper middle class families (SSGs 1-5) acted as masters to a mean of 6.53 apprentices each compared 4.28 for those from lower middle and upper working class origins. The likelihood that CAs who were the sons of parents of limited means could only build a comparatively small and unimpressive practice of their own is also illustrated by the information contained in Table 5.26.

The table shows that a higher proportion of CAs who had fathers in SSGs 6-9 never attained the status of master compared to those from SSGs 1-5. Similarly, a greater percentage of CAs from low status origins contracted only a limited number of apprentices, and those that acted as a master to over 15 SAE recruits were likely to have done so not in firms established by themselves but as a partner or managing clerk in a large firm of long standing.

TABLE 5.26

Cumulative Percentage of Indentures in Which CAs From Various Social Origins Acted as a Master or Joint Master to an SAE Apprentice 1837-1939

Number of Indentures	SSG of CA's Father								
	1	2	3	4	5	6	7	8	9
0	54.8	60.3	61.7	58.5	52.9	63.0	67.9	70.4	100.0
1-4	71.4	69.7	70.0	77.7	73.5	76.5	83.5	77.8	100.0
5-9	78.6	78.7	76.7	84.1	88.2	80.2	89.0	83.3	100.0
10-14	88.1	82.9	78.3	89.4	88.2	85.2	91.8	92.6	100.0
15-29	92.9	90.2	90.0	98.9	94.1	95.1	97.2	96.3	100.0
30 and 30+	100.0	100.0	100.0	100.0	100.0	100.0	100.0	100.0	100.0
N of Cases	42	287	60	94	34	81	109	54	9

CONCLUSIONS

The CA apprentice's ability to enter successfully the profession was heavily reliant upon certain factors relevant to his own individual circumstances. There existed between 1853-1914 a hypothetically ideal route to the achievement of SAE membership.

1. Familial stability was desirable though not essential to success; it was advantageous to the apprentice if his training was not disrupted through becoming orphaned.

2. The apprentice had to derive from a family of such size relative to its income that permitted sufficient financial resources to be allocated to the outlay necessary for qualification.

3. There were advantages in being an eldest son on whom the generational *improvement* of family status primarily rested.

4. The apprentice's parents had to be highly motivated to their son achieving CA and *professional* status.

5. An adequate secondary education was vital and a long period at university desirable particularly in later years as the severity of professional examinations increased and the emphasis moved more towards a *theoretical* professional education.

6. There were benefits in residing away from the parental home though within visiting distance, in accomodation independent of parents and senior relatives during the term of the indenture.

7. A period of pre-apprenticeship employment in an occupation regarded as a *prelude* to the onset of formal training to enter the *profession* was valuable.

8. Perhaps most important of all, an apprenticeship in one of the

largest and most highly respected offices under a master with proven teaching abilities was very significant not only to a successful indenture but also to a prosperous career.

Most of these conditions were essentially available to those with the necessary funds and connections with the CA profession which ensured that apprentices from higher social status origins were in an advantageous position regarding qualification. This is not to say that those without substantial means and multiple associations were at a considerable disadvantage in qualifying. An adequate though cheap secondary education, coupled with a high parental ambition for the upward mobility of their sons, could compensate for a lack of substantial family income (among SAE recruits from lower middle class SSG 6-7 origins for example). It was only in cases where ascriptive and material disadvantages were too overwhelming to be compensated for by other factors (among some SSG 8 and most SSG 9 apprentices) that a successful vocational training was prevented.

The ideal route to membership of the SAE was not generally available to apprentices from low status origins though entry to the profession was possible with considerable parental foresight, enthusiasm and preparation. Once qualification had been achieved, however, the new member of the SAE from social origins in the lower status hierarchy had to contend with a further set of obstacles in order to become a successful member of the professional classes. The legacy of the significance of money and connection assumed equal if not greater post-qualification importance than merit than it had done during vocational preparation. The upward mobile into the SAE from lower middle and working class origins had to contemplate the distinct possibility that having attained professional status, the chances of his achieving eminence within his vocation was considerably limited compared to those of his colleagues from more prosperous social backgrounds.

Notes

1 For a review of the literature on this subject, see A. Heath, *Social Mobility* (London, 1981), chs. 5-6. M. Abrahamson, E.H. Mizruchi and C.A. Hornung, *Stratification and Mobility* (New York, 1976), ch. 9. O.D. Duncan, D.L. Featherman and B. Duncan, *Socioeconomic Background and Achievement* (New York, 1972).

2 Stewart in *Pioneers of a Profession* notes that, during the early years of the SAE, certain members were prone to the non or delayed payment of annual subscriptions (this is borne out by the annual accounts of the SAE in its minute books) indicating that for some CAs membership resulted originally in little financial benefit.

3 Privy Council, "SAE Petition" (1889-90), p. 76.

4 *Ibid.*, p. 77.

5 Finlay, "Speeches by Counsel" (1890), p. 10.

6 Mr Charles Pearson, QC, Privy Council, "Speeches by Counsel", In the Matter of the Petition of the Scottish Institute of Accountants for Incorporation by Royal Charter, (1890), p. 78.

7 Martin, *The Sanctification of the Lie*, pp. 33-4.

8 See G. Anderson, *Victorian Clerks* (Manchester, 1976), pp. 15-20.

9 British *Parliamentary Papers*, 1895, vol XXIV, "Supplement to the Thirty-Eighth Detailed Annual Report of the Registrar General of Births, Deaths and Marriages in Scotland", and: 1906, vol. XXI, "Supplement to the Forty-Eighth Detailed Annual Report of the Registrar General of Births, Deaths and Marriages in Scotland".

10 *Ibid*.

11 Hunter, "Rambling Reminiscences", p. 25.

12 One example of the impact of the death of a parent on an indenture is provided by the apprenticeship of Frederick Falkner, CA, between 1868 to 1879. Within his articles, the following was noted: "The execution of the indenture was delayed owing to the severe and protracted illness of Mr J.P. Falkner, the father of the apprentice, and that ultimately after his death, the matter was neglected".

13 see R.J. Morris, "The Middle Class and the Property Cycle during the Industrial Revolution", in T.C. Smout (ed.), *The Search for Wealth and Stability; Essays in Economic and Social History Presented to M.W. Flinn* (London, 1979).

14 Quoted in Blau and Duncan, *The American Occupational Structure*, p. 367. See A. Dumont, *Depopulation et Civilisation* (Paris, 1890).

15 *Ibid.*, ch. 11. See also Duncan *et al.*, *Socioeconomic Background and Achievement* J. Berent, "Fertility and Social Mobility", *Population Studies* 5 (1952). C.C. Perucci, "Social Origins, Mobility Patterns and Fertility", *American Sociological Review* 32 (1967). G. Hawthorn, *The Sociology of Fertility* (London, 1970). M.E. Sobel, "Social Mobility and Fertility Revisited", *American Sociological Review* 50 (1985).

16 142 separate occupational groups were classified in the published tables of the 1911 Fertility Census for Scotland; 67 of these were usable for accomodation within

the social status group classification used for this study. Information was least available for manufacturers (SSG 3) as owners, managers and operatives were grouped together by industry. The groups comparable with the SSG occupations used in Table 5.7 constitute the fertility of 67,363 marriages. See British *Parliamentary Papers*, 1914, vol. 99, "Census of Scotland 1911", vol. 3, Table XLVII, pp. 284-8.

17 J.H. Goldthorpe, D. Lockwood, F. Bechhofer and J. Platt, *The Affluent Worker in the Class Structure* (Cambridge, 1969), p. 126.

18 See S.R.S. Szreter, "The Decline of Marital Fertility in England and Wales 1870-1914", (Ph.D. Dissertation, University of Cambridge, 1983).

19 "Social Ambitions". p. 550.

20 R.Q. Gray, "Thrift and Working-Class Mobility in Victorian Edinburgh", in A.A. MacLaren (ed.), *Social Class in Scotland: Past and Present* (Edinburgh, 1976), p. 128.

21 See for example, H.T. Himmelweit, "Social Status and Secondary Education", in Glass, *Social Mobility in Britain*. P.M. Blau and O.T. Duncan, "Some Preliminary Findings on Social Stratification in the U.S.", *Acta Sociologica* 9 (1965).

22 *The Scottish Accountant* 1 (1893), p. 115.

23 See Appendix B for the classification of school type used in this table.

24 The figures for annual fees are approximate. The actual fee paid by each scholar depended on the number and particular subjects of classes attended and the fee payable for each. See Appendix B.

25 The distances for this table were calculated on the basis of rail or road distances provided in J. Bartholomew (ed.), *Gazetteer of the British Isles: Statistical and Topographical* (Edinburgh, 1887).

26 Mr Thomas Shaw, QC, Privy Council, "Speeches by Counsel", In the Matter of the Petition of the Scottish Institute of Accountants for Incorporation by Royal Charter, (1896), p. 17.

27 *The Accountant's Journal* 9 (1891), p. 97.

28 *The Accountant's Magazine* 12 (1908), p. 570.

29 *The Accountant's Magazine* 13 (1909), pp. 30-1.

30 *The Accountant's Magazine* 29 (1925), p. 98.

31 Interview with Alexander Harrison, CA (admitted to the SAE in 1914), Edinburgh, 13 December 1984. That a unique and very high standard of professional education was available in the firm of Barstow & Millar is further evidenced by comments on the firm provided in the obituaries of its ex-partners and apprentices. The writer of Robert C. Millar's obituary in 1929 asserted that Millar's brilliant career had "been an inspiration" to his apprentices, and that "For variety of work the office of Barstow & Millar was famed, and fortunate was the apprentice who found himself on the staff." [*The Accountant's Magazine* 33 (1929), pp. 290-1]. The obituary of Robert C. Millar's brother, Thomas J. Millar, CA, who died in 1946, was even more complimentary, stating that: "The office was a good nursery" for Edinburgh CAs and, "was noted for the sound training given to apprentices. Over the years 99 apprentices passed through

the office, and many attained distinction in examination and practice. It produced two Presidents and one Secretary of the Edinburgh Society, and two of the Professors of Accountancy at the University of Edinburgh were former apprentices." [*The Accountant's Magazine* 50 (1946), p. 378.] See also *The Accountant's Magazine* 31 (1927), p. 532.

32 Privy Council, "SIA Petition" (1889–90), p. 15.

33 Sir Horace Davey, QC, MP, Privy Council, "Speeches by Counsel", in the Matter of the Petition of the Scottish Institute of Accountants for Incorporation by Royal Charter, (1890), pp. 98–9.

34 G. Shearer, "The Position and Claims of Provincial Accountants", The *Scottish Accountant* 1 (1894), p. 181.

35 Privy Council, "Brief on Behalf of the Chartered Societies of Scotland", In the Matter of the Petition of the Scottish Institute of Accountants for Incorporation by Royal Charter, (1896), p. 3.

36 Personal letter, 20 November 1984 from a CA apprenticed 1907–12 who wishes to remain anonymous.

37 For estimates of the salary paid to a qualified CA remaining as a clerk see Dicksee, *The Student's Guide to Accountancy; Idem. A Guide to the Accountancy Profession;* Witty, *How to Become a Qualified Accountant.*

38 Cross, *Choosing A Career,* p. 126.

39 From *The Accountant's Journal* 8 (1890), pp. 121–6. See also *The Accountant* 16 (1890), pp. 499–500. See also *The Accountant* 16 (1890), pp. 499–500.

40 Martin, *The Sanctification of the Lie,* p. 35.

41 Walker, *David MacLagan, F.R.C.E.,* p. 44.

42 Davey, "Speeches by Counsel", pp. 108–9.

43 Pixley, *The Profession of a Chartered Accountant,* p. 3.

44 Personal letter, 20 November 1984 from a CA apprenticed 1907–12 who wishes to remain anonymous.

6
The Limits to Self-Recruitment : Marriage and Fertility

There are some other that account wife and children as bills of charges

[Francis Bacon, *Of Marriage and Single Life*]

Although the social structure of the geographical source of recruits, the existence of *connections* between parents and members of the profession, and the system of vocational preparation, were all significant determinants of the expansion and nature of recruitment to the SAE, a further important determinant of the social composition of apprentices remains to be discussed: self-recruitment.

The extent to which the sons of Edinburgh CAs entered their fathers' profession was a potentially important limitation to the recruitment of those from non-SAE backgrounds. The possibility existed that the rate of self-recruitment was so high that upward mobility into the profession was restricted. Conversely, self-recruitment may have been so low that the opportunities for the entrance of sons from inferior status origins were increased.

The actual extent of self-recruitment to the SAE and its effect on the rate of upward social mobility into the profession is discussed in Chapter 7. Meantime, the examination will concern the demographic determinants of Edinburgh CAs' ability to secure the potential for self-recruitment: their marriage and fertility. The rate of and age at marriage were the key regulators of the number of sons born to men in the profession. The prevalence of celibacy (celibacy is used throughout as referring to an unmarried state or a propensity never to marry rather than as meaning total abstinence from sexual activity) was an obvious restriction upon the output of sons and, for those CAs entering wedlock, their age at marriage and that of their wives was a significant determinant of their reproductive capacity and consequently of their potential for securing self-recruitment.

Students of social circulation have long recognized the significance of demographic factors in setting limits to national rates of occupational mobility. The hypothesis can be stated thus:

> Strata in which there are more children born than required to fill positions vacated by mortality (and retirement) as well as new positions created by industrialization and technological innovations become

suppliers of labour and thereby foster social mobility. In contrast, strata in which there are fewer children born than required to fill vacated and newly created positions foster social mobility in that they become consumers of labour.[1]

Particular emphasis has been placed on the effects of the decline of middle class fertility from the mid-later nineteenth century and the existence of class differentials in family size. It has been asserted that the reduced ability of the middle classes to ensure a supply of sons to fill the increasing number of white collar positions in the economy inevitably resulted in the recruitment of sons from among the larger families of the working classes, thus securing their upward mobility.[2]

In order to investigate the potential for self-recruitment in the Edinburgh CA profession between 1853 and 1914, a particular examination was undertaken of CAs entering the SAE from its inception in 1853-4 to 1892. This cohort collectively constituted all members who could have borne sons eligible for recruitment and admission to their own profession by 31 December 1914. This assumes that CAs did not contemplate marriage until they had qualified, an assumption based on the fact that there were no individuals who became SAE members subsequent to 1892 who married previous to qualification and produced sons eligible for membership of the Society by 1914.[3]

The marital and fertility experiences of the 1853-1892 group were investigated using, in part, obituarial sources though primarily utilizing the census, statutory civil registers for Scotland and, in a few cases where vital events occurred before 1855 among some of the older original SAE members, old parish registers.

Before analysing aspects of marital age and fertility among SAE members, investigation of a group of CAs who were in a position to provide no legitimate sons as potential future recruits will proceed: permanent bachelors.

CELIBACY

J. Heiton in *The Castes of Edinburgh* categorized bachelors as a distinct and numerically significant group of citizens in the Scottish capital.[4] The published census returns for Scotland of 1861 showed that at the age of 40 to 44, 16.2% of males in Edinburgh had not married. By 1901, this figure has increased to 19.1%. Heiton was not alone in drawing attention to the apparent prevalence and increasing trend toward non-marriage, particularly among professional men during the nineteenth century. In 1867 'A Bachelor' claimed in *Fraser's Magazine* that:

> We all know, in point of fact, that it is precisely that class of men who can best afford to marry who don't and won't. Imprudent marriages occur occasionally, but they are almost exclusively confined to the operative classes. The well-to-do young men, the wealthy young men, remain single.[5]

Such contemporary concerns were based on 'shrewd suspicions' as to the causes and moral consequences of celibacy. Young men of high social standing were gaining sexual gratification outside wedlock.

> We know for we cannot but know it, how the decrease of marriage is compensated. The polluted streets show it: the evil, born of pride and pride and vain pomp, and show, has ulcerated everywhere. The daughters who are not to wed save when wooed by Cupid and Mammon together, find their purity assailed in the street, the park, at the races, or the hunt, and at the favourite watering place.[6]

Similarly, in an article entitled 'Why are Women Redundant ?' that appeared in *The National Review* in 1862, it was asserted that: " . . . Thousands of men find it perfectly feasible to combine all the freedom, luxury, and self-indulgence of a bachelor's career with the pleasures of female society and the employments they seek for there.[7]

Though some commentators noted that the nature of the matrimonial process and the lack of social contact between the opposite sexes in polite society acted as impediments to marriage, most concurred that the principal causes of male celibacy were pecuniary. The reluctance to sacrifice gentlemanly independence for the constraints of wedlock was propounded as the major explanation for this apparently increasing phenomenon during the mid-late nineteenth century.

A total of 75 of the 352 Edinburgh CAs included in the 1853-92 cohort died unmarried - that is, 21.3% of all members. 5 of these died between the ages of 24 and 29 and 12 between 30 and 40 years. It is impossible to surmise whether these individuals would have married or not. In terms of their contribution to the output of potential self-recruits, however, this consideration is irrelevant as they died without issue. It is similarly difficult to identify the precise causes of celibacy in each of these 75 cases. What is possible is to examine certain dominant characteristics that emerge among permanent bachelors and to reveal the trend in celibacy in order to identify any factors that altered its rate and consequently influenced the capacity for self-recruitment among Edinburgh CAs. Most long surviving bachelors exhibited a combination of traits.

Individual Characteristics of Celibate SAE Members 1853-92

A study of the obituarial information collected for celibate CAs suggests that, compared to SAE members as a whole, most were described as being of a 'retiring disposition' or as 'unassuming'. Comparatively few celibate CAs played an active part in the professional organization as measured by the fact that 43.8% of married CAs in the 1853-92 cohort occupied a position in the SAE organizational elite compared to 26.7% of celibate CAs. Likewise, a number of bachelors appear to have experienced an 'alienated' career, being in practice for most of their professional lives on their own account and outside the major firms.

By contrast to this type of individual was the introverted celibate CA with a high work preference and who was totally dedicated to his career and profession. These essentially *high flyers* had little inclination to marry; wedlock and raising a family formed a potentially disruptive diversion from the achievement of vocational eminence. It was recognized by *The Cornhill Magazine* in 1861, for example, that "many a vigorous career, both in action and in speculation has been cut short by baby fingers."[8] Marriage and the necessity of providing a stable family income was considered detrimental in some quarters to risk-taking and permitted less time and effort to be devoted to the cultivation of advantageous business connections.

> A single man who is independent of his profession can afford to observe its rules, to enter into its spirit, and to study its principles with genuine zeal and interest; but if he marries and has a family, his independence is gone. He must live by his profession and that at once . . . Many a lawyer or doctor who might otherwise have distinguished himself has to put up with half acquaintance with his profession, and an obscure country practice, because he is determined, as he thought magnanimously, in early life to do the brave thing, and marry as he pleased, setting appearances at defiance.[9]

A few examples will suffice to show that certain ambitious and industrious CAs sacrificed marriage for a successful career. Richard Brown, CA (1856-1918) won a £30 fellowship in the SAE examinations, established a leading Edinburgh firm (Richard Brown and Co.), was an SAE council member, secretary, treasurer, examiner, president and acted as the major force behind the organization of the GEB in 1892-3. Similarly, William H. Cook, CA (1851-1928), was a President of the SAE, attained a large and varied business. John S. Tait, CA (1857-1910) was 'one of the Society's most distinguished members', a senior partner who 'never allowed relaxation' and whose existence composed a 'perpetual vigil at the desk'.

Compared to their married colleagues, some celibate CAs appear to have had a high leisure preference, being noted as keen sportsmen, hobbyists, socialites, churchmen and philanthropists. Findlay B. Anderson, CA (1849-1927), for instance, expended considerable time and a large income on photography, his Rolls-Royce, and building an organ and cinematograph into his house. David MacRitchie, CA (1851-1925), a "confirmed bachelor" and author was "associated with almost every society that had for its object the intellectual life, and the betterment of the poor and needy of his native city."[10]

It is extremely difficult to discern whether participation in a long list of recreational pursuits and achievements provides evidence for these being causes of celibacy or its consequences. Certainly, sports and amatuer passions were regarded generally by contemporaries as tending to enhance gentlemanly status which was undoubtedly a more significant aspiration of some CAs than was marital status.

It was a well-documented tendency in Victorian Britain for young professional men to aspire to landed rank by gaining admission to the appropriate social circles through participation in the necessary though costly leisure activities. The consequence of this and the maintenance of *independence* was insufficient funds for marriage. It was extremely expensive for a professional to become a gentleman, it cost much more to also provide for a lady and an appropriate education and career for any offspring. Consequently:

> Men do not marry in our circles as they did years ago. Working men and shop-keepers want wives. Their wives can be of service to them, so marriage is the rule. They have no position to keep up. There are plenty of well-bred, good-looking young men one meets at parties and balls, who maintain their position in consequence of keeping single.[11]

The longer a professional postponed or rejected marriage, the greater were his opportunities for income and wealth accumulation as he reached the zenith of his career in late-middle age. By sacrificing matrimony and family, a CA might be in a position not only to secure his independence but also to purchase a more solid attribute of gentlemanly status – an estate. There is some limited evidence which suggests that certain highly ambitious, career-orientated CAs sacrificed all including wedlock in order to become the first among their professional competitors to illustrate their success through purchasing property.[12]

The status aspiration aspect of celibacy appears to be reflected in the following table.

TABLE 6.1
Social Status Origins of SAE Members Admitted 1853–92
Who Were Never Married at Death

SSG of Father		N Celibate at Death	As % of All CAs in SSG
1	Independent Means	6	19.4
2	Professions	42	26.8
3	Manufacturers	3	25.0
4	Commerce	6	15.4
5	Farmers	3	14.3
6	Distribution & Processing	4	13.8
7	White Collar	7	18.4
8	Skilled Manual	3	16.7
9	Semi & Unskilled Manual	0	0.0
	Not Known	1	
Total/Mean		75	21.3

The rate of celibacy was apparently greatest among the sons of professional men and manufacturers, those who derived from the social groups that were most highly motivated to achieve landed status and preserve *gentlemanly independence* For those CAs from SSG 1 who could already claim independent origins, there was no need to sacrifice marriage and family to social aspiration. Similarly, for those SAE members from origins beyond the margins of upper class status without the prospect of amassing sufficient earned income through professional practice or wealth through inheritance, aspirations to independent status were unrealistic and unattainable.

In considering the possible causes of celibacy, the responsibilities of SAE members to co-residing kin cannot be ignored. Very few celibate CAs appear from the census enumerators' returns to have lived alone. Almost all at some stage resided with spinster sisters or elderly mothers. It would not seem unreasonable to assume that certain of these were obliged, as the major income earners, to provide for such relatives. As Heiton observed in his discussion of celibacy in Edinburgh: "We must remember, too that everyone cannot be always in a state of wedlock; wives die as well as husbands . . . Aunt Beckies and Uncle Tobias' are required to supply the places of parents. Sisters, too, are dependent on brothers."[13]

Celibacy in this form was a symptom of prevailing mortality conditions. Of the 34 celibate SAE members who had died or reached the age of 40 by the 1891 census, only 3 were living in households where another male income earner was resident. 4 resided with an aged mother, 7 with a mother and sisters, 6 with a sister or sisters, and, 4 lived alone. The remaining 10 either died young or emigrated.

The above are some of the likely considerations that individual CAs took into account in deciding whether or not to contemplate marriage. The factors outlined were likely to have explained a relatively stable rate of celibacy among SAE members due to their being essentially individual and personal. The rate of non-marriage among the 1853–92 cohort, however, exhibited wide fluctuation according to the year of admission to the SAE, which indicates that additional considerations were also important; these will now be examined.

The Economics of Celibacy versus Marriage

Marriage for the nineteenth century professional entailed a considerable amount of self-denial; it implied forgoing certain leisure and business pursuits. More importantly, through the reallocation of resources toward dependents, it potentially resulted in incurring a considerable financial burden due to the necessity of preventing a degradation of living standards and status which were its potential consequences.[14] *The Cornhill Magazine* in 1861 asserted that:

> In order to enable the husband to meet the inevitable expenses of almost any liberal profession, it would be necessary that they should live entirely without servants, without change of air or scene, without the society of their equals, without any, or at least any adequate, provision for such emergencies as illness; and with the most minute and rigorous economy in every detail of domestic expenditure. Unless as years went on, their income increased both largely and quickly, they would not have the means of educating their children to fill the same station in life as that in which their own youth was passed.[15]

A year later *The National Review* noted that middle class women adhered to similar ideals, that marriage was only acceptable if it did not result in a decline in social status and standards of consumption; a cause of the "vast amount of super-normal celibacy", it claimed was:

> . . . . The growing and morbid LUXURY of the age. The number of women who remain unmarried, because their marriage – such marriage, that is, as is within their reach, or may be offered them – would entail a sacrifice of that 'position' which they value more than the attractions of domestic life, is considerable in the middle ranks, and is enormous in the higher ranks.[16]

Given that marriage was generally acceptable to potential partners only if sufficient funds had been accumulated to prevent the union from reducing the ability to finance the material necessities of status maintenance, it would appear conceivable that the

rate of celibacy among professionals could have fluctuated according to the state of
their business and competition which could alter the speed of income accumulation.
Indeed, if the celibacy rate of Edinburgh CAs over time is considered this was likely to
have been the case.

TABLE 6.2
**SAE Members Admitted 1853–92 Who Were Never Married at Death
by Year of Membership of the Society**

Year of Admission	N of Celibate CAs	% Celibate	N of New Members
1853–54	12	18.8	–
1855–64	11	26.2	42
1865–74	4	9.1	44
1875–84	23	25.3	91
1885–92	25	22.5	112
Total/Mean	75	21.3	

Although allowances must be made for the small numbers involved, the data
presented in Table 6.2 reveal an interesting trend. The fluctuations in the rate of
non-marriage appear to have been related closely to changes within the profession
which affected career prospects, the level of competition among members and,
consequently, income. That the CA's income was subject to the effects of
competition is beyond dispute. The obsession of the SAE with its exclusive claim to
chartered standing and determination to repel the attempts of the SIA and the
Corporation of Accountants during the 1880s and 1890s to adopt the CA notation due
to its 'high pecuniary value' was ample evidence of this. The design of the Scottish
chartered societies' campaign against rival organizations was, claimed Martin, "in order
to put down competition and secure all professional business for themselves."[17]

The trend in celibacy among SAE members may be explicable in the following terms.
The comparatively low rate of celibacy among the original members of the society
was likely to have been due to the fact that they were the eminent accountants of
their day in Edinburgh who enjoyed a good business as reflected in their residential
location for example. The very earliest members of the Institute of Accountants in
1853 were those practising exclusively as accountants and, given the variety of work
undertaken by accountants of that period, those practising exclusively in the vocation
were likely to have been the most successful.

The high rate of celibacy among the 1855-64 cohort was partly a response to the establishment of the SAE which resulted in a sudden influx of men into accountancy who might now claim equal *professional* status with CA competitors. There was consequently an increase in competition among a greater number of eminent practitioners resulting in pressure on professional incomes. The sudden decline in the proportion of CAs who practised in Edinburgh after 1855 (see Figure 2.2) is evidence of this. Income accumulation for the 1855-64 generation of CAs was slower than previously, and there existed the additional pressure on early members of the organization to exhibit a lifestyle commensurate with the vocation's newly affirmed professional status.

The 1865-74 cohort, by contrast, entered into practice during a period when the CA's workload was expanding while the number of professional competitors (new members) remained static. The introduction of a comprehensive examination system in 1873 increased the number of recruits to the profession and the value of admission to the Society so that the number of new members entering between 1875 and 1884 was double its 1865 to 1874 figure. Each CA of this generation had to contemplate fierce competition for business from fellow members; there was no similar doubling of Edinburgh CAs' potential workload as was shown in Chapter 2. Income accumulation for this and the succeeding cohort was likely to have been slower than it had been previously and, consequently, marriage was rejected by more professionals.

These conclusions are confirmed if examination is made of the celibacy rate among CAs entering the SAE subsequent to 1892. The higher numbers involved permit a greater degree of confidence in the above assertions. 53 or 26.5% of SAE members admitted between 1893 and 1904 remained unmarried at death. These also entered the profession during a period when the number of new members increased markedly compared to the CA's potential business (200 were admitted between 1893 and 1904), and in response to the broadening attractiveness of the profession as a career alternative and the introduction of the GEB examinations in 1893. This cohort embarked on their careers in the period when discussion concerning the overstocking of the CA profession reached its peak.

Celibacy among the entrants of between 1905 and 1914 declined quite dramatically to 16.5% (39 individuals) although the number of new members remained high and increasing at 237. What was different about this group was that their early careers (when marriage was contemplated) took place during and just after the 1914-18 conflict which resulted in a notable expansion in CAs' workload in government departments (primarily in auditing). Additionally, "the change in the general level of taxation on personal incomes and company profits which resulted from the First World War had a marked effect on the volume of accountancy work."[18]

Many SAE members and apprentices also entered the armed forces resulting in a greater decline in professional competition. 171 SAE members and 228 apprentices appear on the Society Roll of War Service (military, and non-military service in government departments). The war resulted in a drastic reduction in the number of indentures contracted and of new members admitted so that, for those who survived the conflict, opportunities for swift income accumulation remained during 1914 to 1918 and until the mid to late 1920s. This is revealed in Table 6.3 below.

TABLE 6.3
The Impact of the 1914–1918 War on SAE Indentures Contracted
and New Members Admitted[19]

Year	Total New Indentures	Total Admissions
1910	35	24
1911	30	32
1912	28	15
1913	38	29
1914	26	26
1915	15	16
1916	22	10
1917	9	3
1918	19	8
1919	122	22
1920	88	58
1921	70	20
1922	93	33
1923	95	38

Considering that a number of the celibate CAs in the 1905-14 cohort died in military service (21 or 8.9% of the intake were killed in the conflict), which exaggerates the celibacy rate, it is apparent that the reduction in the rate of professional competition between 1914 and 1923 had a considerable impact on increasing the propensity of SAE members to marry.

Testing the above hypothesis concerning the relationship between the extent of intraprofessional competition and the rate of non-marriage is not always possible by comparing statistics among different over and understocked professions. This is due to the fact that individual vocations varied during the nineteenth and early twentieth century in the extent to which incomes were affected by competition, and also because of internal conventions concerning marriage in certain professions. Also significant was the state of the occupation with regard to the stage reached in the process of professionalization. Practitioners of a newly organized profession seeking to assert their status were probably more prone than members of an old, established profession to forgo marriage in order to allow expenditure on material consumption at a level associated with that of a professional gentleman.

Consequently, a comparison between the effect of overcrowding, competition and celibacy in the medical profession compared to accountancy might prove fruitless given that the doctor was reputed to "Take his wife as he takes his degree."[20] A higher rate of marriage among the clergy was likely to have been a symptom of non-economic forces. It is therefore more practicable to analyse the potential relationship within the unique context of separate professions. Bearing this point in mind, an investigation of the prevalence of celibacy among Edinburgh lawyers does confirm that abstinence from marriage was affected by the state of intraprofessional competition and overcrowding. Among members admitted to the Faculty of Advocates between 1850 and 1914 24.0% remained celibate at death[21]. The legal profession was notoriously overcrowded during the second half of the nineteenth century:

> Everybody is agreed that the Bar stands not where it did as a money making occupation. Complaints are rife of the falling off of work, and men, who not so long ago were making their thousand a year or thereabouts are now earning barely the half.[22]

There was no certainty that the newly qualified advocate would gain a substantial practice with the consequence that many persisted in a quasi-preoccupation with their profession. In 1873, J. Lorimer commented that the Faculty "at present it consists of about 404 members, not one-fourth of whom are engaged in practice."[23] Certainly, a number of advocates never intended to plead before the Courts; membership of the Faculty was a mark of academic and cultural distinction as well as professional status. Among some sons of landed families who were destined to live a life of economic inactivity, admission to the Faculty was proof of their abilities and social standing. As Chitnis has asserted for eighteenth century Scotland, so it largely remained during the nineteenth that: "Socially the Law appears to have been regarded as a fashionable but useful and respected career in public service rather as Anglican livings were considered for the younger sons of aristocrats and gentry in nineteenth century England."[24]

Other entrants to the Faculty, following the literary interests of illustrious predecessors, such as Henry MacKenzie, Lords Kames, Monboddo, Gardenstone and Cockburn, Sir Walter Scott and later. R.L. Stevenson, determined not on a career in law but in literature.[25] Despite the fact that many advocates were not wholly dependent on income from the practice of their legal profession, and therefore only partly affected by the state of competition for business, there is a discernible relationship between the intake of new members and the rate of celibacy. This is shown in the following table.

TABLE 6.4
Members of the Faculty of Advocates Who Were Never Married
at Death 1850-1914 Admissions

Year of Admission	N Celibate	% Celibate	N of New Members
1850-54	10	24.4	41
1855-64	21	21.2	99
1865-74	21	24.1	87
1875-84	21	22.1	95
1885-94	35	26.5	132
1895-04	24	22.0	109
1905-14	24* (14)	27.3 (17.9)	88 (78)
Total/Mean	156	24.0	651

*Ten of these members were killed young in World War One.

During periods in which there was a notable expansion in the membership of the Faculty such as occurred between 1885 and 1894, celibacy increased and, in periods when a reduction in new admissions occurred, celibacy declined. If those who were killed young and unmarried during the 1914-18 conflict are excluded, it would appear that the expansion of legal work among advocates relative to the reduction in the number of new members (there were only 23 admissions to the Faculty in 1914-18) during the First World War reduced professional competition and the rate of celibacy as it did among Edinburgh CAs.

The upper branch of the Edinburgh solicitor profession was also overstocked during the second half of the nineteenth and early twentieth centuries. The experience of Writers to the Signet also suggests some vulnerability to the effects of changing levels of professional competition in marital decision-making. Overcrowding was reflected in the decline of membership of the Society of Writers to the Signet from 610 in 1850 to 366 by 1885.[24] Of 850 members admitted to the Society between 1850 and 1914, 24.9% are known to have remained unmarried at death, and the social origins of recruits to the profession suggest that WSs were more dependent than advocates on professional practice for their incomes.[26] The proportion of WSs who remained celibate was 28.4% of the 1850-79 intake of members (which were years of acute oversupply) and declined as membership reached its lowest point to 15.7% of admissions between 1880 and 1884. Subsequently, a large influx of members increased the total number of practitioners up to 628 by 1915, and celibacy increased to 23.1% of those admitted to the profession between 1885 and 1914.

AGE AT MARRIAGE

That the age at marriage of CAs and their brides was significant in determining the output of potential self-recruits is evident from the following table.

Table 6.5
**The Relationship Between Age at First Marriage and Marital
Fertility Among SAE Members Admitted 1853-92**

Children Born to Marriage	Mean Age of CA	Mean Age of Bride	N	Sons Born to Marriage	Mean Age of CA	Mean Age of Bride	N
0	39.57	32.45	32	0	36.93	30.00	59
1	34.54	26.52	21	1	33.00	25.97	45
2	32.55	25.37	32	2	31.59	24.28	49
3	33.51	25.53	28	3	31.52	24.94	17
4	30.79	24.62	31	4	30.57	24.10	13
5	29.84	25.11	17	5	28.85	24.20	10
6-10	31.27	24.03	36	6-7	33.40	21.25	4

The marital fertility of Edinburgh CAs who married at later ages or married older brides was below that of those who entered into earlier wedlock. It can be seen from the above table that the age of the CA's bride at marriage was of crucial importance to determining marital fertility.

Given that employment and income considerations in the Edinburgh CA profession were likely to have influenced the decision of whether to marry or not, they were also of potential significance to the determination of when to marry. As Banks has asserted:

> Prudence and postponement became inseparately linked in the middle-class mind, and the notion that no one ought to marry until he was reasonably certain of being able to provide his wife with as high a level of living as she was already enjoying under her parental roof, obtained categorical force in the middle class world.[27]

An appropriate income was necessary to maintain a *suitable establishment* conducive to that of a nineteenth century gentleman of professional status. Marriage was deemed as unaffordable unless personal income was sufficient to ensure that the professional was also not called upon "to make any sacrifice or appreciable reduction in his personal expenses and enjoyments."[28]

It is possible to lend some limited support to this assertion that professionals married at the age at which it was possible to support a wife according to the standards to which she had become accustomed with reference to CAs. The mean age at marriage among SAE members between 1853 and 1892 was 33.14 years in 193 cases where the occupation of the bride's father is known. The mean age at first marriage of 22 CAs who married the daughters of men of independent means (SSG 1) was 34.4 years and among 23 who married the daughters of lawyers, the mean was 33.8. Among 94 CAs who effectively married below their own professional, SSG 2 status, the mean age was 33.04 years (32.34 where the bride's father was in a lower middle or working class status group, SSGs 6-9).

Given the existence of this relationship between the bride's father and the age of the CA at marriage, the social status origins of CAs' brides assumes some limited importance in determining fecundity and, consequently, in determining their capacity for potential self-recruitment.

It was clear from the previous chapter that the ability of a CA to embark on a successful career depended quite heavily on his own social status origins. Income accumulation was likely to have been faster among SAE members who had fathers in higher social status groups. Among CAs who married above their own fathers' social status, it might be expected that it would have taken some time to accumulate sufficient income to support a wife of higher status origins than their own. The information contained in Table 6.6 below reveals that, if measured from the social status of the CA's father, SAE members of low status origins tended to marry the daughters of higher status families more commensurate with their now professional, SSG 2 standing.

The mean age at marriage of 26 CAs who derived from lower middle class or upper working class origins (SSGs 6-9) and who married a daughter from the upper middle classes (SSGs 1-4) was 34.39 years, compared to 33.22 for the 116 CAs from SSGs 1-4 who married into the same status group.

TABLE 6.6
Social Status Origins of SAE Members Admitted 1853–92 Compared to That of Their Brides at First Marriage (where known)

SSG of Father	SSG of CA's Father-in-Law									N
	1	2	3	4	5	6	7	8	9	
1	5	11	1	2	0	0	1	1	0	21
2	13	49	10	9	0	2	3	0	1	87
3	0	3	2	0	0	0	2	1	0	8
4	2	5	2	6	1	3	0	1	0	20
5	1	3	1	2	2	0	1	0	0	10
6	0	4	1	5	0	1	2	3	0	16
7	2	1	3	3	2	2	3	2	0	18
8	0	1	2	3	1	3	1	0	0	11
9	0	1	0	0	0	0	0	1	0	2
N	23	78	22	30	6	11	13	9	1	193

It is apparent from the evidence regarding fluctuations in the rate of celibacy among SAE members that the level of professional competition and its effects on the speed and level of income accumulation could influence the decision on whether to marry or not. Table 6.7 indicates that the same factors had an impact on the age at marriage.

TABLE 6.7
Mean Age at First Marriage of SAE Members Admitted 1853–92 (where known) Relative to the State of Professional Competition

Year of Admission	N of Cases	Age of CA	Age of Bride	Years Between Admission and Marriage	% Celibate	N of New Members
1853–54	49	34.72	28.40	–	18.8	–
1855–64	26	35.74	26.87	8.58	26.2	42
1865–74	28	31.69	23.53	7.08	9.1	44
1875–84	51	33.12	25.50	9.08	25.3	91
1885–92	50	32.61	26.77	8.86	22.5	112

A comparison between the timing and extent of the fluctuations in celibacy and the age at marriage among CAs reveals considerable similarity. The explanations provided for the trend in celibacy would appear to be applicable to that of the age of marriage. Marriage was earlier during periods when the competition among CAs was reduced (1865–74), either by an increase in workload or by a low rate of new admissions – ensuring that the income threshold necessary before wedlock (depending on the bride's social origins) was reached faster. By contrast, marriage was delayed when increases in membership, encouraged by changes designed to improve professional status (the organization of the SAE in 1853–54, the introduction of a sophisticated system of professional examination in 1873, the institution of GEB examinations in 1893), exceeded the rate of expansion in the CAs' potential business and thus reduced the rate of income accumulation.

The relationship between professional competition and the age at marriage is less evident among members of the Faculty of Advocates. As mentioned earlier, the social origins of advocates permitted a lesser degree of reliance upon vocational earnings for total income. Among WSs, however, whose social origins were more akin to those of SAE members, and who were similarly more dependent on professional earnings, the relationship between the number of new members and the age at marriage appears to have been stronger.

TABLE 6.8
Mean Age at First Marriage of Advocates and WSs Admitted 1850–1914 (where known) Relative to Indicators of the State of Professional Competition[29]

Year of Admission	Advocates		Writers to the Signet	
	Age at First Marriage	N of New Members	Age at First Marriage	N of New Members
1850–54	34.53	41	30.90	30
1855–64	34.28	99	32.61	81
1865–74	34.11	87	33.40	96
1875–84	32.82	95	33.42	110
1885–94	34.63	132	34.25	229
1895–04	34.41	109	34.76	153
1905–14	32.92	88	32.86	151
Total/Mean	33.93	651	33.52	850

FERTILITY

The fertility experience of SAE members who entered the profession between 1853 and 1892, as provided by obituarial sources as well as the census, statutory and old parish registers, is outlined in Table 6.9.

It should be noted in this table that fertility by year of marriage after 1900 was particularly low due to the later-than-average age at marriage of members who were admitted before 1893 and that of their wives. Additionally, the two sets of statistics only follow the same trend broadly as marriage took place on average between seven and nine years after admission to the SAE (see Table 6.7). Year of marriage is therefore a more precise indicator of the timing of fluctuations in fertility than year of admission.

The most notable feature of the table is the comparatively unsteady decline in the fertility of Edinburgh CAs, though the small population undoubtedly accounts partly for the intensity of the fluctuations. If decennial cohorts are examined, however, the trend remains evident.

TABLE 6.9
Completed Marital Fertility of SAE Members Admitted 1853-92
(including three ICAEW members practising in Edinburgh)
by Year of First Marriage and Year of Admission

Year of Marriage	Mean Children Born to Marriage	N	Year of Admission	Mean Children Born to Marriage	N
Pre-1845	3.86	22			
	} 4.21				
1845-49	5.00	10			
1850-54	4.25	8	1853-54	3.84	51
	} 4.77				
1855-59	5.20	10	1855-59	5.14	14
1860-64	4.90	10	1860-64	3.33	12
	} 3.90				
1865-69	3.08	12	1865-69	4.00	12
1870-74	5.27	11	1870-74	3.94	18
	} 4.20				
1875-79	3.55	18	1875-79	2.85	21
1880-84	2.64	14	1880-84	2.32	28
	} 2.52				
1885-89	2.45	24	1885-89	1.72	36
1890-94	2.73	23	1890-92	1.68	16
	} 2.34				
1895-99	1.83	18	3 ICAEW		
1900-04	1.50	8	Members	4.66	3
	} 1.11				
1905+	0.77	9			
Total/Mean	3.24	197		3.10	211

Other studies which have investigated the decline of middle class fertility in certain occupational groups have revealed similar fluctuations. Banks, for example, has noted the following for English accountants utilizing the 1911 Fertility Census. Marriages contracted before 1861 produced 5.6 births compared to 5.7 for the 1861-71 cohort (though it has to be remembered that women married pre-1861 and still living in 1911 constituted an odd subset); subsequently, long-term decline became established, marriages contracted between 1871 and 1881 produced 4.5 births and those of 1881 to 1891 produced 3.2.[30] The fertility experience of engineers exhibited similar fluctuation.

These relatively unsteady declines in occupational fertility have remained largely unexplained. While it is not the intention here to provide a thorough investigation of the causes of middle class fertility decline during the second half of the nineteenth century, it is crucial in order to examine the potential for self-recruitment that the determinants of fertility levels among SAE members can be described.

The Long-Run: The Social Origins of Edinburgh CAs and the Economics of Fertility

Tables 6.9 and 6.10 illustrate that long-run fertility decline became established among Edinburgh CAs during the mid-late 1870s.

TABLE 6.10
Completed Marital Fertility of Edinburgh CAs 1853–92 (where known)

Year of First Marriage	Number of Children Born to Marriage										Total
	0	1	2	3	4	5	6	7	8	9	10	
1815-19						1				1	1	3
1820-24	1											1
1825-29		1					1					2
1830-34				2	1							3
1835-39		1		2		1	1		1			6
1840-44	3				3		1					7
1845-49	1		2	1		1	1	1	2	1		10
1850-54	1	1			2	1	1	2				8
1855-59	1		1	1		1	3	1	1	1		10
1860-64	2				1	3		2	2			10
1865-69	2	1	2	2		4	1					12
1870-74				2	3	1	3		1	1		11
1875-79	2	1	3	4	4	1	1		1		1	18
1880-84	1	3	2	2	6							14
1885-89	3	3	8	3	5	1	1					24
1890-94	4	3	5	4	3	2	1				1	23
1895-99	3	4	6	3	2							18
1900-04	2	2	2	2								8
1905-09	4	1	1		1							7
1910-14	1											1
1915-19	1											1
Total	32	21	32	28	31	17	15	6	8	4	3	197

91.2% of CA marriages contracted between 1875 and 1919 produced between 0 and 4 births compared to 48.2% among those contracted between 1815 and 1874. Similarly, only 8.8% of marriages in the later cohort produced 5 or more offspring compared to 51.8% in the earlier one. It is evident, however, that certain *pioneers* of family limitation among Edinburgh CAs began to restrict their fertility from around the 1830s.

The SAE members' marriages contracted between 1815 and 1874 which produced between one and four births are the interesting initiators of small families. Those marriages contracted during this period that remained childless are not included here due to the possibility that infertility was not voluntary (these constitute 13.3% of marriages, a rate slightly above current sterility levels).

The initial point to note concerning the experience of the 31 low fertility marriages contracted between 1815 and 1874 was the impact of mortality on their fecundity. In 4 cases, low fertility can be explained by the early death of the wife, 1 due to the young decease of the CA and, in another, constant debilitating ill health resulting in institutional confinement. In two instances, a first marriage proved infertile followed by a late second marriage with a reduced reproductive capacity. Similarly, one CA married so late that by the time of the birth of his third child, his wife was 45 years old.

If this mortality-influenced group is disregarded, their fertility being involuntarily regulated, the true 22 instigators of fertility decline among Edinburgh CAs are identified. The most significant characteristic of this set of marriages was the social origins of one or both of the partners as compared to those marriages that produced five or more births. In all but one case, at least one partner had a father whose social status was either independent income or traditional, *old* professional (law, medicine, religion or armed forces). 19 (86.4%) of the low fertility CAs had fathers in SSGs 1-2 as a whole compared to 24 (55.8%) of those CAs whose marriages produced more than four births. 13 (30.2%) of the high fertility marriages were contracted between partners of whom neither had independent means, old, or new professional origins.

The marriages of CAs which were contracted before 1875 that restricted their fertility were, thus, predominantly those in which one or both of the partners had been effectively downwardly mobile, or at best whose social status remained static compared to that of their parents. For fathers and fathers-in-laws in SSG 1 or the upper, traditional professions of SSG 2, to have a son or son-in-law as an accountant (pre-1854 marriages) or a CA (post-1854 marriages), entailed a downward social movement. Not only, therefore, had at least one partner in the early low fertility marriages derived from independent means or old professional origins where fertility regulation was likely to have been already established,[31] they also had good socio-economic reasons for having a small family.

As was established earlier in the discussion on the age at marriage, husbands in the upper middle classes were, during the nineteenth century, expected to maintain their wives in the luxury to which they had been accustomed in the parental household. This was likely to have proved difficult to sustain for the CA who had derived from lower status origins than his wife and without his having attained the age of maximum earning capacity (unlike his father-in-law). Similarly, there was pressure on husbands in the professions to maintain a certain standard due to the social convention that sons should commence their married life: "As the saying is, they expect to begin where their fathers left off."[32] That was likely to have proved difficult for the CA in a lower status occupation than that of his father.

In order, therefore, to maintain the levels of consumption necessary to aspire to parental standards, and in the desire to re-assert the family's status though occupying a lower social and economic standing, it is conceivable that this group of Edinburgh CAs were induced to restrict their fertility. A smaller family would not only have permitted the maintenance of desirable standards, it also allowed a greater distribution of resources toward the education and vocational training of fewer sons who might retrieve the family standing in the succeeding generation through entrance to the older professions or through the attainment of economic independence. Just as the marginal social status of the lower middle and artisan classes resulted in aspirations for the upward mobility of sons to the professions achieved by small family size, so with this group of CAs who were placed in a dubious social position through the higher status of their parents or in-laws which encouraged ambitions for intergenerational status improvement which was achievable by restricting their fertility. The data presented in Table 6.11 tend to support these conclusions.

TABLE 6.11
Social Status Origins of CAs' Sons Born to Low and High Fertility Marriages
Contracted Before 1875 (where son's occupation is known)

Intergenerational Social Mobility of Son	1-4	N	5 or 5+	N
Upward (SSG 1 or Higher Professional)	43.3	13	27.9	24
Static (CA or 'New' Professional)	43.3	13	32.6	28
Downward (SSGs 3-9)	13.4	4	39.5	34
Total	100.0	30	100.0	86

The evidence above suggests that, whereas the small CA family could ensure a minimal amount of intergenerational downward mobilty, the large CA family could not. Especially among younger sons of high fertility marriages, there were insufficient resources available to ensure upward movement given the pressure to secure the social advancement of the family through at least one (preferably the eldest) son.

The foregoing analysis of the pioneers of low fertility among CAs would suggest that the social origins of the CA in relation to the status of his vocation and the income derived from it might be crucial in explaining not only the age at marriage but also the level of marital fertility. The following data would appear to confirm this assertion.

TABLE 6.12
**Completed Marital Fertility of Edinburgh CAs According
to Their Social Status Origins (where known)**

SSG of Father	Mean CAs 1853-92	N	Mean Post 1874 Marriages	N	Mean of Members 1853-1914	N
1	2.25	24	2.10	10	2.25	24
2	3.51	90	2.60	45	3.07	119
3	3.12	8	3.00	4	2.60	15
4	3.14	21	2.13	15	2.90	32
5	4.16	12	4.28	7	3.87	16
6	2.70	17	2.16	12	2.06	32
7	2.05	19	1.54	11	2.00	35
8	2.21	14	2.00	10	1.88	25
9	0.00	1	0.00	1	0.00	2
Total/Mean	3.04	206	2.39	115	2.64	300

Even if marriages that were contracted following the onset of general fertility decline are examined (post-1874 marriages), Edinburgh CAs' fertility was generally higher among those who had fathers in high income and status occupational groups. There was evidently (with the exception of SSG 5 where higher than expected fertility was probably the consequence of conventions and traditions concerning the size of farming families), a decline in fertility levels according to social status origins. CAs admitted to the SAE between 1853 and 1892 with upper middle class (SSG 1-5) origins produced 3.3 children per marriage compared to 2.3 for those who had fathers in the lower middle and working classes (SSGs 6-9).

Among CAs who derived from lower middle and working class families, who were upwardly mobile over a great social distance into the profession, the pressure to maintain the material standards required of their professional status was only possible by restricting fertility. This practice, after all, either voluntarily or involuntarily (though most likely the former) by their own parents had secured sufficient resources for their own entrance to the SAE.

The CA who had derived from SSGs 6-9 was confronted with a series of economic dilemmas in his quest to attain levels of consumption commensurate with his now professional, SSG 2 status. It was vital for CAs given the relative infancy of the organized profession to present in themselves, their property, household and family, a front of conspicuous wealth, respectability and integrity. Given also that clientele were primarily based upon a range of *connections*, this presentation had to appear as maintaining a constant or escalating standard; any decline might result in a loss of business confidence. Moreover, the CA had to ensure that there was seen to be a status dichotomy between himself and the competitive non-chartered accountant in order to assert his professional superiority. Davidoff and Hall have summed up a situation relevant to CAs during the second half of the nineteenth century:

> . . . Since it was essential for middle class men to demonstrate credit-worthiness in such a way as to encourage trust from both potential customers and creditors, a respectable household, managed by a dependent wife and staffed by resident servants, became a potent symbol of social status.[33]

The pressure on CAs who had low status origins to attain the required standard was compounded by the fact that they were dependent to a much greater extent than their colleagues from higher status origins on income derived from professional practice. They could not rely on a sizeable inheritance or substantial parental support to build their own business or secure a semi-dependence on vocational earnings. The level of income derived from professional practice was subject to fluctuation according to the state of competition, which could vary markedly over the 1853-1914 period as previous analysis has shown.

There existed an increasing number of CAs from low status origins who, if in practice, were highly dependent on a potentially unstable source of income, with few major business connections; and, if not in practice, were dependent on a comparatively lower salary as a clerk in an established CA firm. It was economically difficult to maintain the necessary standards required of their professional standing. One costly item of non-essential expenditure was the raising of a large family. During periods of relative prosperity in the profession, the need to reduce fertility was less pressing. During years of intense competition for limited business, however, it was essential if standards were not to suffer and limited clientele lost.

The significance of this with regard to the fertility of CA marriages and the potential for self-recruitment was paramount. As the profession was entered increasingly by the sons of lower middle class families (as will be shown in the following chapter) who were heavily reliant on vocational earnings and found the maintenance of professional status difficult to achieve without diverting resources from child bearing, fertility decline among CAs was self-accumulating. As increasing numbers of CAs who had derived from low status origins entered the profession and failed to produce significant numbers of sons, the capacity for self-recruitment was reduced, and the profession was opened hypothetically to those from lower status origins – who, in turn, would provide even fewer future potential recruits relative to the expansion of the SAE.

Additionally, the pressure of professional competition was, particularly after the 1873 examination reforms, increasingly acute. The long-run fertility decline of Edinburgh CAs became established during the same period as professional competition began its more consistent increase (as indicated especially by the emigration of SAE members and the expansion of membership of the Society). This ensured that, not only were future income prospects more unpredictable, particularly among CAs from low status origins (so that it was more difficult to maintain material standards), but also meant that the attractiveness of entering any sons born into one's own occupation was lessened due to its potentially more austere future. Other, more costly-to-enter professions might have to be considered as vocations for any males born to the marriage. Such a course was only feasible through restricting the number of sons that had to be financed through the educational and training systems of the alternative professions and provided with capital to become established in practice.

What is being asserted here is that the fertility levels of the marriages of Edinburgh CAs were to an unquantifiable though significant extent influenced by the socio-economic consequences of their own upward or downward mobility into the CA profession, and that a certain level of material consumption was necessary to maintain professional status and help secure income accumulation. The ability to maintain the necessary standard, and consequently to finance the cost of raising children, depended on the social origins of the CA and the resulting extent to which he was reliant on professionally-derived income which was subject to fluctuation.

Although these propositions may contribute to an understanding of the general trend in the marital fertility of CAs during the period being studied, they only provide a limited explanation for the short-term fluctuations that were revealed in Tables 6.9 and 6.10. In order to explain these, it is necessary to analyse the impact of *intra* professional, institutional changes designed to improve the status of the SAE.

The Short-Run: Professionalization and Fertility

The fluctuations in the fertility of the marriages of Edinburgh CAs in the 1853-92 cohort is revealed further in Figure 6.1. Fertility by the year of the birth of the first child is included for two reasons. Firstly, it removes all involuntarily infertile couples for whom fertility strategies were irrelevant. Secondly, it permits a greater degree of precision in identifying the timing of changes in fertility and their causes, as there existed a delay of 1.8 years on average between the date of the first marriage and the birth of the first child. By both criteria the fluctuations remain. How then can these fluctuations (which will be shown to have been non-random) previous to the mid 1870s be explained ? And, what accounts for the unexpected brief upturn in fertility that occurred among the 1890-4 cohort at a time when long-run fertility decline appears to have become established ?

Structural alterations within the SAE had a significant impact upon its members' status given its relatively short existence during the second half of the nineteenth century. Changes in the SAE's rules were designed not only to improve the standing of members but also to distinguish them from the professionally inferior, unorganized and unqualified accountant. Measures designed to improve professional status and encourage occupational exclusiveness were also heavily motivated by their potential financial rewards; to encourage business into the hands of CAs as against their competitors. The actual effect of status-enhancing measures in the longer run was to increase competition among a greater number of members attracted to the profession - though - from the perspective of the practising member at the time of their introduction, they may have been conceived as being favourable to their own business prospects. More significantly for the fertility considerations of parents, institutional changes may have influenced decisions concerning family size. They did so through their impact on improving professional status, and thus offered the *prospect* of higher future income and an ability to support a larger family due to an improved competitive position in relation to other accountants for the existing and any subsequent generation of CAs.

Additionally, following changes designed to improve vocational standing, any sons born, and later becoming self-recruits, would effectively be admitted to a higher status occupation than that which their fathers had entered. An upper middle class

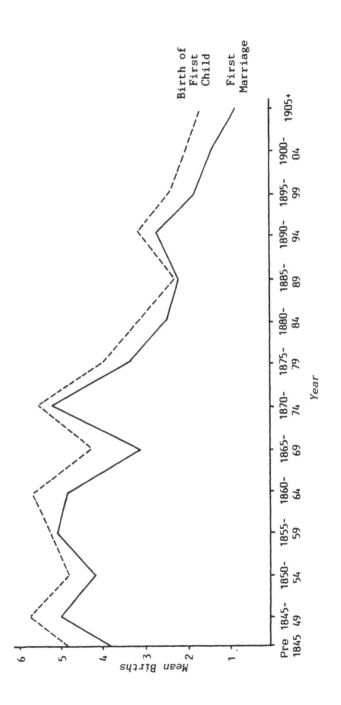

FIGURE 6.1 Completed Marital Fertility of Edinburgh CAs 1853–92 by Year of First Marriage and Year of the Birth of the First Child

convention mentioned by the *Schools Inquiry Commission* of 1867-8 would thereby be satisfied; it referred to a "class of parents" being:

> . . . the great majority of professional men, especially the clergy, medical men, and lawyers; the poorer gentry: all in fact, who having received a cultivated education themselves, are very anxious that their sons should not fall below them.[34]

The peaks and troughs in the fertility of Edinburgh CA marriages from the 1850s onwards are explicable in the following terms. It was not coincidental that the major fluctuations occurred at the same time as the significant events in the history of the SAE which affected the professional status of its members.

The formation of the Institute of Accountants and its incorporation in 1853-4 effectively graded existing Edinburgh accountants into two classes. The SAE attracted the most notable and respectable practitioners, could claim to have professional status, and adopted a notation to recognize the fact. It was organized and recognized by the State. The remaining accountants were occupationally and socially inferior by the absence of these attributes. CAs could envisage the prospect of an increased volume of business at the expense of competitors once this occupational distinction became recognized by clientele. The likelihood of an improved financial and professional position ensured that standards of consumption could be maintained and a large family supported.

From the perspective of an SAE member in the the mid 1850s to the early 1860s, his profession offered excellent prospects for himself and for any sons born compared to its unorganized past, and he was well placed (given the unsophisticated process of entrance and training during this period) to ensure that any sons could adopt his own vocation when decisions concerning occupational destination came to be made in the future. There was, consequently, a double inducement to relax restraints on family size.

Among CAs who were married during the mid to late 1860s the *outlook* for himself and any sons born who might enter the SAE sixteen to eighteen years later, was more uncertain. Alternative, though more-expensive-to-enter, professions may have appeared to CA fathers, anxious to secure the social advance of the succeeding generation, as more attractive for any son born. As explained in Chapter 4, Edinburgh CAs could only partly lay claim during this period to a professional trait of increasing significance: that of practice based upon the acquisition of theoretical knowledge tested by examination. "Between 1855 and 1875", asserts Reader, "examinations, both qualifying and competitive, came into the centre of the stage for the classes which looked for a living either in the public services or to the open professions."[35]

A son's entrance to his father's profession would not therefore result, from the perspective of a mid to late 1860s and early 1870s CA marriage, in the upward mobility of the succeeding generation. Fertility was therefore reduced to permit resources to become available for the vocational preparation of any sons born into higher status professions.

A CA father married during the years immediately following the **introduction of the comprehensive system of professional examinations in 1873** could envisage a brighter future for himself and any offspring. The imposition of a three-tier examination system allowing future generations of SAE members to assert their professional status and superiority on the basis of having gained a *learned* qualification over their competitors ensured greater potential prosperity. Any sons born who might later join the SAE would be entering a profession with a training system comparable to that of alternative vocations and one of higher status than the father had himself entered.

The increased attraction of one's own profession for sons permitted a relaxation of fertility restrictions as it was less costly to train sons to enter chartered accountancy. Fees were comparatively low and only a liberal education was necessary. Moreover, the heavy investment in education, vocational training and establishing a son in practice was more likely to have been rewarded by success, as the father was in an advantageous position to nurse a son through his own occupation and secure for him a clientele after qualification.[36]

The difference in the cost of an educational and vocational preparation for entry to the SAE compared to that of the most desirable alternative higher status profession, the law, is discernible from the following analysis. 22 CA sons became lawyers (14 WSs, 1 SSC, 6 advocates and 1 barrister) and, in 19 of these cases, the major schools attended by each are known. Similarly, 53 CA sons became SAE apprentices; the educational history of 50 is known. The difference between the two sets of sons in terms of school attended and educational costs is revealed in Table 6.13 below.

Equally high proportions of sons attended high class *private* schools in Scotland during their educational careers. The statistics for this group, however, hide considerable differences. 96 (81.4%) of the years spent by future lawyers were at the upper status end of Scottish private schools: Edinburgh Academy (83 years), Loretto (7) and Fettes College (6). This compared to 55.9% of future CA apprentices who attended these expensive schools. Further, none of the future lawyers went to the less costly Scottish *public* schools and a greater proportion (16.4%) spent some time at English schools compared to CA apprentices (9.6%) which implied substantial boarding costs.

TABLE 6.13
School Education of 19 Sons of CAs Who Entered Law Compared to That of 50 Who Entered into SAE Indentures (costs at 1880 prices)

Type of School	Law		SAE	
	Years at	Cost (£s)	Years at	Cost (£s)
Scottish High Class Private	118	2232	290	5307
Scottish High Class Public	0	0	20	244
Great English Public	20	2062	16	1650
Upper Class English	0	0	10	819
English Middle Class/Cathedral or Grammar	4	...	8	598
Foreign School	0	0	1	...
Private Education	4	...	0	...
Total	146	4294	345	8618
Mean	7.68	226.00	6.90	172.36

It can be argued that differences in the schooling received by these sons were largely a reflection of variations in the wealth of CA parents. The differences in the cost of educational preparation between law and chartered accountancy were, however, particularly marked with regard to university attendance which was more likely to have been contemplated after decisions concerning specific career destination had been made. To enter the Bar, a degree was necessary and an adequate period at university was conventional for a writer or a solicitor. All but 3 of the 22 lawyers attended university (for an average of 2.63 years before entering vocational training) and 8 gained a degree. By contrast, only 18 of the SAE apprentices attended university (for a mean of 2.22 years) of whom 6 became graduates. In addition, of the fifty years expended at university by lawyers, 48.0% were at Oxbridge or other English university and 52.0% went to Edinburgh or other Scottish university. This compared to 25.0% at Oxbridge and 75.0% at Edinburgh for the forty years spent by potential CAs. Entrance to a legal training, therefore, required a longer period of higher education at the most costly and distant institutions.

Similarly, the vocational training and entrance costs required were markedly different for chartered accountants compared to lawyers. At 1880 prices, the mean amongst lawyers was £373.81 compared to £157 for CAs. Ignoring the exogenous expenses of subsistence during the periods of education and training, and on the basis of formal school and professional entrance fees, there clearly existed considerable differences between the outlay necessary for entering a son into a higher status occupation than one's own from the perspective of the Edinburgh CA father.

Compared to CA marriages of the early-mid 1870s, those of the late 1870s and 1880s were confronted by a period of vocational insecurity and internal threats to professional status and income. The actual result of the 1873 examination changes was to increase competition among a greater number of SAE members attracted to the profession due to its more *learned* standing. Additionally, the formation of the SIA in 1880, combined with its attempts in 1884 and 1889-90 to obtain a charter of incorporation and adoption of the CA notation, ensured that Scottish chartered accountancy did not guarantee an increasing and stable income in the future which was required to support a large family, and was too vulnerable and uncertain a vocation to consider for any sons born. There was consequently a drastic reduction in the fertility of marriage contracted during the mid to late 1870s and 1880s.

During the 1890s, however, following a decade of threats to future income stability and status, the SAE and the other Scottish chartered societies sought to re-assert their position and fertility temporarily increased as a result. The 1890-3 reaction of the SAE began in 1890 with the successful repulsion of the SIA's second and most concerted attempt to obtain a charter. To this defeat of the rival organizations was added the outcome of the 'CA case' in May 1893 in which the chartered societies gained legal sanction for their exclusive usage of the lucrative CA designation. This decison in the Court of Session was vital to the income stability and status of SAE members. Should the litigation have been unsuccessful, the door was opened effectively for any organized accountant to gain 'CA' status through the use of the notation. The aim of the Corporation of Accountants in challenging the chartered societies was "to appropriate the status and reputation of membership, and the pecuniary and other benefits thence arising", and their success in court would have ensured that "the status of the membership of the chartered societies would be lowered."[37]

The *learned* and *academic* standing of the Scottish CA was improved in 1893 by the introduction of the GEB examinations which affirmed the superior system of training and examination of the CA over his competitors. These campaigns against rival organizations and institutional changes strengthened the links between the chartered societies, and formed the basis of a more united *national* profession geared to the concerted defence of its interests. Parents, imbued with a 'future-time perspective' could envisage during the early 1890s, a brighter, more secure prospect for their own position and for that of any sons born and later entered into a higher status and stronger CA profession. The impact of these apparently favourable changes from the married CA's perspective were temporary. The post-1895 period witnessed renewed attempts by the SIA to gain incorporation (1896) and a succession of parliamentary bills to regulate the British accountancy profession (some of which were specific to Scotland) which were generally unfavourable to the CAs' position. Additionally, the 1893 reforms of the examination system only acted to increase the attractiveness of the vocation and the number of competing practitioners engendered widespread concern by the late 1890s about the overstocked nature of the profession. In these circumstances, the raising of a large family was undesirable and alternative professions for any sons born appeared more attractive to CA fathers wishing to ensure intergenerational upward mobility. There was once again a considerable inducement and socio-economic necessity to reduce fertility.

CONCLUSIONS

It is clear from the above analysis that economic and institutional factors as well as the social derivation of recruits and the status priorities of professional men had a fundamental impact upon their marital and fertility experience and therefore determined their capacity to produce self-recruits. Decisions concerning marriage and child bearing were associated intimately with the state of the individual's profession: his route to it; his social origins and those of his spouse in relation to its social standing; level of dependence on it for income; changes in the earnings derived from it and the prospects it offered for future prosperity; changes in its occupational and social status; and the opportunities it provided for improving family status in the next generation of sons.

It was essentially, internal developments within the Edinburgh CA profession therefore that ultimately determined the ability of its practitioners to secure self-recruitment. The extent to which this was achieved is the question to which the next chapter is directed.

Notes

1 Abrahamson *et al. Stratification and Mobility*, pp. 217–8.

2 For a further discussion of this hypothesis see S.P. Walker, "Occupational Expansion Fertility Decline and Recruitment to the Professions in Scotland, 1850–1914 (with special reference to the Chartered Accountants of Edinburgh)" (Ph.D. Dissertation, University of Edinburgh, 1986), ch. 1.

3 The two exceptions were: Francis J. Moncrieff, CA (admitted 1875) whose first marriage took place on 2 August 1871 aged 21, the son of a Lord Advocate; and, Peter S. Warden, CA (admitted 1890) whose marriage took place at the age of 19 on 18 April 1884 while employed as a CA's clerk – his first vocation. Warden did not originally intend to enter an SAE indenture but did so on the recommendation of his employer.

4 Heiton, *The Castes of Edinburgh,* ch. 15.

5 A Bachelor, "On Some Impediments to Marriage", *Fraser's Magazine* 76 (1867), p. 774.

6 Quoted in M.F. Brightfield, *Victorian England in its Novels 1840–1870* (Los Angeles, 1968), vol. 4, p. 89. See B. Jerrald, *Up and Down in the World* (London, 1863).

7 "Why are Women Redundant ?", *The National Review* 14 (1862), p. 452. See also "The Decline of Marriage", *Westminster Review* 135 (1891).

8 "Keeping up Appearances", *The Cornhill Magazine* 4 (1861), p. 318.

9 *Ibid.,* pp. 311–12.

10 *The Accountant's Magazine* 29 (1925), p. 10.

11 Quoted in Brightfield, *Victorian England in its Novels,* vol. 4, p. 86. See J. Verey, *Martyrs to Fashion* (London, 1868).

12 One such case was mentioned in an interview with Alexander Harrison, CA (admitted to the SAE in 1914), Edinburgh, 13 December 1984. A J.S.T., celibate CA, and fierce business competitor of A.R.D., CA, purchased an estate on the latter inheriting one.

13 Heiton, *The Castes of Edinburgh,* p. 237.

14 For estimates of the domestic expenses of the middle class marital home see Banks, *Prosperity and Parenthood,* ch. 4.

15 "Keeping up Appearances", p. 307. See also A Bachelor, "On Some Impediments to Marriage" on the cost of marriage.

16 "Why are Women Redundant ?", p. 446.

17 Martin, *The Accountant Squabble,* p. 8.

18 ICAS, *History of the Chartered Accountants of Scotland,* p. 58.

19 The total indentures statistics in Table 6.3 were calculated from the indenture registers of the SAE. Total admissions were derived from ICAS, *History of the Chartered Accountants of Scotland,* Appendix 7, p. 173.

20 A Bachelor, "On Some Impediments to Marriage", p. 774.

21 The major sources of information concerning the marriages of advocates was S.P. Walker, "The Faculty of Advocates 1800-1986" (Advocates' Library, Edinburgh, April 1987) for celibacy rates and Grant, *The Faculty of Advocates* for ages at marriage.

22 Stutfield, "Celibacy and the Struggle to Get On", p. 785.

23 J. Lorimer, *A Handbook of the Law of Scotland* (Edinburgh, 1873), 3rd ed., pp. 478-9.

24 A.C. Chitnis, *The Scottish Enlightenment: A Social History* (London, 1976), p. 76.

25 See J. Clive, "The Social Background of the Scottish Renaissance", in N.T. Phillipson and R. Mitchison (eds.), *Scotland in the Age of Improvement* (Edinburgh, 1970), p. 228.

26 The social origins of Writers to the Signet 1850-1914 can be gained from Grant, *History of the Society of Writers to His Majesties Signet.*

27 Banks, *Prosperity and Parenthood,* p. 198.

28 "A Bachelor's Protest", *Chamber's Journal* 15 (1861), p. 385.

29 The age at marriage of Writers to the Signet was calculated from Society of Writers to H.M. Signet, *Register of The Society of Writers to Her Majesties Signet,* (Edinburgh, 1983) which is an updated and revised version of Grant, *History of the Society of Writers to His Majesties Signet.*

30 Banks, *Victorian Values,* pp. 40, 98.

31 See T.H. Hollingsworth, "The Demography of the British Peerage", *Population Studies* 18 (1964). The 1911 Fertility Census of Scotland indicates that fertility decline was earliest among the marriages of higher professionals. The occupational groups enumerated with the lowest mean fertility were: Advocates, Solicitors (3.92 births), Physicians, Surgeons (3.91), Dentists (including assistants) (3.86), Army Officers (effective and retired) (3.76).

32 Stutfield, "Celibacy and the Struggle to Get On", p. 789. See also Banks, *Victorian Values,* p. 47.

33 L. Davidoff and C. Hall, "The Architecture of Public and Private Life; English Middle Class Society in a Provincial Town, 1750-1850", in D. Fraser and A. Sutcliffe, *The Pursuit of Urban History* (London, 1983), p. 328.

34 British *Parliamentary Papers, Reports* vol. 1 "Of the Commissioners Appointed to Inquire into Education", pp. 17-18.

35 Reader, *Professional Men,* p. 99. See also Banks, *Victorian Values,* ch. 6 and Millerson, *The Qualifying Associations,* ch. 5.

36 See Banks, *Victorian Values,* pp. 48-9 and Stutfield, "Celibacy and the Struggle to Get On", pp. 789-90 for a discussion of the costs of educating middle class sons.

37 *Cases Decided in the Court of Session, Court of Justiciary and House of Lords* 20 (1892-3), 4th series, No. 132, p. 756.

7
Self-Recruitment and Social Mobility

> It is a matter of common knowledge in the profession,
> although difficult to prove, that young men get into
> these societies merely because they are the sons of
> their fathers.

[J. Martin, *The Sanctification of the Lie*, 1897]

A study of the potential mobility effects of declining fertility on self-recruitment in the Edinburgh CA profession between 1853 and 1914 requires an analysis of the output of the sons of CAs who were of an eligible age and location to be regarded as potential future recruits. An assessment of whether the supply of such sons was so insufficient as to permit an intake of recruits from alternative social origins, and of the prudence of assuming that CAs did desire the entrance of their sons to their own profession, has to be undertaken. In order to investigate these questions, the following procedure was adopted.

To have entered the SAE by 1914, a son had to be born in or before 1892 as the minimum age of an SAE apprentice on indenture commencement was seventeen years from 1889. The latest date of commencement for an indenture to have been discharged by the end of 1914 was 1909. Reduced periods of service through holding a degree or pre-apprenticeship employment allowing qualification by 1914 and indenture commencement after 1909 were only possible if the son was born well before 1892. Three years of university attendance ensured only a reduced term of one year, as did, for example, two years of previous employment in related occupations.

All CAs who were admitted to the SAE between 1853 and 1892 were considered as having been potential fathers of self-recruits as were 3 ICAEW members who practised in Edinburgh during the same period. 355 potential fathers were thus identified and, of these, a number were excluded as not having been in a position to produce sons for future recruitment to the SAE by 1914. These were:

CAs who remained celibate at death.	75
Migrant CAs who left Scotland and whose sons were highly likely to have joined an alternative CA society should they enter the profession.	69

CAs who were admitted between 1853 and 1892 but
married later than 1892.   51

CAs who married during or before 1892 though
produced no sons until after 1892.   69

Original members of the SAE who were married
with sons but whose occupations were determined
before the formation of the SAE in 1853-4.   4

Total   268

The full significance of professional competition engendering migration, celibacy, postponed marriage and low fertility, as well as the social origins of CAs and their brides that affected these variables, is apparent. Only 87 CAs (24.5%) who became members of the SAE between 1853 and 1892 produced at least one son who was a potential self-recruit to the profession by 1914.

Civil registers of births, census enumerators' books and old parish registers of baptisms for Scotland revealed that 216 sons eligible for recruitment to their fathers' profession were born between 1838 and 1892 to the marriages of these 87 CAs. Their frequency distribution is revealed in Table 7.1.

TABLE 7.1
**Marriages of SAE Members Who Produced Sons Eligible for
Self-Recruitment by 1914**

N of Eligible Sons Born	N of Marriages	Total Eligible Sons Produced
1	28	28
2	26	52
3	11	33
4	11	44
5	8	40
6	2	12
7	1	7
Total	87	216

Only 11 CAs produced 5 or more potential recruits to their own profession - on average, they produced 2.48 sons or, 0.60 sons eligible for self-recruitment for every potential father who entered the SAE between 1853 and 1892.

In order to ascertain the precise number of sons eligible for recruitment by the age of 16 or 17, a search was undertaken to remove all males dying before they reached recruitment age. 22 deaths were discovered leaving a total sample of 194 sons. 16 had died during infancy (4 of prematurity, 3 of meningitis, 2 of broncho-pneumonia, 1 each from cyanosis, cerebral effusion, patency of foramen ovale, disease of the bowels; the cause of death of the remainder were unspecified). 3 were child deaths (caused by whooping cough, diptheria, and teething). The remainder died aged six years, eight years and fifteen years (through 'general delicate health', albuminuria and, meningitis, respectively).

Significantly, for the pool of potential self-recruits, the mortality of sons before recruitment age declined over the whole period. 17.1% of all CAs' sons born between 1850 and 1879 died before that age, compared to 9.4% among those born between 1880 and 1892. Mortality was an increasingly less important factor than fertility in limiting the supply of sons for future recruitment to their fathers' profession.

In order to assess the impact of the CAs' output of sons on their ability to secure self-recruitment three situtaions are posited: potential mobility *assuming* the existence of perfect self-recruitment, potential mobility *not assuming* perfect self-recruitment, and the *real* or *actual* amount of self-recruitment and upward social mobility into the SAE.

Potential Mobility *Assuming* Perfect Self-Recruitment

If it is assumed that all the sons of CAs who survived to recruitment age entered into an SAE indenture (date of birth plus sixteen years for sons entering into apprenticeships before 1889 and date of birth plus seventeen for those entering after 1889), and the numbers are compared to the actual number of indentures contracted each year (see Figure 7.1), then the declining capacity of Edinburgh CAs to secure self-recruitment is evident.

Over the 1854-1909 period, SAE members produced only 194 surviving sons eligible for recruitment compared to a total of 1042 indentures contracted. Only in one year, 1873 (following the high fertility of marriages contracted during the mid-1850s as a response to the organization of the Edinburgh profession), did CAs have sufficient sons available to secure total self-recruitment.

The reproduction rates of the marriages of Edinburgh CAs were required to have been increasingly higher than their actual levels in order to have produced sufficient sons to occupy all the apprenticeships created.

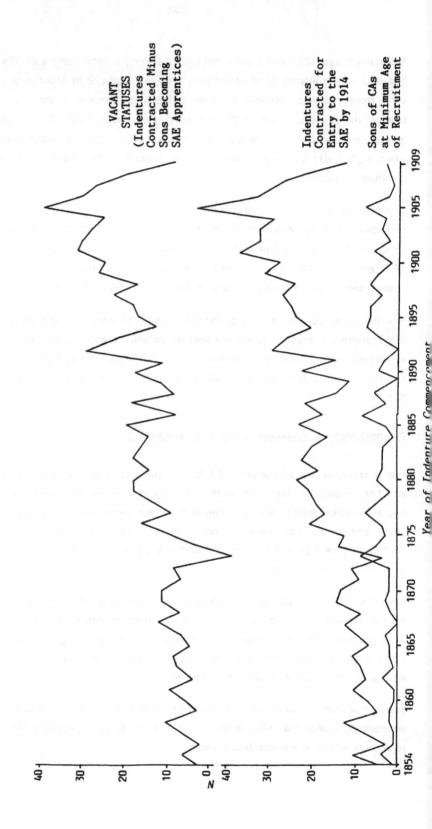

FIGURE 7.1 Hypothetical Number of Vacant Statuses Available to Sons From Non-CA Backgrounds Assuming Perfect Self-Recruitment to the SAE 1854-1909

VACANT STATUSES (Indentures Contracted Minus Sons Becoming SAE Apprentices)

Indentures Contracted for Entry to the SAE by 1914

Sons of CAs at Minimum Age of Recruitment

Year of Indenture Commencement

TABLE 7.2
Number of CAs' Sons Who Survived to Recruitment Age Required to Have
Been Born for CAs to Have Ensured Perfect Self-Recruitment in
SAE Indentures Contracted 1854-1909

Year of Birth of Son	N of Eligible Sons Actually Born	Mean Per Year	N Additional Sons Required	Mean Per Year	Mean Sons Necessary For Perfect Self- Recruitment
1838-42	9	1.80	30	6.00	7.80
1843-47	9	1.80	31	6.20	8.00
1848-52	9	1.80	41	8.20	10.00
1853-57	18	3.60	35	7.00	10.60
1858-62	25	5.00	60	12.00	17.00
1863-67	19	3.80	89	17.80	21.60
1868-72	22	4.40	74	14.80	19.20
1873-77	21	4.20	108	21.60	25.80
1878-82	29	5.80	107	21.40	27.20
1883-87	17	3.40	144	28.80	32.20
1888-92	16	3.20	129	25.80	29.00
Total/ Mean	194	3.52	848	15.41	18.94

The inability of CAs to produce sufficient sons to permit perfect self-recruitment was particularly apparent following the increases in recruitment that occurred due to the introduction of new SAE examinations systems in 1873 and 1893, despite the impact that these events had in temporarily increasing their own fertility. Accounting for the the rate of male mortality before recruitment age (10.2% of births between 1838 and 1892), the 156 Edinburgh CA marriages existing during the period that could have potentially contributed to the pool of eligible sons were required to have produced approximately 1148 male births in order to maintain the capacity to secure perfect self-recruitment (that is, 7.35 male births per marriage compared to the 1.38 that were actually produced).

Under the assumption of perfect self-recruitment there was, therefore, increasing scope for the entrance into SAE indentures of sons from non-CA, alternative social origins.

Potential Mobility *Not Assuming* Perfect Self-Recruitment

If the assumption that all the sons of CAs entered their father's profession is dropped, a more accurate estimation of the mobility effects of the declining fertility of CAs can be ascertained. Middle class parents were keen to preserve a certain degree of occupational inheritance during the nineteenth century:

> . . . commercial men, bankers, businessmen generally, lawyers and doctors, and no doubt others were proud to establish a family line in whatever economic activity they were engaged upon to make a living and they expected that their sons or at least one of their sons would eventually take their place as head of the original firm.[1]

Sources such as civil registers, professional and local directories, obituaries and published educational alumni, suggest that, although Edinburgh CAs were content to enter certain of their sons into their own profession (particularly if they were a partner in a large and prosperous firm), they also looked upon alternative vocations as more attractive options for others. 53 of the 194 sons of Edinburgh CAs studied as eligible recruits to their father's profession entered into an SAE indenture (27.3% of sons and 5.1% of all SAE apprentices between 1854 and 1909) and 41 qualified to membership of the Society (21.1% of all sons and 5.8% of all members admitted between 1858 and 1914).[2] Consequently, 78.9% of the sons of CAs entered alternative vocations to Edinburgh chartered accountancy.

The explanation for this apparent rejection of their own profession as a suitable one for large numbers of sons appears to lie in the quest for status improvement among SAE members. It was discovered in the previous chapter that CAs were more likely to favour the self-recruitment of their sons when institutional changes and the state of intra-occupational business ensured that offspring would be effectively entering a higher status CA profession with greater income stability than they themselves had joined. By contrast, if generational status improvement could not be secured through self-recruitment – then alternative professions were considered as more desirable career options for certain sons. Similarly, some parents whose entrance to the CA profession or marriage to one of its practitioners constituted an effective decline in intergenerational family status were highly motivated toward the return of sons into occupations of higher standing. Such considerations within individual CA marriages acted to limit self-recruitment and increased the supply of SAE apprenticeships filled by sons from alternative social origins.

Table 7.3 provides details concerning the occupational destinations of the 194 sons who were eligible for self-recruitment, and reveals two notable features concerning the career placement of CAs' sons. Firstly, it confirms the significance of occupational and social connections in the nineteenth century vocational decision-making process. 50 of the CAs' sons were found positions in accountancy and 48 in the law, banking, insurance, the actuarial profession or stockbroking and finance, all of which had the closest connections with CAs (60.1% of sons whose occupations are known entered these vocations). Secondly, it reinforces the assertion that status acquisition was an important priority in determining the careers of sons among CAs who were intent on asserting their recently procured professional standing.

TABLE 7.3
Occupations of CAs' Sons Born Between 1838–92 and Eligible for
Recruitment and Entrance to the SAE by 1914

SSG of Son	Occupation of Son	Sons Position in Sequence of Male Births Surviving to Age of Recruitment						
		1	2	3	4	5	6	Total
1	Landed Proprietor	3	2					5
2	Law	11	7	5	1	1		25
2	Religion	4	1		2			7
2	Medicine	3	1	2		1		7
2	Defence	2	1	1		1		5
2	Higher Civil Service	1						1
2	SAE	22	10	3	3	2	1	41
2	Other CA Society	1			1			2
2	Actuary	2	1					3
2	Education		1	1	1			3
2	Scientific		1					1
2	Architect		1			1		2
2	Engineer (Civil or Mining)		4		1			5
2	Artist			1				1
3	Manufacturing	1	1					2
4	Banking or Insurance	3	5	2	1			11
4	Stockbroking or Finance	4	2	2	1			9
4	Merchant	1	2		2	1		6
5	Farming, Planting, Ranching	3	3	3		1		10
7	Accountant or Bookkeeper	3		2	1	1		7
7	Agent or Traveller	1		1				2
7	Clerk or other White Collar	2	3	2				7
8	Craft				1			1
–	Not Known	10	9	4	5	2	1	31
	Total	77	55	29	20	11	2	194

(Left margin, vertical: Social Mobility)

There appears to have been a short and a long-term generational objective among Edinburgh CAs and the upper middle classes in general during the later nineteenth century. The initial objective was to achieve the upward occupational mobility of at least one son in the succeeding generation.[3] This was a first step toward the ultimate long run goal of the ascent of the family in a future generation to landed status, a desire common among the wealthier sections of the Victorian middle class:

> Your son and son's son must seek connection, until the name of
> Nixon has made itself of note, or become but the family name of a

> notable house; such is the open or covert ambition of all rich rising men like you in this free country of ours. Your father is already in treaty for the purchase of landed property.[4]

Although few CAs could envisage owning an estate during their own lifetimes (though a select few did achieve this mainly through inheritance or marriage), the foundations of future family standing could be laid through the entrance of an elder son into the higher status, traditional professions in the hope that, through wealth accumulation or marriage, the succeeding generation might make the ultimate leap. Table 7.3 reveals that elder sons, and particularly the eldest, were the key to the generational status enhancement of CA families. These sons were disproportionately entered into the older professions which had associations with and provided access to, landed circles. The desire for the occupational inheritance of older sons conflicted to some degree with that of long-term status objectives. Consequently, where the first son took over the father's mantle and entered the SAE, the second son appears frequently to have entered an alternative profession or *vice versa*. Other fathers with limited means were satisfied for their sons to become CAs only. Hence, as a proportion of sons whose occupations have been discovered, 62.7% of the first sons of Edinburgh CAs entered chartered accountancy or a higher status, traditional profession (law, religion, medicine, defence, the higher civil service) compared to 43.5% of second sons and 28.0% of third to sixth sons. Second and subsequent sons of Edinburgh CAs tended to enter the newer, though marginally lower status professions, though most were found positions in occupations closely allied to accountancy and which required less expenditure on vocational preparation and training than the professions.

These generational status strategies implied an unequal distribution of intra family resources among sons according to sibling position. In a CA family of more than two sons, depending on individual circumstances, few CAs could envisage entering all of their sons into the professions and providing for the vocational preparation costs required. The possibility exists that the upward mobility of elder sons was only achieved in many families through the downward mobility of middle and younger sons with potential consequences for sibling rivalry. This unequal distribution of intergenerational family status was quite in accordance with the social customs of those occupying a higher place in the status hierarchy. Among landed families, it was the eldest son who inherited the estate and maintained the same social status as his father while the younger sons suffered a decline in standing through having to enter the professions or commerce. A further examination of Table 7.3 shows that compared to their fathers' social status, 68.7% of the first sons of CAs (whose occupations are known) were upwardly or horizontally mobile and 31.4% were downwardly mobile. This compared to 47.8% and 52.2% of second sons, respectively, and 46.0% and 54.0% of third to sixth sons.

The aspirations among Edinburgh CAs for intergenerational status improvement also implied, as was suggested in the previous chapter, the working of *social capillarity* influences on fertility restriction. In order to provide sufficient funds to secure the upward social mobility of at least one son, CAs, according to their individual circumstances, had fewer children. The information presented in Table 7.4 illustrates the point.

TABLE 7.4

Social Status of CAs' Sons Eligible for Self-Recruitment According to the Number of Competing Sons in the Family

SSG of Son		N of Sons Who Survived to Recruitment Age							
		1	2	3	4	5	6	7	Total
1	Independent Means	2	1	0	2	0	0	0	5
2	Professions	13	30	15	18	17	7	3	103
3	Manufacturers	0	0	2	0	0	0	0	2
4	Commerce	1	5	5	6	9	0	0	26
5	Farmers	1	2	2	2	3	0	0	10
6	Distribution & Processing	0	0	0	0	0	0	0	0
7	White Collar	1	3	2	3	3	3	1	16
8	Skilled Manual	0	0	0	1	0	0	0	1
9	Semi & Unskilled Manual	0	0	0	0	0	0	0	0
	Not Known	3	10	2	8	6	1	1	31
Total		21	51	28	40	38	11	5	194
% of Known in SSGs 1-2		83.3	75.6	57.7	62.5	53.1	70.0	75.0	66.3

With the exception of the marriages of CAs that produced six or seven sons whose small numbers limit their significance, as the number of surviving sons increased so did the number who entered below professional status, SSG 3-8, occupations. Those sons that entered commerce, farming and clerking (SSGs 4-7) were derived largely from marriages that produced two or more sons.

The consequences for self-recruitment of CAs' adherence to these status priorities and the entrance of their sons into alternative occupations are evident from Figure 7.2. The number of CAs' sons who became SAE apprentices was consistent and low compared to the overall expansion of recruitment. Only following the introduction of improved systems of professional qualification in 1873 and 1893 was there any discernible increase in self-recruitment. Over the 1854-1909 period, a total of 1042

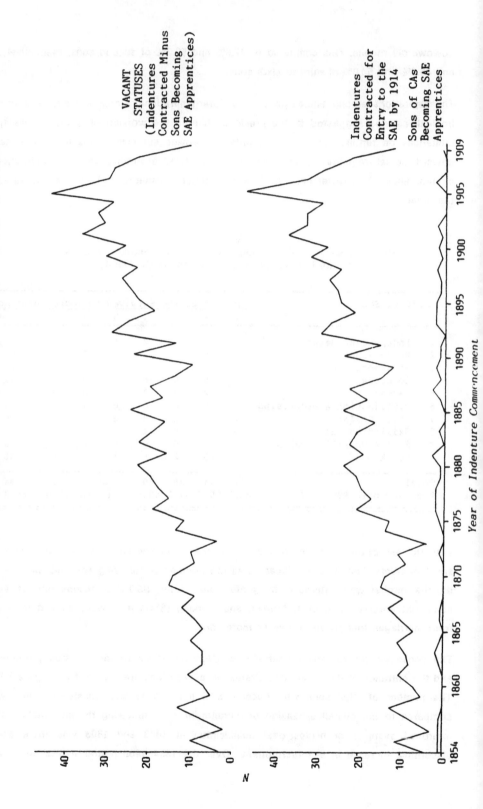

FIGURE 7.2 Actual Number of Vacant Statuses Available to Recruits to the SAE From Non-CA Origins

SAE indentures were contracted, only 53 of these apprentices were the sons of CAs, leaving 989 vacant statuses which were occupied by sons from alternative social origins. The sources of these recruits and the actual extent to which the restricted rate of self-recruitment among CAs permitted upward occupational mobility into the SAE will now be examined.

The Supply of Vacant Statuses and Upward Social Mobility

Although the rate of growth in SAE indentures was too great for all apprenticeships to have been filled by the sons of CAs, the possibility exists that upward social mobility into the Edinburgh CA profession was limited by apprenticeships being occupied by downwardly or horizontally mobile sons. Figure 7.3 shows that - if sons of fathers in the independent means status group (SSG 1) are regarded as having been intergenerationally downward mobiles into SAE apprenticeships, and the sons of fathers in the professions (SSG 2) are assumed to have been horizontally mobile into SAE training, then the rate of upward social mobility increased over the whole period though fluctuated markedly. The number of recruits who derived from SSGs 1-2 was insufficient to fill all the indentures that were created between 1837 and 1911.

Of the 1042 apprenticeships contracted between 1854 and 1909 (that is, those included in the analysis of self-recruitment), 52 (5.0%) were taken by downwardly mobile sons from SSG 1 origins and 365 (35.0%) were occupied by horizontally mobile sons from SSG 2 families (312 if 53 sons of CAs are excluded). 583 (56.0%) of SAE indentures were therefore taken by the sons of fathers in SSGs 3-9 who may safely be regarded as having been upwardly mobile into vocational training for entrance to a professional (SSG 2) occupation. The remaining 42 (4.0%) apprentices derived from families where the fathers' occupation (and therefore his social status group) is unknown, though the majority of these sons were likely to have been upwardly mobile.

Table 7.5 and Figure 7.4 illustrate that the rate of upward social mobility into SAE indentures was particularly marked from the 1870s and early 1890s. Despite the long-run increase in upward circulation, short-term declines were evident between 1875 and 1879 and between 1895 and 1899. An examination of these fluctuations, and of the trends in the recruitment of sons from various social status groups, will identify the precise factors that permitted the occupation of vacant indentures by upwardly mobiles.

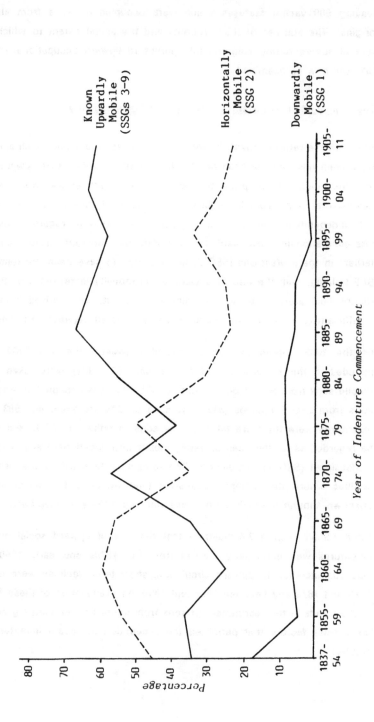

FIGURE 7.3 Social Mobility Into SAE Indentures That Commenced 1837–1911

FIGURE 7.4 Number of Vacant Statuses Occupied by Upwardly Mobile Sons (from SSG 3–9 origins and where father's occupation is not known) 1854–1909 With 9-Year Moving Average

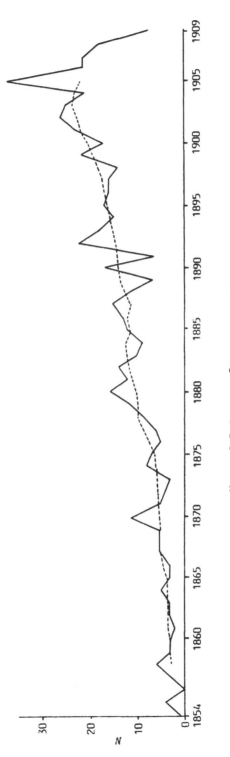

Year of Indenture Commencement

TABLE 7.5
Vacant Statuses (Indentures) Occupied by Upwardly Mobile Sons Into SAE Apprenticeships that Commenced 1854-1909 (from SSG 3-9 origins and those whose father's occupation is unknown)

Year of Indenture Commencement	N of Indentures	As % of All Indentures Contracted
1854-59	17	38.6
1860-64	15	32.9
1865-69	21	38.9
1870-74	31	59.6
1875-79	37	40.2
1880-84	61	59.4
1885-89	63	68.5
1890-94	78	66.7
1895-99	85	62.5
1900-04	112	69.6
1905-09	105	72.4
Total	625	60.0

TABLE 7.6
Social Status Origins of All SAE Apprentices Who Commenced Indentures Between 1837 and 1911

Year of Indenture Commencement	% with Father in SSG:										N
	1	2	3	4	5	6	7	8	9	NK	
1837-54	19.2	46.2	3.9	7.7	11.5	0.0	11.5	0.0	0.0	0.0	26
1855-59	5.0	55.0	2.5	7.5	12.5	2.5	7.5	5.0	0.0	2.5	40
1860-64	6.5	60.9	0.0	8.7	8.7	0.0	4.3	2.2	2.2	6.5	46
1865-69	3.7	57.4	0.0	9.2	5.6	5.6	5.6	7.4	1.8	3.7	54
1870-74	5.8	34.6	5.8	15.4	1.9	15.4	7.7	7.7	3.8	1.9	52
1875-79	8.7	51.1	2.2	9.8	5.4	9.8	6.5	4.3	1.1	1.1	92
1880-84	9.7	31.1	9.7	12.6	3.9	8.8	12.6	5.8	2.9	2.9	103
1885-89	6.5	25.0	10.9	14.1	10.9	7.6	13.0	10.9	0.0	1.1	92
1890-94	6.8	26.5	12.0	13.7	3.4	13.7	12.0	6.8	0.8	4.3	117
1895-99	0.7	36.8	13.2	11.8	5.1	7.4	8.8	9.6	2.2	4.4	136
1900-04	2.5	28.0	6.8	9.9	4.4	13.1	21.1	9.9	0.6	3.7	161
1905-11	2.7	24.3	10.1	15.6	0.0	10.8	18.9	6.1	2.7	8.8	148
1837-69	7.2	56.0	1.2	8.5	9.0	2.4	6.7	4.2	1.2	3.6	166
1870-89	7.9	35.4	7.4	12.7	5.9	9.7	10.3	7.1	1.8	1.8	339
1890-1911	3.0	28.8	10.3	12.6	3.2	11.2	15.7	8.2	1.6	5.4	562
1837-1911	5.3	35.1	8.0	12.0	5.0	9.4	12.5	7.2	1.6	3.9	1067
N of Cases	56	375	85	128	53	100	134	77	17	42	1067

Table 7.6 and Figure 7.5 reveal that there was considerable variation in the timing and rate of the recruitment of sons from different social origins into the SAE professional

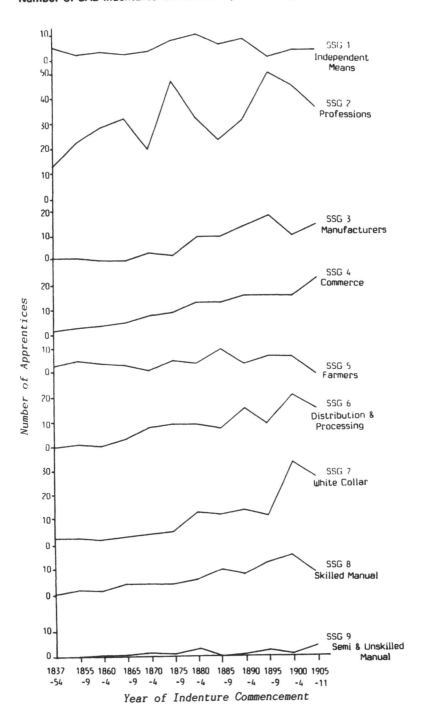

FIGURE 7.5
Number of SAE Indentures Contracted by SSG of Apprentice's Father

training system, if all indentures contracted between 1837 and 1911 are examined.

SSG 1 : Independent Means. The trend in the recruitment of sons from families of independent means to the SAE appears to have been highly reflective of occupational and social connections between those of landed status, in particular, and Edinburgh CAs. The rate or recruitment from these origins declined from the 1890s as the significance of estate management and accounts in the CA's total business was reduced, and as the early nineteenth century landed-law-accountancy recruitment custom mentioned in Chapter 3 became of lesser significance as a result. Recruitment from this source did not respond to institutional changes within the SAE, which contrasts markedly with the experience of the next group, the sons of professional men.

SSG 2 : The Professions. The close network of occupational and social associations between lawyers and Edinburgh CAs accounts largely for the increasing and high proportion of SAE recruits from professional families between 1865 and 1869. The subsequent peaks and troughs in the rate of recruitment from this source correlate closely with internal developments and the state of the SAE. The increases in SSG 2 recruitment that occurred between 1875 and 1879 and between 1895 and 1899 were the direct consequnces of the measures of 1873 and 1893 which were introduced to improve the standard of qualification to the SAE and the professional status of CAs. The decreases that occurred in SSG 2 recruitment between 1870 and 1874, 1880 and 1889 and between 1900 and 1911 correspond identically with the periods in which the SAE and its membership were threatened by competition or rival organizations and the possibility of a consequent diminution of future professional income stability and status.

It is apparent that professional (SSG 2) parents were uniquely and acutely conscious, due to their close occupational and social proximity to their own and other professions, of the significance of internal organizational developments designed to improve occupational standing. The precise professional vocation entered by their sons was heavily dependent on the relative opportunities for income and status acquisition or maintenance offered by each alternative. Additionally, the ability of a professional training system to take full advantage of the expensive education that had been provided for the sons of professional men, in the form of comprehensive examination procedures thus permitting a claim to professional status based on the acquisition of *theoretical* and specialized knowledge was also a significant consideration of these parents during the second half of the nineteenth century. For these reasons, the SAE was highly favoured by the local professional class during the mid to late 1870s and 1890s as a desirable organization in which to enter sons. In other periods, alternative professions offered brighter opportunities and appropriate forms of vocational preparation.

It is clear from this that it was primarily the sons of professional men who were responsible for the great increases in SAE recruitment that initially followed the introduction of the 1873 and 1893 changes in the system of examination and qualification. It also follows that these institutional measures, which at first sight appear as having increased the meritocratic basis of recruitment, did not open the profession to sons from a broader range of social origins but had exactly the opposite effect. Hence, upward mobility to SAE apprentice status declined significantly between 1875 and 1879 and 1895 and 1899.

SSGs 3-4 : **Manufacturers and Commerce.** The recruitment of sons from manufacturing and commercial families exhibited similar trends particularly from the 1870s, and suggest the importance of occupational and social connections in career determination. The small number of apprentices from manufacturing families until the 1880s reflected the trend in Edinburgh CAs' business toward company auditing (see Table 2.1). The more consistent increase in the recruitment of sons from commercial origins from the earliest period is indicative of the heavy involvement of CAs in insurance and banking. There was also an expansion of commercial auditing during the later nineteenth century among SAE members, and a *revelation* effect among merchants employing accountants and who resided in the Newington and Morningside districts of Edinburgh in close spatial proximity to CAs and who were ambitious for the entrance of their sons into the professions.

Apart from an increase in apprentices from manufacturing families between 1895 and 1899, the number of recruits from SSGs 3 and 4 sources was unresponsive to internal SAE developments of which parents in these groups would have had limited knowledge.

SSG 5 : **Farmers.** The intake of SAE apprentices from farming families followed a similar trend to that in the recruitment of sons from independent means (SSG 1) origins thus indicating that recruitment from this, mainly rural source, was heavily dependent on interpersonal and occupational associations with CAs or others connected with the profession.

SSGs 6-8 : **Distribution and Processing, White Collar and Skilled Manual.** Among SAE apprentices who had lower middle or upper working class origins, a different set of factors appear to have been instrumental in explaining their similar trends. Fathers in

SSGs 6-8 had many fewer immediate occupational and social connections with CAs until perhaps the 1900s when the auditing of small businesses became a more common component of CAs' business. These parents were, however, given their marginal social status, highly motivated to the social advancement of their sons. Before the sons of these parents could enter the professions, however, the educational infrastructure had to become available in order that they could satisfy their liberal schooling and entrance requirements. Among parents in the upper middle classes (SSGs 1-5), the receipt of a suitable education for entry to desirable occupations was an accepted and affordable norm for their sons; the lower middle and upper working class parent could make no such assurances for their sons.

It was apparent from the evidence presented in Chapter 5 that a secondary education, preferably at a private school was highly desirable for the successful completion of an SAE indenture. The trend in the number of apprentices from lower middle and upper working class origins can be explained largely by the increasing availability to them of a relatively cheap and high quality secondary education in Edinburgh, enabling an increasing supply of sons to satisfy the educational standards of entrance required for a CA indenture and its successful completion.

It was from the 1870s that consistently high and increasing numbers of the sons who entered on an SAE training derived from SSGs 6-8, the initial upturn commencing earlier according to social status (1870 to 1874 for SSG 6, 1880 to 1884 for SSG 7 and 1885 to 1889 for SSG 8). This development occurred at the same time as major changes in the provision of private secondary education in Edinburgh.

The crucial event was the passing of the Endowed Institutions (Scotland) Act 1869 which permitted the Merchant Company of Edinburgh to apply for an order to alter the terms of the trust deeds of the foundations of the schools under its supervision with the object of improving their efficiency. This the Merchant Company did in 1870 with the result that two previously minor endowed hospital schools with a restricted intake of foundationers from among impoverished parents opened as low fee, secondary day schools. George Watson's Hospital had 83 boys in 1869, in 1870 as George Watson's College, the school roll stood at 800, and at 1722 by 1900. Similarly, Daniel Stewart's Hospital had between 60 and 70 boys during the 1860s which increased to 300 during the 1870s following the conversion to a college; the figure peaked at 890 in 1889-90.

That these schools aimed for and succeeded in attracting the sons of the aspiring lower middle classes of Edinburgh is evidenced by their low fees (£2 per quarter in the early 1870s); the heavy representation of sons who attended them from

Newington and similar districts, and; the nature of the subjects taught, being comparable with those available in the established, high fee, middle class secondary sector. Before the Endowed Schools Commission of 1875 the Merchant Company claimed that its colleges "have been able to offer to the middle classes of Edinburgh a cheap and good elementary and secondary instruction, of which upwards of 3900 pupils enjoy the benefit."[5] The Commission itself reported that in Edinburgh there now existed ample accomodation for the secondary instruction of the middle classes:

> The opening of the Merchant Company Hospital Day Schools had put a good secondary education within the reach of all but the poorest classes. For those who could afford the larger fees, there were the High School of Edinburgh, the Edinburgh Academy, and a considerable number of Adventure Schools of good repute.[6]

Although the expansion of Watson's and Stewart's was detrimental to the numbers of pupils attending the Academy and other institutions at the high class end of the local educational hierarchy, their major impact was not only one of greater accomodation. Also, in increasing competition between lower-medium status secondary schools they led a more general reduction in fees.[7] By 1893 the Headmaster of Daniel Stewart's College was obliged to report that a diminution in the school roll had taken place and that this had been caused by:

> . . . The opening as a day school of Heriot's Hospital (in 1886) with fees half those charged at Stewart's. He showed that Gillespie's, the Established Church Normal School and the Free Church Normal School had all added three year courses in higher subjects . . . The opening of Craighall School, now Trinity Academy, at Leith, a school offering free secondary education to university entrance level also hit us hard . . . Fees at the Royal High School had been lowered.[8]

With regard to recruitment to the SAE, the availability of an appropriate education for entrance to an indenture and a successful period of training was open increasingly to the sons of the lower middle and artisan classes of Edinburgh. The gradual expansion of secondary school places and the consequent reduction in fees brought a post elementary education within the reach first of SSG 6 sons, followed by those from SSG 7 and those from SSG 8. Additionally, the relative decline in the cost of obtaining a good education potentially permitted a diversion of greater familial resources to the expense of the vocational preparation of sons.

The impact of the expansion of cheap, high quality private secondary education in Edinburgh on the recruitment of sons from the lower middle and upper working classes to the SAE can be ascertained from the data in Table 7.7.

TABLE 7.7
Percentage of SAE Apprentices Who Commened Indentures 1874-1911 and Who Attended the Expanding, Low Fee, Secondary Education Sector in Edinburgh by Social Origins (where known)

SSG of Father	Institution and Year of Opening as a Low Fee Secondary School					
	Watson's & Stewart's (1870)	Church Normal Schools (1880)	George Heriot's (1886)	James Gillespie's (1890)	Royal High (1890)	Total
1	9.7	0.0	0.0	0.0	5.9	15.6
2	27.5	0.0	1.3	0.0	4.5	33.3
3	19.7	0.0	1.5	0.0	5.2	26.4
4	27.8	0.0	1.2	1.4	2.8	33.2
5	21.6	0.0	0.0	0.0	0.0	21.6
6	53.9	0.0	8.8	12.7	7.9	83.3
7	43.3	0.9	8.3	7.9	7.9	68.3
8	24.2	4.8	24.1	8.7	6.5	68.3
9	14.3	0.0	33.3	11.1	11.1	69.8
N of Cases	252	4	35	21	29	341

What is evident with regard to SAE recruitment from SSG 6-8 families is that their marginal middle class status acted as a potent motivation for achieving the upward mobility of their sons. From the 1870s, the educational infrastructure was becoming available for the satisfaction and reinforcement of these ambitions. Increasing numbers of sons entered an educational milieu that was highly geared to the social progress of its pupils which was a means of enhancing institutional reputations in a period of acute competition between schools for fee paying pupils. Once obtained, a good secondary education could be utilized to gain entrance to an increasingly visible and relatively attractive career alternative of professional status - chartered accountancy.

SSG 9 : Semi and Unskilled Labour. The expansion of the secondary education sector and reduction in private school fees that occurred in Edinburgh from the 1870s did not generally bring a post elementary schooling within the reach of the semi and unskilled sections of the local working class. Indeed, the opening of Merchant Company Hospitals and George Heriot's as fee paying schools reduced the number of places in what had been institutions for the education of poor, deserving boys. Representatives of the Edinburgh Trades Council claimed in 1875 that the fees charged in the Merchant Company colleges were at a level "beyond the power of working men to pay them."[9] Despite this, the low fees imposed at Heriot's, in particular, undoubtedly opened doors to the sons of fathers in SSG 9 who received a stable income and who were prepared to sacrifice expenditure on alternative items of consumption.

The recruitment of sons to the SAE from semi and unskilled manual origins remained relatively low throughout the whole 1837 to 1911 period. Apprentices from these families represented the ability of a few select parents and sons to gain an appropriate education and amass sufficient funds to enter an occupation from which they were occupationally and socially distant. Recruitment to the local professions was only possible from lower working class origins if parents practised considerable restraint particularly in terms of limiting the number of children among whom limited resources were to be distributed. Alternatively, an SSG 9 son could enter the CA profession through having raised sufficient funds himself by clerking in accountancy or in a related occupation before entering an indenture.

Thus far the analysis has been concerned with social mobility to the vocational training system of the SAE providing the *opportunity* for the achievement of full professional status through membersip of the society. It was established in Chapter 5, however, that although qualification to the SAE was attainable by all in varying degrees according to their social origins, a large number of apprentices failed to gain admission and entered alternative occupations that were potentially of lower status than chartered accountancy or than that of their fathers' vocation. It is therefore necessary to examine the final status achieved by recruits to the SAE.

Excluding 79 original members, 711 apprentices who had undergone an SAE registered indenture were admitted to the society between 1855 and 1914. Of these 31 (4.4%) were derived from independent means (SSG 1) origins and can therefore be regarded as having been downwardly mobile into the profession. 246 (34.6%) of members were the sons of fathers in the professions (SSG 2) and were essentially intergenerationally horizontally mobile so that 434 (61.0%) of CAs can be regarded as having been upwardly mobile into membership of the SAE (417 or 58.6% if those whose father's occupation is not known are excluded).

If indentures contracted between 1854 and 1909 only are considered (as was necessarily done in the previous analysis of self-recruitment capacity), 694 apprentices became CAs (admitted between 1858 and 1914). 41 (5.9%) of these were self-recruits leaving 653 members who were derived from alternative social origins. 27 (3.9%) were downwardly mobile sons from SSG 1, a further 201 (29.0%) were the sons of professionals and were horizontally mobile, so that 425 (61.2%) can be regarded as having been intergenerationally mobile into the Edinburgh CA profession (408 or 58.8% if the father's occupation unknown category is excluded).

If the total membership of the SAE is examined, including the original members of the society (all admissions between 1853 and 1914) then 42 (5.3%) of CAs were derived from SSG 1, 287 (36.3%) from SSG 2 and 461 (58.4%) from families of below professional status (441 or 55.8% if the father's occupation unknown category is excluded).

By all these criteria, a majority of the membership of the SAE were upwardly mobile into the CA profession over the whole period. Figure 7.6 reveals that, despite the obstacles to membership, upward mobility into the Edinburgh CA profession was subject to a long-run increase punctuated only by the temporary impact of the recruitment of large numbers of sons from the professional classes following internal status enhancing alterations to the qualification process.

Table 7.8 and Figure 7.7 attempt to identify more precisely the trends in the social origins of SAE members between 1853 and 1914.

TABLE 7.8
Social Status Origins of All SAE Members Admitted 1853-1914

Year of Admission	% with Father in SSG:										
	1	2	3	4	5	6	7	8	9	NK	N
1853-54	17.2	50.0	1.6	6.2	4.7	6.2	7.8	1.6	0.0	4.7	64
1855-59	17.4	43.5	4.4	8.7	8.7	4.3	13.0	0.0	0.0	0.0	23
1860-64	0.0	63.2	0.0	10.5	0.0	0.0	15.8	10.5	0.0	0.0	19
1865-69	0.0	81.3	0.0	12.5	0.0	0.0	0.0	6.2	0.0	0.0	16
1870-74	3.6	53.6	0.0	7.1	14.3	3.6	3.6	7.1	3.6	3.5	28
1875-79	6.7	46.7	3.3	13.3	3.3	13.3	6.7	6.7	0.0	0.0	30
1880-84	4.9	45.9	1.6	9.8	3.3	14.8	14.8	3.3	1.6	0.0	61
1885-89	9.2	32.9	5.3	14.5	6.6	9.2	13.1	6.6	1.3	1.3	76
1890-94	9.5	23.8	11.1	14.3	8.0	11.1	11.1	11.1	0.0	0.0	63
1895-99	3.7	26.2	11.3	16.2	5.0	11.3	20.0	3.8	0.0	2.5	80
1900-04	2.1	39.8	14.0	9.7	4.3	8.6	6.5	11.8	1.1	2.1	93
1905-09	1.0	28.7	9.9	9.9	3.0	13.8	21.8	6.9	1.0	4.0	101
1910-14	1.5	26.5	9.6	14.7	0.7	12.5	17.6	8.8	2.9	5.2	136
1853-74	10.7	54.7	1.3	8.0	6.0	4.0	8.7	3.3	0.7	2.7	150
1875-94	7.8	35.7	5.7	13.0	5.7	11.7	12.2	7.0	0.9	0.4	230
1895-14	2.0	30.0	11.0	12.7	2.9	11.7	16.6	8.0	1.5	3.7	410
1853-1914	5.3	36.3	7.6	11.9	4.3	10.3	13.8	6.9	1.1	2.5	790
N	42	287	60	94	34	81	109	54	9	20	790

The full range of factors that determined the ability of apprentices to qualify according to their social origins that were discussed in Chapter 5 as well as the influences

FIGURE 7.6 Social Mobility Into SAE Membership 1853-1914

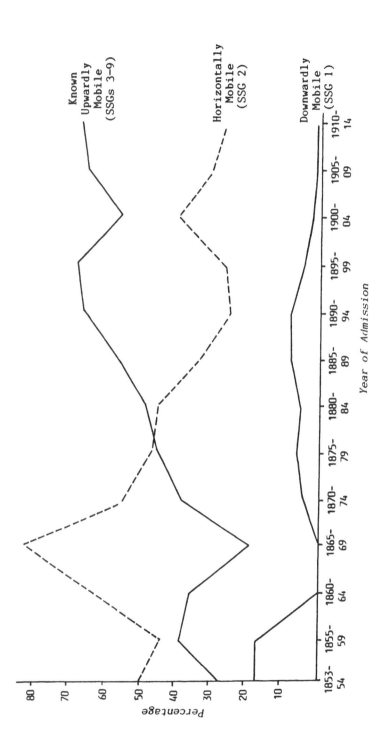

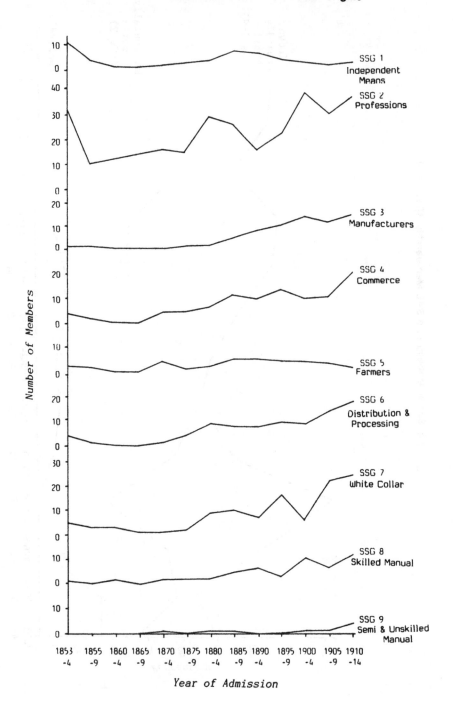

FIGURE 7.7
Number of SAE Members From Various Social Origins

mentioned recently that encouraged or discouraged recruitment to the SAE are apparent. The proportion of Edinburgh CAs who were derived from lower middle and working class origins increased from the late 1870s with the greater availability of secondary education and declined during periods when the sons of professional men entered the SAE in large numbers, or, when the standard of GEB examinations became increasingly severe in the 1900s.

If attention is directed to the occupations followed by apprentices who failed to become CAs, only a certain proportion can be regarded as having been upwardly mobile: this is shown in Table 7.9. 41 failing apprentices or 19.8% of those whose occupation is known achieved, through entrance to the independent means status group (SSG 1) or traditional professions, a higher status than they would otherwise have done should they have become CAs. A further 12 (5.8%) managed to enter an alternative, though slightly lower status profession than Edinburgh chartered accountancy. The remaining 154 (74.4%) unsuccessful apprentices can be regarded as having entered occupations of below professional status.

TABLE 7.9
Major Occupations of SAE Apprentices 1837–1911 Who Failed to Enter the SAE (excluding apprentices who failed due to death or ill health)

	SSG of Apprentice	Occupation	N	% of Known Cases in SSG
↑	1	Independent Means	13	6.3
	2	Law	5	19.3
S	2	Religion	5	
o	2	Medicine	6	
c	2	Defence	10	
i	2	Higher Civil Service	2	
a	2	ICAEW or Incorporated Accountant	4	
l	2	Actuary	3	
	2	Engineer (Civil or Mining)	1	
M	2	Artist or Actor	4	
o	3	Manufacturing	20	9.7
b	4	Banking or Insurance	11	14.0
i	4	Stockbroking or Broking	11	
l	4	Merchant	7	
i	5	Farming	9	11.6
t	5	Planting or Ranching	15	
y	7	Accountant or Bookkeeper	50	37.2
	7	Agent or Traveller	2	
	7	Clerk or Other White Collar	25	
↓	8	Craft	4	1.9
	-	Not Known	123	
Total			330	100.0

The above statistics do not necessarily preclude failing apprentices from having been intergenerationally upwardly mobile. Despite their non-qualification, they may still have entered occupations of a higher status than those of their fathers. Table 7.10 throws light on this question.

TABLE 7.10
Social Status of SAE Apprentices 1837–1911 Who Failed to Achieve SAE
Membership Compared to That of Their Fathers
(where occupation is known and excluding those apprentices who
failed to qualify due to death or ill health)

SSG of Father	SSG of Son (Failing Apprentice)									N
	1	2	3	4	5	6	7	8	9	
1	8	3	0	2	4	0	5	0	0	22
2	4	19	2	12	9	0	24	1	0	71
3	0	7	7	2	0	0	2	0	0	18
4	1	2	2	5	4	0	6	1	0	21
5	0	4	0	2	5	0	4	0	0	15
6	0	2	0	0	0	0	7	0	0	9
7	0	0	2	0	0	0	14	0	0	16
8	0	1	2	1	2	0	9	2	0	17
9	0	1	0	0	0	0	4	0	0	5
N	13	39	15	24	24	0	75	4	0	194
% Downward Mobile	63.3	67.6	22.2	52.4	26.7	77.8	0.0	0.0	0.0	

45.4% of SAE apprentices who failed to qualify as CAs suffered a decline in intergenerational social status. Among apprentices from working class origins (SSGs 8–9) who exhibited a high rate of non-qualification, failure to enter the profession did not prevent some upward social mobility. An SAE indenture at least permitted such sons to move into non-manual occupations, particularly clerking. Sons from SSG 1–6 origins who did not become SAE members clearly suffered a greater decline in social status through failing to qualify and gain professional (SSG 2) status as the major alternative employment was to become a non-professional accountant or clerk, both SSG 7 occupations.

46 SAE apprentices who did not qualify to membership were known to have been intergenerationally upwardly mobile into alternative occupations. If this figure is added to the total of 417 apprentices from SSGs 3–9 who did achieve CA status having completed an SAE registered indenture that commenced between 1837–1911, then 463 of all Edinburgh CA apprentices or 43.4% are known to have achieved upward intergenerational social mobility, 119 (11.2%) were downwardly mobile, and 306

FIGURE 7.8 **Model of Recruitment and Self-Recruitment to the SAE 1837-1911**

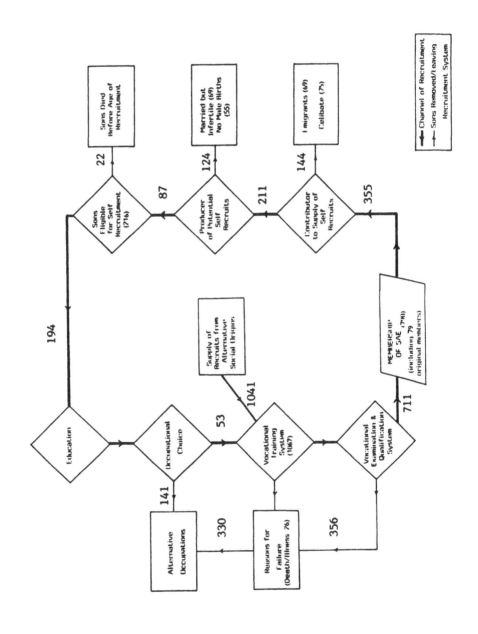

(28.7%) were known to have been horizontally mobile or of static intergenerational social status. The process of recruitment to the SAE between 1837 and 1911, taking into account the potential for, and the actual extent of, self-recruitment to the profession, is illustrated in Figure 7.8.

CONCLUSION : COMPARATIVE RATES OF SOCIAL MOBILITY
IN TWO EDINBURGH PROFESSIONS

If upward social mobility to the Edinburgh CA profession is compared to that which occurred in the second profession studied, the Faculty of Advocates, then the SAE appears to have been considerably the more open of the two vocations. The rate of upward mobility in the *new* profession was double that of the *old*.

TABLE 7.11
Upward Social Mobility in Two Edinburgh Professions 1855-1914

Year of Admission	Percentage of Members Known to Have Derived From SSGs 3-9	
	Faculty of Advocates	Society of Accountants
1855-64	30.3	38.1
1865-74	23.0	31.8
1875-84	37.9	48.4
1885-94	36.4	61.2
1895-04	42.2	61.3
1905-14	40.9	66.7
1855-1914	35.4	58.3
N of Cases	216	423
% Upwardly Mobile From SSGs 3-5	80.6	42.6
% Upwardly Mobile From SSGs 6-9	19.4	57.4

The data provided in Table 7.11 above reveals that during the 1855-74 period, rates of upward circulation were not dramatically different in the two professions but that, subsequently, there was a significant divergence in the social sources of recruits. It is also evident that the distance of upward mobility into the SAE was much greater than to the Scottish Bar. Chartered accountancy offered opportunities for the recruitment of sons from lower middle and upper working class origins whereas upward mobiles to the Faculty were derived predominantly from manufacturing and commercial families who occupied a social position on the fringes of professional status, and who desired for their increasing economic significance to be socially and culturally represented by the entry of certain of their sons to the most esteemed professional organization in Scotland.

There was also a considerable divergence in the rate of self-recruitment to the two professions. Whereas 5.8% of CAs' sons entered their fathers' new and rapidly expanding occupation between 1858 and 1914, a proportion which declined during those years, male succession to the old and slow growing profession of advocate remained at a static 11.7% of members admitted during the same period.

Notes

1 Banks, *Victorian Values*, p. 127.

2 See A.K. Cairncross, "The Social Origins of Chartered Accountants", *The Accountant* 97 (1937), p. 374. Cairncross discovered a similar rate of self-recruitment to the profession in a study of 445 Glasgow CAs between 1931–7. He concluded that "about one in five of the sons of accountants becomes an accountant."

3 Banks, *Victorian Values*, p. 127.

4 Quoted in Brightfield, *Victorian England in its Novels*, vol. 2, p. 60. See J. Tautphoeus, *Quits* (London, 1857).

5 British *Parliamentary Papers*, 1875, vol. XXIX (*Reports*, vol. 1), "Report (third) of the Commissioners appointed to inquire into the Endowed Schools and Hospitals (Scotland)", appendix, p. 21.

6 *Ibid.*, vol. 1, p. 42. See Anderson, *Education and Opportunity in Victorian Scotland*, pp. 180–1.

7 See Magnusson, *The Clacken and the Slate: the Story of Edinburgh Academy*, pp. 210–13.

8 J. Thomson, *A History of Daniel Stewart's College 1855–1955* (Edinburgh, 1955), p. 50.

9 British *Parliamentary Papers*, 1874, vol. XVII (*Minutes of Evidence*), "Report (second) of the Commissioners appointed to inquire into the Endowed Schools and Hospitals (Scotland)", p. 108.

8
Conclusions

Detailed investigation of recruitment and self-recruitment to the Edinburgh CA profession during the second half of the nineteenth and early twentieth centuries reveals that the rate of upward social mobility to the occupation was dependent upon several intraprofessional developments and general socio-economic changes in the geographical source of potential recruits.

With reference to the social changes which occurred during the 1850–1914 period and which were noted in Chapter 1 as likely to have affected rates of upward social mobility to the professions, study of the SAE suggests that the following conclusions may be arrived at.

The emergence of a *new* profession as an additional career option for sons provided opportunities for increased upward mobility. In the early existence of the organization, however, those recruited to the profession tended to derive predominantly from occupational groups which had close employment and social connections with the vocation and its membership. The absence, during the nineteenth century, of a sophisticated infrastructure for the provision of vocational advice ensured that career decision-making was greatly influenced by parents; their status priorities for their sons, and the occupations in which they had an associate or influence. In Edinburgh chartered accountancy, this meant that early recruits to the profession were drawn heavily from families occupied in the law so that rates of upward mobility into the SAE were limited. Those parents and sons who were outwith the occupational and social milieu of the practitioners of the new profession had limited access to information concerning the vocation as a career alternative and fewer associations which would provide a post-qualification clientele for a son.

These factors, together with the limited role played by educational institutions in the career determination process, effectively restricted the social origins of the pool of potential recruits who aspired, and were financially able, to enter the vocation. This state persisted until the membership and scale of operations of the new profession expanded and its practitioners undertook a broader variety of business. By these means, the number of occupational and social connections between Edinburgh CAs and parents from a range of social groups increased, and so did cognizance of the vocation and its conditions of entry among sons with aspirations to enter a professional occupation.

The high rate of growth in the membership of the *new* profession of chartered accountancy certainly provided greater opportunities for upward social mobility when compared to the local, slow growing, *ancient* professions. Given the decline of fertility in the marriages of professional men during the nineteenth century, members of the fast growing profession were unable to maintain levels of self-recruitment. In the slow growing professions, the evidence available for the Faculty of Advocates suggests that levels of self-recruitment could be preserved.

The expansion of membership of the CA (and other) professions was not solely the consequence of increased demand for occupational services caused by the increasing sophistication of the industrial-urban economy as is often assumed. Such factors placed only indefinite, long-term limits on rates of vocational recruitment and sustained growth that was determined primarily by the supply of recruits desirous, and qualified, to enter the system of professional education. The supply of potential recruits to the professions was determined by social pressures on parents to enter sons into vocations with professional and learned standing and by the inferior status attached to alternative occupations in commerce, manufacturing and trade. The ability of a profession to satisfy the demands of parents that their sons should enter a *learned* occupation was also an important regulator of recruitment levels. The output of sons from educational institutions which provided scholars with the qualifications and motivation to enter professional vocations was also significant in increasing the supply of potential recruits.

The supply of available recruits was permitted to enter the unregulated new professions (especially those which were organized on a local and small scale), due to: the desire for the assertion of occupational presence and status through an increasing membership; the need to accumulate financial resources from entrants and members; and attempts to secure a monopoly of business for the membership in order to exclude the unqualified competitor from the performance of professional functions. The necessary imposition of increasingly complex tests of the academic abilities of potential members in order to maintain professional status, ensured that large numbers of recruits were required to enter the vocational training system as increasing numbers would fail to qualify.

The process of professionalization and the meritocratization of the system of vocational preparation and entry had highly significant, short-term impacts on the social origins of recruits and on the rate of upward mobility to the profession. Intraprofessional events designed to effectively improve the status of qualified members tended to have a deleterious effect on the rate of upward circulation.

Following the introduction of increasingly sophisticated systems of vocational training and entry, recruitment to the CA profession became more highly desirable to parents in the professional classes who sought the entrance of their sons to vocations which thoroughly tested academic abilities and thus provided the successful recruit with *learned* professional standing. Such parents were in close social proximity to the members of the various professions and, therefore, had greater access to information concerning internal developments which improved (or were likely to improve) the status of individual vocations which consequently became more alluring career alternatives for their sons.

The increases in recruitment to the SAE of the sons of professional men which occurred following status-enhancing changes restricted the intake of upwardly mobile recruits to the vocational training system. Among fathers who were members of the profession, internal developments also greatly influenced the extent to which self-recruitment was desired. Following the introduction of more comprehensive entrance systems which meant that membership of the CA profession was more selective, the attraction of entering a son into one's own occupation was increased as the son would effectively be recruited to a higher status vocation than that which his father had entered.

The expansion in educational provision was of considerable importance in increasing rates of upward mobility into the Edinburgh CA profession. The aspirations of local parents in marginal middle class occupations for the social advancement of their sons tended to increase accomodation in the private secondary sector of the educational system. The expansion of provision in Edinburgh from the 1870s and competition between an increasing number of schools tended to reduce fees which permitted greater numbers of sons from the lower social ecshelons to be sufficiently qualified and motivated to enter local professional training systems.

General changes in the distribution of income and wealth also played a significant part in determining the social composition of recruits to the professions. Those whose economic superiority was not reflected in a commensurate social status (particularly where the source of their income was profits) had a powerful inducement to enter sons into the respectable professions. The wealthy manufacturers and merchants of Edinburgh preferred to enter sons into the most esteemed and expensive-to-enter vocations – particularly the law, though chartered accountancy was an alternative option with which increasing numbers had occupational and social connections.

The decline of middle class fertility in relation to the rate of expansion of the new professions acted to severely restrict the potential for securing persistant levels of self-recruitment. The decline in the fertility of Edinburgh CAs has to be understood in the context of their social origins, the changing status of their vocation, the opportunities offered by it for generational status improvement and the level of competition for business between members. These factors, in relation to the expansion of the profession, ensured that self-recruitment to the SAE declined over the 1853-1914 period, thus leaving vacant statuses available to sons from inferior social origins.

It would be unwise to provide any further generalized conclusions concerning recruitment to the British *new* professions on the basis of information collected and analysed for one highly localized branch of a developing vocation. Perhaps the inevitable result of an intensive investigation of this nature is to conclude that each profession and each of its local branches was likely to have exhibited unique characteristics in the recruitment of its members. The sources of recruits to the professions were likely to have depended on the social composition of the location of the professional organization and the relationships between the social strata; the period of the vocation's organized existence and, therefore, awareness of its as a career option; the timing and nature of internal professional developments affecting the status and *learned* standing of the membership; and educational provision and its costs in the geographical source of potential recruits.

Clearly, a great deal more detailed investigation is required of individual professions and branches of those professions before further assertions may be made concerning the complex nature of recruitment to the professions during the nineteenth and early twentieth centuries. Further study is however necessary if a greater understanding of the origins and behaviour of those at the head of the British middle class is to be gained.

Appendix A
Occupational and Status Group Classification

The problem of occupational classification is one common to all studies of social stratification. Particularly in a mobility-orientated project, it is vital to be able to assess definable social movement and measure the extent of social circulation.

It was apparent during the research stage of this investigation that the great majority of occupational titles to be analysed were, in broad terms, middle class. A simple breakdown on the basis of social class or in terms of the Registrar-General's classification was clearly innappropriate, and would only serve to produce a huge amorphous, undifferentiated group in its middle sections and an extremely low frequency of manual occupations. The precise classification adopted had to be based upon the nature, objectives, period and, location of the study.

As a social mobility investigation, a number of distinctive and hierarchically-ordered macro-social status groups had to be identified. In order to study more intensive issues (such as the importance of occupational connections in the career decision-making process, and in discovering minor status distinctions within the professions) a micro-orientated breakdown reflecting similar occupations was necessary. The classification essentially had to be flexible in order that minor occupational divisions could be aggregated into major status groups as required. Additionally, the classification adopted had to reflect the status distinctions conceived by contemporaries in the major location of the study, Edinburgh, during the nineteenth and early twentieth centuries.

It was decided initially, therefore, to code related occupations together in minor groups which were then aggregated and coded according to their position in the major social status hierarchy.[1] For example, bakers, pastry bakers and confectioners were classified under a minor group of 'bakers' which was then included in the major social status group of 'distribution and processing'. Similarly, MDs, GPs, physicians, surgeons, army and navy medical officers and dentists were classified in the occupational sub-group 'medicine' of the 'professions' status group.

The formation of principally middle class occupational titles into status groups reflecting the objective prestige ascribed to them by the local population is a difficult enough exercise for modern sociological studies. Historical investigations do not have the benefit of conducting interviews and constructing occupational ranking orders.

There has to be reliance on contemporary impressionistic (often highly subjective) and qualitative evidence concerning the major social status divisions which existed in a locality, and utilize available quantitative indicators to support assertions and value judgements.

In attempting to construct a social status classification, it is essential initially to assess what were the determinants of social prestige and standing. Clearly, a whole range of contributory factors mainly relating to consumption are potentially relevant: the nature of the individual's occupation, the income derived from it and the source of that income; type, size, district of residence as well as the standards of comfort and acquisitions of the household; education; and membership of organizations. Recent studies have revealed that in modern industrial societies some of these factors are of greater importance than others in determining ascribed status.[2] In descending order of significance, the most important indices are said to be occupatation, source of income, house type, and dwelling area. In the construction of an "index of status characteristics", these factors were weighted 4,3,3,2 respectively by Warner[3] for the United States during the 1940s – that is, as four simple characteristics upon which social status may be evaluated. It appears reasonable to base a status classification on an examination of these prestige-determining criteria using available historical sources. This would appear to be a valid procedure given the results of recent American research which suggests that the relative importance of the determinants of prestige appear to alter little over time and between different industrial societies.[4] Treiman in 1977 observed that: "Wherever prestige data are available for two or more periods, the prestige hierarchy appears to be virtually unchanged."[5]

The next stage is to identify the major social status divisions that existed in nineteenth and early twentieth century Edinburgh firstly by examining the most important determinant, the prestige of the individual's occupation.

OCCUPATIONAL STATUS

The status divisions within Edinburgh society during the 1854-1914 period were particularly complex. James Bone in 1911 noted that: "One hears that the divisions and cross-divisions in Edinburgh society are more difficult to follow than elsewhere".[6] Occupational distinctions were minute in a city with a relatively small industrial base. "Our beautiful Modern Athens", claimed J. Heiton in 1861, "is in a swarm of castes, worse than ever was old Egypt or is modern Hindostan".[7] There were between ten and twelve "well defined castes in our city, from the titular Lord to the Applewoman."[8]

A similar series of occupational schisms had been present during the eighteenth century. Commentators such as Heiton and Cockburn,[9] observed that the distinctions between the strata became more intense and acute during the nineteenth century. In the eighteenth century, within the confines of the 'Old Town', all ranks and orders were regarded as having been socially integrated, necessarily due to their close geographical proximity to one another. The construction of the 'New Town' during the late eighteenth and early nineteenth centuries, and the movement to London of the literary and intellectual foci, ensured the movement out of the 'Old Town' of the resident gentry and middle orders. Social divisions were also exaggerated by the increasing dichotomy between landed and commercial wealth, between professions and trade, and by the increasing significance of material consumption and wealth accumulation in status acquisition. Consequently, claimed Heiton: "There is war among the castes, but it is a war which increases them, hardens them and vexes them."[10] The major occupational status divisions discernible from Heiton's commentary and similar qualitative sources which appear suitable for the purposes of this study were as follows.

1) Independent Means

The nobility, gentry and others whose wealth was based on land ownership or similar independence from the means of their income were at the head of the Edinburgh and Scottish status structure. Vestiges of the old resident aristocracy of the capital remained during the nineteenth century. There was a constant presence of resident or semi-resident gentry in the city. According to Bone, Edinburgh contained: "per acre and per mile, more baronets, K.C.B.'s, knights and people in *Who's Who* than any other city outside Westminster."[11]

2) The Professions

The traditional professions were associated and connected particularly with landed society. According to Cockburn[12], the nobility, gentry, the law, the college, the Church and medicine formed during the late eighteenth century a "local aristocracy". The most dominant group of professionals in terms of wealth and prestige during the 1854–1914 period were the lawyers. The higher eschelons of law were integrated closely with the landed interest through marriage, recruitment and business. Within this group was a series of hierarchical gradations, ranging from the advocate at the top, followed by the Writer to the Signet, the Solicitor to the Supreme Court and the solicitor or writer at the bottom. Similar divisions existed among the clerics between the Established, the Episcopal, the Free, the United Presbyterian and the smaller sects.[13] Likewise,

physicians were ranked above surgeons. The teaching profession assumed a high
standing due to the eminence of the University and local public schools. Other
professional men could expect a higher standing in Edinburgh than elsewhere:

> There are only two places in Britain, an eminent architect from the
> west once remarked, where they know how to treat an architect –
> London and Edinburgh. In Glasgow they treat you like a damn clerk of
> the works.[14]

Civil and mining engineers, administrators and executives in the home and foreign civil
service and armed forces officers were also included in this group. Scientists, the
majority of artists and authors who again assumed a relatively high status in
Edinburgh due to the eminence of certain of their predecessors and the general high
standing of professional men in the city, were also classified in this group.

3) Manufacturers

Given their comparative numerical insignificance in Edinburgh, manufacturers receive
only cursory mention by contemporary commentators of the local social structure.
Heiton includes some Edinburgh manufacturing families under his classification of
merchants. Indeed, many appear to have conceived that manufacturing and commerce
were indistinguishable in a city where the latter was more prevalent. In order to
accomodate for this, and because the data suggested that their experiences were
often similar, manufacturers and commercial men have been amalgamated in certain
parts of the study. A separate status group of owners and managers of substantial
manufacturing concerns was, however, deemed necessary due to the scale of the
operations of manufacturers (information from the census suggests that they
employed on average 140.7 hands), and their apparent wealth compared to that of
those in commercial occupations (as shown later in Tables A.2-3 and A.4-6).

By the late nineteenth century, Edinburgh and its environs had a small class of
wealthy manufacturers who owned or managed large-scale concerns in brewing,
paper, and india rubber production. Despite their wealth, however, these individuals
stood below the professionals in the social scale mainly due to their income being
derived from *profits*. Though occupationally and socially distinct from professionals,
manufacturers were of higher local standing than commercial men. Their greater
wealth and economic power permitted manufacturers to assert and institutionalize
their status through connecting themselves with landed and professional society by
marriage, estate purchase, and through acts of municipal altruism and benevolence.

Of the manufacturing families of Edinburgh who produced sons who entered the local chartered accountancy training system, the following can be noted. The Ushers, brewers, gave the city £100,000 in 1896 to build the Usher Hall; the McEwans, brewers, and MPs built the McEwan Hall at a cost of £115,000 and presented it to the University of Edinburgh; and generations of Cowans, paper manufacturers, were parliamentary representatives for the city.

4) Commerce

This group contains merchants, bankers, insurance officials, dealers and brokers. According to Heiton: "The Merchants – not great with us – stand between the Professionals and the Shopkeepers".[15] Most bankers and insurance officers were of greater standing than merchants due to Edinburgh being the centre of Scottish banking and insurance yet, despite the dazzling salaries paid to their managers, they, like merchants, were tainted by the business and money-handling tag. The merchants of Edinburgh, despite their corporate organization, dominance of local politics and gentlemanly presumptions, claimed Heiton, "however rich they may be, are overshadowed by many castes."[16]

5) Farmers

It is particularly difficult to accomodate farmers in an occupational status hierarchy which is essentially urban-orientated. Farmers, planters and market gardeners assume as great a standing in rural society as the manufacturer in the city: "The Lothian farmer was a very definite figure; canny and competent, a professional farmer, a keen businessman, a man of substance, influential and respected in local society."[17] In terms of the major determinant of occupational status, however, the wealth that accrues from it, farmers appearing in this study were by all indicators on a lower prestige level than the urban manufacturing and commercial groups. Their standing also suffered from the manual connotations of farming, and from the fact that few owned the land that was the source of their income.

6) Distribution and Processing

Individuals with occupations in this status group can be difficult to distinguish from certain merchants. Their concerns were, however, on a smaller scale and characterized mainly by shopkeeping and a dependence upon those in higher strata for the major component of their clientele. This group included a wide range of retailers from grocers, drapers and tobacconists to those preparing and selling their products (such as bakers and butchers); as well as similar services such as those provided by hotelkeepers, publicans and cab proprietors.

7) White Collar

This was a group of clerks, non-professional accountants, bookkeepers, cashiers, travellers and minor agents. They were distinguished from the strata below them by the non-manual nature of their employment despite the possibility of lower income. This group included a gradation of occupational statuses from the cashier, the salesman and the traveller within, for example, a retail establishment; or the gradation from the cashier to the junior teller in a bank.

8) Skilled Manual

This group comprised craftsmen or artisans and makers in relatively small workshops. Again, they were largely in the service of groups 1 to 6 above them and heavily dependent on their patronage. They were distinguished from groups 6 and 7 by the essentially manual nature of their work tasks, and from group 9 by their greater skill and employer or self-employed status. According to Heiton, the shopkeepers "expel the Tradesmen, who erect a *nez re-trousse* against the labourers."[18] Examples of occupations classified in this group include tailors, shoemakers, cabinetmakers, gunmakers, and printers.[19]

9) Semi and Unskilled Labour

This group comprised manual labourers and workers employed by others and waged including domestic servants.

Having outlined the proposed nine-fold social status groups, and their ordering according to contemporary evaluations of occupational prestige, the validity of this classification will now be tested according to other, quantitative indicators of social status. The major sources utilized here are the occupations of SAE members and apprentices' fathers as compared to information concerning the household structure and residence from census schedules. The occupations and census data used were those closest to the age at which the son became a CA apprentice – which roughly corresponds to the stage at which the father experienced maximum earning capacity and occupational status.

The frequency distribution of the 1146 CAs' or CA apprentices' fathers or guardians enumerated in the study of occupational status groups is outlined in Table A.1.

TABLE A.1
**Number of SAE Apprentices' Fathers Enumerated
by Occupational Status Group**

Occupational Status Group of Father or Guardian	N of Cases
1 Independent Means	67
2 Professional	416
3 Manufacturers	86
4 Commerce	134
5 Farmers	56
6 Distribution and Processing	105
7 White Collar	141
8 Skilled Manual	79
9 Semi and Unskilled Manual	17
Not Known	45
Total	1146

SOURCE OF INCOME AND EMPLOYMENT STATUS

Source of income has been claimed to be an equally good or better determinant of social status than the amount of income.[20] This is especially advantageous for historical analysis as the latter is difficult to determine for individual occupations and practitioners. The source of income which, during the 1854–1914 period offered greatest status rewards was inherited wealth, especially that derived from the inheritance of land:

> Land is the real root and nucleus of the aristocratic caste, retaining, in its wonderful influence on the sentiments of the proprietors as on the regards of the public, its perfect independence of the means by which it is acquired.[21]

Similarly, income derived from wealth created within one's own lifetime was a next best – that is, in the form of returns on investments and annuities both of which, like inherited wealth, secured *independence* from employment. The professional's fee paid for learned services and advice was regarded with more respect than the profits of business and trade, while salary implied the status of employee and dependence. At the bottom of the source of income hierarchy was the wage paid for labour. Table A.2 shows that the occupational status grouping adopted above reflected the major perceived status divisions on the basis of income source and employment status.

TABLE A.2
Source of Income and Employment Status of Occupational Status Groups

Occupational Status Group	Source of Income	Employment Status of Majority in Group
1 Independent Means	Inherited/Earned Wealth	Independent
2 Professional	Fee or Salary	Employer/Self-Employed
3 Manufacturers	Profits	Employer
4 Commerce	Profits/Salary	Employer
5 Farmers	Profits	Employer
6 Distribution and Processing	Profits	Employer/Self-Employed
7 White Collar	Salary	Employee
8 Skilled Manual	Profits/Wages	Employer/Self-Employed
9 Semi and Unskilled	Wages	Employee

TYPE OF RESIDENCE

The best historical indicator of the standard of the individual's housing is the information provided by the censuses from 1861 concerning the number of windowed rooms of the household. This can be taken as a proxy indicator of house size. Table A.3 illustrates that the occupational status classification correlates closely with the number of windowed rooms.

TABLE A.3
Mean Number of Windowed Rooms in the Total Households Enumerated in 1861–91 Censuses by Occupational Status Group of SAE Apprentices' Fathers or Guardians

Occupational Status Group of Father or Guardian	Total Cases Where Information Available	Mean Number of Windowed Rooms
1 Independent Means	73	17.1
2 Professions	515	13.7
3 Manufacturers	99	14.6
4 Commerce	170	12.5
5 Farmers	59	10.6
6 Distribution and Processing	137	8.2
7 White Collar	150	6.7
8 Skilled Manual	88	6.9
9 Semi and Unskilled Manual	24	4.0

RESIDENTIAL AREA

Most towns and cities can be divided into districts of high and low prestige; certain areas are considered more desirable than others as indicated, for example, by property evaluations. A comparison of occupational status and residential areas was made possible for Edinburgh by utilizing information concerning the registration district in which a CA apprentice's family lived.

Fortunately, during the second half of the nineteenth century and the early twentieth, the five registration districts of Edinburgh encompassed and reflected generally the major divisions of ecological area status. The major spatial status divide was between the New Town and the Old. The West side of the former (St. George registration district) was considered more desirable than the east (St. Andrews). Increasingly favoured were the villas and suburban districts of the south in Morningside, Braid and Newington (Newington registration district). The least desirable residences were those of the Old Town, the worst being in the east side (Canongate), while those of the west (St. Giles) were only marginally more attractive for the inclusion of some respectable middle class residences in George Square and Laurieston.

This five-fold division of the city according to residential desirability is lent some support by the work of Gordon.[22] He considered that, on the basis of valuation rolls in 1855-6 and 1914-15 there were five grades of residences in Edinburgh. It is clear that Gordon's grading corresponds generally with the registration district hierarchy. Most of his Grade 1 residences were located in St. George registration district, the majority of Grade 2 residences were located in St. Andrews, most of Grade 3 were in Newington, and most Grade 4 and 5 residences appeared in the St. Giles and Canongate registration districts. Table A.4 shows that standards of housing and the income of inhabitants were distributed according to the above grading.

TABLE A.4

Mean Number of Windowed Rooms and Domestic Servants in the Households
of CAs' and CA Apprentices' Father's or Guardian's Residence
by the Registration Districts of Edinburgh

Registration District	Mean Windowed Rooms (1861-91)	Mean Domestic Servants (1841-91)
Grade 1: St George	13.9 (265)	3.2 (279)
Grade 2: St Andrew	11.4 (290)	2.2 (311)
Grade 3: Newington	10.6 (351)	1.7 (355)
Grade 4: St Giles	7.9 (48)	1.3 (51)
Grade 5: Canongate	7.8 (13)	1.1 (13)

Table A.5 shows further that, with the exception of occupational groups with a small number of cases (such as 8 and 9), those of higher occupational status tended to live in the most desirable districts of the city. 78.3% of fathers contained in the independent income group who resided in Edinburgh, lived in the New Town (as did 66.1% of those in the professions) compared to between 28.6% and 48.8% of those in occupational groups 3 to 7. The majority of the latter resided in middle-grade Newington. The relatively high numbers of working class fathers who resided in the higher grade areas does not imply that they lived in spacious or desirable residences; the figures reflect the inclusion of some inferior housing in the registration districts, and the employment of groups 8 and 9 in districts close to their clientele (artisans), or, within the households of higher-status employers (domestic servants).

TABLE A.5
Percentage of CAs' and CA Apprentices' Fathers or Guardians Who Resided in the Registration Districts of Edinburgh Graded According to Desirability by Occupational Status Group

Occupational Status Group	Graded Registration District					N
	1 (St George)	2 (St Andrew)	3 (Newington)	4 (St Giles)	5 (Canongate)	
1	30.4	47.8	17.4	4.4	0.0	23
2	40.4	25.7	30.7	2.5	0.7	280
3	17.6	21.6	54.9	0.0	5.9	51
4	19.0	29.8	47.6	3.6	0.0	84
5	23.8	4.8	61.9	9.5	0.0	21
6	13.1	23.0	50.8	9.8	3.3	61
7	16.7	23.5	54.9	2.9	2.0	102
8	19.2	28.8	36.6	11.5	3.9	52
9	20.0	50.0	20.0	0.0	10.0	10
Not Known	16.7	22.2	61.1	0.0	0.0	18

LEVEL OF INCOME AND CONSUMPTION

The information amassed for this study permitted a testing of the validity of the hierarchy of occupational status groups against a further quantitative variable: one that was a particularly significant indicator of family income, comfort and consumption and of general social standing; that is, the number of domestic servants employed in the household. Table A.6 would appear to confirm the usefulness of the classification adopted.

TABLE A.6
Mean Number of Domestic Servants in the Households Enumerated in 1841–91 Censuses by Occupational Status Group of CAs' or CA Apprentices' Fathers or Guardians

Occupational Status Group of Father or Guardian	Total Cases Where Information Available	Mean Number of Domestic Servants
1 Independent Means	83	3.8
2 Professions	555	3.0
3 Manufacturers	101	2.8
4 Commerce	175	2.4
5 Farmers	68	1.6
6 Distribution and Processing	146	1.1
7 White Collar	158	0.7
8 Skilled Manual	88	0.8
9 Semi and Unskilled Manual	23	0.0

CONCLUSIONS

It would appear that the *occupational* status divisions and hierarchy derived from contemporary qualitative and impressionistic sources were largely valid when tested with quantitative data, and were therefore a reasonably accurate description of *social* status groups. There was a clear relationship between occupational status and other indicators of social prestige. It can therefore be asserted with some degree of confidence that occupational standing was a reliable indicator of general social status and that the grouped classification adopted in this study is a reasonably precise division and ordering of the nineteenth and early twentieth century social structure of Edinburgh by social status. Consequently, it forms a usable measure of the distance of social movement.

Notes

1 The coding of related occupations into minor groups was greatly assisted and based on a classification of middle class occupational titles by Dr. R.J. Morris which was slightly modified according to the nature and location of this study. See R.J. Morris, "The Leeds Middle Class, 1820-1850", end-of-grant report to the SSRC, 1983 (Grant No. b/00/24/003/1). *Idem.*, "Property Titles and the use of British Urban Poll Books for Social Analysis", *Urban History Yearbook* (1983).

2 See, for example: W. Lloyd Warner, *Social Class in America: The Evaluation of Status* (New York, 1960). D.J. Treiman, *Occupational Prestige in Comparative Perspective* (New York, 1977). J.A. Kahl, *The American Class Structure* (New York, 1957). J.H. Goldthorpe and K. Hope, *The Social Grading of Occupations: A New Approach and Scale* (Oxford, 1974).

3 Warner, *Social Class in America.*

4 See R.W. Hodge, D. Treiman and P.H. Rossi, "A Comparative Study of Occupational Prestige" in R. Bendix and S.M. Lipset, *Class, Status and Power,* 2nd ed., (London, 1967). *Idem.*, "Occupational Prestige in the US", *American Journal of Sociology* 70 (1964).

5 Treiman, *Occupational Prestige in Comparative Perspective,* p. 74.

6 Bone, *Edinburgh Revisited,* p. 251.

7 Heiton, *The Castes of Edinburgh,* p. 1.

8 *Ibid.,* p. 6.

9 H.T. Cockburn, *The Journal of Henry Cockburn being a Continuation of the Memorials of His Time* (Edinburgh, 1874 ed.).

10 Heiton, *The Castes of Edinburgh,* p. 6.

11 Bone, *Edinburgh Revisited,* p. 241.

12 Cockburn, *The Journal of Henry Cockburn,* vol. 2., pp. 194-201.

13 See Heiton *The Castes of Edinburgh,* p. 6 and p. 138.

14 Bone, *Edinburgh Revisited,* p. 232.

15 Heiton, *The Castes of Edinburgh,* p. 7.

16 *Ibid.,* p. 281.

17 L.J. Saunders, *Scottish Democracy, 1815-40: The Social and Intellectual Background* (Edinburgh, 1950), p. 38.

18 Heiton, *The Castes of Edinburgh,* p. 17.

19 Most of those included in this occupational group are studied in Gray, *The Labour Aristocracy in Victorian Edinburgh.*

20 See Warner, *Social Class in America,* p. 139.

21 Heiton, *The Castes of Edinburgh,* p. 25.

22 G. Gordon, "The Status Areas of Edinburgh: A Historical Analysis", (Ph.D. Dissertation, University of Edinburgh, 1971).

Appendix B
Classification of Schools Attended by
SAE Apprentices

Information concerning the educational institutions attended by SAE apprentices had to be classified according to school type and location. 345 individual educational titles were collected and these required ordering into manageable groups for analysis.

The location of each school, if not obvious from its title, was derived from gazetteers and educational directories.

Classification of schools by their type was centred around information concerning the status of each in 1880 as derived from these sources:

1. For Scotland the 1880 *Report on School Supply.*[1] This provided information concerning the status of each institution, that is, whether it was elementary/secondary and public/private.

2. For England and Wales *The Educational Year-Book, 1881* was consulted. This provided comprehensive information relating to the major secondary schools (their type, size and fees) beyond those listed in *The Public Schools Year-Book.*[2]

3. The 1875 *Return Respecting Secondary Schools in the twelve Parliamentary Burghs of Scotland.* This provided information for some pre-1880 schools, particularly those in Edinburgh (the major centre of SAE apprentices' education) run by private individuals which frequently suffered a short existence.[3]

4. After 1880 a major problem was to determine which schools were to be classed as public/board schools and which were private; many of the latter were eventually taken over by the school boards. The 1897 *Report on School Supply (Scotland)* provided lists of the board schools as did a similar series of reports for England and Wales in 1906.[4]

On the basis of these sources the following classification was adopted.

SCOTTISH SCHOOLS

1. **High Class Public Schools**: these provided a secondary education and were supervised by the school boards from the Education (Scotland) Act 1872. Instruction was provided beyond reading, writing and arithmetic in the *classic* or *modern* subjects. Examples which were attended by SAE apprentices included the Royal High School of Edinburgh (fees £ 12.8s.2d. *per annum* in 1875), Stirling

High School (£3.1s.6d.) and Dumfries Academy (£1.10s.).

2. **High Class Private Schools**: these secondary schools were run by private institutions or individuals and financed by endowments, fees and subscriptions. They exhibited considerable variation in the emphasis placed on the classical or modern side and in their status and fees. For instance between the Edinburgh Academy (£16 *per annum* in 1875), Newington Academy (£6) and Hart's Private School (£1.10s.) in Edinburgh.

3. **Technical Schools or Colleges**: for example, Heriot-Watt College, Edinburgh.

4. **Public (Board) or Parish Schools**: these were concerned principally with providing an elementary instruction. For example, Kirkwall Burgh School, Kelso Parish School, Canonmills School (Edinburgh). Fees varied though were generally around £1-2 during the late 1870s.

5. **State-Aided Elementary Schools**: these were run by private individuals or institutions with financial aid (and therefore some control) from the state. Examples attended by SAE recruits included Bathgate Academy, Edinburgh Free Church Training College, Dr. Bell's School (Edinburgh).

6. **Private Elementary Schools**: for example the United Industrial School (Edinburgh), Dr. Begbie's School.

ENGLISH AND WELSH SCHOOLS

1. **The Nine Great Public Schools**: of the Public Schools Commission of which SAE apprentices attended Harrow, Eton, Winchester, Charterhouse and Rugby. Characterized by their high status and high fees.

2. **Other Upper Class Schools**: these were secondary, proprietary and more recently founded than the great public schools though close to them in status. Fees ranged from fifteen to thirty guineas a year in 1881. Examples included Repton, Leamington and Haileybury.

3. **Grammar, Cathedral, Middle Class and County Schools**: this group comprised a large number of secondary schools including London Company Schools (such as Gresham's and Tonbridge) and non-endowed grammar and cathedral schools of three grades. i) **First Grade** - offered a classical education at a minimum fee of £10 *per annum*, scholars left the school at the age of nineteen. Lancaster Grammar School is an example. ii) **Second Grade** - provided a classical and modern curriculum for a minimum fee of £5, for under seventeen year olds. Sedbergh is an example attended by an SAE apprentice. iii)**Third Grade** - provided secondary instruction primarily in modern subjects for a minimum of £3 a year for scholars up to the age of 15 years. For example, the City of London School. Middle class and county schools such as Hereford County School and Norfolk County School were

included in this group due to their comparable status and range of fees to grammar and cathedral schools.

4. **Other Private Secondary Schools**: these included denominational schools (such as Ley's School), foundations for the sons of professional men (such as Epsom College which catered for the sons of doctors).

5. **Professional and Scientific Institutions**: such as Woolwich and Sandhurst.

6. **Public (Board) Elementary Schools**: Eccles Public School and Hertford Board School for instance.

7. **Private or Voluntary Elementary Schools**: such as Culmington School.

OTHER

1. **Foreign Institutions**: a few apprentices received some of their education overseas, in France (College Chaptal, Paris), Germany (Royal Gymnasium, Dresden), Switzerland (Ecole Cantonal, Lausanne), Russia, South Africa, India (Bishop Cotton's School, Punjab) and Canada (Winnipeg Public School).

2. **Non-Institutional Private Education**: received at home, instruction by parents or private tutors.

For the purposes of data analysis, each school was coded according to its geographical location, type in the above classification, its estimated annual fees (where available), and was provided with an individual identification number. The school and educational titles were then sorted alphabetically and by location to identify any duplication. For example, some schools changed their names though their structure and type remained unaltered. Others were known by their address or by their owner/headmaster (the Southern Academy in Edinburgh was often referred to as Park Place Academy; the Edinburgh Collegiate School was frequently called Dr Bryce's School).

SCHOOL FEES

In order to apply a uniform standard and indicator of school type and status, information concerning fees was collected for as close as possible to 1875 to 1881. *The Educational Year-Book* provided considerable detail relating to the fees of many secondary schools (mainly those in England). The 1875 *Return* for secondary and high class schools provided comprehensive information for the twelve Scottish burghs.

Fearon's estimates for 1877 given in Anderson *Education and Opportunity in Victorian Scotland,* as well as works relating to individual Edinburgh schools, also proved to be of assistance.[5]

It should be noted that statistics concerning the level of school fees are subject to approximation which limit their use and renders it extremely difficult to estimate the precise expense incurred in the schooling of each SAE apprentice. Average school fee figures provided in published sources can hide considerable variation in individual schooling costs according to:

- The number of subjects or classes taken by the scholar. In many Scottish schools especially, fees were paid not by the term or the session but according to the number of individual classes or subjects taken.

- Age and whether in the junior/lower department of the school or the senior/upper department.

- Whether the scholar was a boarder or a day boy. Fearon estimated that the cost of lodgings was between £25-40 per year in 1877.[6]

- Whether or not the scholar was in receipt of an award, bursary or scholarship.

EDUCATIONAL INSTITUTIONS ATTENDED BY SAE MEMBERS 1853–1914 AND APPRENTICES CONTAINED IN THE STUDY PREVIOUS TO THE COMMENCEMENT OF THEIR INDENTURES

Scottish Schools and Colleges

COUNTY OF/ COUNTRY	LOCATION	INSTITUTION	N
Aberdeen	Aberdeen	Aberdeen Grammar School	6
Aberdeen	Aberdeen	Ashley Public School	1
Aberdeen	Aberdeen	Bon-Accord School	1
Aberdeen	Aberdeen	Marywell Street Public School	1
Aberdeen	Aberdeen	Robert Gordon's College	5
Aberdeen	Aberdeen	St John's Episcopal School	1
Aberdeen	Aberdeen	Town School	1
Aberdeen	Ardallie	Ardallie Public School	1
Aberdeen	Cultercullen	Cultercullen Public School	1
Aberdeen	Huntly	Huntly Public School	1
Aberdeen	Towie	Towie Free Church School	1
Aberdeen	Towie	Towie Parochial School	1
Angus	Arbroath	Arbroath High School	2
Angus	Brechin	Brechin Public School	2
Angus	Broughty Ferry	Seafield House School	1
Angus	Dundee	Ancram Road Public School	1
Angus	Dundee	Dundee High School	5
Angus	Dundee	East of Scotland Institution	2
Angus	Forfar	Forfar Academy	1
Angus	Kettins	Kettins Parish School	1
Angus	Kirriemuir	Burnside of Inchewan Public School	1
Angus	Montrose	Montrose Academy	2
Argyll	Islay	Bowmore Parish School	1
Argyll	Campbeltown	Campbeltown Grammar School	6
Argyll	Oban	Oban School	1
Ayr	Ayr	Ayr Academy	5
Ayr	Dreghorn	Dreghorn College	1
Ayr	Irvine	Irvine Academy	1
Banff	Banff	Banff Academy	1
Banff	Banff	Banff Grammar School	1
Berwick	Duns	Berwickshire High School	1
Berwick	Duns	Duns/Wellfield Academy	2
Berwick	Eyemouth	Berwickshire Free Church School	1
Berwick	Lauder	Lauder School	1
Berwick	Leitholm	Leitholm School	1
Berwick	Whitsome	Whitsome Public School	1
Bute	Rothesay	Rothesay Academy	1
Caithness	Wick	Patteneytown Academy	2
Clackmannan	Alloa	Alloa Academy	1
Clackmannan	Dollar	Dollar Academy	10
Dumfries	Annan	Annan Academy	1
Dumfries	Closeburn	Wallace Hall Academy	1
Dumfries	Dumfries	Dumfries Academy	6
Dumfries	Dumfries	Glasgow Street Public School	1
Dumfries	Halfmorton	Halfmorton Parish School	1
Dumfries	Moffat	Moffat Academy	1

Dumfries	Moffat	St Ninians	6
Dumfries	Moffat	Warriston College	1
Dunbarton	Dunbarton	Burgh Academy	1
Dunbarton	Glen Douglas	Glen Douglas School	1
Dunbarton	Helensburgh	Larchfield Academy	1
Dunbarton	Lenzie	Lenzie Academy	1
Dunbarton	Row	Row Parish School	1
Elgin	Elgin	Elgin Academy	2
Elgin	Fochabers	Fochabers School	1
Elgin	Knockando	Knockando Public School	1
Fife	Crail	Crail School	1
Fife	Culross	Culross Public School	1
Fife	Cupar	Bell Baxter School	1
Fife	Dunfermline	Dunfermline High School	2
Fife	Dunfermline	St Leonard's Public School	2
Fife	Dysart	Dysart Public School	2
Fife	Kirkcaldy	Burgh School	1
Fife	Kirkcaldy	Kirkcaldy High School	5
Fife	Kirkcaldy	Viewforth	1
Fife	Leslie	Leslie Public School	1
Fife	Leven	Leven Public School	2
Fife	Markinch	Markinch Public School	1
Fife	St Andrews	Abbey Park School	3
Fife	St Andrews	Cleghorn's Private Academy	2
Fife	St Andrews	Clifton Bank School	3
Fife	St Andrews	Edgecliffe	1
Fife	St Andrews	Madras College	7
Fife	St Andrews	St Salbatus School	1
Haddington	Dunbar	Dunbar School	1
Haddington	Gifford	Gifford Public School	1
Haddington	Haddington	Haddington Burgh School	1
Haddington	Haddington	Knox Institute	1
Haddington	North Berwick	Abbey School	1
Haddington	North Berwick	North Berwick School	1
Haddington	Stenton	Stenton Parish School	1
Haddington	Tranent	Tranent Public School	2
Inverness	Croy	Croy Public School	1
Inverness	Inverness	Herr Waack's Preparatory School	1
Inverness	Inverness	Inverness Board School	1
Inverness	Inverness	Inverness High School	3
Inverness	Inverness	Inverness Royal Academy	6
Inverness	Inverness	Raining's School	2
Inverness	Inverness	The College	5
Inverness	Kingussie	Kingussie School	1
Kincardine	Laurencekirk	Laurencekirk Public School	1
Kincardine	Stonehaven	Mackie Academy	1
Kinross	Kinross	Kinross Public School	3
Kirkcudbright	Buittle	Buittle Public School	1
Kirkcudbright	Castle Douglas	Castle Douglas School	1
Kirkcudbright	Kirkcudbright	Kirkcudbright Academy	1
Lanark	Biggar	Biggar Public School	2
Lanark	Dolphinton	Dolphinton School	3
Lanark	Glasgow	Garnethill Public School	1
Lanark	Glasgow	Glasgow Academy	4
Lanark	Glasgow	Glasgow High School	1
Lanark	Glasgow	Hutcheson's Grammar School	1
Lanark	Glasgow	Longcroft Public School	1

Linlithgow	Bathgate	Bathgate Academy	1
Linlithgow	Broxburn	Broxburn Public School	1
Linlithgow	Linlithgow	Landward Public School	1
Midlothian	Corstorphine	Corstorphine Parish School	1
Midlothian	Cramond	Cargilfield Preparatory School	13
Midlothian	Crichton	Crichton Public School	3
Midlothian	Currie	Currie Parish School	1
Midlothian	Dalkeith	Mr Simpson's School	1
Midlothian	Edinburgh	Aird House	6
Midlothian	Edinburgh	Albany Street Academy	1
Midlothian	Edinburgh	Bonnington Institute/Academy	2
Midlothian	Edinburgh	Bruntsfield Public School	2
Midlothian	Edinburgh	Canonmills School	1
Midlothian	Edinburgh	Chalmers Private School	1
Midlothian	Edinburgh	Circus Place School	6
Midlothian	Edinburgh	Clare Hall Academy, Causewayside	3
Midlothian	Edinburgh	Coltbridge School	1
Midlothian	Edinburgh	Craigmount	10
Midlothian	Edinburgh	Daniel Stewart's Hospital/College	62
Midlothian	Edinburgh	Douglas Private School, Gt King Street	2
Midlothian	Edinburgh	Dr Begbie's School	3
Midlothian	Edinburgh	Dr Bell's School	1
Midlothian	Edinburgh	Dr Cameron's School, Gayfield Square	1
Midlothian	Edinburgh	Dr Thomson's School	5
Midlothian	Edinburgh	Edinburgh Academy	201
Midlothian	Edinburgh	Edinburgh Collegiate School	46
Midlothian	Edinburgh	Edinburgh Institution	65
Midlothian	Edinburgh	Episcopal Church Normal School	1
Midlothian	Edinburgh	Ewart's High School	1
Midlothian	Edinburgh	Fettes College	25
Midlothian	Edinburgh	Free Church Normal School, Moray House	7
Midlothian	Edinburgh	George Heriot's Hospital/School	43
Midlothian	Edinburgh	George Watson's Hospital/College	203
Midlothian	Edinburgh	Gorgie Public School	1
Midlothian	Edinburgh	Grange Academy	6
Midlothian	Edinburgh	Hamilton Place Academy	1
Midlothian	Edinburgh	Hay's Academy	1
Midlothian	Edinburgh	Henderson's School, India Street	7
Midlothian	Edinburgh	Heriot-Watt College	4
Midlothian	Edinburgh	James Baillie's School, Marmion Terr.	4
Midlothian	Edinburgh	James Gillespie's School	24
Midlothian	Edinburgh	Leith Walk Board School	3
Midlothian	Edinburgh	Lods Private School	1
Midlothian	Edinburgh	Lothian Road School	2
Midlothian	Edinburgh	McLean's School, Thistle Street	1
Midlothian	Edinburgh	Merchiston Castle School	34
Midlothian	Edinburgh	Milne's Private School	1
Midlothian	Edinburgh	Minto House	1
Midlothian	Edinburgh	Morelands	4
Midlothian	Edinburgh	Morningside College/Academy	2
Midlothian	Edinburgh	Morningside Public School	1
Midlothian	Edinburgh	Mr Adam's, Young Street	1
Midlothian	Edinburgh	Mr Crerar's School	1
Midlothian	Edinburgh	Mr Hunter's, York Place	7
Midlothian	Edinburgh	Mr Munro's, Minto Street	2
Midlothian	Edinburgh	Mr Oliphant's School	10
Midlothian	Edinburgh	Newington Academy	5

Midlothian	Edinburgh	Newington Free Church School	1
Midlothian	Edinburgh	Normal Private School, Johnston Terr.	3
Midlothian	Edinburgh	Ramsey Law School	2
Midlothian	Edinburgh	Heriot School, Rose Street	1
Midlothian	Edinburgh	Royal High School	78
Midlothian	Edinburgh	Sciennes Public School	2
Midlothian	Edinburgh	Skerry's Civil Service College	2
Midlothian	Edinburgh	South Side High/Drummond St. Academy	2
Midlothian	Edinburgh	Southern Academy, Park Place	4
Midlothian	Edinburgh	St Bernard's Public School	1
Midlothian	Edinburgh	St George's Institution/Day School	4
Midlothian	Edinburgh	St John's Episcopal School	1
Midlothian	Edinburgh	St Leonard's School	1
Midlothian	Edinburgh	Stockbridge School	1
Midlothian	Edinburgh	United Industrial School, High Street	2
Midlothian	Edinburgh	Viewpark School	4
Midlothian	Edinburgh	Warrender Park Public School	2
Midlothian	Granton	Granton Public School	1
Midlothian	Lasswade	Lasswade Public School	1
Midlothian	Leith	Convent School	1
Midlothian	Leith	Leith Academy	3
Midlothian	Leith	Leith High School	4
Midlothian	Leith	Leith Episcopal School	1
Midlothian	Leith	Lorne Street School	1
Midlothian	Leith	Miss Grove's Private School	1
Midlothian	Leith	Private School	2
Midlothian	Musselburgh	Loretto	20
Midlothian	Musselburgh	Musselburgh Grammar School	4
Midlothian	Newbattle	Newbattle School	2
Midlothian	Penicuik	Penicuik Public School	2
Midlothian	Portobello	Portobello Board School	2
Midlothian	Portobello	Windsor Academy	4
Nairn	Moyness	Moyness School	1
Orkney	Kirkwall	Kirkwall Burgh School	1
Peebles	Peebles	Burgh and County High School	1
Perth	Aberfeldy	Aberfeldy Board School	1
Perth	Acharn	Acharn Public School	1
Perth	Bridge of Earn	Bridge of Earn Board School	2
Perth	Collace	Collace Parochial School	1
Perth	Crieff	Arvrick School	2
Perth	Crieff	Madras Academy	1
Perth	Crieff	Morrison's Academy	5
Perth	Glenalmond	Trinity College	11
Perth	Monzievaird	Monzievaird Public School	1
Perth	Muthill	Muthill Public School	2
Perth	Perth	Knox Institute	1
Perth	Perth	Perth Academy	6
Perth	Perth	Sharpe's Educational Institution	4
Perth	Perth	William Street Public School	1
Ross & Cromarty	Dingwall	Dingwall Parish School	1
Ross & Cromarty	Fortrose	Fortrose Academy	1
Ross & Cromarty	Invergordon	Invergordon Academy	1
Ross & Cromarty	Stornoway	Nicholson Public School	1
Ross & Cromarty	Stornoway	Stornoway School	1
Ross & Cromarty	Tain	Tain School	1
Roxburgh	Bowden	Bowden Village School	1
Roxburgh	Hawick	Teviot Grove Academy	1

Roxburgh	Jedburgh	Jedburgh Grammar School	1
Roxburgh	Kelso	Kelso High School	2
Roxburgh	Kelso	Kelso Parish School	2
Roxburgh	Kelso	North School	1
Roxburgh	Melrose	Highfield House	3
Roxburgh	Melrose	St Mary's	2
Roxburgh	St Boswells	St Boswells Public School	3
Stirling	Bridge of Allan	Kelvingrove House	1
Stirling	Bridge of Allan	La Villa	1
Stirling	Bridge of Allan	Mr Braidwood's Academy	1
Stirling	Bridge of Allan	Stanley House	4
Stirling	Polmont	Blair Lodge School	10
Stirling	Stirling	Stirling High School	2
Wigtown	Stranraer	Stranraer School	1

English, Welsh and Irish Schools and Colleges

Bedford	Bedford	Bedford School	1
Berkshire	Theale	Bradfield College	1
Berkshire	Reading	Amersham School	1
Berkshire	Sandhurst	Royal Military Academy	1
Berkshire	Crowthorne	Wellington College	3
Buckingham	Eton	Eton	2
Buckingham	Lathbury	Lathbury Park	1
Cambridge	Cambridge	Ley's School	5
Channel Islands	Guernsey	St Elizabeth College	1
Denbigh	Ruthin	Ruthin Grammar School	1
Derby	Repton	Repton	2
Derby	Tideswell	Tideswell Grammar School	1
Devon	Exeter	Exeter Grammar School	1
Devon	Exeter	Norwood Preparatory School	1
Durham	Barnard Castle	PEC School	1
Durham	Durham	Bow Preparatory School	1
Durham	Durham	Durham School	1
Essex	Wanstead	Wanstead School	1
Gloucester	Bristol	Clifton College	4
Gloucester	Cheltenham	Cheltenham College	6
Gloucester	Cheltenham	St John's School	1
Gloucester	Cirencester	Royal Agricultural College	1
Hampshire	Bournemouth	Bournemouth School	1
Hampshire	Fareham	Stubbington House School	2
Hampshire	Southampton	Bitterne Government School	1
Hampshire	Southsea	Vickery School	1
Hampshire	Winchester	Winchester College	2
Hampshire	Winchester	Wistow House	1
Hereford	Hereford	Hereford County School	1
Hertford	Berkhampstead	Berkhampstead School	1
Hertford	Hertford	Hertford Board School	1
Hertford	Hertford	Hertford Grammar School	1
Hertford	Hoddeston	Grange School	1
Hertford	Hoddeston	Haileybury College	5
Ireland	Dublin	Dublin High School	2

Ireland	Kildare	Liexlip High School	1
Isle of Man	Castletown	King William College	2
Kent	Cranbrook	Cranbrook Grammar School	1
Kent	Tonbridge	Tonbridge School	2
Lancashire	Eccles	Clarendon House School	1
Lancashire	Eccles	Eccles Public School	1
Lancashire	Fleetwood	Rossall School	2
Lancashire	Lancaster	Royal Grammar School	1
Lancashire	Manchester	Fullerton House School	1
Lancashire	Rochdale	H. Patrick's School	1
Lincoln	Burgh	Lincolnshire Grammar School	1
London	London	Christ's Hospital	2
London	London	City of London School	1
London	London	King's College School	1
London	London	Middle Close School	1
London	London	Oakfield	1
London	Westminster	St John's Wood School	1
London	Westminster	United Westminster School	1
London	Woolwich	Royal Military Academy	1
Middlesex	Harrow	E.R. Hasting's Preparatory School	1
Middlesex	Harrow	Harrow	4
Middlesex	Mill Hill	Mill Hill Grammar School	1
Norfolk	Elmham	Norfolk County School	1
Norfolk	Great Yarmouth	Rev. Shelley Boarding School	1
Norfolk	Holt	Gresham's School	1
Northampton	Wellingborough	Wellingborough Grammar School	1
Nothumberland	Berwick	Avenue Academy	2
Northumberland	Berwick	Berwick Grammar School	2
Northumberland	Berwick	Berwick Preparatory School	1
Northumberland	Berwick	Corporation Academy	1
Northumberland	Newcastle	Mr Marchbank's School	1
Rutland	Uppingham	Uppingham School	3
Shropshire	Culmington	Culmington School	1
Stafford	Tettenhall	Tettenhall College	1
Stafford	Walsall	Aldridge School	1
Surrey	Addiscombe	Addiscombe College	1
Surrey	Epsom	Epsom College	1
Surrey	Godalming	Charterhouse	4
Surrey	Surbiton	Bramham House School	1
Surrey	Surbiton	Surbiton	1
Surrey	Wimbledon	Prackenbury's and Wynnes	1
Surrey	Wimbledon	Wimbledon	1
Sussex	Brighton	Brighton and Hove High School	1
Sussex	Brighton	Private School	1
Warwick	Knowle	Brisbane Academy	1
Warwick	Leamington Spa	Leamington	2
Warwick	Rugby	Rugby	2
Warwick	Warwick	Coten End Board School	1
Warwick	Warwick	King's Grammar School	1
Warwick	Warwick	King's Middle School	1
Westmoreland	Kendal	Stranongate School	1
Worcester	Malvern	Malvern College	1
York	Doncaster	Doncaster Grammar School	1
York	Giggleswick	Giggleswick School	1
York	Northallerton	Northallerton	1
York	Sedbergh	Sedbergh	3
York	Sheffield	Sheffield High School	1

Foreign Schools and Colleges

Canada	Winnipeg	Winnipeg Public School	1
France	Paris	College Chaptal	1
Germany	Berlin	Handelshule	1
Germany	Dresden	Royal Gymnasium	1
Germany	Hiedelberg	Nevenheim College	1
Germany	Wiesbaden	H.B. Cotterill's School	1
India	Simla	Bishop Cotton's School	1
South Africa	Cape Town	South African College	1
South Africa	Kimberley	Kimberley High School	1
Switzerland	Basle	Gymnasium	1
Switzerland	Lausanne	Ecole Cantonal	1

Universities

Edinburgh	166
Glasgow	2
Aberdeen	4
St Andrews	8
Dundee	1
Oxford	8
Cambridge	8
Samonigh	1

Notes

1 British *Parliamentary Papers*, 1880, vol. LV, "Return showing by counties for each School District in Scotland, Rateable Value, School Rate, Population, number of Children of School Age (5-13), and Accomodation in Public Schools, in State-aided Schools (not-Public), in other Elementary Schools recognized as efficient, in Higher Class Public Schools, and in Higher Class Schools (not Public)".

A further return is available for 1888, vol. LXXXVIII.

2 The *Educational Year-Book, 1881,* (London, 1881). Unfortunately, this useful parents, guide to the major secondary schools was published in 1879-82 and 1885 only.

3 British *Parliamentary Papers*, 1875, vol. LX, "Return respecting the secondary and higher class schools in each of the twelve Parliamentary Burghs referred to in the Second Report of the Board of Education for Scotland (p. 35), stating the population of each burgh; and showing separately for boys' and girls' schools, the number of pupils which each school could accomodate; the average number of pupils on the roll for the school year closing in 1875; the average daily attendance, and also the average amount of the fees &c."

4 British *Parliamentary Papers*, 1897, vol. LXXI, "Return showing by Counties for each school District in Scotland, the Rateable Value, the School Rate, the Population, the Number of Children of School Age (5-14), and the Amount of Accomodation, and the Number in Average Attendance in Public Schools, State-aided Schools (Non-Public), and other Elementary Schools, recognized as Efficient, Higher Class Public Schools, Higher Class Schools (Non-Public), Technical Schools under the Management of the School Board, and Technical Schools not under the Management of the School Board".

British *Parliamentary Papers*, 1906, vol. LXXXVI, "List of Public Elementary Schools in England and Wales on 1 January 1906". Vols. LXXXVII-III, "Return of the Schools in England and Wales recognized on the 1st day of January 1906 as Non-Provided Public Elementary Schools".

5 Anderson, *Education and Opportunity in Victorian Scotland,* p. 143.

6 *Ibid.,* p. 142.

Appendix C
Place of Birth of SAE Members and Apprentices
1837–1914

This appendix is included for three reasons. Firstly, it reveals the system of classification used in the study for the coding of geographical variables. Secondly, it is hoped that the information provided concerning the place of birth of SAE members and apprentices, which was not significant to the mainstream discussion of recruitment, will be of some interest to readers interested in the origins of members of the Edinburgh profession. Thirdly, when a comparison is made between the places of birth of apprentices and the addresses of their parents and guardians at indenture commencement, a certain degree of migration is revealed. The latter figure is given in parenthesis in the following table.

Whereas 4.3% of apprentices were known to have been born outside the British Isles, only 0.7% of the parents of recruits still resided abroad when their sons' indentures were signed. If Scotland alone is considered, a considerable amount of internal migration is evident. There was clearly a gravitation towards Midlothian (Edinburghshire), the organizational centre of the SAE and the major location of professional training. Whereas 57.7% of apprentices were born in Edinburghshire, 77.6% had parents or guardians resident in that county 16 to 19 years later. 20.3% of recruits to the SAE contained in the study were born in the four regions bordering South Eastern Scotland (East Midland, West Midland, South Western and Southern Scotland), but only 9.9% of apprentices' parents resided in these areas at the commencement of their sons' vocational training.

PLACE OF BIRTH OF SAE APPRENTICES 1837-1911 BY BRITISH
CENSUS DISTRICT IN 1891 OR CONTINENT

Scotland

Northern			
Shetland	1		
Orkney	2		
Caithness	2		
		5 0.4 (0.0)	
North Western			
Ross & Cromarty	8		
Inverness	10		

Inverness-shire	2			
		20	1.9	(1.6)
North Eastern				
Elginshire	6			
Banffshire	6			
Aberdeen	5			
Aberdeenshire	8			
Kincardineshire	1			
		26	2.4	(1.6)
East Midland				
Arbroath	1			
Dundee	12			
Angus	19			
Perth	12			
Perthshire	20			
Dunfermline	3			
Kirkcaldy	4			
Fife	25			
Kinross-shire	4			
Clackmannanshire	4			
		104	9.7	(5.6)
West Midland				
Falkirk	4			
Stirling	3			
Stirlingshire	6			
Dunbarton	1			
Dunbartonshire	2			
Argyll	9			
Bute	1			
		26	2.4	(1.1)
South Western				
Greenock	3			
Paisley	1			
Renfrewshire	2			
Ayr	3			
Ayrshire	11			
Glasgow	17			
Partick	4			
Airdrie	1			
Hamilton	2			
Lanarkshire	14			
		58	5.4	(1.2)
South Eastern				
Linlithgowshire	12			
Edinburgh	522		{48.9}	{65.8}
Leith	43			
Edinburghshire	51			
Haddingtonshire	13			
Berwickshire	14			
Peebleshire	5			
Selkirkshire	1			
		661	61.9	(80.9)

Southern
Hawick	1			
Roxburghshire	12			
Dumfries	2			
Dumfriesshire	7			
Kirkcudbrightshire	8			
		30	2.8	(2.0)

England, Wales and Ireland

South Eastern
London	13			
Surrey	1			
Sussex (Brighton)	2			
Hampshire (Southampton)	2			
		18	1.7	(1.2)

South Midland
Hertfordshire	2			
		2	0.2	(0.1)

Eastern
Essex	2			
Suffolk	1			
		3	0.3	(0.0)

South Western
Dorset	1			
Plymouth	2			
Devon	2			
		5	0.4	(0.1)

West Midland
Bristol	1			
Gloucestershire	1			
		2	0.2	(0.3)

North Midland
Leicestershire	1			
Derbyshire	2			
		3	0.3	(0.1)

North Western
Cheshire	2			
Manchester	1			
Liverpool	2			
Lancashire	1			
		6	0.6	(0.3)

Yorkshire
Middlesbrough	1			
Yorkshire	6			
		7	0.6	(0.1)

Northern

Newcastle	4			
Northumberland	6			
Cumberland	2			
Westmoreland	1			
		13	1.2	(0.2)

Unspecified England

	4	0.4	(0.0)

Wales

	0	0.0	(0.1)

Ireland

Belfast	2			
Northern Ireland	1			
Dublin	3			
Southern Ireland	7			
		13	1.2	(0.2)

Overseas

Europe

France (Paris)	1			
Russia	1			
		2	0.2	(0.4)

South Africa

Cape Colony (Cape Town)	1			
Orange Free State	1			
		2	0.2	(0.2)

Asia

Calcutta	3			
Bombay	2			
Madras	3			
India	9			
Ceylon	3			
Burma	1			
Shanghai	1			
China	3			
Hong Kong	1			
Malay States	1			
Dutch East Indies	1			
		28	2.6	(0.1)

Australasia

Sydney	3			
New South Wales	1			
Melbourne	1			
New Zealand	1			
		6	0.6	(0.0)

North America

Newfoundland	2			
Ontario	1			
USA	1			

		4	0.4	(0.0)
Central and South America				
West Indies	1			
Brazil	1			
Argentina (Buenos Aires)	1			
Falkland Islands	1			
		4	0.4	(0.0)
Not Known		15	1.4	(2.6)
Total		1067	100.0	(100.0)

Scotland		930	87.2	(94.0)
England, Wales and Ireland		76	7.1	(2.7)
Overseas		46	4.3	(0.7)
Not Known		15	1.4	(2.6)
Total		1067	100.0	(100.0)

**PLACE OF BIRTH OF THE ORIGINAL MEMBERS OF THE INSTITUTE OF
ACCOUNTANTS IN EDINBURGH AND OF THOSE MEMBERS ADMITTED
TO THE SAE 1855–60 WITHOUT HAVING SERVED
AN SAE REGISTERED INDENTURE**

Scotland

Northern
Caithness	2		
		2	2.5

North Eastern
Elginshire	1		
Aberdeenshire (Aberdeen)	2		
		3	3.8

East Midland
Arbroath	1		
Angus	1		
Perth	1		
Perthshire	1		
Dunfermline	2		
Fife	4		
		10	12.6

West Midland
Stirlingshire	1		
		1	1.3

South Western
Ayrshire	1		
		1	1.3

South Eastern
Edinburgh	48		
Edinburghshire	4		
Haddingtonshire	3		
Berwickshire	2		
		57	72.1

Southern
Roxburghshire	2		
Dumfriesshire (Dumfries)	1		
Kirkcudbrightshire	1		
		4	5.1

England, Wales and Ireland

South Eastern
London	1		
		1	1.3

Total		79	100.0

Scotland	78	98.7
England, Wales and Ireland	1	1.3
Total	79	100.0

Appendix D
Selected Documents Illustrative of the Organizational Development of the SAE and the System of Recruitment and Qualification

Details concerning the precise organizational structure of the SAE have only been provided in the mainstream text where they have been highly relevant to recruitment, examination and professional status. The following papers will provide a greater insight into events that were of great significance in the development of the SAE and to its membership over the 1853 to 1914 period.

1. Institute of Accountants in Edinburgh – Constitution and Laws, 1853. The first published set of regulations of the new professional organization were clearly very unsophisticated when compared with later constitutions, and as article 14 suggests, have the appearance of comprising an interim list of rules which would require refinement following an application for incorporation. The principal concern of the Institute's founders was to establish a basic organizational structure and to provide for its management.

The elementary nature of the Institute's Constitution did not pass unnoticed in Edinburgh legal circles. The 1853 issue of *Index Juridicus* (see preface, pp. x–xii) welcomed the establishment of the organization due to its "comprising nearly all the respectable Accountants in Edinburgh" but expressed some disquiet on a number of points regarding its *Constitution and Laws*. The absence of regulations of admission and training, which were alluded to in Chapter 4, were particularly noted: "There is no sufficient provision made for controlling the admission of members". A further source of contention was the dual nature of the membership – its separation into *Ordinary* and *Honorary* members:

> . . . we find that the management of the new Institute is entirely in the hands of the Ordinary Members, although the Honorary Members are called upon to contribute to the funds. This, surely cannot have been properly considered. The Honorary Members must either be admitted to a share in the management, or exempted from annual payments.

In conclusion, it was stated that:

> Altogether, the "Rules and Regulations" bear unmistakable evidence of having been hastily and crudely concocted. For the credit of the profession, and the prosperity of the Institute the Members (including

the Honorary ones) should meet at an early day, to consider the Rules and Regulations under which they are at present bound together.

The next two documents illustrate that this advice was taken, within two years the founders of the Institute of Accountants had established a more substantial organizational infrastructure and the dual status of the membership was removed.

Source: *Index Juridicus, The Scottish Law List and Legal Directory, 1854,* pp. 174-177. The *Constitution and Laws* also appear in the 1853 edition.

2. Royal Charter Incorporating the Society of Accountants in Edinburgh, 1854. This document reveals the names of the founders of the Edinburgh professional organization of CAs and also the strong legal component of their business. Note the heavy emphasis which was placed on the assertion of the professional respectability of Edinburgh accountants through their connections with the lawyers, and entrance based on the attainment of a *liberal education*.

Source: Privy Council. "In the Matter of the Petition of the Scottish Institute of Accountants for Incorporation by Royal Charter" (1889-90). Appendix to Petition, pp. 100-104.

3. Constitution and Laws of the Society of Accountants in Edinburgh, 1855. The Constitution drafted by the SAE following incorporation and ratified by a General Meeting of 7 February 1855. The document contains 46 articles compared to 14 in the 1853 Constitution. Regulations concerning recruitment and qualification were established – a final examination was instituted.

Source: *Index Juridicus, The Scottish Law List and Legal Directory, 1856,* pp. 593-602.

4. Rules and Regulations of the Incorporated Society of Accountants in Edinburgh, 1889. This paper reveals the precise nature of the 1873 to 1893 system of examination and entrance, and the introduction of the compulsory attendance of apprentices at university law classes. The changes in the dues of admission to the SAE following the establishment of the Endowment and Annuity Fund, which effectively blocked the membership of some recruits of lesser means, are contained in article 39.

Source: Privy Council. "In the Matter of the Petition of the Scottish Institute of Accountants for Incorporation by Royal Charter" (1889-90). Appendix to Petition, pp. 105-111.

5. Nature of the Chartered Societies' Examinations, 1889-90. This provides more details concerning the content of SAE examinations during the 1873 to 1893 period. The qualification system of the Edinburgh CA Society is compared to that of the Glasgow Institute, and clearly, are more sophisticated and thorough than those established in article 39 of the *Constitution and Laws* of 1855. (For a comparison of the two systems of examinations see also *The Accountant* 19 [1893] pp. 150-1).

Source: Privy Council. "In the Matter of the Petition of the Scottish Institute of Accountants for Incorporation by Royal Charter" (1889-90). Opponent's Case, pp. 7-9.

6. Scottish Institute of Accountants – Scheme for Admission of Associates, 1887. This reveals that the competing SIA's system of examination was inferior to that of the chartered societies during the 1880s. The Institute's establishment of comprehensive provisions for the examination of recruits were clearly at a rudimentary stage. Even *The Accountant* (which adopted a pro-SIA stance during this period), on inspecting the SIA's examinations for the admission of Associates, had to admit that "As far as the papers go they are very good; but it certainly occurs to us that they are far below the standard of the Scottish Chartered bodies." (*The Accountant* 15 [1889] p. 29).

Source: Privy Council. "In the Matter of the Petition of the Scottish Institute of Accountants for Incorporation by Royal Charter" (1889-90). Appendix to Petition, p. 140.

7. Scottish Institute of Accountants – Prospectus of Examinations, 1892. The new, codified and upgraded system of examinations introduced by the SIA in October 1892 was designed to equalize standards of admission between itself and the Scottish chartered societies. The likeness of the Institute's examination procedure to the three-tier SAE system would negate the CA societies' argument that the SIA did not deserve a charter of incorporation on the basis that its qualification system was less exacting and comprehensive. Note also that the SIA examinations were to be *open* to all apprentices of professional accountants in Scotland whereas the examinations of the chartered societies were *closed* – restricted to recruits trained in the offices of their members. This was a point that the SIA was to stress in its 1896 application for incorporation.

Source: *The Scottish Accountant* 1 (1892), p. 59.

8. Agreement Entered Into in 1893 Between the Three Chartered Societies Constituting the General Examining Board. This agreement, in introducing a uniform system of recruitment and qualification to the chartered societies was the first major event in the development of a national, *Scottish* CA profession. The significance of this concord in asserting the superior status of CAs, and in raising standards of entry was shown in its effects on increasing recruitment to the SAE and its impact on the marital and fertility experiences of the membership.

Source: Privy Council. "In the Matter of the Petition of the Scottish Institute of Accountants for Incorporation by Royal Charter" (1896). Appendix to Petition, pp. 70–76.

9. **Syllabus of Examinations by General Examining Board, 1895.** This document provides an example of an early syllabus of the GEB which was to undergo several alterations from 1893 to 1914. Note that the content of examinations of the early GEB differed little from those of the SAE in 1889.

Source: Privy Council. "In the Matter of the Petition of the Scottish Institute of Accountants for Incorporation by Royal Charter" (1896). Appendix to Petition, pp. 77–79.

10. **Chartered Accountants of Scotland – Syllabus of Examinations, 1913.** This reveals details of the system of professional examinations for qualification to the SAE at the end of the period studied. Note the new form of *preliminary qualification* which replaced the GEB matriculation examination and also the two division structure of the final examination.

Source: *Scottish Chartered Accountants, Official Directory, 1913-14,* pp. 227–234. (Reproduced with the permission of The Institute of Chartered Accountants of Scotland).

Institute of Accountants in Edinburgh

CONSTITUTION AND LAWS

SECTION I
Constitution and Objects

1. The Institute of Accountants in Edinburgh is an Association constituted for the purposes of uniting together the Accountants in that City, and of advancing those objects in which they have a common professional interest.

2. The Institute consists of Ordinary and Honorary Members. The Ordinary Members are Gentlemen who are engaged in practice in Edinburgh as professional Accountants. The Honorary Members consist of Gentlemen who have formerly practised as Accountants in Edinburgh but who are now engaged in the management of Life Assurance or other Public Companies in Edinburgh or elsewhere, or who hold Official Appointments in connection with the Courts.

SECTION II
Annual General Meeting and Election of Office-Bearers and New Members

3. A General Meeting of the Members is held on the first Wednesday in February of each year, to elect out of the Ordinary Members the Office-Bearers for the following year, and to dispose of all questions relating to the objects of the Institute, the Rules and Management thereof, and disposal of Funds.

4. The Management of the Institute is intrusted to a Council, consisting of the President, and eight Ordinary Members; any four are a quorum. The Chairman of the meeting has both a deliberative and casting vote. The President retires annually, and are not eligible for election till they have been out of office for one year. The Secretary and Treasurer attend all Meetings of Council, but has no power to vote thereat.

5. The Council has power to make Regulations or Bye-Laws for its own guidance, and for the management of the affairs of the Institute, subject to review and alteration by any General Meeting of Members.

6. New Members are admitted into the Institute at any General Meeting, annual or special. They must be proposed by one Member, and seconded by another, and their election shall be carried by the votes of three-fourths of the Members present, ascertained by ballot.

SECTION III
Payments by Members

7. Each Ordinary Member pays an annual subscription of £2, 2s., and each Honorary Member an annual subscription of £1, 1s., payable in advance on the first day of January annually.

8. Any Member whose annual subscription shall be in arrear for two years, shall, after three months' notice, be liable to be declared a defaulter; and unless reponed by the Council on payment made, he shall at the next General Meeting be struck from the Roll of Members.

9. Any Member may withdraw from the Institute by giving written notice to that effect to the Secretary, and on payment of any arrears of subscriptions which may be due by him.

SECTION IV
Duties of Office-Bearers

10. The President shall preside at all Meetings of the Institute and Council, and exercise, if necessary, a deliberative and casting vote. In his absence, a Chairman, with the like powers, shall be appointed by the Meeting.

11. The Secretary shall conduct all Correspondence, and attend all Meetings of the Institute and Council, and keep a record of the proceedings. The Treasurer shall receive the Contributions of Members, and lodge the same in Bank. He shall keep an account of his receipts and disbursements. In the discharge of their respective duties, the Secretary and Treasurer shall be under the direction of the Council.

SECTION V
Special General Meetings and Meetings of Council

12. Special General Meetings of the Institute may be called at any time by the Council, or on the requisition of any five Ordinary Members; in which case ten days' notice at least shall be given to each Member of the proposed Meeting, and the object of the Meeting specified in the notice. At General Meetings twelve shall form a quorum.

13. The Council shall meet at such times as they may themselves appoint.

SECTION VI
Power to Apply for Charter

14. It shall be hereafter competent to apply for a Royal Charter or Act, incorporating the Members of the Institute into a body corporate and politic, with the usual powers and privileges.

ROYAL CHARTER INCORPORATING THE SOCIETY OF
ACCOUNTANTS IN **EDINBURGH**, DATED 23RD OCTOBER,
AND REGISTERED AND SEALED 11TH DECEMBER, 1854.

Victoria R.

VICTORIA, by the Grace of God of the United Kingdom of Great Britain
and Ireland, Queen, Defender of the Faith.

To all to whom these presents shall come, Greeting.

Whereas, We, considering that an humble Petition has been presented to
us by James Brown, Donald Lindsay, Thomas Robertson Chaplin, Thomas
Mansfield, Henry George Watson, Archibald Borthwick, Ralph Erskine Scott,
Archibald Horne, Thomas Scott, William Moncreiff, Charles Murray Barstow,
David Robertson Souter, George Auldjo Esson, Alexander Weir Robertson,

Kenneth Mackenzie, James Wilkie, Thomas Goldie Dickson, Robert Christie, junior, John Spence Ogilvie, George Mitchell, Archibald Gibson, George Murray, George Auldjo Jamieson, Alexander Thomas Niven, James Ogilvie, Frederick Hanes Carter, Charles Pearson, Robert Spottiswoode, John Charles Fraser, Alexander Jamieson, Charles Wodrow Thomson, David Cormack, William Russell, John Menzies Baillie, Christopher Douglas, James Adam Brown, Patrick Morison, James Jobson Dickson, Samuel Raleigh, Donald Smith Peddie, Thomas Martin, Richard Gordon, Joseph Mack Liddell, William Low, William Wood, George Meldrum, George Todd, James Maclean Macandrew, John Hunter, George Dundas, Andrew Murray Paterson, Henry Callender, John Scott Moncrieff, David Marshall, George Ramsay, James Howden, John Maitland, John Barron, Robert Balfour, David Maclagan, and Thomas Grant, all Members of the Institute of Accountants in Edinburgh, setting forth that the profession of Accountants, to which the Petitioners belong, is of long standing and great respectability, and has of late years grown into very considerable importance:

That the business of Accountant, as practised in Edinburgh, is varied and extensive, embracing all matters of account, and requiring for its proper execution, not merely thorough knowledge of those departments of business which fall within the province of the Actuary, but an intimate acquaintance with the general principles of law, particularly of the law of Scotland; and more especially with those branches of it which have relation to the law of merchant, to insolvency and bankruptcy, and to all rights connected with property;

That in the extrication of those numerous suits before the Court of Session, which involve directly and indirectly matters of accounting, an Accountant is almost invariably employed by the Court to aid in eliciting the truth:

That such investigations are manifestly quite unsuited to such a tribunal as a Jury, yet cannot be prosecuted by the Court itself without professional assistance on which it may rely, and the Accountant, to whom in any case of this description a remit is made by the Court, performs in substance all the more material functions which the Petitioners understand to be performed in England by the Masters in Chancery:

That Accountants are also largely employed in Judicial Remits, in cases which are peculiar to the practice of Scotland, as, for instance, in Rankings and Sales, in processes of Count and Reckoning, Multiplepoinding, and others of a similar description:

That they are also most commonly selected to be Trustees on Sequestrated Estates, and under Voluntary Trusts, and in these capacities they have duties to perform, not only of the highest responsibility, and involving large pecuniary interests, but which require, in those who undertake them, great experience in business, very considerable knowledge of law, and other qualifications which can only be attained by a liberal education:

That, in these circumstances, the Petitioners were induced to form themselves into a Society called the Institute of Accountants in Edinburgh, with a view to unite into one body those at present practising the profession, and to promote the objects which, as members of the same profession, they entertain in common; and that the Petitioners conceive that it would tend to secure in the members of their profession the qualifications which are essential to the proper performance of its duties, and would consequently conduce much to the benefit of the public if the Petitioners who form the present body of practising Accountants in Edinburgh were united into a body corporate and politic, having a common seal, with power to make rules and bye-laws for the qualification and admission of members, and otherwise:

And the Petitioners thereby humbly prayed that We would be graciously pleased to grant them a Royal Charter, incorporating them and such persons as may hereafter be duly admitted Members, into one body corporate and politic, by the name, style, and title of "The Society of Accountants in Edinburgh," with perpetual succession and power to acquire and hold property, and to make rules and bye-laws, and with such other powers, privileges, and authorities as are usually given to other bodies corporate and politic of the like nature, in such manner as to us in our Royal wisdom shall seem proper:

And whereas such Petition has been referred to the Lord Advocate of Scotland to consider thereof, and report his opinion what may properly be done therein, and We having taken the said Petition and report thereon into our Royal consideration, and being satisfied that the intentions of the Petitioners are laudable, and deserving of encouragement, Therefore We have constituted, erected, and incorporated, as We by our prerogative Royal, and of our special grace, certain knowledge, and mere motion, by these presents, for us and our Royal successors, constitute, erect, and incorporate the said James Brown, Donald Lindsay, Thomas Robertson Chaplin, Thomas Mansfield, Henry George Watson; Archibald Borthwick, Ralph Erskine Scott, Archibald Horne, Thomas Scott, William Moncreiff, Charles Murray Barstow, David Robertson Souter, George Auldjo Esson, Alexander Weir Robertson, Kenneth Mackenzie, James Wilkie, Thomas Goldie Dickson, Robert Christie, junior, John Spence Ogilvie, George Mitchell, Archibald Gibson, George Murray, George Auldjo Jamieson, Alexander Thomas Niven, James Ogilvie, Frederick Hanes Carter, Charles Pearson, Robert Spottiswoode, John Charles Fraser, Alexander Jamieson, Charles Wodrow Thomson, David Cormack, William Russell, John Menzies Baillie, Christopher Douglas, James Adam Brown, Patrick Morison, James Jobson Dickson, Samuel Raleigh, Donald Smith Peddie, Thomas Martin, Richard Gordon, Joseph Mack Liddell, William Low, William Wood, George Meldrum, George Todd, James Maclean Macandrew, John Hunter, George Dundas, Andrew Murray Paterson, Henry Callender, John Scott Moncrieff, David Marshall, George Ramsay, James Howden, John Maitland, John Barron, Robert Balfour, David Maclagan, and Thomas Grant, and such other persons as shall hereafter be admitted as Members of the said Society into one body politic and corporate, by the name of "The Society of Accountants in Edinburgh," under which name they shall have perpetual succession, and shall have a common seal, with power to alter and renew the same at discretion, and shall by the same name sue and be sued, implead and be impleaded, and answer and be answered in all our Courts:

As also, We will and ordain that the said Society shall be capable in law to take, purchase, and hold to them and their successors, any goods, chattels, and personal property whatsoever, and shall also be capable in law to take, purchase, and hold in the said corporate name such land, buildings, and heritages as may be necessary for the purposes of the Society, with power to alienate, dispone, and dispose of all or any such lands, buildings, and heritages, goods, chattels, or personal property, and also to raise and receive such sums of money for the purposes of the Society as they may think necessary, by annual contributions, fees on Entrants, or otherwise from the Members thereof, and to do all other acts or things incidental or appertaining to a body corporate—declaring that all deeds and other writings whatsoever affecting heritable or movable property, shall be valid and effectual in all respects, if conceived in name of the corporation, and sealed with the seal, and subscribed by the President, and by the Secretary and Treasurer of the corporation for the time:

And We, also, for ourselves and our Royal successors, give and grant to the Petitioners, and to those persons who shall hereafter compose the said Society, full power and authority, at their ordinary General Meeting, as after appointed, to constitute, make, and ordain, such bye-laws, rules, and regulations, as they, or the majority of them at the time assembled, shall consider proper and necessary for the better administration of the affairs and funds of the Society, and provided that the same are not inconsistent with this Charter, or contrary to the laws of the realm, and to alter and abrogate the said bye-laws, rules, and regulations, as to the majority of the Society present at such meeting shall seem proper:

And We will and ordain that such bye-laws, rules, and regulations so to be made shall be duly kept, observed, and obeyed:

And We hereby will and ordain that a Stated General Meeting of the Corporation shall be held once in every year in Edinburgh, on the first Wednesday in February, at twelve o'clock noon, or at such other time and place as the Corporation shall from time to time determine, and that General Meetings of the Corporation may also be held at such other times and places as may from time to time be fixed, at the Stated Annual General Meeting in February, and that Special General Meetings may also be held (provided the same are duly called in terms of the bye-laws, rules, and regulations for the time) at such times and places as may be necessary or expedient, and that at each Stated Annual General Meeting in February, the Society shall choose out of the Members thereof hereby incorporated, a President, Council, Secretary, and Treasurer, and such other officers as the Society may find hereafter to be necessary and proper:

And We will and ordain that the Corporation shall have power from time to time, and in such manner as may be fixed by the bye-laws, rules, and regulations, to constitute and appoint a Committee of Examinators for the purpose of regulating and conducting such Examination of Entrants and others as the Corporation may from time to time direct, and in such manner as they may appoint, in furtherance of the objects of the Society ; and that the course of education to be pursued, and the amount of general and professional requirements to be exacted from Entrants, shall be such as the Corporation shall from time to time fix :

And We further hereby will, grant, and declare, that the present President, Council, Secretary, and Treasurer of the said Institute shall hold their offices and discharge their functions respectively as President, Council, Secretary, and Treasurer of the Society hereby incorporated until the Stated Annual General Meeting in February, Eighteen hundred and fifty-five, and that they and their successors in office, to be chosen according to the bye-laws, rules, and regulations of the Society, shall have full power to manage, direct, order, and appoint, in all matters and things touching and concerning the said Society, in terms of and conform to the bye-laws, rules, and regulations thereof :

And We, for ourselves and our Royal Successors, declare that this our present Charter shall be in and by all things valid and effectual in law, according to the true intent and meaning of the same ; and it shall be accepted and understood in the sense most favourable and beneficial to the said Corporation, notwithstanding any mis-recital, defect, uncertainty, or imperfection in the same :

And Her Majesty doth further will and command that this Charter do pass the Seal appointed by the Treaty of Union to be kept and used in Scotland in place of the Great Seal thereof formerly used there, without passing any other seal or register ; for the doing whereof these presents shall be to the Director of Her Majesty's Chancellary in Scotland for writing the same, as well as to the Keeper of the said Seal, for causing the same to be appended thereto, a sufficient warrant.

> Given at Her Majesty's Court at St. James's, the 23rd day of October, Eighteen hundred and fifty-four, in the Eighteenth year of Her Majesty's reign.

> By Her Majesty's Command.

> > PALMERSTON.

> > Written to the Seal and Registered the eleventh day of December, 1854.

> > > ARCHD. M'NEILL, C.D.

Sealed at Edinburgh the eleventh day of December, in the year One thousand eight hundred and fifty-four.

> J. GIBSON, Jun., *Depute*.

312

3
Constitution and Laws of the Society of Accountants in Edinburgh, 1855

Society of Accountants in Edinburgh

CONSTITUTION AND LAWS

Stated and Special General Meetings

1. The stated Annual General Meeting of the Society shall be held in Edinburgh on the first Wednesday in February, at Twelve o' clock noon, at such place as the Council shall appoint.

2. Special General Meetings may be called whenever deemed necessary or expedient, by order of the President, or, in his absence, on the requisition of any three Members of the Council, or, in case of his or their refusal so to do, on the requisition of any ten Members of the Society, on notice to that effect given to the Secretary.

3. Each Member shall receive at least two days' previous notice of every Meeting – such notice to be by printed circular, shortly stating the business to be brought before the Meeting; and it shall not be competent to take up any business which is not specified in the circular.

4. The minutes and transactions of the Society shall be engrossed in a Minute-book, to be kept by the Secretary.

5. At all General Meetings, the President of the Society shall take the chair: in his absence, the Member of Council first in rotation on the list of Council present shall preside; and in the absence of the President and all the Members of Council, the Meeting shall elect a Chairman out of the Members present.

6. Any number of Members present at Annual General Meetings shall form a quorum. At Special General Meetings fifteen Members shall form a quorum.

7. After the Chairman of a Meeting has taken the chair, the minute of the previous General Meeting shall be read by the Secretary before proceeding to other business, and thereafter it shall be engrossed in the Sederunt-book, and subscribed by the Preses of the Meeting at which the minute is approved.

8. All questions brought before General Meetings shall be determined by a majority of votes of Members present, the Chairman of the Meeting having, in case of equality, a casting vote in addition to his deliberative vote.

9. No Member who is in arrear for two years of his contributions to the Society shall be entitled to attend or vote at any General Meeting.

Office-Bearers

10. At the stated Annual General Meeting on the first Wednesday of February, as

appointed by the Charter, the Society shall elect from among the Members a President, a Secretary, and a Treasurer.

11. At said stated Annual General Meeting, the Society shall also, as appointed by the Charter, elect a Council. The Council shall consist of eight Members in addition to the President. The two Members at the top of the list of eight Members at the time, shall not be eligible for re-election till they have been one year out of office.

12. The Society shall also at said stated Annual General Meeting elect three Members, who, with the President and Council, shall form the Committee of Examinators (of whom three shall be a quorum) for regulating and conducting the examination of entrants.

13. The Society shall also at said stated Annual General Meeting elect an Agent, who shall transact all legal business connected with the affairs of the Society, under the direction of the Council.

14. At said stated Annual General Meeting, the Society shall also select an Auditor for the ensuing year, who shall audit and report on the Treasurer's accounts, previous to the same being laid before the next stated Annual General Meeting for approval.

15. All vacancies in said offices by death, resignation, or other causes, shall be filled up by a new election at the next stated or special General Meeting of the Society.

Duties and Meetings of Council

16. The Duties of the President and Council shall be to manage and direct all matters which concern the Corporation, in terms of and conform to these Bye-Laws, and to deliberate and advise on all matters affecting its interests.

17. The Council shall meet as often as may be requisite, at such time and place as the President, or a quorum of Council, may appoint. At all Meetings of Council three Members shall be a quorum. The President shall preside, and in his absence the Member of Council first in rotation on the list who may be present shall act as Chairman. The Chairman shall have, in addition to his deliberative vote, a casting vote in case of equality.

18. The minutes and transactions of the Council shall be engrossed in a separate Minute-Book kept for them, and shall be subscribed by the Preses of the Meeting.

19. The Secretary shall attend all Meetings of the Council *ex officio,* but shall have no vote thereat.

Treasurer

20. The Treasurer of the Society for the time being shall find caution, for his intromissions to such extent as the Members present at a General Meeting may fix. The Bond to be prepared at the expense of the Society, and to be approved of by the Council.

21. The Treasurer shall collect the Admission-Fees, Annual Contributions, and other funds arising due to the Society, and shall be entrusted with the custody of the Title-Deeds, Bonds, and other Vouchers belonging to the Society.

22. He shall pay the Funds, as received, into an account to be kept in name of the Society with such Bank as the Council may appoint till they be otherwise invested; and he shall not at any time keep in his possession more than £20 of said Funds for a longer period than one month.

23. The accounts of the Treasurer shall be closed on the thirty-first day of December annually, They shall thereafter be audited by the Auditor of the Society, and, along with a full State of the Affairs of the Society made up by the Treasurer, shall be laid for approval before the stated Annual General Meeting appointed to be held on the first Wednesday of February.

24. The annual allowance of the Treasurer shall be fixed by the Council, subject to the approval of the Society.

Secretary

25. The Secretary, or, failing him, any Member of Council named by the President for the purpose, shall summon Meetings of the Society, and of the Council, and of Committees.

26. The Secretary shall keep the Minute-Books of the Society, and of the Council, and shall cause to be engrossed therein all Minutes of General Meetings, and of Meetings of Council, and of Committees. He shall also conduct any correspondence which may be necessary, under the direction of the President and Council.

27. He shall record in a Register to be kept for that purpose all Indentures and Discharges thereof lodged with him for registration.

28. Generally, he shall perform the whole business of the Society connected with his office, and shall execute any duty with which, as Secretary, he may be entrusted by the President and Council.

29. The annual allowance to the Secretary shall be fixed by the Council, subject to the approval of the Society.

Apprentices

30. No person who is under sixteen years of age shall be taken by any Member of the Corporation as an Apprentice. The period of service shall be five years except in the cases provided for under Bye-Law No. 31.

31. It shall be competent to a Member to take an Apprentice for a shorter period of service than five years, where the person entering into indenture has been previously in the business chambers of a Member of the Corporation, or of a Member of the Society of Writers to the Signet, or of a Member of the Society of Solicitors before the Supreme Courts of Scotland, or of a Member of the Incorporated Society of Solicitors-at-Law, - such shorter period to be computed on the principle of deducting one year from the term of service under indenture for each two years during which such person has been previously employed as above; but in no case shall the term of service under indenture with a Member of the Corporation be less than three years.

32. No Apprentice shall be taken except under regular deed of Indenture; the form of indenture to be approved by the Council.

33. The Apprentice-Fee shall be One Hundred Guineas, and shall be paid when the indenture is entered into.

34. All indentures shall be lodged with the Secretary, for the purpose of being recorded by him, within six months from the commencement of the apprenticeship. The dues of recording shall be £1, 1s., payable to the General Fund of the Society.

35. On the expiration of the term of apprenticeship, the indenture shall be discharged by the Master, and the discharge forthwith recorded by the Secretary. Immediately on the discharge being recorded, an Apprentice may apply for examination.

36. The above regulations shall not apply to Apprentices serving or having served under indenture to a Member of the Society at the date of the adoption by the Society of these Bye-Laws, further than that they shall produce their indentures within six months, from 1st January 1855, to the Secretary, for the purposes of being recorded by him, and shall pay the above dues of recording, and shall also produce their indentures, when discharged, that the discharge may be recorded in terms of the preceding article, No. 35.

Candidates for Admission

37. Till the expiry of five years from the date of the adoption by the Society of these Bye-Laws, persons who shall produce evidence to the satisfaction of the Council that they fall under one or other of the following classes shall alone be eligible as Candidates for examination and admission into the Society:-

1. Persons who have served as apprentices under indenture to a Member of the Society, duly recorded and discharged.

2. Persons who have served the usual term of apprenticeship with a Member of the Society of Writers to the Signet, or with a Member of the Society of Solicitors before the Supreme Courts of Scotland, or with a Member of the Incorporated Society of Solicitors-at-Law, and who, after completing such term of apprenticeship, shall have been employed for three years at least in the business chambers of a Member or Members of the Society.

3. Persons who have not served an apprenticeship with a Member of the Society, or elsewhere, as specified under the preceding class, but who, at the date of application for examination and admission, shall not be under twenty-three years of age, and who shall have been employed for six years at least in the business chambers of a Member or Members of the Society.

38. After the expiry of five years from the date of the adoption by the Society of these Bye-Laws, no person shall be eligible as a Candidate for examination and admission into the Society who has not served as Apprentice with a Member of the Society, conform to the provisions of Bye-Laws Nos. 30 and 31, under an indenture duly recorded and discharged.

39. Candidates for admission shall undergo examination by the Examinators at such time and place as they may appoint. The Examinators shall examine Candidates for admission in such form and to such extent as they may consider necessary upon

subjects usually occurring in the practice of the profession, such as algebra, including the use of logarithms – annuities – life assurances – liferents – reversions – book-keeping – framing of states under sequestrations, trusts, factories, executries – the Law of Scotland, especially that relating to Bankruptcy, private trusts and arbitration, rights and preferences of creditors in rankings.

40. All applicants who are found qualified shall receive a certificate from the Examinators to that effect; and they shall be admitted as Members of the Society at the stated Annual General Meeting, held on the first Wednesday of February yearly, or at any special General Meeting; and they shall receive a Commission signed by the President, under the seal of the Society; and shall continue Members so long as they observe and comply with the Bye-Laws, Rules, and Regulations made and enacted by the Society.

41. The dues of admission shall be as follows:- Every Candidate who, at the date of the adoption by the Society of these Bye-Laws, has been employed for six years at least in the business chambers of a Member or Members of the Society, or who at said date has served an apprenticeship with a Member, and whose indenture has been duly recorded and discharged in terms of these Bye-Laws, shall pay Twenty Guineas to the General Fund of the Society. Every Candidate entering the Society after said date who has served an apprenticeship with a Member, and whose indenture has been duly recorded and discharged in terms of these Bye-Laws, shall pay Fifty Guineas to the General Fund of the Society. Every Candidate, otherwise qualified in terms of these Bye-Laws, entering the Society after said date, shall pay Seventy-five Guineas to the General Fund of the Society.

Funds

42. Every Member shall pay the sum of £2, 2s. annually into the General Fund of the Society, and said annual contribution shall be payable on the first Wednesday of February.

43. Any Member who shall be four years in arrear of his annual payment shall cease to be a Member of the Society.

44. The Funds of the Society shall be invested in the purchase of heritable property, or lent out on heritable securities; in the purchase of Government stocks; or stock of the Bank of England; or of any of the Chartered Banks in Scotland at the sight and to the satisfaction of the Council. Till so invested, the funds shall be deposited in such bank as the Council may select, in an account in the name of the Society, to be operated upon by cheques signed by the Treasurer.

45. After paying all necessary expenses, the funds of the Society shall, from time to time, be applied to such purposes as a majority of Members present at any General Meeting may determine.

Alteration of Bye-Laws, Rules, and Regulations

46. It shall not be competent to alter any of the existing Bye-Laws, Rules, and Regulations till a motion for such alteration has been made and seconded at a stated Annual General Meeting. Such motion shall lie on the table till the next stated Annual General Meeting, when it shall be disposed of.

Edinburgh, 7th February 1855

The foregoing Bye-Laws, Rules, and Regulations were approved of and adopted at a stated General Meeting of the Society, held this day, in terms of the Charter, and ordered to be printed and circulated among the Members.

Extracted from the Records of the Society by

ALEX. W. ROBERTSON,
Secretary

4
**Rules and Regulations of the Incorporated Society of
Accountants in Edinburgh, 1889**

RULES AND REGULATIONS OF THE INCORPORATED SOCIETY OF ACCOUNTANTS IN **EDINBURGH**. INCORPORATED BY ROYAL CHARTER. 1854.

STATED AND SPECIAL GENERAL MEETINGS.

1. The stated Annual General Meeting of the Society shall be held in Edinburgh on the first Wednesday in February, at Twelve o'clock noon, at such place as the Council shall appoint.

2. Special General Meetings may be called whenever deemed necessary or expedient, by order of the President, or, in his absence, on a requisition signed by not less than three Members of the Council, or by not less than ten Members of the Society, addressed to the Secretary.

3. Notice of every General Meeting shall be given by printed circular, which shall shortly state the business to be brought before the Meeting: and shall, at least seven days before the holding of the Meeting, be dispatched, prepaid, by post, to each Member of the Society, directed to him at his address last known to the Secretary; and it shall not be competent to take up at the Meeting any business which is not specified in the circular.

4. At all General Meetings the President of the Society shall take the chair; in his absence, the Member of Council first in rotation on the list of Council present shall preside; and in the absence of the President and all the Members of Council, the Meeting shall elect a Chairman out of the Members present.

5. At Annual General Meetings, any number of Members present shall form a quorum. At Special General Meetings fifteen Members present shall form a quorum. At General Meetings summoned for the purposes stated in Section No. 49 hereof, thirty Members present shall form a quorum.

6. After the Chairman of an Annual General Meeting has taken the chair, the Minute of the previous Annual General Meeting, and of any intervening Special General Meetings, shall be read by the Secretary before proceeding to other business, and if aproved of shall thereafter be engrossed in the Society's Minute Book, and subscribed by the Preses of the Meeting at which the Minute is approved of.

7. All questions brought before General Meetings shall be determined by a majority of votes of members present, the Chairman of the Meeting having, in case of equality, a casting vote in addition to his deliberative vote.

OFFICE-BEARERS.

8. At the stated Annual General Meeting on the first Wednesday of February, as appointed by the Charter, the Society shall elect from among the Members a President, a Secretary, and a Treasurer. Should any Member be elected to the office of President at three consecutive Annual General Meetings, he shall not again be eligible for re-election until he shall have been one year out of office.

9. At said stated Annual General Meeting, the Society shall also, as

appointed by the Charter, elect a Council. The Council shall consist of eight Members, in addition to the President, who shall, *ex officio*, be a Member thereof. Neither of the two Members whose names stand at the top of the list of the eight elected Members of Council, as adjusted at the last Annual General Meeting, shall be eligible for re-election, as Members of Council, till they have been one year out of office, but either of them shall be eligible for the office of President.

10. At said stated Annual General Meeting the Society shall also elect four Members, who, with the President and Council, shall form the Committee of Examinators (of whom three shall be a quorum) for regulating and conducting the examination of intending Apprentices, and of Candidates applying for admission into the Society. The Committee of Examinators shall have power to call in such assistance as they shall consider necessary for the proper conduct of said examinations, and they shall also have power to issue from time to time a Syllabus of the subjects upon which intending Apprentices and Candidates for admission into the Society shall be examined.

11. At said stated Annual General Meeting, a sum may be voted to the Committee of Examinators for allowances and expenses connected with the conduct of the Examinations.

12. At said stated Annual General Meeting, the Society shall also elect a Law Agent, or Agents, who shall transact all legal business connected with the affairs of the Society, under the directions of the Council.

13. At said stated Annual General Meeting, the Society shall also elect an Auditor for the ensuing year, who shall audit and report on the Treasurer's accounts previous to the same being laid before the next stated Annual General Meeting for approval.

14. All vacancies in said offices by death, resignation. or other causes, shall be filled up by the Council, and the persons appointed to fill such vacancies shall hold office until the next Annual General Meeting of the Society.

DUTIES AND MEETINGS OF COUNCIL.

15. The duties of the President and Council shall be to manage and direct all matters which concern the Society in terms of and conform to these Rules and Regulations ; and to deliberate and advise on all matters affecting its interests.

16. The Council shall meet as often as may be requisite at such time and place as the President, or a quorum of three Members of Council, may appoint. At all meetings of Council three Members of Council shall be a quorum. The President shall preside, and in his absence the Member of Council first in rotation on the annual list who may be present shall act as Chairman. The Chairman shall have, in addition to his deliberative vote, a casting vote in case of equality.

17. The Council shall watch over all Parliamentary and other proceedings affecting the interests of the profession, and shall report thereon to Meetings of the Society, when such proceedings appear of sufficient importance.

18. The Minutes and Transactions of the Council shall be engrossed by the Secretary in a separate Minute-Book kept for them, and shall be subscribed by the Preses of the Meeting of Council at which they are approved.

19. The Secretary shall attend all Meetings of the Council *ex officio*, but shall have no vote thereat.

TREASURER.

20. The Treasurer shall find caution for his intromissions to such extent as the Members present at a General Meeting may fix ; the Bond to be prepared at the expense of the Society, and to be approved of by the Council.

21. The Treasurer shall collect the Admission-Fees, and other funds arising due to the Society, as the same shall fall due, and shall be intrusted with the custody of the Title-Deeds, Securities, and other Vouchers belonging to the Society.

22. The Treasurer shall pay the funds, as received, into an account to be kept in name of the Society with such Bank as the Council may appoint, to be operated upon by him, and he shall not at any time keep in his possession more than £50 of said funds for a longer period than one month.

23. The Accounts of the Treasurer shall be closed on the thirty-first day of December annually. They shall thereafter be audited by the Auditor of the Society, and shall be laid for approval before the stated Annual General Meeting, and an Abstract thereof shall previously be circulated among the Members.

24. The annual allowance to the Treasurer shall be fixed by the Council, subject to the approval of the Society.

SECRETARY.

25. The Secretary, or failing him, any Member of Council named by the President for the purpose, shall summon Meetings of the Society, and of the Council and of Committees.

26. The Secretary shall keep the Minute-Books of the Society, and of the Council, and shall cause to be engrossed therein all Minutes of General Meetings, and of Meetings of Council, and of Committees. He shall also conduct any correspondence which may be necessary, under the direction of the President and Council.

27. The Secretary shall record, in a Register to be kept for that purpose, all Indentures and Discharges thereof lodged with him for registration.

28. Generally, the Secretary shall perform the whole business of the Society connected with his office, and shall execute any duty with which, as Secretary, he may be entrusted by the President and Council.

29. The annual allowance to the Secretary shall be fixed by the Council, subject to the approval of the Society.

APPRENTICES.

30. No person who is under seventeen years of age shall be taken by any

Member of the Society as an apprentice. The period of service shall be five years, except in the cases provided for under Rule and Regulation No. 31.

31. It shall be competent to a Member to take an Apprentice for a shorter period of service than five years, where the person entering into indenture has previously served in the business chambers of a Member of the Society, or of a Member of the Society of Writers to the Signet, or of a Member of the Society of Solicitors before the Supreme Courts of Scotland,—in which case there may be deducted from the regular term of service, under indenture as before prescribed, a portion thereof equal to one-half of the time during which such person having been over seventeen years of age shall have been engaged as above, prior to the date of his indenture : but in no case shall the term of service under indenture with a Member of the Society be less than three years.

32. Every Applicant, before entering into an indenture with a Member of the Society, shall undergo an examination in regard to his general education, to be entitled the Preliminary Examination ; such Examination shall be conducted in such manner as may from time to time be prescribed or approved of by the President and Council. Each Applicant shall, on intimating to the Secretary his desire to be examined, pay an Examination fee of £2 2s. Any Applicant who may have taken a degree of B.A. or M.A. at any University in Great Britain or Ireland, or who may have obtained the Government School Leaving Certificate, consisting of three subjects, including Mathematics, shall be exempt from the Preliminary Examination.

33. No Apprentice shall be taken except under regular deed of indenture ; the form of indenture to be approved of by the Council.

Note.—On application, the Secretary will furnish printed Forms of Indenture.

34. The Apprentice-Fee shall be One Hundred Guineas, and shall be paid when the indenture is entered into.

35. All indentures shall be lodged with the Secretary, for the purpose of being recorded by him, within six months from the commencement of the apprenticeship. The dues of recording shall be £1 1s., payable to the General Fund of the Society.

35a. Every Apprentice shall, after the commencement of the third year of his apprenticeship, undergo an intermediate Examination in such professional subjects as the President and Council may from time to time prescribe ; and in the event of any Apprentice failing to pass such Examination to the satisfaction of the Committee of Examinators at the time fixed for such Examination, it shall be competent for him to present himself for re-examination at any time during the remainder of his Apprenticeship, it being provided that an interval of one year shall always elapse between the date of the intermediate Examination and the final one required to be passed before admission into the Society.

36. All Apprentices, in order that they may be eligible to become candidates for admission as Members of the Society, are required, before coming up for their final examination, to attend the Classes of Scots Law and Conveyancing in the University of Edinburgh for one complete session, and such Lectures on special subjects as the Society may in General Meeting approve.

Apprentices are recommended to attend also the Class for Political Economy and Commercial Law in the University of Edinburgh.

CANDIDATES FOR ADMISSION.

37. All Apprentices who have passed the intermediate examination provided for under Rule 35a, whose terms of Apprenticeship have expired, whose indentures have been discharged, and the discharge thereof duly intimated to the Secretary, and who have produced Certificates to the Secretary that they have attended the Classes of Scots Law and Conveyancing in the University of Edinburgh for one complete session, and such Course of Lectures as may be prescribed under preceding Article, all prior to the diet fixed for the Examination of Candidates for admission into the Society in any year, shall be entitled to come forward for examination at said diet, having previously given notice of their intention to do so to the Secretary.

38. Candidates for admission shall undergo examination at such time and place as the Committee of Examinators may appoint. The following are the subjects for examination :—

First, The "Law of Scotland." This examination shall be conducted by an examiner to be selected by the Committee of Examinators, and shall consist of written papers, as well as a *viva voce* Examination.

Second, "Actuarial Science." This examination shall be conducted by a gentleman of actuarial attainments, to be selected by the Committee of Examinators.

Third, "The general business of an Accountant." This examination shall be conducted by Members of the Society exclusively, under arrangements to be made by the Committee of Examinators, and shall consist of written papers, as well as a *viva voce* examination before a Board of not less than three of the Committee of Examinators.

39. All Candidates who have been found duly qualified by the Examinators shall receive Certificates from them to that effect, and shall, subject as hereinafter provided, be entitled to be admitted Members of the Society at the next ensuing stated Annual General Meeting, or at any earlier Special General Meeting which may be called for the purpose. Provided always, that no Candidate shall be admitted a Member of the Society until after he shall have paid his Entrance Fee of £52 10s. to the General Fund of the Society, and also his first Annual Subscription of £2 2s. to the said Fund, if he shall have entered into indenture prior to 29th March, 1887 ; or until after he shall have paid his Entrance Fee of £52 10s. to the said General Fund, also his first Annual Subscription of £2 2s. to the said Fund, and also his first Annual Contribution of £5 5s. to the Endowment and Annuity Fund of the Society, if he shall have entered into indenture subsequently to 29th March, 1887, but prior to 31st July, 1888 ; or until after he shall have paid his Entrance Fee of £105 to the said General Fund, and also his first Annual Contribution of £5 5s. to the said Endowment and Annuity Fund, if he shall have entered into indenture subsequently to 31st July, 1888. All Candidates shall, on admission, receive Commissions signed by the President, under the seal of the Society, and shall

thereupon be and continue Members of the Society, so long as they observe and comply with the Rules and Regulations made by the Society.

LIBRARY.

40. It shall be one of the objects of the Society to form a Library of professional works, for consultation and reference, the Arrangements and Regulations in regard to which shall be intrusted to the Council, subject to the approval and control of the Society.

41. Apprentices may have access to the Library, under such Regulations as the Council may from time to time resolve on.

SOCIETY'S HALL.

42. For the purpose of Meetings, and for the preservation of the Society's Library, it shall be competent to the Council to purchase or lease suitable premises.

FUNDS.

43. The dues of admission shall be as follows :—Every Candidate before being admitted a Member of the Society shall pay an Entrance Fee of One Hundred Guineas to the General Funds of the Society, if he shall have entered into indenture subsequent to 31st July, 1888. Every Candidate who shall have entered into indenture prior to that date shall, before being admitted a Member of the Society, pay an Entrance Fee of Fifty Guineas to the said General Funds, and a first Annual Subscription thereto of £2 2s., and shall thereafter, subsequent to admission, pay within one calendar month after the Annual General Meeting of the Society an Annual Subscription of £2 2s. to the said Funds, for the five consecutive years immediately succeeding the year of his admission.

44. The Funds of the Society shall be invested under the direction, at the sight, and to the satisfaction of the Council, but only in the purchase of or in loans on the stocks, funds, and securities or other property, real or personal, heritable or moveable, in which gratuitous trustees are, by any public Act applicable to England or Scotland, empowered to invest their Trust Funds, or in the purchase of Stock or Shares of any Bank in Scotland, incorporated by Royal Charter or Act of Parliament, or in loans or debentures of, or deposits with, any Joint-Stock Company having its head office in Great Britain, and authorised to take money on debenture or deposit, which has paid dividends on its ordinary share capital for five consecutive years immediately preceding the date of the investment.

45. After paying all necessary expenses, the Funds of the Society shall, from time to time, be applied to such purposes as a majority of Members present at any General Meeting may determine.

ALTERATION OF RULES AND REGULATIONS.

46. It shall not be competent to repeal or alter any of the existing or to

make any new Rules and Regulations, till after a motion for such purpose shall have been made and seconded at a General Meeting, and shall thereafter have lain on the table till another General Meeting, convened for the purpose, shall have disposed of it; which other General Meeting shall be called for a day not earlier than one month, nor later than three months, after the Meeting at which the motion shall have been made and seconded. Notice of the motion shall, within eight days after the meeting at which it shall have been made and seconded, be dispatched, prepaid, by post to each Member of the Society, directed to him at his address last known to the Secretary.

BYE-LAWS.

47. The Council may, from time to time, make Bye-Laws for conducting the affairs of the Society, and for the better carrying out, in detail, of the Society's Rules and Regulations, and may, from time to time, repeal or alter any such Bye-Laws; provided always that such Bye-Laws shall not be inconsistent with the Rules and Regulations of the Society in force for the time.

GENERAL.

48. No Member of the Society shall be entitled to plead exemption from the operation of any of the Society's Rules and Regulations, on the ground of not being aware of the existence or purport thereof.

49. In the event of any Member being, in any Court of competent jurisdiction, convicted of falsehood, fraud, and wilful imposition, or embezzlement, or forgery, or uttering any forged document, knowing it to be forged, or of any other crime or misdemeanour, it shall be in the power of the Society, at any General Meeting, to expel such Member from the Society; and in the event of any Member of the Society being publicly accused of any such crime or misdemeanour as aforesaid, or having notoriously absconded from the United Kingdom, with the object of defrauding his creditors or fleeing from justice: and written information thereof being given to the President or Secretary of the Society, it shall be the duty of the President and Council to serve on such Member, at his address last known to the Secretary, intimation in writing that they will proceed on some day, not less than ten days after such written information shall have been received, to consider the accusation against such Member, and if, after such inquiry as they shall deem sufficient, and after considering any explanations which such Member may tender, they shall come to be of opinion that the Member accused is guilty of such crime or misdemeanour, or of having so absconded, they shall report the conduct of such Member to the first Annual General Meeting of the Society, or to any Special General Meeting to be called for the purpose, in terms of the Society's Rules and Regulations; and on a motion of expulsion being made and carried at such Annual General or Special General Meeting, such Member shall be expelled from the Society in the same manner as if he had been convicted of such crime or misdemeanour.

NATURE OF THE CHARTERED SOCIETIES' EXAMINATIONS.

Specimens of the examination papers are produced along with this Case. No person is admitted to any of the Societies who does not take a high percentage of marks in each of the required subjects; and the tendency is to raise the standard of the Societies' requirements. The regulations in force in Edinburgh and Glasgow are given below. The Aberdeen rules are similar:

A.—*Edinburgh.*

Before an applicant is indentured he must have attained the age of seventeen, and must be examined in general knowledge, unless he has obtained a University degree or the Government school leaving certificate, involving examination in three subjects, including mathematics. The subjects included in the general knowledge examination are the following:—English composition, arithmetic, elementary mathematics, history, geography, Latin, and French or German.

During apprenticeship, the apprentice has to undergo an examination to test the progress made by him. This examination consists of the following subjects:—

I.—*Arithmetic.*

Including decimals, simple interest, discount, &c.

II.—*Mathematics.*

Including quadratic equations, arithmetical and geometrical progressions, and the use of logarithms.

III.—*Professional knowledge.*

(A) Framing accounts, interest states, &c.;
(B) Writing and acknowledging letters;
(c) Bookkeeping, including the framing of balance sheets and profit and loss accounts.

The apprentice is required to attend the classes of Scots Law and Conveyancing, in the University of Edinburgh, and such lectures on special subjects as may from time to time be approved of by the Society. He is also recommended to attend the classes of Political Economy and Commercial Law, in the University of Edinburgh.

On the expiry of his apprenticeship, which extends over a period of five years, the apprentice has to pass an examination in the following subjects, viz. :—

I.—*Law of Scotland.*

(A) The dates, import and effect of the statutes on which the original Bankrupt Law of Scotland was founded, and the principles thereby established applicable to alienations by insolvents in favour of parties related to the granters, and to transactions involving preferences to particular creditors;

(B) The dates, import and effect of the modern sequestration statutes, and the leading rules of law applicable to the administration of bankrupt estates;

(C) Specially the rules of the ranking of creditors, secured and unsecured, at common law and under the statutes ; and the mode of treating claims against companies and individual partners, and upon accommodation bills ;

(D) The dates, import and effect of the statutes and Acts of Sederunt relating to the estates and affairs of minors and incapacitated persons, and to property subject to judicial factory, and the legal principles applicable to the powers and duties of trustees and of officers appointed by the Court to manage trust estates;

(E) The principles of the law relating to joint stock companies and the powers and duties of liquidators;

(F) The law of partnership, succession in moveables, arbitration, insurance, bills of exchange, sale of goods, and cautionary obligations.

II.—*Actuarial Science.*

(A) Compound interest and annuities certain;

(B) The elementary theory of probabilities;

(C) The elementary principles of life annuity and assurance calculations.

III.—*General professional knowledge of Accounting Business,* embracing—

(A) The theory and practice of book-keeping;

(B) The framing of trust and factorial accounts and states, joint adventure and consignment accounts, and interest states, &c. ;

(C) The procedure and requisites in the audit of accounts and books, specially those of public companies and private firms;

(D) The management of sequestrated estates, private trusts, landed estates, curatorial and judicial factories, &c. ;

(E) The procedure under judicial references, remits and proofs.

B.—*Glasgow.*

No restriction is put upon applicants as to the age at which they may enter the offices in which they are to receive their training, nor are they restricted to offices of Members of the Institute, service in the office of a member of any chartered body being held to qualify.

Before, however, they can apply for admission as Associates they must have attained eighteen years of age. They must then present themselves for examination in the following subjects, which may be taken in two (or more) stages, as applicants may prefer, unless they hold a university degree, or have obtained the Government school leaving certificate.

SYLLABUS OF EXAMINATIONS, 1890.

ASSOCIATES.

I.—*Arithmetic and Mathematics.*

    (A) Arithmetic, including the use of logarithmic tables ;
    (B) First three books of Euclid;
    (C) Algebra, as far as and inclusive of quadratic equations;

II.—*General Knowledge.*

    (D) Geography of the British Empire ;
    (E) British History.

English Composition.

III.—*Elements of Book-keeping and Framing of Accounts.*

The examinations under Branches I. and II. are conducted by a professional educationalist, and under Branch III. by a Member or Members of the Institute.

After passing in these subjects, applicants are admitted as Associates of the Institute. Associates not under twenty-two years of age, who have served for four years at least as clerks or apprentices, and have been Associates for not less than one year, may present themselves for examination for membership in the following subjects :—

I.—*The Law of Scotland.*

    (A) Principles of bankrupt law;
    (B) Bills and promissory notes;
    (C) Partnerships and companies.

II.—*Actuarial Science.*

    (A) Compound interest and annuties, certain;
    (B) General knowledge of the theory of probabilities, with special reference to its application, in the form of life annuity and assurance tables;
    (C) Practical use of annuity and assurance tables.

III.—*General Business of an Accountant.*

    (A) Administration of estates under sequestration and voluntary trusts;
    (B) Factorships under the Court and Pupils Protection Act;
    (C) Public audits;
    (D) Liquidation of public companies;
    (E) Book-keeping and accounts.

328

SCOTTISH INSTITUTE OF ACCOUNTANTS.—SCHEME FOR ADMISSION OF ASSOCIATES.

That with the view of promoting the training and qualification of young men engaged as apprentices or clerks in the offices of Members of the Institute, and of such other young men as may, in the opinion of the Council, be under satisfactory professional training, it is expedient that provision be made for their admission to the Institute as Associates on the following conditions, viz. : —

I. Applicants shall not be under 18 years of age and shall have served for at least three years as apprentices or clerks in the offices of Members of the Institute or of other public Accountants.

II. They shall be recommended by at least two Members.

III. They shall pass a written examination by Examiners appointed by the Council on such subjects as the Examiners may from time to time determine, special reference being always had to

1. Arithmetic and English Composition.
2. The principles of Book-keeping.
3. Preparation of Factorial and other Accounts.
4. Framing of States of Affairs in insolvency and bankruptcy.
5. A general knowledge of bankruptcy law and forms.

IV. Candidates on being recommended for admission by the Examiners, and being approved by the Council, shall, before admission as Associates, pay to the Treasurer a subscription of five shillings and a like sum on 1st October annually thereafter. The subscriptions shall be applied in defraying all expenses incidental to the admission of Associates, and otherwise on their account as the Council may approve.

V. Associates on commencing business on their own account shall be eligible for election as Members, provided they have been Associates for at least two years and pass the final examination. Unless within two years of their commencing business they qualify as Members they shall, on the expiry of that period, *ipso facto*, cease to be Associates.

VI. The Council shall give every encouragement to the Associates to unite as far as that may be practicable for mutual advancement in the knowledge and study of Accountantcy, and the latter shall have access to such books and documents relating to the profession as may belong to the Institute.

JAMES L. SELKIRK,

Secretary and Treasurer.

82, WEST REGENT STREET,

GLASGOW, *September*, 1887.

Scottish Institute of Accountants.

PROSPECTUS OF EXAMINATIONS.

With the view of rendering the Examinations for Membership still more thorough and complete the Examiners appointed by the Council of the Institute have prepared and approved of the following scheme of subjects of examination for candidates. It is proposed to hold the Examinations in three stages: a general knowledge or preliminary examination, on commencement of apprenticeship, and two professional examinations.

The Council may appoint experts as independent examiners in particular subjects, and may discharge a candidate from examination on any subject who produces a certificate from a public examining body with whose standard of pass they are satisfied.

The Examinations will be open to the apprentices of professional accountants in Scotland, whether members of the Institute or not, and to professional accountants, including those who, though not becoming members of the Institute, may wish to undergo the Examinations.

The object of the Council is to ensure that every member of the Institute shall be thoroughly grounded in the subjects common to accountancy work, and that those who wish to devote themselves more exclusively to special branches of such work may have the opportunity of doing so in the choice of subjects provided for examination.

Candidates are recommended to attend the Scotch Law and Conveyancing Classes at any University, College, or Institution. The Examiners may, in conducting the examination, have regard to such attendance.

JAMES L. SELKIRK, *Secretary*.

I.—PRELIMINARY.

Compulsory Subjects.

1. Latin.
2. English Language and Composition, History and Geography.
3. Mathematics:—
   (a) Arithmetic.   (b) Algebra.   (c) Euclid.

Optional Subjects.

Two Subjects to be selected by the Candidate from following group—
   (a) Physical and Mathematical Science.
   (b) Natural Science.
   (c) Mental and Moral Science, including Logic.
   (d) Shorthand.
   (e) Greek or Modern Languages.

II.—INTERMEDIATE AND FINAL.

Compulsory Subjects.

1.—*Book-keeping and Accounts.*
   (a) Theory and Practice of Book-keeping.
   (b) Factorial, Trust and Executry Accounts, and Accounts of Private Firms, Companies, and Public Corporations.
   (c) General Commercial Knowledge of Businesses and Trades, and the Style of Books best adapted to each kind of Business.
   (d) Costs Accounts of Manufacturing Businesses; different methods of allocation of general oncost charges and depreciation to particular contracts; Charging of materials, wages, and stores to particular contracts, and corresponding credits of General Accounts.

2.—*Actuarial Science.*
Compound Interest and Annuities certain.

3.—*Business of Accountants.*
   (a) Auditing.
   (b) Factors, Judicial and Voluntary.
   (c) Trustees for behoof of Creditors, Judicial and Voluntary.
   (d) Trustees and Executors under Deeds of Settlement *inter vivos* and *mortis causa*, and Administrators appointed by the Court.
   (e) Tutors and Curators.
   (f) Liquidators of Incorporated Companies.
   (g) Arbiters and Judicial Referees.

4.—*Law of Scotland, and Conveyancing.*

1. Law of Scotland.—General knowledge of the law, and a more advanced knowledge of the following special expositions:—
   (a) Constitution, transmission, and extinction of obligations.
   (b) Contracts of sale, hiring, loan, pledge, and deposit; retention and lien; stoppage *in transitu.*
   (c) Agency and guarantee.
   (d) Bills of exchange, promissory notes, and bank cheques.
   (e) Bankruptcy: 1. Insolvency; 2. Notour bankruptcy; 3. Cessio and sequestration proceedings.
   (f) Liquidation of joint stock companies.
   (g) Trusts; constitution, administration, and extinction. Legal and equitable estates.
   (h) Guardian and ward.
   (i) Landlord and tenant.
   (j) Provident, industrial, and building societies.
   (k) Fire and life insurance.
   (l) Succession, testate and intestate, in heritable and moveable rights.

2.—*Conveyancing.*
   (a) Structure, authentication, and execution of deeds.
   (b) Deeds relating to constitution and transmission of heritable and moveable rights.

Optional Subjects.
One Subject to be selected by the Candidate from the following group—
   (a) Political Economy.
   (b) Law of Evidence and Process.
   (c) Actuarial Science (Advanced).
   (d) Banking and Stock Exchange Operations.

AGREEMENT entered into in 1893 between the three CHARTERED SOCIETIES constituting General Examining Board.

This Agreement entered into between the parties following, viz. :—The Society of Accountants in Edinburgh, incorporated by Royal Charter, of the first part; The Institute of Accountants and Actuaries in Glasgow, incorporated by Royal Charter, of the second part ; and The Society of Accountants in Aberdeen, incorporated by Royal Charter, of the third part (all hereinafter collectively described as " the Societies," or " the parties hereto "), witnesseth that, whereas the objects contemplated by the said respective Royal Charters would be further promoted if uniform Rules were made for qualification for and admission to membership of their respective Corporate Bodies, and if a General Examining Board were established common to the three Societies : Therefore the parties hereto agree to, and hereby undertake, each to the other. to carry out, implement, and fulfil, each and all of the following provisions, and to make such Bye-laws, Rules and Regulations as may be necessary for carrying out and enforcing the same, and to repeal or alter any existing Bye-laws, Rules and Regulations which may be inconsistent therewith, viz.:

Apprentices.

1. No person who is under seventeen years of age shall be taken by a Member of any of the Societies as an Apprentice. Except in the cases hereinafter provided for, the period of service shall be four years, or such longer period as may be prescribed by the Rules of the Society which the Apprentice desires to enter.

2. It shall be competent to a Member of any of the Societies to take an Apprentice for a shorter period of service than four years, where the person entering into indenture has previously served in the business chambers of a Member of one of the Societies, or of any enrolled Law Agent in Scotland, in which case there may be deducted from the regular term of service under indenture as before prescribed, a portion thereof equal to one-half of the time during which such person while over seventeen years of age shall have been engaged as above, prior to the commencement of his apprenticeship; but in no case shall the term of service under indenture with a Member of any of the Societies be less than

three years. When, owing to the retirement from business, death, bankruptcy, or insolvency of the Member with whom an indenture of apprenticeship shall have been entered into, the whole period of apprenticeship under such indenture cannot be completed with him, the remainder of the period may be completed with another Member of any of the Societies; and a Member may permit his Apprentice to serve any part of the period of apprenticeship, not exceeding two years, with another Member of any of the Societies; but such change of Master during the currency of an apprenticeship shall not make an Apprentice eligible for admission to any Society other than the Society of which the Master named in his original indenture is or was a Member.

3. Except in the cases aftermentioned, every person desirous of serving an apprenticeship with a Member of any of the Societies, shall, before commencing his apprenticeship, or within six months thereafter, pass an examination in regard to his general education, to be entitled the Preliminary Examination, and such examination shall be conducted by the General Examining Board, to be constituted as hereinafter provided for, and which is hereinafter called 'the Board.' Each Applicant shall, on intimating to the Secretary of the Board his desire to be examined, pay to him an Examination Fee of £1, 1s., and in the event of re-examination an Examination Fee of 10s. 6d. on each occasion on which he may be re-examined. But any Applicant who may have taken a degree at any University of the United Kingdom, or who may have obtained the Government School Leaving Certificate, including three subjects, one of which shall be Mathematics, or who may have passed an examination which in the opinion of the Board is equivalent to the Preliminary Examination, shall be exempt from the said examination.

4. No apprenticeship shall be served except under regular deed of indenture, and no indenture shall be executed until after the Apprentice named therein has passed his preliminary examination, or has satisfied the Board that he is exempt therefrom. The form of indenture used by the Members of each Society shall be approved of by the Council thereof.

5. All indentures shall within six months from the date thereof be lodged with the Secretary of the Society to which the Apprentice is qualifying for admission, for the purpose of being recorded, along with a certificate of the date of birth of the Apprentice.

6. Every Apprentice shall, after the commencement of the second year of his apprenticeship, undergo an examination by the Board on such subjects as may be prescribed by the Board, to be called the Intermediate Examination; and in the event of any Apprentice failing to pass such examination to the satisfaction of the Board on first presenting himself, it shall be competent for him to present himself for re-examination at any time before the expiry of his apprenticeship, it being provided that an interval of one year shall always elapse between the date of the Intermediate Examination and the Final Examination required to be passed

before admission into any of the Societies. Every Apprentice, on intimating to the Secretary of the Board, through the Secretary of the Society to which he is qualifying for admission, his desire to undergo his Intermediate Examination, shall pay to the Secretary of the Board an Examination Fee of £1, 1s., and in the event of re-examination an Examination Fee of 10s. 6d. on each occasion on which he may be re-examined.

7. Every Apprentice, in order that he may be eligible to become a candidate for admission as a Member of any one of the Societies, shall be required, before coming up for final examination, to attend the Class of Scots Law in any of the Scottish Universities for one complete session, or such Extra-Mural Classes on Scots Law as the Board may have previously approved of as equivalent, together with such other Lectures as the Society to which he is seeking admission may in General Meeting prescribe.

Candidates for Admission

8. Every Apprentice who has passed the Intermediate Examination, whose term of Apprenticeship has expired, whose indenture has been discharged, and the discharge thereof duly intimated to the Secretary of the Society he desires to enter, and who has produced Certificates to such Secretary that he has attended the Scots Law Class and any other Classes prescribed by the Rules of that Society, all prior to the diet fixed for the Final Examination in any year, shall be entitled to come forward for examination at said diet, having previously given notice of his intention to do so to the Secretary of the Board through the Secretary of the Society he desires to enter, and having paid to the Secretary of the Board an Examination Fee of £2, 2s., and in the event of re-examination an Examination Fee of £1, 1s. on each occasion on which he may be re-examined.

Candidates for admission shall undergo examination at such time and place as the Board may appoint. The following shall be the subjects of examination :—

First, The Law of Scotland.
Second, The Elements of Actuarial Science.
Third, The Elements of Political Economy.
Fourth, The general business of an Accountant.

9. Every Candidate who has been found duly qualified by the Board shall, subject as hereinafter provided, be eligible to be admitted a Member of the Society for which he shall have qualified at a General Meeting thereof. Provided always, that no candidate shall be admitted a Member of any of the Societies until he shall have paid any Entrance Fees and first year's Subscription due under the Rules of that particular Society, and any other fees or sums of money required by any law in force for the time. Every Candidate shall, on admission to any

of the Societies, receive a Commission or Certificate signed by the President of such Society, under the seal thereof, and shall thereupon be and continue a Member of that Society, so long as he shall observe and comply with the Rules and Regulations thereof.

10. The Secretary of the Board shall issue a Certificate to each person who passes the Preliminary, Intermediate, or Final Examination, certifying that he has passed such Examination.

11. The Board shall, on the recommendation of the Council of the particular Society concerned, have power to modify, in special circumstances, the foregoing Regulations, so far as they relate to the periods at which persons may present themselves for Examination.

12. The foregoing General Regulations shall not apply to persons who, at the date of the adoption thereof, have entered upon their apprenticeship or service, and have conformed to the Rules of the Society to which they are seeking admission, but in the Examinations which they have still to pass, they shall do the papers set by the Board.

13. Whereas the Institute of Accountants and Actuaries in Glasgow have had in force a Rule providing that Accountants who have been ten years in practice may, under certain conditions, be admitted Members of that Institute without serving an apprenticeship or passing the ordinary examinations, and whereas there may in the future be other Accountants in exceptional circumstances whom it might be right and proper to admit to membership of the said Institute; Therefore, it is hereby declared that it shall be competent for the said Institute, notwithstanding this Agreement, to admit Members in terms of such rule, or of any similar rule which may hereafter be adopted by said Institute, provided that the said Institute shall not admit any person to membership under such rule unless and until his name and proposed admission shall have been submitted to and approved of by the Board.

General Examining Board.

14. The Board, to whom shall be delegated, and who alone shall exercise the whole rights and powers and perform the whole duties hitherto exercised and performed by the Committees of Examinators appointed by the parties hereto respectively, shall consist of five members of the Society of Accountants in Edinburgh, to be elected by that Society at each annual general meeting thereof; five members of the Institute of Accountants and Actuaries in Glasgow, to be elected by that Institute at each annual general meeting thereof; and two members of the Society of Accountants in Aberdeen, to be elected by that Society at each annual general meeting thereof; together with the Presidents, for the time, of each of the said

Societies and Institute respectively, who shall severally be *ex officio* Members of the Board.

15. Seven Members of the Board shall form a quorum thereof.

16. In the event of the resignation, incapacity, or death of any elected Member of the Board, his place may be filled up by the Council of the Society or Institute, as the case may be, of which he is or was a member; but the acts and proceedings of the remaining Members of the Board, or of a quorum thereof, shall be valid and effectual, notwithstanding the existence of any such vacancy.

17. At all meetings of the Board held in Edinburgh, the chair shall be taken by the President of the Society of Accountants in Edinburgh; or, in his absence, by the President of the Institute of Accountants and Actuaries in Glasgow; or, in the absence of both of them, by the President of the Society of Accountants in Aberdeen; at all meetings of the Board held in Glasgow, the chair shall be taken by the President of the Institute of Accountants and Actuaries in Glasgow; or, in his absence, by the President of the Society of Accountants in Edinburgh; or, in the absence of both of them, by the President of the Society of Accountants in Aberdeen; at all meetings of the Board held in Aberdeen, the chair shall be taken by the President of the Society of Accountants in Aberdeen; or, in his absence, by the President of the Society of Accountants in Edinburgh; or, in the absence of both of them, by the President of the Institute of Accountants and Actuaries in Glasgow; and at all meetings of the Board, whether held in Edinburgh, Glasgow, or Aberdeen, the chair shall, in the absence of all three of the said Presidents, be taken by such Member of the Board as shall be appointed to do so by the Members of the Board present, or by a majority of them.

18. The Meetings of the Board shall be held alternately in Edinburgh and Glasgow, or as may be otherwise arranged. All questions shall be decided by a majority of the votes of those present, and in the case of an equality of votes, the Chairman shall have a casting as well as a deliberate vote.

19. The Board shall—subject to the rules of the Societies, have full power to regulate and conduct the Preliminary, Intermediate, and Final Examinations of applicants for admission to any of the Societies. The Board shall be responsible for all papers set, and for the values attached to the replies of the candidates, and shall finally decide whether or not a candidate shall be certified as having passed an examination satisfactorily.

20. The Board shall superintend the diets of Examination (at each of which at least one Member of the Board shall be present), and shall fix the places and dates of such diets. If deemed necessary by any one of the Societies, diets of Examination shall be held in Edinburgh, Glasgow, and Aberdeen; but in all cases where the same Examination is conducted in more than one place, the day and hour of the Examination shall be the same.

21. The Board shall have power to employ and remunerate special Examiners, whether members of one or other of the Societies or not, and to employ and remunerate a Secretary and Treasurer. The Board shall also have power to pay its own Members such remuneration for their trouble, as Examiners or otherwise, as the Councils of the Societies may jointly approve, and the Board shall repay its Members all personal outlay incurred by them in attending meetings or examinations.

22. The Income of the Board shall consist of fees paid by candidates for examination, and of such contributions to be made by the three Societies, in proportion to their Membership at the time, as are necessary to meet any balance of Expenditure. If any sum shall accumulate in the hands of the Board, in excess of what, in the opinion of the Board, is necessary for the purposes thereof, it shall be paid to the three Societies in proportion to their Membership at the time. The Accounts of the Board shall be made up annually, and shall be submitted to the Councils of the three Societies within two months of the date to which they are made up.

23. The Board may be dissolved at the end of six months from and after intimation having been given by any one of the Societies to the other two of the Societies of intention to withdraw from this Agreement, but such intimation shall not be competent until after a motion of withdrawal made at a General Meeting of any one of the Societies (which shall be considered a motion for an alteration of the Rules of that Society), shall have been passed in the manner, and with the majority necessary to effect an alteration in its Rules according to its Constitution.

IN WITNESS WHEREOF, these presents, consisting of this and the five preceding pages, written (in so far as not printed) by Robert Muil, Clerk to John Clerk Brodie and Sons, of Edinburgh, Writers to the Signet, are—along with other three copies hereof—executed by or on behalf of the parties hereof, as follows, *videlicet* : —Are sealed with the Common Seal of the Society of Accountants in Edinburgh, and are subscribed for and on behalf of said Society by James Howden, President, and Richard Brown, Secretary and Treasurer of said Society, at Edinburgh, on the second day of February in the year Eighteen hundred and ninety-three, before these Witnesses :—John Hamilton Buchanan and Thomas Barnby Whitson, both Chartered Accountants in Edinburgh : And are sealed with the Common Seal of the Institute of Accountants and Actuaries in Glasgow, and are subscribed for and on behalf of said Institute as follows :—by Alexander Sloan, Secretary of said Institute, at Glasgow, on the third day of said month of February in the year last mentioned, before these Witnesses :—John Henry Cochran, Cashier, and James Miller, Clerk, both to the said Alexander Sloan, at Number One hundred and forty Hope Street, Glasgow ; by James Wyllie Guild, Treasurer of said Institute, also at Glasgow, on the said third day of February in the year last mentioned, before these Witnesses :—Robert Nelson and Charles Hugh Drew, both Clerks to the said James Wyllie Guild, at Number Sixty-three St. Vincent Street, Glasgow ; and by Walter Mackenzie, President of said Institute, at Bournemouth, on the sixth day of said month of February in the year last mentioned, before these Witnesses :— Robert Duncan Mackenzie and Margaret Mackenzie, both of Caldarvan, Dum-

336

bartonshire : And are sealed with the Common Seal of the Society of Accountants in Aberdeen, and are subscribed for and on behalf of said Society as follows :—by Alexander Ledingham, President of said Society, at Aberdeen, on the eighth day of said month of February in the year last mentioned, before these Witnesses :— Alexander Troup and William MacBain, both apprentices to Messrs. Edmonds and Ledingham, Advocates in Aberdeen : And by Walter Alexander Reid, Secretary and Treasurer of said Society, also at Aberdeen, on the said eighth day of February in the year last mentioned, before these Witnesses :—James William Barclay and James Barclay Rennet, both Chartered Accountants in Aberdeen.

J. Hamilton Buchanan, *Witness.*

Thomas B. Whitson, *Witness.*

SEAL OF THE SOCIETY OF ACCOUNTANTS IN EDINBURGH.

JAMES HOWDEN, *President.*

RICHARD BROWN, *Secretary & Treasurer.*

R. D. Mackenzie, *Witness.*

M. Mackenzie, *Witness.*

John Henry Cochran, *Witness.*

James Miller, *Witness.*

Robert Nelson, *Witness.*

Charles H. Drew, *Witness.*

SEAL OF THE INSTITUTE OF ACCOUNTANTS AND ACTUARIES IN GLASGOW.

WALTER MACKENZIE, *President.*

ALEXANDER SLOAN, *Secretary.*

J. WYLLIE GUILD, *Treasurer.*

Alex. Troup, *Witness.*

Will. MacBain, *Witness.*

James W. Barclay, *Witness.*

James Barclay Rennet, *Witness.*

SEAL OF THE SOCIETY OF ACCOUNTANTS IN ABERDEEN.

A. LEDINGHAM, *President.*

WALTER A. REID, *Secretary & Treasurer.*

SYLLABUS OF EXAMINATIONS by
GENERAL EXAMINING BOARD.

CHARTERED ACCOUNTANTS OF SCOTLAND.

The Society of Accountants in Edinburgh, ... Incorporated by Royal Charter, 1854.
The Institute of Accountants and Actuaries in Glasgow,   Do.   Do.   1855.
The Society of Accountants in Aberdeen, ...   Do.   Do.   1867.

SYLLABUS.

Candidates are required to intimate their intention of presenting them-selves for examination to the Secretary of the Board through the Secretary of the Society with which they are connected, not later than the 15th day of the month preceding that in which the Examination is to be held. Seven days' notice at least of the dates and places of Examination will be given to each Candidate who has made due intimation and paid the Examination Fee.

I.—PRELIMINARY EXAMINATION.

NOTE.—This Examination, which occupies one day, is held half-yearly, in the months of June and December, and each Candidate is charged a fee of £1, 1s.

Any Applicant who may have taken a degree at any University of the United Kingdom, or who may have obtained the Government School Leaving Certificate (Lower Grade), or have passed the Junior or Senior Local Examinations conducted by any of the Universities, in all cases including three subjects, one of which shall be Mathematics, will be exempted from passing this Examination.

I. Writing to Dictation, English Grammar and Composition. (Book recommended—Nichol's *Primer of English Composition.*)

NOTE.—Special Marks will be awarded for handwriting.

II. Arithmetic (elementary); including Vulgar and Decimal Fractions, Practice, Proportion, and Interest.

Candidates will be examined in the foregoing subjects; and in *three* of the *six* following subjects, each Candidate having the right to select the three he may prefer.

I. British History. (Books recommended—Creighton's *The Tudors and the Reformation*; and Oscar Browning's *Modern England* (Longmans' Epochs of English History).)
II. Geography of the World; with special reference to the Geography of Great Britain, its Colonies, and the Continent of Europe. (Mill's *Elementary Commercial Geography*, chapters vii. to xvii. inclusive.)

III. Geometry; Euclid, Book I., with Deductions.
IV. Shorthand; Dictation and Transcription of Notes.
V. Latin; including Grammar and short Translations.
VI. French or German, do. do.

II.—Intermediate Examination.

Note.—This Examination, which occupies two days, is held in June and December in each year, and must be passed after the commencement of the second year, and before the expiry, of the apprenticeship. One year at least must elapse between the date of passing the Examination and the date when an Apprentice is entitled to come up for the Final Examination. The Examination Fee payable is £1, 1s.

I. *Mathematics :—*

   (a.) *Arithmetic (Advanced)—*
      Including Vulgar and Decimal Fractions, Practice, Proportion, Simple and Compound Interest, and Discount.

   (b.) *Algebra—*
      Including Quadratic Equations, Arithmetical and Geometrical Progressions, and the nature and use of Logarithms.

II. *Professional Knowledge :—*

(Special attention to be given to neatness of handwriting and style.)

   (a.) Book-keeping, including the framing of Balance-Sheets and Profit and Loss Accounts.
   (b.) Framing Accounts, Interest States, etc.
   (c.) Correspondence.

III.—Final Examination.

Note.—This Examination, which occupies four days, is held in the months of June and December in each year. The Examination Fee payable is £2, 2s.

I. *Law of Scotland :—*

   (a.) Bankruptcy.
   (b.) Judicial Factories.
   (c.) The Companies' Acts.
   (d.) Partnership.
   (e.) References and Arbitrations.
   (f.) Bills, Cheques, and Deposit Receipts.
   (g.) Sale, Insurance, and Cautionary Obligations.

II. *Actuarial Science :—*

   (a) Compound Interest and Annuities certain.
   (b) The Elementary Principles of Life Annuities, Assurances, and Reversions.
      Books recommended—King's *Theory of Finance*, Glen's *Manual of Actuarial Science.*

III. *Political Economy :—*

The Examination will involve an elementary knowledge of economic principles, and more special knowledge of one or more of the following topics, to vary from time to time :—Statistics, Rate of Interest and Investments, Currency, Banking, Credit, Commercial Crises, National and Municipal Debts, Taxation.

Until further notice the following books are recommended :—

Marshall's *Economics of Industry* (New Edition).

Bagehot's *Lombard Street* (10th Edition, edited by E. Johnstone).

Apprentices whose Indentures were executed, or who, in the case of the Institute of Accountants and Actuaries in Glasgow, had entered upon their term of service with a Member of that Institute, prior to the adoption by the respective Societies of the new Regulations regarding examinations provided for in the Joint Agreement between the three Societies, dated 2nd, 3rd, 6th, and 8th February 1893, may, in lieu of Political Economy, take a second and more advanced Actuarial paper covering :—

(*a*) Probabilities.
(*b*) Mortality Tables.
(*c*) Life Contingencies.

IV. *General Business of an Accountant :—*

(*a.*) The Theory and Practice of Book-keeping.
(*b.*) Preparation of Balance-Sheets and Profit and Loss Accounts.
(*c.*) The procedure and requisites in the Audit of Accounts and Books ; including those of Public Companies, Private Firms, and Trust Estates.
(*d.*) The framing of Trust and Factorial Accounts and States, Joint Adventure and Consignment Accounts, Interest States, etc.
(*e.*) Schemes of Division.
(*f.*) The Management of Bankrupt and Sequestrated Estates, Private Trusts, Heritable Estates, Curatorial and Judicial Factories, etc.
(*g.*) Formation, Administration, and Liquidation of Public Companies.
(*h.*) The procedure under Judicial and Private References, Remits, and Proofs.

By Authority of the General Examining Board.

RICHARD BROWN, C.A.

Secretary and Treasurer.

23 St. Andrew Square, Edinburgh,
January 1895.

Chartered Accountants of Scotland.

◆

The Society of Accountants in Edinburgh,
Incorporated by Royal Charter, 1854.

The Institute of Accountants and Actuaries in Glasgow,
Incorporated by Royal Charter, 1855.

The Society of Accountants in Aberdeen,
Incorporated by Royal Charter, 1867.

— ◆ ◆ —

SYLLABUS OF EXAMINATIONS

BY GENERAL EXAMINING BOARD.

The Examinations are held half-yearly, near the beginning of the months of June and December, on dates which will be intimated in The Accountants' Magazine *of 1st May and 1st November. Candidates are required to intimate their intention of presenting themselves for examination to the Secretary of the Board through the Secretary of the Society with which they are connected, not later than 15th May for the June Examinations, and 15th November for the December Examinations. Seven days' notice at least of the dates and places of Examination will be given to each Candidate who has made due intimation. and paid the Examination Fee.*

I.—Preliminary Qualification.

Every person desirous of serving an apprenticeship shall, before commencing his apprenticeship, or within six months thereafter, pass the Examinations in English, in one other language, ancient or modern, and in Mathematics, set as part of the Preliminary Examination for Graduation in Arts at the Scottish Universities —the lower standard in Latin or Greek and in Mathematics being accepted.

These examinations take place half-yearly, usually in March and September, and entry must be made at the University where the Candidate desires to be examined. Fee payable, 10s. 6d. The dates for receiving entries and other particulars may be obtained from the University Calendars.

Exemptions.

Persons who have passed one or other of the following Examinations will be entitled, on production of their Certificates, to exemption from the above Examination :—

(1) The Intermediate Certificate Examination of the Scotch Education Department, provided the following subjects are endorsed on the Certificate :—Mathematics, English (covering History and Geography), and one other language.

(2) The Leaving Certificate Examination of the Scotch Education Department, provided the subjects entered on the face of the Certificate include Mathematics, English, and one other language.

(3) Lower or Higher Grade passes at the Intermediate or Leaving Certificate Examination of the Scotch Education Department in Mathematics, English, History, Geography, and one language other than English, provided that in

the case of Lower Grade passes all these subjects have been taken at one Examination.

(4) The Junior or Senior Local Examinations of the Universitie of Oxford or Cambridge, provided the Certificate includes Arithmetic, Algebra and Geometry, English, History, and Geography, and one language other than English, and provided that in the case of the Junior Examination all these subjects have been taken at one examination.

(5) The Examinations of the Oxford and Cambridge Schools Examination Board, covering Mathematics (Elementary or Additional), English, English History, and Geography, and one language other than English.

(6) The Responsions Examination of the University of Oxford (provided the Candidate pass the Examination of the Joint Board in English) or the Previous Examination of the University of Cambridge.

(7) Any Examination which is accepted by the Scotch Universities as entitling to exemption from the Preliminary Examination for Graduation in Arts in the subjects of Mathematics, English, and one other language.

II.—Intermediate Examination.

NOTE.—This Examination occupies two days, and must be passed at some time during the last three years of the apprenticeship, and after at least one year thereof shall have been served. One year at least must elapse between the date of passing the Examination and the date when an Apprentice is entitled to come up for Final Examination. The Examination Fee payable is £1, 1s.

First Day. *Mathematics :—*

    Paper No. 1. *Arithmetic—*

        Including Vulgar and Decimal Fractions, Practice, Proportion, Simple and Compound Interest, and Discount.

    Paper No. 2. *Algebra—*

        Including Quadratic Equations, Arithmetical and Geometrical Progressions, Compound Interest and Annuities-certain, and the nature and use of Logarithms. (Books recommended for Compound Interest and Annuities-certain—Glen's *Manual of Actuarial Science*, Chaps. I. and II.; King's *Theory of Finance*, Chaps. I. and II. (1 to 28).)

Second Day. *Professional Knowledge :—*

    (Special marks will be given for neatness of handwriting and style.)

    Paper No. 3.

        Book-keeping, including the framing of Balance Sheets and Profit and Loss Accounts.

    Paper No. 4.

        (*a.*) Framing Statements of Accounts, Interest States, etc.

        (*b.*) Correspondence and Précis-writing.

III.—Final Examination.

Note.—This Examination occupies four days, and cannot be undergone until the Candidate has completed his apprenticeship, and has attended the prescribed classes. The Examination is in two divisions, which may be taken separately, in either order, or together. No Certificate will, however, be issued until the Candidate has passed in both divisions, and a Candidate who has passed in one division must pass in the other within a period of twenty-six calendar months. If he fails to do so and desires to present himself again, he will require to undergo Examination in both divisions. In the case of any Candidate who undergoes both divisions of the Examination at one time, the Board may hold him to have passed in one division and to have failed in the other. The names of those who have passed in only one division of the Examination will not be published until they have also passed in the other division.

The Fees of Examination are as follows:—For those who enter for the whole Examination, £2, 2s.; for either division, £1, 1s.

First Division.

First Day.

Paper No. 1. *Actuarial Science:—*

(*a.*) Annuities - certain, Sinking Funds, Loans repayable by Instalments, etc.

(*b.*) The Principles of Life Annuities, Assurances, and Reversions. (Books recommended — King's *Theory of Finance*, Glen's *Manual of Actuarial Science.*)

Paper No. 2. *Political Economy:—*

(*a.*) General Economic Principles.

(*b.*) Statistics, Rate of Interest and Investments, Currency, Banking, Credit, Commercial Crises, National and Municipal Debts, Taxation.

(Books recommended—*Elements of Political Economy*, by J. Shield Nicholson (A. & C. Black); *Principles of Political Economy*, by Charles Gide, translated by Dr. Veditz (D. C. Heath & Co., London, 1907); *An Elementary Manual of Statistics*, by Arthur L. Bowley (Macdonald & Evans, London, 1910).

SECOND DAY.

PAPER NO. 3. *The Law relating to the following Subjects :—*

(*a.*) Partnership.

(*b.*) Bills, Cheques, and Deposit Receipts.

(*c.*) Sale, Insurance, and Cautionary Obligations.

(*d.*) Trusts.

(*e.*) Judicial Factories.

(*f*) Fee and Liferent.

PAPER NO. 4. *The Law relating to the following Subjects, and the Procedure usually devolving upon Professional Accountants in connection therewith, excluding all questions as to Book-keeping, Accounts, and Auditing:*—

    (*a.*) Insolvency and Bankruptcy.

    (*b.*) Joint Stock Companies.

    (*c.*) References, Remits, and Arbitrations.

Second Division.

THIRD DAY.

    PAPER No. 5. *Book-keeping:*—

        The Theory and Practice of Book-keeping, including the Preparation of Balance Sheets, Trading Accounts, and Profit and Loss Accounts.

    PAPER No. 6. *Partnership Accounts, etc.:*—

        The adjustment of Partners' Accounts; Joint Adventure and Consignment Accounts; States of Affairs for Creditors; Cost Accounts; Income-tax Returns and Claims.

FOURTH DAY.

    PAPER No. 7. *Auditing:*—

        The procedure and requisites in the Audit of Balance Sheets, Accounts, and Books; including those of Public Bodies, Companies, Firms, and Trust Estates.

PAPER No. 8. *Trust Accounts, etc.:—*

The framing of Executry and Factorial
Accounts, Rentals, Schemes of Division,
and Interest States; Apportionments;
Estate and Farm Accounts; Accounts
of Municipal and Local Authorities,
etc.

By Authority of the General Examining Board.

RICHARD BROWN, C.A.,
Secretary and Treasurer.

23 ST. ANDREW SQUARE, EDINBURGH.
October 1913.

———

NOTE.—Candidates desiring copies of past Examination
Papers are informed that they are reprinted in the
Accountants' Magazine of 1st January and 1st July.
(W. Blackwood & Sons, Edinburgh and London. Price
6d. each number, or 5s. per annum.)

List of Abbreviations

ACA   Associate of the Institute of Chartered Accountants in England and Wales

CA   Chartered Accountant

GEB   General Examining Board (of the Scottish CA Societies)

IAAG   Institute of Accountants and Actuaries in Glasgow

ICAEW   Institute of Chartered Accountants in England and Wales

ICAS   Institute of Chartered Accountants of Scotland

SAA   Society of Accountants in Aberdeen

SAE   Society of Accountants in Edinburgh

SIA   Scottish Institute of Accountants

SSC   Solicitor to the Supreme Courts

SSG   Social Status Group

WS   Writer to the Signet

Selected Bibliography

MAJOR SOURCES OF BIOGRAPHICAL INFORMATION

Manuscript

Society of Accountants in Edinburgh (Institute of Chartered Accountants of Scotland, 27 Queen Street, Edinburgh):

Agenda Book, 1894–1919.

Annual Reports and Accounts, 1902–26.

Council Sederunt and Minute Books, 1853–1928.

General Meeting Minute Books, 1854–1946.

Letter Books, 1877–1903.

Register of Apprentices, 1900–23.

Register of Examination Candidates, 1873–1906.

Register of Indentures, 1855–1941.

Register of Members, *c.*1855–1923.

General Register Office for Scotland (New Register House, Edinburgh):

Census Returns for Scotland, 1841–91.

Statutory Registers of Births, Marriages and Deaths for Scotland, 1855–1984.

Old Parochial Records of Baptisms, Banns and Burials (mainly for Edinburgh and district).

Special Collections Department of Edinburgh University Library (George Square, Edinburgh):

Matriculation Registers of the University of Edinburgh, 1780–1914.

The Faculty of Advocates (Advocates' Library, Parliament House, Edinburgh):

Advocates' Widows Fund Register, 1830–1914.

Birth and Marriage Certificates and Correspondence of the Advocates' Widows Fund, 1850–1914.

Minute Books of Faculty, 1843–1930.

Treasurer's Accounts, 1850–1914.

Periodicals

The Accountant (London).

The Accountant's Magazine (Edinburgh).

The Scotsman (Edinburgh).

The Times (London).

Directories – Local

Oliver and Boyd, *New Edinburgh Almanac* (Edinburgh, annual).

Annual Post Office Directories of: Edinburgh and Leith, Glasgow, Dundee, Aberdeen and London.

Directories and References Works – Accountants

Brown, R. *A History of Accounting and Accountants* (Edinburgh, 1905).

Index Juridicus: The Scottish Law List and Legal Directory (Edinburgh, annual).

Scottish Chartered Accountants *Official Directory* (from 1951 *Institute of Chartered Accountants of Scotland Official Directory*) (Edinburgh, annual).

Society of Incorporated Accountants and Auditors *List of Members &c.* (from 1904 *The Incorporated Accountant's Yearbook* (London, annual).

Stewart, J.C. *Pioneers of a Profession* (Edinburgh, 1977).

Directories and Reference Works – Lawyers

Foster, J. *Men–at–the–Bar. A Biographical Handlist* (London, 1885).

Grant, Sir F.J. *The Faculty of Advocates, 1532–1943* (Edinburgh, 1944).

Grant, Sir F.J. *History of the Society of Writers to His Majesties Signet* (Edinburgh, 1936).

Society of Writers to HM Signet *Register of the Society of Writers to Her Majesties Signet* (Edinburgh, 1983).

Walker, S.P. "The Faculty of Advocates 1800–1986. A Biographical Directory of Members", Advocates' Library, Edinburgh.

Directories and Reference Works – Clergymen

The Clergy List (London, annual).

Lamb, J.A. *The Fasti of the United Free Church of Scotland, 1900–1929* (Edinburgh, 1956).

Scott, H. *Fasti Ecclesiae Scoticanae. The Succession of Ministers in the Church of Scotland from the Reformation,* new ed. (Edinburgh, 1915).

Directories and Reference Works – Medical

General Council of Medical Education and Registration of the United Kingdom. *The*

Dentists Register (London, annual).

The Medical Directory (formerly *The London and Provincial Medical Directory* until 1870), (London, annual).

General Council of Medical Education and Registration of the United Kingdom. *The Medical Register* (London, annual).

Directories and Reference Works – Armed and Foreign Services

Drew, R. (ed.) *Commissioned Officers in the Medical Services of the British Army, 1660-1960* (London, 1968).

East India Register and Directory (from 1861 *Indian Army and Civil Service List* (London, annual).

O'Byrne, W.R. *A Naval Biographical Dictionary* (London, 1849).

Directories and Reference Works – Engineers

Bell, S.P. *A Biographical Index of British Engineers in the Nineteenth Century* (New York, 1975).

Directories and Reference Works – Commerce

Bassett, H.H. *Men of Note in Finance and Commerce. A Biographical Business Directory* (London, 1900-1).

Bourne's Insurance Directory (London, annual).

Jeremy, D.J. *Dictionary of Business Biography: A Biographical Dictionary of Business Leaders Active in Britain in the Period 1860-1980* (London, 1984-5).

The United Kingdom Stock and Shareholders Directory (London).

Directories and Reference Works – General

Eddington, A. *Contemporary Biographies: Edinburgh and the Lothians at the Opening of the Twentieth Century* (Edinburgh, 1904).

Findlay, J. *Directory to Gentlemen's Seats, Villages &c. in Scotland* (Edinburgh, 1843).

Scottish Biographies 1938 (London, 1938).

Schools – Scottish

Cargilfield Register, 1873-1927 (Leith, 1928).

Connell, E.O. (ed.) *Merchiston Castle School Register, 1833 to 1962,* 5th ed. (Edinburgh, 1962).

The Edinburgh Academy Register 1824-1914 and War Supplement (Edinburgh, 1921).

The Fettes College Register, 1870 to 1932 (Edinburgh, 1933).

George Heriot's School *Roll of Honour 1914-19* (Edinburgh, 1921).

George Watson's College *A Memorial Record of Watsonians who served in the Great War 1914-1918* (Edinburgh, 1920).

The Glenalmond Register 1847-1954 (Edinburgh, 1955).

The Loretto Register 1825 to 1925 (Edinburgh, 1927).

Royal High School of Edinburgh *Roll of Honour, 1914-1918* (Edinburgh, 1920).

Watt, T. *Aberdeen Grammar School Roll of Pupils 1795-1919* (Aberdeen, 1923).

Young, R.S. (ed.) *Edinburgh Institution 1832-1932* (Edinburgh, 1933).

Schools - English

Charterhouse Register 1872-1910 (London, 1911).

Borwick, F. (ed.) *Clifton College Annals and Register 1862-1925* (Bristol, 1925).

Christopher, H.S. *King William's College Register, 1833-1904* (Glasgow, 1905).

Courtenay Welch, R. (ed.) *The Harrow School Register 1801-1893* (London, 1894).

Pigg, C.H. *Cheltenham College Register 1841-1951* (Cheltenham, 1953).

Wainewright, J.B. (ed.) *Winchester College 1836-1906. A Register* (Winchester, 1907).

Wellington College Regsiter January 1859 to December 1973, 9th ed. (London, 1975).

Universities

Addison, W.I. *A Roll of the Graduates of the University of Glasgow From 31st December 1727 to 31st December 1897* (Glasgow, 1898).

Addison, W.I. *The Matriculation Albums of the University of Glasgow From 1728 to 1858* (Glasgow, 1913).

Anderson, J.M. (ed.) *The Matriculation Roll of the University of St Andrews 1747-1897* (Edinburgh, 1905).

Anderson, P.J. (ed.) *Officers and Graduates of University and King's College Aberdeen 1495-1860* (Aberdeen, 1893).

Foster, J. *Alumni Oxonienses. The Members of the University of Oxford 1715-1886* (later series, Oxford).

Johnston, W. *Roll of the Graduates of the University of Aberdeen 1860-1900* (Aberdeen, 1906).

MacKenzie, J.E. (ed.) *University of Edinburgh Roll of Honour 1914-1919* (Edinburgh, 1921).

Venn, J.A. *Alumni Cantabrigienses, Part II From 1752 to 1900* (Cambridge, 1940).

Watt, J.A. *Roll of the Graduates of the University of Aberdeen 1901-1925* (Aberdeen, 1935).

ACCOUNTANTS AND ACCOUNTANCY

A Guide to the Accountancy Profession (London: Gee & Co., 1895).

The Accountant's Student Journal (from 1886 *The Accountant's Journal*) (London).

Balfour-Melville, B. *The Balfours of Pilrig* (Edinburgh, 1907).

Begg, R.W. *Interim Account of a Going Concern, some essays on the History of the Firm of Mann, Judd, Gordon and Co., C.A.'s, Glasgow, 1817-1967* (Glasgow, 1967).

Briston, R.J. and Kedslie, M.K.M. "Professional Formation the case of Scottish Accountants - some corrections and some further thoughts", *British Journal of Sociology* 37 (1986).

British *Parliamentary Papers.* Report on the Judicial Statistics of Scotland (annual, 1868-1914).

British *Parliamentary Papers.* Return of the names, objects &c. of all Joint Stock Companies formed. Board of Trade.

Cases Decided in the Court of Session, Court of Justiciary and House of Lords, 4th series. 20 (1892-3), No. 132.

The Chartered Accountants of Scotland. "Interdict Case". The Chartered Accountants of Scotland against the Corporation of Accountants Ltd. 1892-3. (Manuscript sheets in the Institute of Chartered Accountants of Scotland Collection, National Library of Scotland, Edinburgh).

Cowan, J.J. *From 1846-1932* (Edinburgh: By the Author, 1933).

Crew, A. *The Profession of an Accountant* (London, 1925).

Davidson, A.R. *The History of the Faculty of Actuaries in Scotland, 1856-1956* (Edinburgh, 1956).

Dicksee, L.R. *The Student's Guide to Accountancy,* 1st and 2nd eds. (London, 1897 and 1907).

Dunlop, A.B.G. "Scottish Chartered Accountants", *The Scottish Genealogist* 12 (1965).

Garrett, A.A. *History of the Society of Incorporated Accountants, 1885-1957* (Oxford, 1961).

Gynther, R. *Practising Accountants in Australia* (Queensland, 1967).

Harrison, A. SAE member admitted 1914. Interview 13 December 1984.

Hopkins, L. *The Hundredth Year; The Story of the Institute of Chartered Accountants of England and Wales* (Plymouth, 1980).

Hunter, A.T., CA "Rambling Reminiscences of an Old Edinburgh Citizen", *The Weekly Scotsman* (October-December 1936, Edinburgh).

Institute of Chartered Accountants of Scotland. *A History of the Chartered Accountants of Scotland to 1954* (Edinburgh, 1954).

i

The Incorporated Accountant's Journal (London).

Jones, E. *Accountancy and the British Economy 1840-1980. The Evolution of Ernst & Whinney* (London, 1981).

Kapadia, G.P. *History of the Accounting Profession in India* (New Delhi, 1973).

McClelland, J., CA *The Origin and Present Organization of the Profession of Chartered Accountants in Scotland* (Glasgow, 1869).

Macdonald, K.M. "Professional Formation; the case of Scottish Accountants", *British Journal of Sociology* 35 (1984).

Macdonald, K.M. "Professional Formation: a reply to Briston and Kedslie" *British Journal of Sociology* 38 (1987).

McDougall, E.H.V. *Fifth Quarter-Century: Some Chapters in the History of the C.A.'s of Scotland* (Edinburgh, 1980).

Martin, J. *The Accountant Profession: A Public Danger* (Glasgow, 1896).

Martin, J. *The Accountant 'C.A.' Case. Was There a Misapplication of the Law* (Glasgow, 1896).

Martin, J. *Did the Devil Win the Toss, or, The Lie Triumphant in the Law Courts: An Exposure* (Glasgow, 1897).

Martin, J. *The Sanctification of the Lie. Grace, Grace Unto It. A Tribute to the Queen's Sixty Years Reign* (Glasgow, 1897).

Martin, J. *The Accountant Squabble: The Government and the C.A. Case, Were the Law Courts Bribed ? A Scathing Exposure* (Glasgow, 1908).

Maxtone-Graham, M.E. *The Maxtones of Cultoquhey* (Edinburgh, 1935).

Murray, D. *Chapters in the History of Bookkeeping, Accountancy and Commercial Arithmetic* (Glasgow, 1930).

Personal letters from an SAE Member apprenticed 1907-12. November to December 1984.

Pixley, F.W. *The Profession of a Chartered Accountant* (London, 1885).

Previts, G.J. and Merino, B.D. *A History of Accounting in America* (New York, 1979).

Privy Council. In the Matter of the Petition of the Scottish Institute of Accountants for Incorporation by Royal Charter (1889-90). (ICAS Collection, National Library of Scotland, Edinburgh). A slightly different copy is available in the Scottish Department of Edinburgh Central Public Library.

Privy Council. "Speeches by Counsel". In the Matter of the Petition of the Scottish Institute of Accountants for Incorporation by Royal Charter (1890). (Scottish Department of Edinburgh Central Public Library).

Privy Council. In the Matter of the Petition of the Scottish Institute of Accountants for Incorporation by Royal Charter (1896). (Scottish Department of Edinburgh Central Public Library).

Privy Council. "Speeches by Counsel". In the Matter of the Petition of the Scottish Institute of Accountants for Incorporation by Royal Charter (1896). (Scottish Department of Edinburgh Central Public Library).

Pryce-Jones, J.E. *Accounting in Scotland. A Historical Bibliography* (Edinburgh, 1974).

Registers of the Registrar of Companies for Scotland. (Scottish Record Office, West Register House, Charlotte Square, Edinburgh. BT.1 series).

Reports (annual) of the Accountant in Bankruptcy. (Scottish Record Office, West Register House, Charlotte Square, Edinburgh, CS.322 series).

Reports (annual) of the Accountant of Court. (Scottish Record Office, West Register House, Charlotte Square, Edinburgh. CS.322 series).

The Scottish Accountant (Glasgow).

Smith, W.H., C.A., *From Constable to Commissioner* (London, 1910).

Society of Writers to Her Majesty's Signet. "Report of the Committee . . . to consider the Details and report upon a Bill . . . for the Appointment of an Accountant-General in the Court of Session" (1834). (Special Collections Department, Edinburgh University Library, George Square, Edinburgh).

Solomons, D. and Berridge, T.M. *Prospectus for a Profession: The Report of the Long Range Enquiry into Education and Training for the Accountancy Profession* (London, 1974).

Stacey, N.A.H. *English Accountancy; A Study in Social and Economic History* (London, 1954).

Transactions of the Chartered Accountants Students' Society of Edinburgh (Edinburgh).

Usher, Family of. *The History of the Usher Family in Scotland* (Edinburgh: By the Authors, 1956).

Walker, Revd. N.L. *David MacLagan, F.R.C.E.* (London, 1884).

Walker, S.P. "Occupational Expansion, Fertility Decline and Recruitment to the Professions in Scotland 1850-1914 (with Special Reference to the Chartered Accountants of Edinburgh)". Ph.D. Dissertation, University of Edinburgh, 1986.

Witty, R.A. *How to become a Qualified Accountant* (London, 1895).

Woolf, A.H. *A Short History of Accountants and Accountancy* (London, 1912).

Worthington, B. *Professional Accountants* (London, 1895).

THE PROFESSIONS

Barber, B. "Some Problems in the Sociology of the Professions", *Daedulus* 92 (1963).

Ben-David, J. "Professions in the Class System of Present Day Societies", *Current Sociology* 12 (1963-4).

Carr-Saunders A. and Wilson, P.A. *The Professions* (London, 1933).

Elliot, P. *The Sociology of the Professions* (London, 1972).

Hickson, D. and Thomas, M. "Professionalization in Britain", *Sociology* 3 (1969).

Holland, P.A. "A Strategic Approach to Occupational Developments Amongst Architects". Ph.D. Dissertation, University of Edinburgh, 1974.

Hughes, E.C. "Professions", *Daedulus* 92 (1963).

Jackson, J.A. (ed.) *Professions and Professionalization* (Cambridge, 1970).

Johnson, T.J. *Professions and Power* (London, 1972).

Lewis, R. and Maude, A. *Professional People* (London, 1952).

Millerson, G. *The Qualifying Associations: A Study of Professionalization* (London, 1964).

"The Outlook of the Professional Classes", *The Spectator* 63 (1889).

Reader, W.J. *Professional Men* (London, 1966).

Vollmer, H.M. and Mills, D. *Professionalization* (New Jersey, 1966).

VOCATIONAL DECISION MAKING

A Veteran Journalist. "Journalism as a Career", *National Review* 32 (1898–9).

Atkinson, R.W. *Popular Guide to the Professions* (London, 1895).

Cross, D. *Choosing a Career* (London, 1908).

Devanant, F. *What Shall My Son Be ? Hints to Parents* (London, 1870).

Devanant, F. *Starting in Life: Hints to Parents on the Choice of a Profession or Trade for their Sons* (London, 1881).

Dickens, C. *Bleak House* (London, 1862).

The Guardian. "Our Sons: Their Start in Life". (reprinted from The *Guardian,* 1903).

Guide to the Government, Civil Service, East India Service, the Leading Professions, Scholarships &c. With Salaries from £80 to £500 a Year (London, n.d. *c.*1850).

Gully, W.C. *Careers for Our Sons: A Practical Handbook for Parents* (Carlisle, 1904).

Haystead, J. "Social Structure, Awareness Contexts and Processes of Choice", *Sociological Review* 19 (1971).

Jones, H. *Guide to the Professions and Business* (London, 1898).

Kelly College, Tavistock. *On the Choice of a Profession* (Oxford, 1891).

MacLeane, D. "The Church as a Profession", *National Review* 33 (1899).

Marsland, F. *Occupations in Life* (London, 1905).

"Maxims by a Man of the World", *Chamber's Journal*, 4th series, 45.

Mercator. *Reasons for Failure and Roads to Success* (Walsall, 1900).

"On Relatives and Connections", *Temple Bar* 1 (1861).

Open University. *Occupational Structure and Placement* (Milton Keynes, 1976).

Orwell, G. *The Road to Wigan Pier* (London, 1937).

Pechell, M.L. *Professions for Boys and How to Enter Them* (London, 1898).

"The Professions versus Trade", *The Spectator* 75 (1895).

"Prospects in the Professions", *Cornhill Magazine* n.s. 13-15 (1902-3).

Roberts, K. "The Entry Into Employment", *Sociological Review* 16 (1968).

Slocum, W.L. *Occupational Careers* (Chicago, 1966).

The Student's Annual and Guide to Employment (Dublin, 1897-8).

Timperley, S.R. and Gregory, A.M. "Some Factors Affecting the Career Choice and Career Perceptions of Sixth Form School Leavers", *Sociological Review* 19 (1971).

Tozer, B. "The Unemployed Gentleman", *National Review* 49 (1907).

What Shall I Be ? (London, 1900).

"What to do With My Sons", *Chamber's Journal* 4th series, 5 (1868).

Williams, W.M. (ed.) *Occupational Choice* (London, 1974).

SOCIAL MOBILITY, OCCUPATIONAL AND SOCIAL STRUCTURE

Abrahamson, M., Mizruchi, E.H. and Hornung, C.A. *Stratification and Mobility* (New York, 1976).

Anderson, G. *Victorian Clerks* (Manchester, 1976).

Berent, J. "Fertility and Social Mobility", *Population Studies* 5 (1952).

Besant, W. "The Upward Pressure", *Scribner's Magazine* 13 (1893).

Blau, P.M. "The Flow of Occupational Supply and Recruitment", *American Sociological Review* 30 (1965).

Blau, P.M. and Duncan, O.D. "Some Preliminary Findings on Social Stratification in the U.S.", *Acta Sociologica* 9 (1965).

Blau, P.M. and Duncan, O.D. *The American Occupational Structure* (New York, 1967).

Booth, C. *The Occupations of the People: England, Scotland and Ireland 1841-81* (London, 1886).

Boudon, R. *Mathematical Structures of Social Mobility* (London, 1973).

Carlsson, G. *Social Mobility and Class Structure* (Lund, 1958).

Checkland, S.G. *The Rise of Industrial Society in England, 1815-1885* (London, 1964).

Clark, C. *The Conditions of Economic Progress* (London, 1957).

Davidoff, L. and Hall, C. "The Architecture of Public and Private Life: English Middle Class Society in a Provincial Town, 1780-1850". In Fraser, D. and Sutcliffe, A. *The Pursuit of Urban History* (London, 1983).

Duncan, O.D., Featherman, D.L. and Duncan, B. *Socioeconomic Background and Achievement* (New York, 1972).

Erickson, C. *British Industrialists: Steel and Hosiery, 1850-1950* (Cambridge, 1959).

Featherman, D.L. and Hauser, R.M. *Opportunity and Change* (New York, 1978).

Garnsey, E. "Occupational Structure in Industrial Societies", *Sociology* 9 (1975).

Glass, D. (ed.) *Social Mobility in Britain* (London, 1954).

Goldthorpe, J.H. *Social Mobility and Class Structure in Modern Britain* (Oxford, 1980).

Goldthorpe, J.H. and Hope, K. *The Social Grading of Occupations: A New Approach and Scale* (Oxford, 1974).

Goldthorpe, J.H., Lockwood, D., Bechhofer, F. and Platt, J. *The Affluent Worker in the Class Structure* (Cambridge, 1969).

Goode, W.J. "Family and Mobility". In Bendix, R. and Lipset, S.M. (eds.) *Class, Status and Power.* 2nd ed. (London, 1967).

Gray, R.Q. "Thrift and Working-Class Mobility in Victorian Edinburgh". In McLaren, A.A. (ed.) *Social Class in Scotland: Past and Present* (Edinburgh, 1976).

Halmos, P. *The Personal Service Society* (London, 1970).

Hall, R.H. *Occupations and the Social Structure* (London, 1969).

Halsey, A.H. (ed.) *Trends in British Society Since 1900* (London, 1972).

Heath, A. *Social Mobility* (London, 1981).

Hodge, R.W., Treiman, D. and Rossi, P.H. "Occupational Prestige in the U.S.", *American Journal of Sociology* 70 (1964).

Hodge, R.W., Treiman, D. and Rossi, P.H. "A Comparative Study of Occupational Prestige". In Bendix, R. and Lipset, S.M. (eds.) *Class, Status and Power* (New York, 1966).

Hope, K. (ed.) *The Analysis of Social Mobility: Methods and Approaches* (Oxford, 1972).

Kaeble, H. *Historical Research on Social Mobility* (London, 1977).

Kahl, J.A. *The American Class Structure* (New York, 1957).

Lawton, R. (ed.) *The Census and Social Structure* (London, 1978).

Lewis, R. and Maude, A. *The English Middle Classes* (London, 1949).

Lipset, S.M. and Bendix, R. *Social Mobility in Industrial Society* (Berkeley, 1959).

Lloyd Warner, W. *Social Class in America: The Evaluation of Status* (New York, 1960).

Lockwood, D. *The Blackcoated Worker: A Study in Class Consciousness* (London, 1958).

Marsh, D.C. *The Changing Social Structure of England and Wales, 1871-1951* (London, 1958).

Marsh, R.M. "Values, Demand and Social Mobility", *American Sociological Review* 28 (1963).

Matras, J. "Differential Fertility, Intergenerational Occupational Mobility and Change in the Occupational Distribution", *Population Studies* 15 (1961).

Millar, R. *The New Classes* (London, 1966).

Morris, R.J. "The Middle Class and the Property Cycle during the Industrial Revolution". In Smout, T.C. (ed.) *The Search for Wealth and Stability* (London, 1979).

Musgrove, F. *The Migratory Elite* (London, 1963).

Parry, N. and J. "Social Closure and Collective Social Mobility". In Scase, R. (ed.) *Industrial Society: Class Cleavage and Control* (London, 1977).

Payne, G. "Occupational Transition in Advanced Industrial Societies", *Sociological Review* n.s. 25 (1977).

Payne, G., Ford, G. and Robertson, C. "Changes in Occupational Mobility in Scotland", *Scottish Journal of Sociology* 1 (1977).

Perkin, H. *The Origins of Modern English Society, 1780-1880* (London, 1969).

Perucci, C.C. "Social Origins, Mobility Patterns and Fertility", *American Sociological Review* 32 (1967).

Preston, S.H. "Differential Fertility, Unwanted Fertility and Recent Trends in Occupational Achievement", *American Sociological Review* 39 (1974).

Reid, I. *Social Class Differences in Britain: A Sourcebook* (London, 1977).

Ridge, J.M. *Mobility in Britain Reconsidered* (Oxford, 1974).

Rogoff, N. *Recent Trends in Occupational Mobility* (New York, 1953).

Sibley, E. "Some Demographic Clues to Stratification", *American Sociological Review* 7 (1942).

Sobel, M.E. "Social Mobility and Fertility Revisited", *American Sociological Review* 50 (1985).

"Social Ambitions", *Blackwood's Magazine* 101 (1867).

Sorokin, P. *Social Mobility* (New York, 1927).

Sorokin, P. *Social and Cultural Mobility* (New York, 1964).

Taylor, L. *Occupational Sociology* (London, 1968).

Treiman, D.J. *Occupational Prestige in Comparative Perspective* (New York, 1977).

Westergaard, J. and Resler, H. *Class in a Capitalist Society* (London, 1975).

Zweig, F. *The Worker in an Affluent Society* (London, 1961).

FERTILITY, MORTALITY AND NUPTIALITY

A Bachelor. "On Some Impediments to Marriage", *Fraser's Magazine* 76 (1867).

"A Bachelor's Protest", *Chamber's Journal* 15 (1861).

Ansell, C. "On the Rate of Mortality". In Benjamin, B. *Rates of Mortality* (Farnborough, 1973).

Banks, J.A. *Prosperity and Parenthood* (London, 1965).

Banks, J.A. *Victorian Values: Secularism and the Size of Families* (London, 1981).

Brightfield, M.F. *Victorian England in its Novels, 1840-1870* (Los Angeles, 1968).

British *Parliamentary Papers.* Censuses of Scotland, 1851-1921.

British *Parliamentary Papers.* Supplements to the Thirty-Eighth and Forty-Eighth Detailed Annual Reports of the Registrar General of Births, Deaths and Marriages in Scotland (1895 and 1906).

"The Decline of Marriage", *Westminster Review* 135 (1891).

Flinn, M. (ed.) *Scottish Population History* (Cambridge, 1977).

Freedman, R. "The Sociology of Human Fertility", *Current Sociology* 10 (1961).

Hawthorn, G. *The Sociology of Human Fertility* (London, 1970).

Hollingsworth, T.H. "The Demography of the British Peerage", *Population Studies* 18 (1964).

"Keeping Up Appearances", *Cornhill Magazine* 4 (1861).

Stevenson, T.H.C. "The Fertility of the Various Social Classes in England and Wales from the Middle of the Nineteenth Century to 1911", *Journal of the Royal Statistical Society* 83 (1920).

Stutfield, H.E.M. "Celibacy and the Struggle to Get On", *Blackwood's Magazine* 156 (1894).

Szreter, S.R.S. "The Decline of Marital Fertility in England and Wales, 1870-1914". Ph.D. Dissertation, University of Cambridge, 1983.

"Why are Women Redundant ?", *National Review* 14 (1862).

EDUCATION

Anderson, R.D. *Education and Opportunity in Victorian Scotland* (Oxford, 1983).

Archer, R.L. *Secondary Education in the Nineteenth Century* (Cambridge, 1921).

British *Parliamentary Papers*. Report of the Commissioners appointed to Inquire into the Education given in the Schools in England (1867-8).

British *Parliamentary Papers*. Reports of the Commissioners appointed to Inquire into the Endowed Schools and Hospitals (Scotland) (annual 1873-5).

British *Parliamentary Papers*. Return respecting the Secondary and Higher Class Schools in each of the twelve Parliamentary Burghs of Scotland (1875).

British *Parliamentary Papers*. Returns Showing by Counties for each School District in Scotland Accomodation in Schools (1880, 1887, 1897).

British *Parliamentary Papers*. List of Public Elementary Schools in England and Wales on 1 January 1906 (1906).

British *Parliamentary Papers*. Return of the Schools in England and Wales recognized on 1 January 1906 as Non-Provided Public Elementary Schools (1906).

Craigie, J. *A Bibliography of Scottish Education Before 1872* (London, 1970).

Craigie, J. *A Bibliography of Scottish Education, 1872-1972* (London, 1974).

The Educational Year-Book (London, 1881).

Grant, A. *The Story of the University of Edinburgh* (London, 1884).

Himmelweit, H.T. "Social Status and Secondary Education". In Glass, D. (ed.) *Social Mobility in Britain* (London, 1954).

Law, A. *Education in Edinburgh in the Eighteenth Century* (London, 1965).

Logan Turner, A. (ed.) *History of the University of Edinburgh, 1883-1933* (Edinburgh, 1933).

Magnusson, M. *The Clacken and the Slate: The Story of Edinburgh Academy* (London, 1974).

"Middle Class Education in England", *Cornhill Magazine* 10 (1864).

Musgrove, F. "Middle Class Education and Employment in the Nineteenth Century", *Economic History Review* 2nd series, 12 (1959-60).

Musgrove, F. "Middle Class Education and Employment in the Nineteenth Century: A Rejoinder", *Economic History Review* 2nd series, 14 (1961-2).

Perkin, H. "Middle Class Education and Employment in the Nineteenth Century: A Critical Note", *Economic History Review* 2nd series, 14 (1961-2).

The Public Schools Year Book (London, annual).

Sanderson, M. *The Universities and British Industry 1850-1970* (London, 1972).

Scotland, J. *The History of Scottish Education* (London, 1969).

Staunton, H. *The Great Schools of England* (London, 1865).

Steven, W. *History of George Heriot's Hospital* 3rd ed. (Edinburgh, 1872).

Steven, W. *The History of the High School of Edinburgh* (Edinburgh, 1849).

Strong, J. *A History of Secondary Education in Scotland* (Oxford, 1909).

Thomson, J. *A History of Daniel Stewart's College, 1855-1955* (Edinburgh, 1955).

Waugh, H.L. (ed.) *George Watson's College, 1724-1970* (Edinburgh, 1970).

EDINBURGH AND SCOTLAND

Bell, W. *A Dictionary and Digest of the Law of Scotland* (Edinburgh, 1861).

Bone, J. *Edinburgh Revisited* (London, 1911).

Checkland, S. and O. *Industry and Ethos. Scotland 1832-1914* (London, 1984).

Chitnis, A.C. *The Scottish Enlightenment: A Social History* (London, 1976).

Cockburn, H. *Memorials of His Time* (Edinburgh, 1856).

Cockburn, H.T. *The Journal of Henry Cockburn being a Continuation of the Memorials of His Time* (Edinburgh, 1874).

Gordon, G. "The Status Areas of Edinburgh: A Historical Analysis". Ph.D. Dissertation, University of Edinburgh, 1971.

Grant, J. *Cassell's Old and New Edinburgh: Its History, its People and its Places* (London, 1882).

Gray, R.Q. *The Labour Aristocracy in Victorian Edinburgh* (Oxford, 1976).

Groome, F.H. *Ordnance Gazetteer of Scotland* (London, 1885).

Heiton, J. *The Castes of Edinburgh* 3rd ed. (Edinburgh, 1861).

Institute of Public Administration. *Studies in the Development of Edinburgh* (London, 1939).

Keith, A. *Edinburgh of Today* (Edinburgh, 1908).

Lockie, K.F. *Picturesque Edinburgh* (Edinburgh, 1899).

Lorimer, J. *A Handbook of the Law of Scotland* 3rd ed. (Edinburgh, 1873).

McDowall, T. and W. *McDowall's New Guide in Edinburgh* (Edinburgh, 1849).

Phillipson, N.T. and Mitchison, R. (eds.) *Scotland in the Age of Improvement: Essays in Scottish History in the Eighteenth Century* (Edinburgh, 1970).

Saunders, L.J. *Scottish Democracy, 1815-40: The Social and Intellectual Background* (Edinburgh, 1950).

Shaw, J.S. *The Management of Scottish Society 1707-64* (Edinburgh, 1983).

Smith, C.J. *Historic South Edinburgh* (Edinburgh, 1978-9, 1987).

Smout, T.C. *A History of the Scottish People 1560-1830* (London, 1969).

Youngson, A.J. *The Making of Classical Edinburgh* (Edinburgh, 1966).

WORKS USEFUL IN DATA PREPARATION AND ANALYSIS

Balan, J., Browning, H.L., Jelin, E. and Litzler, L. "A Computerized Approach to the Processing and Analysis of Life Histories Obtained in Sample Surveys", *Behavioural Science* 13 (1969).

Bartholomew, J. (ed.) *Gazetteer of the British Isles: Statistical and Topographical* (Edinburgh, 1887).

Blalock, H.M. *Social Statistics* (New York, 1960).

Dyos, H.J. (ed.) *The Study of Urban History* (London, 1968).

Floud, R. *An Introduction to Quantitative Methods for Historians* (London, 1973).

Morris, R.J. "The Leeds Middle Class, 1820-1850". End-of-Grant Report to the SSRC. 1983 (Grant no. b/00/24/003/1).

Nie, N.H., Hull, C.H., Jenkins, J.G., Steinbrenner, K. and Bent, D.H. *Statistical Package for the Social Sciences* 2nd ed. (New York, 1975).

Wrigley, E.A. (ed.) *Nineteenth-Century Society: Essays in the Use of Quantitative Methods for the Study of Social Data* (Cambridge, 1972).

Zeller, R.A. and Carmines, E.G. *Statistical Analysis of Social Data* (Chicago, 1978).

Name Index

Subject Index